The Art of Authorial Presence

The Art of

Authorial Presence

Hawthorne's Provincial Tales

G. R. Thompson

DUKE UNIVERSITY PRESS   Durham and London 1993

For Elizabeth

Contents

Acknowledgments

Although I am always respectful of the feat of writing a sustained critical-scholarly study, I do not of course find all studies of Hawthorne equally valuable. Some with which I find fault, however, have been of major importance to me. It is my hope that those scholars with whom I most strongly disagree will appreciate the fact that my frequently citing and attempting to refute or modify their positions indicates the value of their work for mine and their influence on my argument, which I offer in the spirit of critical debate.

Among my colleagues at Purdue University and elsewhere whom I should like to acknowledge for both general and specific help, the first place goes to Leonard N. Neufeldt, whose continuing dialogue with me over the last fifteen years has sharpened my awareness of critical issues in American literature, American historiography, and theoretical criticism. He has reviewed the manuscript meticulously from first to last; those recommendations of his that I finally did not take probably constitute a mistake on my part.

I owe as much in a more general way to two of my theoretical colleagues at Purdue. Virgil L. Lokke, my collaborator on *Ruined Eden of the Present* and other works, and with whom I have also several times team-taught, has more than any other single person kept me aware of the "current in criticism," chiding me with ironic good humor when he found me becoming "retrograde." His pungent assessments of *everything*, combined with his own recurrent miscalculations, have kept me saner than I otherwise might be. My good friend David M. Miller, a true Renaissance man, has reminded me over and over again that there is a larger world than that of Poe and Hawthorne scholarship — such as the world of Donne, Milton, and Shakespeare — and that a tradition of ethical understanding still manages to survive.

These colleagues, along with Wendy Stallard Flory and Donald A. Seybold of Purdue University, Frederick Newberry of Duquesne University, and Rolf Meyn of Universität Hamburg, read the opening chapters of the manuscript and, like Len Neufeldt, made so many good suggestions that I was forced to rewrite again. Howard Mancing, former head of the Department of Foreign Languages and Literatures at Purdue University, read the manuscript from the point of view of a Cervantean and comparatist and helped me see some of the issues of American provincialism in a more cosmopolitan way; not the least appreciated of his efforts has been his unflagging encouragement. My former colleagues, Djelal Kadir, now chair of the program in comparative literature at the University of Oklahoma, and Robert C. McLean of Washington State University, editor of *ESQ: A Journal of the American Renaissance*, have also been unfailingly supportive over the years.

Leonard Neufeldt, Howard Mancing, and Rolf Meyn, along with John T. Irwin of Johns Hopkins University, Patrick F. Quinn of Wellesley College, Eric S. Rabkin of the University of Michigan, Barton Levi St. Armand of Brown University, and William Veeder of the University of Chicago supported my successful applications for fellowships in the Center for Humanistic Studies at Purdue University in 1984 and 1990. These fellowships, combined with sabbatical leave, enabled me to complete the present work and a draft of the longer work on nineteenth-century fiction of which it was originally a part. I am most grateful to Purdue University and the Humanities Center selection committees. Judith Musser, a student in my Hawthorne seminar in the spring of 1990, acted as my research assistant during the summer of that year. Would that one could always have such efficient and capable help.

A special word of thanks must go to Reynolds Smith of Duke University Press, who encouraged the work, dealt with the initial draft stage with sensitivity and aplomb, kept the project going despite delays, and throughout dealt with me in a kindly and respectful manner which authors do not always experience. I wish also to thank the readers of Duke University Press — Cynthia S. Jordan, Edgar A. Dryden, and Terence Martin — for their time and criticism, and particularly for their willingness to read a penultimate draft of a very long manuscript.

Finally, this book is written for — and at the insistence of — Elizabeth Boyd Thompson. Having discovered her even later in life than Nathaniel his Sophia, I am all the more appreciative. Only she knows the full story of the long delayed completion of this work. As a professional editor as well as a nineteenth-century specialist, she was the severest of all my readers. She read the manuscript in bits and parts and as a whole more times than I like to think about. Without her, this book would not have been completed, and to her it is dedicated with love.

West Lafayette, Indiana
April 1990
October 1991

Citations in the Text

Citations to Hawthorne will be given parenthetically in the text in double form.

(A) By volume and page number to *Works,* ed. George Parsons Lathrop (Boston and New York: Houghton Mifflin "Riverside" Edition, 1879).

(B) By page number to *Tales and Sketches,* ed. Roy Harvey Pearce (New York: Library of America, 1982), hereinafter cited as *T&S.* This edition reprints the texts of the *Centenary Edition of the Works of Nathaniel Hawthorne,* ed. William Charvat, Roy Harvey Pearce, Claude M. Simpson, et al. (Columbus: Ohio State University Press, 1962–present), abbreviated as *CE* in citations.

Unless otherwise indicated, the quotations are from the Riverside Edition, which, though normalized in spelling and punctuation, for the most part represents an actual historical text. The Centenary Edition, following the Greg-Bowers principles of textual editing, at times presents a "composite text." I have compared all the passages and comment in the notes where appropriate. In the parenthetical notes to other frequently cited works, I use a shortened form (e.g., *E&R* for Poe's *Essays and Reviews*).

Given the massive summaries of scholarship and criticism by Lea Bertani Vozar Newman, *A Reader's Guide to the Short Stories of Nathaniel Hawthorne* (Boston: G. K. Hall, 1979), and Michael Colacurcio in his notes to *The Province of Piety: Moral History in Hawthorne's Early Tales* (Cambridge, Mass.: Harvard University Press, 1984), it seems redundant to recapitulate it all. In my notes I frequently refer the reader to Newman (abbreviated as LBVN) and Colacurcio. To cut down on repetitive citation, a comprehensive bibliography of secondary material is appended. Its order is alphabetical by author (or, for edited works, by title) and within that (for the author of more than one work) by date of publication. References in the notes are in shortened form and keyed to this bibliography by last name of the author, sometimes followed by a short title or simply date of publication, whichever is most appropriate.

Related reference material appears in a work I have found necessary to cite frequently: *Romantic Arabesque, Contemporary Theory, and Postmodernism*, a monograph on Poe and Schlegel, published as nos. 3 and 4 of *ESQ* 35 (1989). Here I set forth the theory of the arabesque romance in some detail in terms of romantic aesthetics and American literature, along with parallels to (and divergences from) later twentieth-century critical theory. Citations are abbreviated as *Romantic Arabesque*. Further amplification may be found in certain other of my works as listed in the bibliography.

All Shakespearean references and quotations are from G. B. Harrison's edition of 1948.

All titles, proper names, and place names occurring in the main text are cataloged in the index, as are "historical" (essentially pre-twentieth-century) names in the notes. The names of twentieth-century scholars appearing in the notes (many of them with great frequency) are not indexed unless a particular note constitutes a significant gloss on a topic of special interest to students of Hawthorne or romantic narratology.

The Robin's my Criterion for Tune —
Because I grow — where Robins do —
But, were I Cuckoo born —
I'd swear by him —
The ode familiar — rules the Noon —
The Buttercup's, my Whim for Bloom —
Because, we're Orchard sprung —
But, were I Britain born,
I'd Daisies spurn —
None but the Nut — October fit —
Because, through dropping it,
The Seasons flit — I'm taught —
Without the Snow's Tableau
Winter, were lie — to me —
Because I see — New Englandly —
The Queen, discerns like me —
Provincially —

— Emily Dickinson
(c. 1861)

Introduction: Romantic Context
of the "Hawthorne Question"

In one word, the world is mistaken in this Nathaniel Hawthorne. He himself must often have smiled at its absurd misconception of him. . . . The truth seems to be, that like many other geniuses, this Man of Mosses takes great delight in hoodwinking the world, — at least with respect to himself. . . . But with whatever motive, playful or profound, Nathaniel Hawthorne has chosen to entitle his pieces in the manner he has, it is certain that some of them are directly calculated to deceive — egregiously deceive, the superficial skimmer of pages.
— Herman Melville, "Hawthorne and His Mosses" (1850)

If we used to think the question of Edgar Allan Poe's artistry, works, life, and overall significance vexed, the question of Nathaniel Hawthorne seems in some ways even more so. Just as we now see more clearly the social and historical concerns embedded in Poe's writings, so also we should be able to acknowledge, once again, the aesthetic focus of Hawthorne the artist. Whatever else he has to offer us, we need to rediscover a sense of his radical literary experimentation.

What has come to be called the "Hawthorne Question" dogs his literary valuation. Ranging from phrases that parody his most famous novel and his best-known short story as the "Scarlet A-Minus" and "Young Goodie Two-Shoes" to reiterated perplexities about his personality and life, the critical formulation of the so-called Hawthorne Question queries his status as a major writer from a variety of sophisticated and not so sophisticated critical positions. Critics not only insist on asking where he *stands* on various philosophical, moral-ethical, religious, and political issues — as if he were one of those nineteenth-century reformist lecturers he despised; they also ask whether he actually lived in this world or a fantasy world of pure imagination — as if he were a version of the myth of the pure poet of the "other-worldly." As with Poe, these worldly questions somehow cast doubt upon

Hawthorne's artistry. Such criticism especially calls into question his aesthetic distance, control, and intent in the early "provincial" tales. Covering a problematic interpretative miscellany, the Hawthorne Question seems an almost haphazard mix of aesthetic, narratological, ideological, and biographical elements, with more than a dash of politics and psychoanalysis thrown in.[1]

Edgar A. Dryden puts the matter sensibly and succinctly:

> Who is Nathaniel Hawthorne? This question puzzled Hawthorne's contemporaries — even his family and friends — has perplexed his biographers and critics, and continues to be asked by students who read his work. . . . Why is it, a student once asked me during a discussion of *The Scarlet Letter*, that Hawthorne introduces his book with such a long discussion of himself and his problems when the book itself seems completely unrelated to the history, biography, or psychology of Nathaniel Hawthorne?
>
> The last twenty years of Hawthorne scholarship make clear that there are a number of ways one could try to answer such a question. The symbolic readings of Roy Male, Richard Fogle, Hyatt Waggoner, and others, the psychoanalytic perspective of Frederick Crews, the psycho-poetic approach of Jean Normand: all are in one way or another attempts to describe the form of Hawthorne's presence in his work, to connect the biographical and literary selves.[2]

Dryden notes that "novelists traditionally have been preoccupied with the issues of pseudonymity and anonymity, with the relationship between their real and fictive selves." From "Cervantes through Defoe and Richardson, three writers who were important to Hawthorne, concern with the nature of the writer's identity is so central that it becomes more a thematic than simply a biographical or psychological issue. So too with Hawthorne." Dryden urges that "the writer's self" be thought of as "a thematic self, a self that may be defined simply as the organizing principle or conceptual center of his work" (p. 11).

Although this definition may be a little reductive, Dryden has concisely identified a key interpretative problem: the fictionalizing of the authorial self. When does the author speak *in propria persona*? How does one know? Dryden observes that "to suggest that the writer's self is his major theme . . . is not to imply that he is immediately available to his reader. Like a name, the surface of a text may conceal as much as it expresses. Hawthorne, more than most writers perhaps, is fascinated by the ways in which a writer's work is at once a disguise he wears and a manifestation of his most intimate concerns" (p. 11).

The conventional wisdom on Hawthorne's authorial identity sees the narrative voice of his early "provincial" tales as identical with that of the "young Nathaniel," presumed inheritor of New England Calvinism: mired in Puritanism, the green youth had not yet developed his mature style and was embarrassingly nationalistic. This aspect of the Hawthorne Question continues to the present day, even in the face of persuasive newer critical arguments for the simultaneity of Hawthorne's preoccupation with the moral and ethical issues of the political history of America *and* his aesthetic distance in his first tales and sketches.[3] In this book I am only tangentially concerned with a biographical Hawthorne. My focus is the figured authorial self of Hawthorne's works, the representation of the artist figure worrying about his audience, puzzling over the interaction of waking life and a dream life, and musing on the relation of fiction and history—especially American history. Hawthorne's ethical psychology, politics, historiography, and metaphysics are bound up in the questions of his aesthetic distance, deployment of narrators, and figured authorial presence.

Pared down, the Hawthorne Question is exemplified by the critical perplexity over his provincial texts and his sometimes provincial narrators in the first period of his career. Conventionally, the first phase is identified as the twelve years or so from about 1825 to just after the publication of the first edition of *Twice-told Tales* in 1837. Although the focus of my argument is on this early period, its actual scope is wider. This book addresses problems of narratology and historiography, ethics and psychology, romanticism and realism, and the cultural mythoi of America. Embedded in it is the interpretative tradition regarding Hawthorne. Indeed, Hawthorne studies and criticism on nineteenth-century fiction in general and romance narrative in particular may be called the "extended text" of Hawthorne's works.[4] In terms of the broad questions of Hawthorne the writer, this book attempts to demonstrate the validity of four claims: (1) that he early perfected the art of the open-ended "twice-told" tale and sketch dominated by an insistent but ironic authorial presence; (2) that this skeptical authorial presence frames and foregrounds the problematic function of Hawthorne's narrators; (3) that it aesthetically contextualizes and complicates any "interpretation" of American history to be found in his works; and (4) that the "shape of Hawthorne's career" is consistent along aesthetic lines that he developed from the beginning.

Consequently, this book makes an argument against a sizable group of scholar-critics of the last thirty years or so and modifies a number of others. I take issue with interpretations of Hawthorne based narrowly on conventional preconceptions concerning his biography, human psychology, New England Puritanism, or the American experience. What Benjamin Disraeli called the "psychobiographical" is of least interest; and I argue against those interpretations, older and newer, that cast the younger Hawthorne into the role of perpetual mother-dependent adolescent and, by a curious logic, thereby deny narrative complexity to Hawthorne's early prose. On the other hand, I privilege critical commentary that leads to a *dialogue* about Hawthorne in a "provincial" American context (whether I agree with it or not) and Hawthorne in a "cosmopolitan" European context.

The overall organization unfolds in seven chapters of varying length. The introduction and the next chapter are intended to provide a historical and especially a theoretical frame around close readings of representative provincial tales in chapters two through five. These four exegetical chapters are followed by a concluding frame chapter that attempts to draw together the various themes of history, fiction, romance, dreamvision, narrative technique, genre, authorial presence, and self-reflexivity in Hawthorne's early works and to open out the implications of the study for the next cycle of Hawthorne's career.

The general question of provinciality provides a critical-historical context in which to address the Hawthorne Question; and Hawthorne's notion of the provincial is central to a study of his fictional concerns and techniques prior to the publication of *Twice-told Tales*. Hawthorne's early "American" tales were originally designed to be part of a story-collection or narrative-cycle. There were principally three such projected (but unpublished) collections: *Seven Tales of My Native Land* (c. 1827), *Provincial Tales* (ante 1832), and *The Story Teller* (c. 1832–34). The themes of naive earnestness versus aesthetic distance in these so-called provincial tales[5] are intricately involved in the relation of ethics and irony in Hawthorne and the major opposition posed in Hawthorne studies of *history* versus *romance*. Along with these issues comes a host of related binarial "romantic" problems: truth and fiction; actual and imaginary; dreaming and waking; and the indeterminate and unsettling relationships between conscious/unconscious or unconscious/subconscious or conscious/subconscious mental activity. Binaries of a formal literary nature, most particularly the distinction between *tale* and *sketch*, so insisted upon by Poe, are for Hawthorne points on a generic continuum rather than discrete or opposed modes.

This book is intended as a more-or-less formalist corrective, or at least an aesthetic counter, to psychological, biographical, and overly historicist approaches to a "Hawthorne," the "shape" of his career, and the "question" of America.[6] It explores how Hawthorne addresses the complex relationships of an "author" to a "narrator" and an "audience" at several levels of figuration. These matters are not only implicit, but also explicitly foregrounded by Hawthorne in *Provincial Tales* and *The Story Teller*. From the

Provincial Tales I extract a paradigmatic set of eight representative "provincial" narratives ranging from dreamvision sketches to historical romance tales. Narratival paradigms are adapted to Hawthorne from narratology theory, especially the semiotics of narratological mediation and transaction. These paradigmatic narratives illustrate differing techniques of authorial presence and mediation and the indeterminacy of genre boundaries. From *The Story Teller* papers I extract (in the last chapter) a self-reflexive portrait of the artist as simultaneously romantic and ironic.

Romanticism itself, properly conceived, is a corrective to one-sided, provincial views — particularly that accommodative, more or less harmonious confluence of romantic theories of narrative as transgeneric and dialogical. The importance of recovering the concept of romantic dialogics (as distinguished from dialectics) cannot be overemphasized. The open-ended binary of monological and dialogical was specifically articulated by romantic aesthetic theorists in the 1790s and early 1800s; and in discussing the romantic context of the Hawthorne Question, I play off against the problem of "provinciality" a series of related romantic aesthetic concepts. These include (1) a special meaning of *twice-told*; (2) the constructs *psychological romance*, *negative romance*, and *negative romanticism* (along with the attendant terms *negative closure*, *negative allegory*, *negative apocalypse*, and *negative epiphany*) as major components of romantic narratology; (3) romantic dialogics and author-narrator relationships; and (4) the author figure or storyteller as romantic trope. These aspects of romantic narratology radically modify concepts of "provinciality."

Provincialism: A Two-Edged Sword

Critical assumptions of Hawthorne's unmediated provincialism are not hard to understand. For, as if in response to the call for literary nationalism in the 1820s and 1830s, Hawthorne seems to have been intent on producing a thoroughly American volume as his entrée to the provincial literary scene. Certainly the titles of his first two planned collections would seem to indicate some such intention. And, in fact, we should *not* underestimate the deliberate provinciality of Hawthorne's early tales and sketches.

To say "deliberate" is, in this context, to separate oneself from critics who see the early Hawthorne trapped inside an inherited Puritanism, a painfully earnest youth lacking objective distance from provincial American history.[7] In this view, New England Puritanism and the American Revolution form not only a *history* but also a *mythos* — an all-containing, thoroughly limited text that Hawthorne could not get outside — in essence a cage. In such an approach, the word *provincial* is especially appropriate, meaning more than its literal signification of something characteristic of or restricted to a particular locale, away from the center. In general, the word connotes naiveté, narrowness, ignorance, immaturity, bias, one-sidedness. From a specifically literary point of view, it suggests that the writer's material is somehow inadequate or that the writer has not appropriately developed the material. A further implication is that the artist has not developed or matured sufficiently to get outside the containing, restrictive boundaries of his culture. Theoretically this provincialist view is problematical in that it glosses over the inside/outside cultural dilemma of any literary production, including Hawthorne's early and later work, by simply separating inside and outside. In Hawthorne's case, the provincialist answer to an old aesthetic-philosophical question is to separate his works chronologically and designate them immature and mature respectively. The result is a triangulation of large interchangeable constructs in characterizing Hawthorne's early work: the inside view of cultural containment, provinciality, and immaturity.[8]

"Provincialism," however, is double-edged, and the term does in fact describe a major aspect of Hawthorne's art. Roy Harvey Pearce has argued that provincialism, far from being a constraint on Hawthorne's imagination, opened up a world of creative possibilities but that Hawthorne's later European experiences "tended to make him see the differences between Europe and America as almost black and white" so that as an older man "his latent provinciality" came "to dominate his mind and his sensibility" in a negative way. This formulation uncritically adopts the familiar perception of Hawthorne's flagging creative powers after 1852, and it reflects in the critic the latent provinciality that is charged to Hawthorne. For the American writer's creative energies, Europe is bad, America good. Hawthorne should give up false European models and use the provincial materials of his "dear native land." Pearce argues that Hawthorne's interpretation of America was centrally informed by a mythic sense of New World history as proleptic of the fulfillment (in American independence) of the Puritan errand into the wilderness to found the City of God, so that when Hawthorne strayed from his grand provincial theme to write Europeanized romances, his artistry suffered. Provincialism was the source of Hawthorne's creative power and his "American" works his best.[9]

David A. Hollinger's remarks in *In the American Province* are pertinent to a less constrained consideration of provincialism in Hawthorne. Hollinger points out that two typical reactions of "provincials" tend to be opposite:

> The recognition that one is "in a province" can inspire conflicting sentiments. Some people celebrate the particularity of the province,

and advance provincialism as a doctrine. In this view, the virtue of a province is its sustaining homogeneity, its distance from the varied social world beyond provincial borders. Others recoil from this potential confinement, and advance the cause of cosmopolitanism against the imperatives of provincial life. Then, the point of being in a province is to get beyond it, to encounter and absorb a range of experience by means of which one can cease to be "provincial."

But there is a third position, one which embraces Hawthorne and is embraced by Hawthorne. Hollinger continues:

> In between these two abstractions—provincialism and cosmopolitanism—spans a field of concrete possibilities. Somewhere amid these real options most of us try to have it both ways, avoiding at once the constraints of a province too narrowly defined and the discomforting instability of a universe too vast and varied for us to make our own. Having it both ways depends, of course, on finding the right spot along the spectrum from the local to the universal. . . . The insight that America is a province of a civilization that also embraces the national cultures of Europe is hardly new, but the historiographical implications of this truism have been slow to take hold.[10]

Hollinger is referring in the last remark to twentieth-century intellectuals. But in fact the ambiguity of being provincial was recognized much earlier by major writers of the American renaissance. Emerson, for example, not only wrote a classic essay in affirmation of a kind of provincialism in "The American Scholar" (1837) but also directly addressed the double nature of provincialism in "New England Reformers" (1844) and *Society and Solitude* (collected 1870). So did Thoreau, in a more prickly way, wryly understating (and overstating) the matter in the opening of *Walden* (1854): "I have travelled a good deal in Concord." Some years later Emily Dickinson gave puckish expression to the double perspective of provincialism. The narrator of a poem composed circa 1861 (J.285) observes that the "Robin's my Criterion for Tune — / Because I grow—where Robins do," in New England. The local habitation becomes habituation. What the narrator calls the "ode familiar" is what "rules" perception; that is, she sees "New Englandly." The provincial vision is to be found everywhere, even back in the cosmopolitan center, Old England: "The Queen, discerns like me — / Provincially—." Such a recognition is very much in the Hawthorne mode.[11]

Problematizing the province of New England piety, Michael Colacurcio reformulates the Hawthorne Question as the "Hawthorne Problem" (the title of his first chapter). He takes exception to the mythic, oneiric, escapist-fantasy critics and defends Hawthorne as social critic and moral historian. In particular, he tries to counter such pronouncements as Nina Baym's that "history" was a "constraint" on Hawthorne's "imagination" and reaffirms in a more critically sophisticated way the basic position of Roy Harvey Pearce. Colacurcio formulates the "Hawthorne Problem" around Herman Melville's and Henry James's estimates of their compatriot, depending subsequent criticism from their two views. James saw Hawthorne as remote from the actual and the historical — an aesthete. Melville saw at Hawthorne's center his Calvinist sense of "the power of blackness." Colacurcio asks the basic question: why could not Hawthorne be both the American Calvinist and the aesthete? What if Hawthorne intended to "get up" his Puritan ancestors as a "quasi-academic subject, as part of a quasi-historical attempt to 're-cognize' the authorial intentions of writers like John Winthrop and Cotton Mather"? As self-conscious artist, Hawthorne "might well have enjoyed a certain doctrinal distance from his Puritan ancestors and have managed a certain esthetic distance from his Calvinist subject" (pp. 12–13). Thus, despite his emphasis on Hawthorne the romance writer as moral historian, Colacurcio also emphasizes his aesthetic distancing, suggesting that Hawthorne as well as any twentieth-century philosopher-historian understands that we are always dealing with "texts," not raw truth or fact.

This recognition is congruent with the idea that Hawthorne was carefully playing on the double implications of "provincial" when he answered the call for a native literature. He did so in a calculatedly duplicitous way; and, as with all ironists, he was misread by some readers. Others, however, understood his irony and therefore recognized the dialogical quality of his fiction. In part, this effect was what the *Dublin University Magazine* called in 1855 Hawthorne's technique of "negative suggestion."

The Dublin review is a particularly interesting and historically useful piece, for it is an early appreciation of Hawthorne's deliberate duplicity not only in regard to the question of simplistic provinciality, but also in regard to the question of literary form and effect in the early shorter narratives. The reviewer notes that, beyond the three major romances then published, "the rest of Hawthorne's works consist principally of tales and sketches." In these, "allegory is frequently employed, with masterly effect." Hawthorne combines the "quaint, nervous simplicity" of that "prince" of dreamers and allegorists John Bunyan, with "his own rich vividness of descriptive power, and quiet under-current humor." But many of Hawthorne's compositions "sound as incomplete half utterances, hinting but vaguely at the meaning intended to be conveyed, though we are not sure if we should call this indefiniteness a defect — the *power of negative suggestion* thus displayed being often perfectly magical." This "power of negative suggestion" apparently applies even to form. "On the whole," the reviewer remarks, the "walk" in which Hawthorne may most excel is "that blending of the essay, sketch, and tale, for which we have no definite term as yet — a style which . . . is perhaps the most difficult of all. . . ."[12] This description applies quite well to the works examined in the exegetical chapters, where precisely these intertwined ideas of "provinciality" and "negative suggestion" are discussed in terms of the "blending of essay, sketch, and tale."

Hawthorne demonstrates such irony, negative suggestion, and aesthetic distance from the first. That his early narratives are loosely known as the "provincial tales" is wonderfully ironic in itself; for although they are indeed provincial in subject, they also constitute an early embodiment of religious-theological, moral-ethical, cultural-historical, and aesthetic-philosophical *perspectivism* in Hawthorne's writings. Hawthorne's historical and psychological "romances" are anti-absolutist; and neither the destiny of the Puritans as the chosen of God, nor the "rising glory of America" are chauvinistically celebrated. He wrote tales and sketches that *seem* to be romantic nationalistic evocations of an American mythos — of American history, of American manifest destiny, of American legend, and of American heroes. But within or alongside the provincialist element, in tension with it, runs a line of skepticism and ambiguity, so that when Hawthorne uses the word "provincial" to describe his tales and sketches he does so with a knowing look, and sometimes the sly wink of an authorial Merry Andrew. It is his way of having it both ways: the way of the romantic ironist who is both seriously engaged with his subject matter, caught by it, and aesthetically and critically disengaged from it at the same time — the double vision of the teller of the twice-told provincial tale or sketch.

This view is not universally accepted by Hawthorne scholars, several of whom, though sympathetic to the interpretative perspectivism Hawthorne brings to historiography, still struggle with "having it both ways" on the "question of America." In poststructuralist terms, the question is one of being contained or imprisoned within one's culture, within its concepts of history and categories of valuation. Hawthorne not only acknowledges the "iron cage" — the inside view; he also emphasizes it. And yet, through the art of romantic narrative, Hawthorne suggests that one can attain the liberating outside view too. And, what is more liberating, both simultaneously.[13]

Negative Romanticism, Psychological Romance, Negative Romance

The idea of a symbolic representation or even allegory of the discovery of a hidden self or of an "other" realm of psychic existence is highly suggestive for the reading of the mythic drama of romantic texts. When recontextualized in a romantic frame, some more-or-less psychological emphases yield various insights. Unfortunately, psychological criticism has been dominated by the biographical—and vice versa. The principal model has been unreconstructed literary Freudianism. This enterprise is suspect when psychoanalytic constructs like Oedipal conflict and sibling incest are applied without mediation to the *author*, rather than employed as aspects of a particular methodology of reading *texts* (with their many conventions). Most psychological and biographical approaches tend to be naive regarding both psychoanalysis and literature and frequently are offered as a substitute for engagement with the literary text. Easy to do badly, biographical criticism is difficult to do well.

Distortions of Hawthorne's familial and political orientation and of his position in the publishing trade in America are promulgated without recourse to the available data. Amateur psychoanalyses of the biographical subject flat-footedly tramp across the faint fossil record of a human being's life. Misconceptions of Hawthorne's concept of vocation and his literary praxis in his early phase are repeated uncritically. Of more legitimate psychological and of much more intrinsic critical interest are questions of Hawthorne's conscious artistry as a romantic skeptic in the genre that he himself called in the 1851 preface to *The Snow-Image* "psychological romance."[14]

By this term, as he was at pains to observe in the same preface, Hawthorne did not mean direct self-revelation. Instead, psychological romance was for him a complex inquiry (via the romance form) into human psychology conceived historically, philosophically, and ethically. Psychological romance deals with human experience that is specific in place and time but partakes of what Hawthorne calls "our common nature." Hawthorne's earliest works throw into high relief his concerns with the special problems of his "dear native land" in relation to the common, possibly archetypal, nature of humankind and the unfolding of time as conceived by the age. The American, specifically the New England, experience is complicated by the perception of the New World as a "province" of the Old, both separate from and part of Europe. It is further complicated by the particular American vision of an ideal society in terms of a concept of the providential and messianic meaning of history in which the chosen province is revealed to be not marginal but central.

For Hawthorne, however, the Great Plan was not so clear. And whatever else universal human nature might be, it was ultimately mysterious. It was something into which Hawthorne said he wanted to "burrow" so deep as to penetrate into the dusky province of an "other" existence. This realm was indistinct, indirectly accessible, and destabilizing: it was the sphere of what was then called the "nightside of nature." Any theory of romanticism must include this perception of a negative other side of existence, no matter how benign the orientation of a particular romantic writer. The nightside was not purely negative; it included imaginary visions, fantasies, dreams. It was — as in the poetry of Poe — sometimes supernally beautiful as well as nightmarish. It was the province of the nonrational and the irrational, collectively, the unconscious of the human race. The province of the mysterious Other was, somehow, related to the conscious, waking, daytime life, but it worked in unknown or half-known ways. Comfortable neoclassical concepts of an intentionally controlled life and a unified or at least unitary self were eroding.[15] The borders between the conscious, the subconscious, and the unconscious, between the apparitional and real, waking and dreaming, were uncertain and wavering. The borderland itself constituted what Hawthorne called a "ghostland" that "romance," rather than the "novel," might reveal. In addition to the relation of ethics and irony, a central concern of the present study is the intersection of "dreamvision" and "actuality," and of psychology and history, as components of "romance," whether as tale or sketch.

The term *romance* stems from the example of the long medieval narrative, either verse or prose, in the local, provincial language. Romance is conventionally defined as aggressively fictitious narrative (i.e., legendary) of the idealized loves and adventures of great heroes (especially princes and knights) involved in some great quest and characterized by extraordinary, mysterious, or marvelous events. Applied to modern prose narrative after 1740, such definitions are inadequate not just in terms of the novel of everyday life, but also for description of the new forms of the romance. By the 1790s the romance had undergone a variety of transmutations. Romantic narrative was not conceived as merely tales of heroic adventure, patriotic triumph, idealized love, or noble idealism. Neither was the supernatural a necessary or even a distinguishing characteristic — not even of the gothic romance. Nor was romance restricted to conventional allegory or parable affirming traditional values.[16]

Instead, the new prose romance was becoming in avant garde Continental and American romanticism — in the writings of Denis Diderot, Jean Paul Friedrich Richter, Ludwig Tieck, Friedrich Schlegel, Clemens Brentano, E. T. A. Hoffmann, Mary Shelley, Thomas De Quincey, James Hogg, Charles Brockden Brown, Washington Irving, Edgar A. Poe, Herman Melville, and Nathaniel Hawthorne — somehow inherently and simultaneously "negative," in a special meaning of that term. The negative romance included countercurrents to an upper surface of idealized character, motive, and theme. Beneath ringing phrases of the right, the true, the noble, the eternal, and the providential were — apart from the horrific, the disgusting, the degraded — unresolved inconsistencies and contradictions, meaningless or confusing paradox — and not merely at the level of the gothic tale, but also at the level of national epic.

As a contemporary term for the new literature, *romance* implied a narrative form of complicated design, in which the modern version of the quest was to incorporate the irregular, the conflictual, the incomplete, the half-known with their opposites. The opposite of the known is the unknown; the opposite of the half-known, in one sense, is the half-known: its own mirror image. The romantic theory of the romance suggested that the new form was to go beyond the symmetries, social surface, mundane ambiance, and conventional didacticism of the eighteenth-century novel. The romance was to plumb "depths" as well as soar to "heights": psychological turbulence as well as spiritual aspiration, ennobling idealism alongside (possibly metaphysical) iniquity. Eschewing simplistic didacticism (or ironically undercutting it), the new romance sought to embody the positive and the negative in a self-reflexive form that subverted even itself. In the hands of Hawthorne, Melville, or Poe, the romance doubled back on itself and called into question its own status as "romance."[17]

From Negative Romance to Negative Allegory

Although the literary avant garde (especially in Europe) often designated the ironic text of complex design by the term *romance*, for clarity I shall use the term *negative romance* to describe certain of Hawthorne's American "provincial narratives." The phrase has several advantages, one of which is suggesting forcibly the tension between idealized romantic elements and negating countercurrents deliberately embodied in the same text. Works like "The Gray Champion" or "Endicott and the Red Cross" are highly qualified romantic tales of the author's native land. Somber or earnest enough on the surface (ostensibly tales of devotion, determination, or courage in the face of adversity), they are informed by overall ironic authorial mediation. In this way, a seemingly tragic romance, like "Roger Malvin's Burial," is doubly negative. In an expanded sense, the old charge of Hawthorne's sentimentality also applies inversely; these sentimental and provincial texts are often intertwined, as in "The Gentle Boy." Hawthorne often deliberately constructs a sentimental narrative and then deconstructs it — just as he constructs a version of American historical myth and deconstructs it.[18]

The connection of negative romance with Morse Peckham's original formulation of "negative romanticism" should be readily apparent. The series of key "negated" terms that I employ — *negative suggestion* (after the Dublin review), and *negative closure, allegory, apocalypse,* and *epiphany* — depends from the broad rubric *negative romanticism* as an umbrella term for Hawthorne's aesthetic and philosophical orientation. Peckham's basic concept is that the negative romantic is "lost" between the world views of neoclassic static mechanism and the dynamic organicism of the romantics; I mean to use the term as modified by Peckham's followers. Michael J. Hoffman, for example, uses the phrase "negative romanticism" to mean something like "subverting irony," very much akin to "romantic irony."[19] The romantic ironist, rather than being "lost," acknowledges and embraces contradiction, opposition, and paradox in a deliberate aesthetic embodiment of indeterminacy in tension with determinacy.[20] Thus "negative" romanticism does not mean *anti*-romanticism, but the negative side of *romanticism.* My intent in using such terms as *negative romanticism* and *negative romance* is not so much to resolve anything as to accommodate multiplicity in a critical discourse that recognizes the polyvalence of romanticism. I use the term *negative romanticism* in its multifaceted and subversive sense to mean a work that is predominantly the *conscious* embodiment of the indeterminate and the conflictual as opposed to a *sub*conscious (re)enactment of unresolved oppositions and contradictions in the culture.[21]

By analogy with negative romance, then, terms like *negative closure* and *negative allegory* are advanced. By *negative closure* I mean that technique of abrupt, truncated, inconclusive denouement by which dreaming and waking, the imagined and the actual, are left ambiguously blurred in a narrative form that undercuts the reader's preconceived (genre) expectations. This effect is present to some degree in almost all of Hawthorne's provincial tales, but it is especially evident in dreamvision sketches like "An Old Woman's Tale" and "The Wives of the Dead." In Hawthorne's employment of negative allegory, an old form of moral didacticism and the whole system of moral-historical-ethical-social-political-psychological-aesthetic relationships is called to mind only to be contested, countered, or deconstructed in turn. Although not a provincial American tale, "Rappaccini's Daughter" is perhaps the most vivid example of Hawthorne's negative allegory. Among the early provincial tales, "My Kinsman, Major Molineux" most clearly incorporates elements of the negative romance in the service of dismantling allegory in the sense of undermining the fixed correspondence on which traditional allegory depends.

The problem of allegory looms large in the criticism of Hawthorne's work. The most elaborate consideration of Hawthorne's "historical" allegory is that of John E. Becker, who is especially concerned about the clarity of a fixed allegorical meaning. Becker ambitiously attempts to distinguish different kinds of allegory as conceived by Hawthorne, the Puritans, and "traditional allegorists":

> The Puritans exercised their allegorical bent chiefly in the interpreta-
> tion of history, and history is also Hawthorne's favorite arena of fic-
> tional speculation. This conjunction of history and allegory suggests
> the possibility that some form of biblical typology, that is, the inter-
> pretation of historical events in terms of past events and future expec-
> tations rather than abstract concepts, is the literary characteristic
> which binds Hawthorne to his Puritan ancestors and distinguishes him
> from traditional allegorists.[22]

But it turns out that something more or less the opposite of Hawthorne's employment of "biblical typology" is Becker's thesis. He writes that his own study "was initially undertaken to question" Ursula Brumm's thesis that "typology is the distinguishing characteristic of the Puritan literary tradition in America." Close reading of Hawthorne, Becker says, has forced him "to the conclusion that typology is not as relevant to his technical apparatus as a more traditional form of allegory" (p. 4). Yet just a page earlier he writes that Hawthorne "is certainly not an allegorist in the traditional sense." Hawthorne "seems too skeptical, too unsure; he rejects the systems of thought he knew, both scientific and religious." Nevertheless, allegory is "still the closest approximation to a correct critical designation of Hawthorne's best work" but it is allegory "reshaped and redefined" (p. 4). This new allegory somehow includes older allegory, Puritan typology, romantic symbolism, a combination of realism and fantasy, ironies of various kinds. Becker's promising thesis is never precisely worked out, suggesting that the critic has been victimized more than mentored by the subversive character of Hawthorne's "allegory."[23] In my view, Hawthorne deploys allegory and typology *against* themselves and against the tradition of typological inter-pretation of American "manifest destiny" as the glorious possession of the North American continent by a capitalist Protestant nation. Thus we have "negative" allegory.[24]

   Closely related to the self-collapsing effect of negative allegory is that of negative apocalypse or negative epiphany. In works like "Young Goodman Brown" and "Alice Doane's Appeal," a prophetic revelation seems to con-stitute the narrative climax, if not also the denouement; but the vision is deliberately qualified, undercut, or incomplete. Sometimes Hawthorne creates a series of revelations, each one seemingly the ultimate unveiling of the truth, but each turning out to be only a kind of permanently penulti-mate apocalypse: the promised final meaning is always deferred. So too the literary idea of "epiphany," as borrowed from theology by James Joyce to describe the reader's or character's sudden transcendent recognition of the comprehensive symbolic meaning of a situation or scene, or of a whole text, may in Hawthorne be only a promised revelation, the "final" meaning always remaining just out of reach — as in the "Revelation" chapter of *The Scarlet Letter* — literally, in fact, the penultimate one. As with Hawthorne's negative allegory, so Hawthorne's apocalyptic scenes are "twice-told."

Twice-told: Dialogical Author-Narrator Relationships

Analogous to Hawthorne's techniques of deferring or denying a final "answer" in a narrative is the aesthetic theory of romantic dialogics. In contrast to previous studies of Hawthorne's first phase, here seeming inconsistencies or contradictions regarding the human psyche or the meaning of American history are seen as interestingly problematized — not just in critical retrospect but by Hawthorne himself. The discussion, therefore, is informed by a concept of the dialogical as rearticulated in our century by M. M. Bakhtin.

At its most basic level, the dialogical is acknowledgment that all intentionary discourse has conflictual or contradictory elements competing for dominance. In part, this recognition is the key to the meaning of the "twice-told" in Hawthorne. The literal meaning of *Twice-told Tales* is always taken to mean that the volume constituted their second publication and little more.[25] But in so titling his first published collection, Hawthorne opened the door wide for metaphorical implications of doubleness of various kinds. I am convinced that by "twice-told" he meant to indicate a double narrative quality and a capacity for redoubled interpretation. The *artist* of the dialogical does not seek "dialectical" unity or final "resolution" (a major twentieth-century misunderstanding of romantic aesthetics) but aesthetic accommodation and incorporation of contestatory elements. As an aesthetic principle, the dialogical derives from that negative romanticism, incorporating self-subversion, articulated a century and a half before Bakhtin by Friedrich Schlegel and Adam Müller as the foundation of romanticism itself.[26]

In Hawthorne, the dialogical applies not only to the multiple voices of various characters played off against one another, but also to competing narratival voices. These include that (or those) of an "authorial" narrator — and by implication those of narratees and audience, spoken or not. Central to Hawthorne's narrative aesthetics — particularly his deployment of the negative romance and the romantic sketch — is the complex nature of the foregrounded narrator as figured "author" and his intricate relation to the structure of narrator-narratee transactions, including the analogous ones of author and reader, implied or otherwise. The *author*-narrator as a fully or half fictionalized literary figure is precisely what most historicist and biographical critics leave out or tend to play down. This author-narrator figure is an integrating element of framed-narrative, a "figure" who creates a variety of frames (or framing effects) to produce an overall ambiguity of structure and tone in the provincial tales. As in the "Aubé-pine" frame of "Rappaccini's Daughter," the "author figure" is simultaneously taken seriously and satirized by the overarching authorial voice we call Hawthorne.[27]

The sometimes contradictory "Story Teller" figure lurks behind the now disassociated individual works of Hawthorne's first two framed-narrative collections, *Seven Tales of My Native Land* and *Provincial Tales*. As the surviving fragments of the third collection — the *Story Teller* cycle — reveal, the figure of the young narrator-author is frequently treated with humor and irony. Speaking in the first person, his narrative voice modulates from apparent univocal seriousness to deadpan self-parody. Reading sketches and tales from Hawthorne's early period as separate pieces radically decontextualizes them and generates major hermeneutical problems. We must therefore make some effort to recover at least part of the self-reflexive intertextuality of these early works through partial restoration (to the best of our ability) of Hawthorne's original design, with all its framing strategies and variations on "authorial" presence.[28]

That a distinction must be made between the flesh and blood author and his narrators is a basic tenet of many schools of criticism; but that distinction has come to seem to some recent critics less obvious (more problematic) than it was, say, to the American New Critics. Is there really any axiomatic reason to assume, prior to reading any text, that the narrative voice of a text is to be taken as distinct from the author named on the title page? Some critics have questioned the reasonableness of such a presumption unless, and only unless, the narrator is explicitly marked in some way as not congruent with the author: by being a first-person narrator-character in a narrative, by being named with a different name, by expressing attitudes contrary to or different from those somehow "known" to be held by the author, and so forth.[29] Nick Carraway narrates the story of *The Great Gatsby*; a vizier tells a story through Scheherazade; a knight tells his own story to Harry Bailey and the assembled Canterbury pilgrims through yet some other narrative presence; a Poe narrator, insisting that he is not mad, tells a story about murder and ghostly return and opium addiction. Does the "I" narrator of the frame of *Heart of Darkness* stand for Conrad? Is Marlow, through the frame "I," the mouthpiece of Conrad?

To take a more difficult question, does the author of *The Scarlet Letter* have Hester Prynne return to New England to "expiate" her "sin" because he is a male chauvinist consciously or unconsciously playing out his gender bias, or does Hawthorne present a psychological case study of a woman culturally and institutionally trapped in necessary yet unnecessary guilt? Does the narrator of *The Blithedale Romance*, the writer Coverdale, some-how embody the concealed misogynist attitudes of the author, Hawthorne, because Hawthorne's narrative of Coverdale's narrative leads to the death of the outspoken Zenobia? Or is Coverdale, the failed writer, presented dramatically and ironically by his "author" in a story *about*, among other things, misanthropy and misogyny?[30]

Vexed as some of these questions may be, there are others more vexed, such as those seemingly third-person narrators who use the pronoun "I" who are not directly characterized other than as "authors," who yet from text to text by the same author express different views. What are we to make of a chronicler-narrator, who is not especially particularized and is not a character in the dramatic world of the narrative, who contradicts himself or herself? Shall we, whenever some epistemological, moral, or ethical prob-lem, ambiguity, or contradiction presents itself, assume "loss of control" or attribute a set of "unfortunate" attitudes and cultural entrapment to the author? Even an unnamed "I" chronicler-narrator who more or less "sounds" like what we conceive the author to be from reading various texts may be a fictional character at some level; and it is here that biographical-interpretative problems become more tangled. Some critics, taking Haw-thorne's narrator in "The Gray Champion" as Hawthorne and presuming that Hawthorne is a proponent of the New World "democratic" experi-ment, an opponent of Old World "tyranny," conclude that Hawthorne would not be critical of the American colonists. Some critics refuse, writes Nina Baym, to acknowledge Hawthorne's "unqualified nationalism" be-cause they find it "unpleasant and inconsistent with what they take to be Hawthorne's true feelings" (*Shape of Hawthorne's Career*, p. 80). The trouble is that this criticism turns back upon the critic; the criticism that readers reject what they somehow take to be the author's unacceptable "true feel-ings" applies to Baym as much as to any other reader. As Colacurcio says, there is always "some *text* interceding": historical, biographical, and liter-ary — including the "conventions" of authorship.[31]

Author as Romantic Trope

Hawthorne himself has articulated a caveat for the reader regarding the identity of the flesh and blood author and any narrator, even those pretend-ing to be "Hawthorne" in the prefaces to some of his books. In the preface to *Mosses from an Old Manse*, he remarks that in his works: "So far as I am a man of really individual attributes I veil my face" (2:44). In the 1851 preface to *The Snow-Image and other Twice-told Tales*, dedicated to Horatio Bridge, the "author" writes:

> My Dear Bridge, — Some of the more crabbed of my critics, I understand, have pronounced your friend egotistical, indiscreet, and even impertinent, on account of the Prefaces and Introductions with which, on several occasions, he has seen fit to pave the reader's way into the interior edifice of a book. In the justice of this censure I do not exactly concur.... [Despite] *whatever appearance of confidential intimacy*, I have been especially careful to make *no disclosures respecting myself* which the most indifferent observer might not have been acquainted with, and which I was not perfectly willing my worst enemy should know....
>
> ... There is no harm, but, on the contrary, good, in arraying some of the ordinary facts of life in a slightly idealized and artistic guise. I have taken facts which relate to myself, because they chance to be nearest at hand, and likewise are my own property. And, as for egotism, a person, who has been burrowing, to his utmost ability, into the depths of *our common nature*, for the purposes of *psychological romance*, — and who pursues his researches in that dusky region, as he needs must, as well by the tact of *sympathy* as by the light of *observation*, — will smile at incurring such an imputation in virtue of a little preliminary talk about his external habits, his abode, his casual associates, and other matters entirely upon the surface. These things *hide the man, instead of displaying him*. You must make *quite another kind of inquest*, and look through the *whole range* of his fictitious characters, good and evil, in order to *detect any of his essential traits*. (3:385–86; my italics)

Is the narrator of *The Scarlet Letter*, characterized in the first person by himself in "The Custom-House" preface, Nathaniel Hawthorne? Is Coverdale Hawthorne? Some critics argue as if it were so, or as if the answer were obvious and simple. But Hawthorne is more often than not manipulating the convention of the "storyteller" as author-narrator. This manipulation adds another layer of narrative ambiguity to the text. As readers, not only do we need to be alert for relatively conventional unreliable narrators like the madman narrator of Poe's "Ligeia" or the possibly hallucinating narrator of "The Fall of the House of Usher" or the "safe" lawyer of Melville's "Bartleby" or the earnest governess in James's *The Turn of the Screw*, but also we need to pay very careful attention to the many possible self-reflexive variations on the convention of the author-narrator.

The figure of the author-narrator as a trope in Hawthorne's early works has been underemphasized and generally misunderstood, especially in its close alliance with the author-foregrounding genre associated with romantic irony, the *Rahmenerzählung*, the framed-narrative.[32] The presumption throughout the present work is that the inscribed author-figure trope is recoverable in a way that a biographical author is not. A simplified semiotic model of narratological transaction assists a more "romantic" reading of Hawthorne's "provincial" tales and sketches. A narratological approach also throws into high relief Hawthorne's careful paralleling of the political and moral beliefs in the culture at large with the psychological conflicts of particular individuals in his sketches and tales. What Hawthorne allegorizes, if anything, is the cultural and psychological *muddle* of the seventeenth and eighteenth centuries. Hawthorne gives us consciously crafted dramatic portrayal, not just unconscious self-revelation. More than the portrayer of individual psychology that most critics focus upon and more than the moral historian Colacurcio emphasizes, Hawthorne is also the psychoanalyst of relative cultural ethics, speaking with shifting layers of irony, through various authorial personae.[33]

Hawthorne's great subject may be, as Pearce and Colacurcio argue, "moral history." But Colacurcio is closer to the mark than Pearce in his perception that Hawthorne's moral history is focused on the *impact* of moral assumptions and codes upon culture and individuals rather than some sort of quasi-metaphysical moral thesis about the destiny of America. Hawthorne's attitude toward culturally codified morality exhibits that very aesthetic distance that critics have fretted over or downright denied in the early works. The narratological structures of these pieces and the authorial presence worked into them make quite clear that the traditional distinction between "moral" and "ethical" is Hawthorne's as well. The "moral" is conceived as those laws and axioms of right conduct deriving from revelation or some other authoritative source outside social practice. The "ethical" is defined as concepts of right conduct derived from ideas of the relation of human beings to human beings. Hawthorne is, in my view, more accurately described as the ethical analyst of "moral situations" as they become constituted in individuals (often through guilt) by current circumstances and cultural memory.

The mediating author persona — the figure of the *author*-narrator — is by no means a totally positive figure. Indeed, the artist is frequently the con artist, whose craft is to be suspected or at least examined. This figure is concerned not only with the narratees' perception of the relation of the conscious and the subconscious, the waking life and the dream life, but also with the writing down of "facts" in terms of the interpretative coherence of "fiction." Complicating the life of Hawthorne's storyteller, the genres are not neoclassically neat and clean. Governed by various (sometimes competing, sometimes overlapping, sometimes identical) conventions, the genres include *romance* and *history* in such a way as to foreground the fictionality of history and the ironies and ambiguities of romance. Hawthorne's provincial narratives exhibit considerable self-reflexivity in their presentation of the "author" as "narrator" in his many guises as "storyteller": chronicler, interpreter; wise man, fool; negative romantic, romantic ironist.

Oberon and Arabesque

Hawthorne's works are highly artificed, self-reflexive examples of contemporary romance congruent with the most sophisticated theories of the time. His presence in them is not personal in any conventional biographical sense, but figural or iconic: thus my insistence that the focus of this study is not the biographical subject of the author, but the figured literary self as authorial construct. The biographical is seen as a romantic trope, in the sense of a thematic self. Romantic authorial presence was intimately bound up in contemporary concepts of the artist self, interpenetrating but distinguished from a biographical self, manifest in the "new fiction." The authorial self is itself a romantic fiction.

The way a narrative is told by narrators — authorial and otherwise — not only shapes the hermeneutics of particular texts but also foregrounds the problematics of history, truth, and ethics. Among my central concerns are the relations of the tone, mode, and form of a text to ideological components, particularly ethical and moral ideologies intersecting the political and historical in the psychology of the individual. Rhetorical and formal elements are part of the narratological structuration of levels of ideology. The semiotics of narratology as defined here includes not only the idea of narratological transactions between and among author, implied author, narrator, narratee, implied reader, and reader, but also degrees of ethical and epistemological mediation presented by an explicit or implicit narrator presence and by explicit or implicit frames.[34]

This narratival authorial presence, implicitly or explicitly appearing in some guise as an author figure, mediates or conducts negotiations among the conflictual, the contradictory, the contestatory. To this amalgamating presence Hawthorne gives the general name of *Oberon*, his own nickname in college and first authorial pseudonym. By this naming of the storyteller, Hawthorne invokes the night world of imagination ruled by the fairy king of medieval and Renaissance legend and literature. And as all kings have their fools, so we have Oberon's antic alter-ego, Puck. The dynamic of the two entwined figures (paralleled in *The Story Teller* by figures specifically identified with Don Quixote and Sancho Panza) frequently generates a species of romantic irony. The embodiment of the romantic artist-self in the new romance is no simple thing, and Hawthorne's works exhibit a high degree of self-reflexivity focused on this theme/figure.

In Hawthorne's case, the problem of authorial mediation is further complicated by his particular position as a romancer who was also a serious historian, an interpreter of American history in ethical-psychological terms. While making recurrent use of the psychological and moral historicism of certain influential critics, I attempt to reconfigure Hawthorne's provincial narratives within romantic aesthetics of authorial presence. Throughout this book I try, not really to balance, but to integrate the literary and the historical, as is appropriate to the spirit of Hawthorne's own works. But at the present juncture of Hawthorne studies, the self-reflexive is a surprisingly neglected aspect. This is an especially curious phenomenon in view of the importance of self-reflexivity and metafiction in contemporary criticism.[35] Hawthorne's relation to romanticism is an aspect of his work that historical critics have virtually ignored. The view presented here is more thoroughly romantic; and (not surprising to romanticists) that makes it more contemporary.

Romantic aesthetics, especially as rediscovered and redefined since the 1970s, is not merely a topic of scholarly inquiry and historical interest. Romantic theories of narrative provide a viable way of conceptualizing the intersection of art as order or structure, however open-ended, and the world as chaotic or indeterminate, however provisionally patterned. The artistic theories of negative romanticism, when seen in their full complexity, have strong resonances with contemporary chaos theory and, to a surprising degree, with the destabilizing theoretical reevaluations of poststructuralism. Redefining romantic narrative in more contemporary terms while simultaneously recognizing its key differences from postmodern fictional praxis and poststructuralist aesthetics is a key to my approach in this study of Hawthorne. For throughout the present book, and especially toward its close, I employ a number of constructs and metaphors of symmetry, balance, and harmony that may seem incongruent with the aesthetics of unstable irony and indeterminacy detailed here. But the combination of chaos and structure, of pattern and randomness — what Friedrich Schlegel called "ein gebildetes, künstliches Chaos" — is in fact the point.

This large point may be clarified by reference to what Friedrich Schlegel was describing by the phrase "structured, artistic chaos": the *arabesque*. Hawthorne's provincial narrators are in the European tradition of the self-reflexive narrator; his narratives are in the tradition of the polyphonic narrative. As such, they demonstrate, not American exceptionalism, but

American continuity with the national cultures of Europe. Throughout, I attempt to point some new directions in narratological analysis that are of unsuspected importance for the recovery of a neglected and misunderstood distinction between "tale proper" and "sketch" in romantic aesthetics. In this, the Americans were exploring paths blazed by European writers. In America as in Europe the romantic sketch and the narrative cycle sometimes called a "sketch-book" are concentrated on the ever-present romantic artist self.[36] For a romantic writer like Hawthorne, the fine art of telling a story depends on a pervasive, carefully wrought fiction of authorial presence. This trope of the authorial self ties one story to another in an unfolding, aesthetically framed sequence that was known among the avant garde in the romantic era as the arabesque.

Thus, while not making much use of the term per se, I place central emphasis on the concept of romantic arabesque as a form and mode foregrounding the artist self and featuring aesthetically framed indeterminacy and perspectivity. By framing, aesthetic control of chaos is, if not realized, closely approached, achieving a kind of "neutral territory." Neither meliorist nor nihilist, Hawthorne was also not a complete relativist. He was instead given to fundamental traditionalist values of *caritas* and *sympathia* within a general acknowledgment of the primacy of *perspectiva*. The utter simplicity of the values of love and sympathy should not obscure Hawthorne's complexity or the paramount importance of perspectivity. Acknowledgment of the subjective is a step toward "higher" objectivity in the romantic sense; and combining subjectivity with objectivity means combining fundamental human values with perspectivity. The dialogical form most congenial to the aesthetic containment of the oppositional elements of subjective involvement and objective distance is what Schlegel called alternately *Arabeske* and *Roman* — that is, the new romantic fiction as opposed to the neoclassic. I contend that these concepts and forms are parallel to what Hawthorne called the "twice-told" and "psychological romance."[37] Such combined simplicity and complexity characterizes the figured, self-conscious romantic artist self. In this sense, Hawthorne's complex and subtle art of "Oberonic presence" in the *Provincial Tales*, as well as his other works, is the inclusive subject of this book.

1 Paradigmatics of *Provincial Tales:*
Narratological Transaction and Dialogical Framing

May not a man have several voices . . . as well as two complexions?
—Nathaniel Hawthorne, "My Kinsman, Major Molineux" (1832)

Hawthorne, despite his voluminous output, did not begin his career in a particularly auspicious way. For years he had no name as an author, no literary identity. Neither *Seven Tales of My Native Land* nor *Provincial Tales* ever saw publication as originally planned; nor, for that matter, did the more metafictional, satiric, and author-foregrounding collection *The Story Teller.* Rather, the bulk of these projected framed-narrative collections was subsumed in *Twice-told Tales* in a radically rearranged (actually dismantled) form in two separate installments in 1837 and 1842, and to a lesser extent in *Mosses from an Old Manse* in 1846 (revised 1854). Moreover, Hawthorne's first tales and sketches appeared without direct credit to him in a variety of periodicals from 1830 to 1837 before the first edition of *Twice-told Tales* came out in his name through the agency of a friend. Although Hawthorne seems to have been ambivalent about his anonymity in these early days, scholars have felt that he was victimized by editors and publishers. Both the editor of the gift annual *The Token* and the editor of the *New-England Magazine* filled their pages with Hawthorne's works but kept the author's name obscure via nonattribution and pseudonyms, possibly so that readers would not know that there were so many pages by one author in a single issue. From 1831 through 1836, nearly every volume of *The Token* contained from one to four Hawthorne pieces, and the 1837 volume contained at least eight. But he had been unable to get a volume published in his own name.[1]

Composition of Provincial Tales

By printing Hawthorne's early tales separately and out of sequence from the design of his projected framed-narrative collections, magazine editors altered contextualized meanings of some of the individual pieces. When the publisher to whom he had sent the *Seven Tales of My Native Land* seemed indifferent to his work, Hawthorne, like his author-character Oberon in "The Devil in Manuscript" (1835), retrieved the manuscripts and committed most of them to the flames — or so tradition has it — leaving only two manuscripts to survive in "kinder custody" than the author's.[2] But Hawthorne continued to experiment with projected narrative sequences. His next effort was the *Provincial Tales*. In December 1829, he submitted some of these to Samuel G. Goodrich, editor of *The Token*, for advice on how to get them published as a group. He commented that they were founded on the superstitions of his part of the country and were rather "wild" and "grotesque." We know from Goodrich that these pieces included "Roger Malvin's Burial," "The Gentle Boy," and "My Kinsman, Major Molineux," along with "The Wives of the Dead" and "Alice Doane's Appeal." Goodrich responded to Hawthorne's request for advice on his *Provincial Tales* manuscript on 19 January 1830, singling out "Alice Doane's Appeal" as the one piece that he doubted would get "public approbation." After some initial resistance, Hawthorne was persuaded to let Goodrich publish the other four works. "The Wives of the Dead," "My Kinsman, Major Molineux," "Roger Malvin's Burial," and "The Gentle Boy" were published in that order in the 1832 *Token* volume (again without Hawthorne's name). "Alice Doane's Appeal" did not appear until three years later in the 1835 *Token*.[3]

Based on these works and some fragments of contemporary testimony, we can say that the narratives of the *Provincial Tales* are of two major subject types: (1) historical, romance or otherwise; (2) legendary, tending toward gothic, supernatural or otherwise. Almost all of them have a nimbus of the supernatural and the oneiric; subjective and objective reality blend one into the other; and historical romance bleeds into supernatural legend.[4] Moreover, the distinction between the "sketch" and "tale proper," in Poe's sense of the latter term in his 1842 review of Hawthorne (*E&R*, p. 573), is deliberately blurred. Nevertheless, we can conveniently separate the narratives into these two groups of historical tale and gothic sketch for discussion of narrative technique. Both the historical romances and the gothic romances are "provincial," being firmly rooted in the history and culture of colonial America and set in a circumscribed New England locale.

Scholarly guesses as to what other surviving early pieces were part of *Provincial Tales* have enlarged the possible canon in various ways, though almost any of the earliest tales and sketches involving American folklore and colonial history of New England are likely candidates. "We do not know precisely what Hawthorne meant to imply by his title," Nina Baym writes in *The Shape of Hawthorne's Career* (p. 30), "nor how the tales were to be arranged and interrelated. If Hawthorne had a unifying scheme in mind, it is not implicit in the known stories. Critics' attempts to identify a thematic focus in *Provincial Tales* have often involved assigning additional fictions to the group or removing one or more stories from it." Indeed, Elizabeth Lathrop Chandler proposes adding adding "Dr. Bullivant," "The Gray Champion," "The May-Pole of Merry Mount," and "Young Goodman Brown" for a total of nine narratives. Nelson F. Adkins proposes "The Gray Champion," "Young Goodman Brown," "The May-Pole of Merry Mount," and "The Minister's Black Veil." Richard P. Adams, seeking collective unity around the theme of initiation, rejects "The Wives of the Dead" and "Alice Doane," but adds "The Gray Champion," "The May-Pole of Merry Mount," and "Young Goodman Brown." Alfred Weber, emphasizing the Puritan context of *Provincial Tales*, adds "The May-Pole of Merry Mount" and "The Gray Champion" and suggests that the seven stories were chronologically arranged. Baym suggests that a conservative approach is best: she will "stick with the known group, and reject the others because they were all written [*sic*] later than the original four or five."[5] I myself do not reject any of the above named works; most of them seem quite likely possibilities, if not probabilities. I observe merely that three of the very earliest works seem to make a paradigmatic pattern with those pieces definitely known to have been part of the disassembled manuscript. In the first category of historical romance, I suggest, speculatively, the addition of only a single historical work (itself somewhat legendary). This is the 1830 tale "The Gray Champion," added by all other commentators. In the second category of gothic romance, I suggest the likely inclusion of Hawthorne's two earliest printed pieces (one collected in *Twice-told*), both involving New England legend and folklore from the colonial period: "The Hollow of the Three Hills" and "An Old Woman's Tale."

All three pieces were published prior to the first volume of *Twice-told Tales* in 1837. The historical-legendary tale of "The Gray Champion" (1835) significantly stands as the introductory piece of *Twice-told Tales*; and Hawthorne's first two published sketches (both 1830) deal with native legends of witchcraft and the supernatural and with the psychology and epistemology of dreamvision in a manner similar to the blurring of fact and fiction in "Alice Doane's Appeal." With the addition of these works to those identified by Goodrich as part of the *Provincial Tales* manuscript, we have a group of eight narratives that gives us a paradigmatic representation of Hawthorne's early experimentation with genre, mode, and ambiguity and exemplifies the variations in his deployment of a storyteller narrator and attendant framing techniques. I do not mean to confine the *Provincial Tales* to these eight, nor do I pretend to suggest the precise contents of the volume. ("Young Goodman Brown," "The Minister's Black Veil," and "The May-Pole of Merry Mount," along with "Endicott and the Red Cross," are all likely candidates.) The eight narratives I have singled out offer, I emphasize, paradigms. Also the phrase "provincial tales" applies generally in Hawthorne criticism to any of the early narratives with recognizable American (New England) settings or concerns. But the three additional works suggested here — and I am not the first to suggest them — adumbrate the pattern of the volume.[6]

Of particular interest is the narratival structure of "The Gray Champion" (including the double narrative voice and the implied double narratee), partly because so many critics take it to be a plain and simple, completely unmediated nationalistic and pietistic yarn. Of the early pieces definitely known to be part of the *Provincial Tales*, the most highly metafictional narrative is "Alice Doane's Appeal." Although it "tells" an interior gothic story, it is, in its recurrent interpenetration by an intrusive narrator, more centrally a treatment of authorship and audience. The narrator is an author, who tells the story of how he reads one of his "tales" (merely "sketched" in) to two "young ladies." The interior story, previously written as part of a series (the narrator says) in the *Token* and (the narrator says) forgotten, is told from the retrospect of the disappointed author commenting on this second attempt at the same tale. The author's struggle to tell his story to an unresponsive audience comes to be the central narrative event and the term "intrusive" thus a misnomer. Between these two narratives are six other early works clearly illustrating the range of deployment of a narrator and narrator-character and the range from the tale proper to the indeterminate area of the romantic sketch.

Altogether the eight narratives suggest something of the nature of the framed tale-sketch ensemble that Hawthorne had originally planned. Cut loose from their narrative frames in which the character of the "Story Teller" was a foregrounded feature, the surviving *Provincial Tales* as we have them are generally less overt (certainly on a first reading) in insinuating the presence of an "author" than "Alice Doane's Appeal." But the Story Teller figure is there in all of them, mediating the text in various ways, modulating with varying degrees of irony the tonality and meaning of these "American" tales. To understand Hawthorne's narrative art, we must turn to a consideration of the narrator of a tale or sketch as a narrative figure.

Semiotics of Narratological Transaction

John M. Ellis, in his introduction to *Narration in the German Novelle* (1974), makes the elementary yet profound point that "narration is an essential part of the meaning of the story, and not a matter of technical value only."[7] His study of eight different narrative techniques in representative stories by Kleist, Tieck, Hoffmann, Grillparzer, Keller, Storm, Hauptmann, and Kafka focuses on the key question of narration as the "relation of the narrator to his story" (p. 25). Ellis assumes narrator not only to be distinct from author, but also to be "a distinct figure in his own right . . . not like any other character in the story." The narrator is a "highly conventional figure, to whom the convention of narration allows, on occasion and depending on the particular case, the ability to read other people's minds, to be present during conversations which could not have been overheard, to show extraordinary powers of memory, and so on. . . . The degree to which these conventional abilities are drawn upon in particular cases varies greatly, but without the existence of the convention in general no fiction is possible . . ." (p. 28).

Ellis is at pains to critique the naive assumptions of most theories of the *Novelle*. His very basic point is that "emergence of distinct characters to tell a story has often been taken as a means of guaranteeing the 'truth' of it. . . . Nothing could be further from the point of narration by distinct characters, who . . . do exactly the reverse; they limit the degree to which we can accept the story at face value by the fact that their own concerns, intelligence and stake in the story are delimited for us" (p. 37). Telling the story from the point of view of a character does not mean "any *necessary* sharing of attitude" between narrator and character (p. 39; my italics).

If this last point seems obvious, his next is not. The same lack of absolute continuity holds true for a seemingly omniscient narrator (and one might add for the implied author beyond the narrators). In fact, Ellis suggests that omniscience in narrators is "exceedingly rare." They usually have "distinct areas of knowledge, delimited in specific ways, for example limited as to type (knowledge of facts, of minds, of values of the story), or as to extent (knowledge of the facts as experienced by one character or group of characters, or knowledge of the minds of only one or a group)." Of central importance is the recognition that "it is very common for the conventional story-teller to have a distinct, limiting relationship with his story as far as his attitude to it is concerned." The point Ellis derives from this observation is of major importance and is subscribed to in the present study. The "attitude of the narrator is offered to us as part of [the story's] thematic material, *not* as a *key* to it; something for us to think about and evaluate, *not to accept as the attitude of the work as a whole*."[8]

Rather than "subscribe to any standard typology of narration," says Ellis, he prefers to ask a series of questions of the narrator of any work. (The narrators of the works he discusses in the rest of the volume are all presumed male.) The first question is: "To what extent does he emerge as a distinct character?" The narrator "may be one character among others, an actor in the story but not an especially important one." Or he may be "the central character of the book, . . . a story-teller having real physical existence within the story as a writer though not directly an actor in it"; or he may be "a story-teller having no physical existence in the story but still projected as a distinct figure through his explicit comments and thoughts." At the other "end-point of the spectrum," he may be "the distant unidentified narrator who makes no comment from the viewpoint of an observer, but who nevertheless can be endowed with a distinct outlook through the emphases he gives to what he reports" (pp. 32–33). Other important questions include: "How much does he intervene? Why does he intervene? How much does he know? What kind of knowledge does he have of people (their appearances or their thoughts) or of the universe in which they live? Where is he — always in the company of one character, more than one, or no-one in particular? And most importantly: What are his concerns, and the emphases which predominate in his story?" Any one of these questions, Ellis adds, "may have to be answered in different ways at different points in any one story."

Ellis does not deal much with the movement back and forth from an "author-figure" narrator to a character narrator involved to different degrees in the action of the narrative, though he does hint at this movement in E. T. A. Hoffmann, who is "concerned with the clash of different mental worlds, and thus narrates from several points of view" (p. 34). Hoffmann's multiple points of view habitually include that of a putative or fictive author (as in Hawthorne) fretting over the best way to marshal his story for the reader, highlighting the author-reader collaboration. (See, for example, the narrator's intrusion a third of the way into "The Sandman.") Hoffmann, writes Ellis (p. 35), "demands constant action, interpretation, and then reinterpretation on the part of his readers." That is, this demand is thematic, as in Hawthorne.

Hoffmann and Hawthorne radically reconceive not only point of view but also concepts of dramatic or narrative unity — especially those prescriptions derived (as the neoclassicists thought) from Aristotle. Romantic writers came to emphasize the principle that narrative unity is shaped by multiple point of view and by authorial-narratorial relationships that both constitute and frame exponentiating point of view. And genre is yet another kind of frame or point of view, especially pertinent to romantic concepts of the effects and purposes of the "sketch" and "tale proper." Although I discuss the dreamvision sketches before I discuss the historical tales, the basic paradigms are generated from the more fully developed "Freytag" pattern of drama and "tale proper." That is, the norm of the unified story or novel is taken to be the exposition :: complication :: crisis (climax) :: denouement (reversal - catastrophe) pattern of the conventional Aristotelian narrative as we have come to know it since the Renaissance.[9] By this I mean to say that the narratival paradigms suggested here as helpful to understanding Hawthorne's story-telling technique are based on Hawthorne's variations on that standard pattern from a taxonomic or paradigmatic point of view.

Thus the exegetical chapters take up the narratives in an order that highlights the relative presence or absence of a narrator or narrator-author and the employment of exterior or interior, explicit or implicit framing devices. This strategy marshals a cumulative weight of evidence for reading even so seemingly straightforward a tale as "The Gray Champion" as an ambiguous narrative employing a complicated author persona with at least two masks, one obtuse, one satiric, and suggests the possibility of an ambivalent symbolic figuration of author and reader in the narrative of "My Kinsman, Major Molineux." Each of the four historical narrative-tales has an interior introduction in which a technically first-person narrator or author figure sets the story to follow in the context of colonial history and proceeds to tell the narrative *as though* from the third person. These introductions vary in length and tone, but each does more than contextualize its tale historically. The historical "preface" (as one of Hawthorne's narrators calls it) may also set up a hermeneutical tension between a narrator's interpretation and the structure of the ensuing tale, so that the whole system of structures suggests, often inversely and ironically, an overarching theme not immediately evident on the surface of the story. The eight texts fall into two categories of four each, ranging from "sketch" to "tale proper." They represent the tensions of dream and actuality, romance and history. The four sketches tend toward dream and legend; the four tales tend toward history. Insofar as legend reflects some kind of historicity of place, all eight partake of history. All eight also partake of romance. They resist neat categorization. Each pushes toward a deformation of its apparent genre.

In general (and only in general), as we move from tales to sketches, the focus on the narrator as author figure and upon the art of narrating the narrative to various narratees is sharpened, and the art of closure is more implicitly involved in understanding the nature of the narrative mode employed by this author figure. The tendency of Hawthorne's narratives is to move from one end of the received generic spectrum toward a middle of some kind, a form "for which we have no definite term as yet." The narratives dealt with here may be conceived as exhibiting a tendency toward an

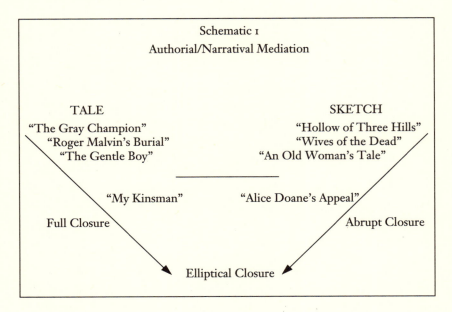

Schematic 1
Authorial/Narratival Mediation

TALE

"The Gray Champion"
"Roger Malvin's Burial"
"The Gentle Boy"

SKETCH

"Hollow of Three Hills"
"Wives of the Dead"
"An Old Woman's Tale"

"My Kinsman"   "Alice Doane's Appeal"

Full Closure   Abrupt Closure

Elliptical Closure

axis of "authorial/narratival mediation" and "elliptical closure," bounded on either side by norms of tale and sketch, and by observed norms of conventional closure (full closure) and violated norms of closure (abrupt closure). Thus the theoretical-formal relations and narratological organization of the present book may be represented by the diagram in schematic 1. In his sophisticated experimentation with narrative paradigms, genre conventions, and manipulation of narrators and narrative voices, Hawthorne was in his narrative aesthetics so startlingly contemporaneous with us that he anticipates concepts of semiotic "transaction" articulated by later-twentieth-century narratologists.[10]

As a first-stage consideration, we may go back to the simplified paradigm offered in M. H. Abrams's *The Mirror and the Lamp*. This is the AUTHOR-TEXT-READER-WORLD paradigm of the "Orientation of Critical Theories" section of that book.[11] To this model I have added "Literary Convention" in brackets (schematic 2).

The schematic is seductively simple. Booth, Chatman, Prince, Iser, and Lanser, however, suggest that our ideas of the "real" reader and the "real" author are represented in a text by substitute agents: particularly (1) the *implied author*, (2) the *implied reader*, (3) the *narrator(s)* telling the story to some (4) *narratee* (which may or may not be, directly, us). The implied author is inevitably assembled by a reader from all the components of a text (the design of the whole). The implied author is not only separate from a rhetorical narrator and from a narrator who is a character literally in the

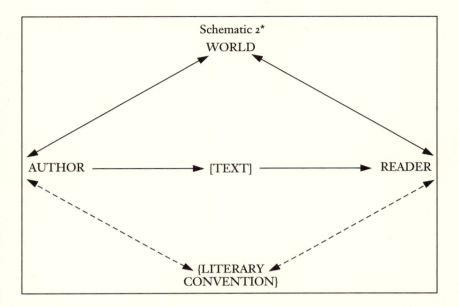

dramatic world of the text (for example, the "I" narrator-character in a typical Poe story of a murderous maniac), but also from the historical or biographical "real" author (that is, a Nathaniel Hawthorne or an Edgar Poe). The "simple" schematic of Author-Text-Reader or even of Author-Narrator-Text-Reader is thus radically problematized, as shown in schematic 3. A different (more linguistically oriented and simplified) diagram might look something like the one in schematic 4.

One of the first things one notices is the immediate exponential gain in complexity graphically illustrated even by so relatively simple a schematization. The relations of multiple narrators to *each* different multiple narrative to *each* different narratee (and their multiples) are not even represented. (All figures are potentially variables.) Hawthorne, I am claiming, is as a literary artist not only aware of these implicit relationships in narrative as represented by schematic 3 but in fact foregrounds them over and over again. He thematically heightens their epistemological implications, frequently in the manner of mid-twentieth-century metafictionists like Jorge Luis Borges, Thomas Pynchon, John Hawkes, or John Barth. Hawthorne particularly attacks the juncture of implied author and narrator speaking to a shifting narratee, especially evident in "Alice Doane's Appeal."

The trickiest concept to employ is that of different levels of *narratee* in

*From the basic paradigm of M. H. Abrams with emphasis on the "reception" of narrative "flow" to the "reader."

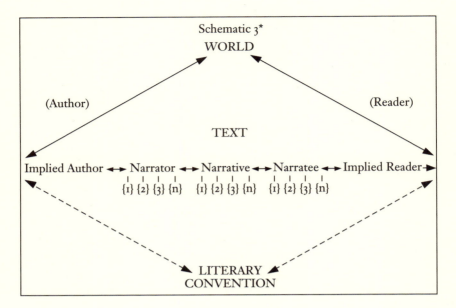

Schematic 3*
WORLD

(Author)   (Reader)

TEXT

Implied Author ↔ Narrator ↔ Narrative ↔ Narratee ↔ Implied Reader→
                 {1} {2} {3} {n}   {1} {2} {3} {n}   {1} {2} {3} {n}

LITERARY
CONVENTION

relation to different levels of implied narrators or author-narrators. The terminology can quickly become confusing, and indeed there is no absolute agreement among narratologists on either the terminology or the structural relationships. In framing Hawthorne's works by reference to narratology theory, I propose some revised terms that, while they may contribute to the terminological confusion of the larger field, will, I hope, simplify and clarify the basic points I wish to make about Hawthorne's narrative technique.

First, the "implied author" in the sense that it is used by Booth and Chatman is supplemented in Hawthorne by the concept of an "author figure" (not *quite* the same thing as what Booth designates "dramatized narrators," some of whom may be "authors"). The author figure may be more precisely termed "*author*-narrator" or "*narrator*-author," depending upon which role is emphasized: that of *author* primarily concerned about narrative and audience or that of an abstract *narrator* making occasional and conventional references to authorship ("the biographical sources I have relied upon only partially reveal the truth"), or to narrative ("we shall now leap ahead to the crisis of our story"), or to readership ("dear reader"). The author figure may be explicit or implied; but if explicit, he (almost always "he" in Hawthorne) stands textually in a special relationship to his reader. He may specifically refer to himself as author or chronicler, historian, or

*Simplified paradigm derived from Booth, Chatman, Prince, Iser, Lanser, et al.

Schematic 4

$$\text{IA} \left[\left\{ \begin{array}{c} \text{Nr}^1 \\ \text{Nr}^2 \\ \text{Nr}^3 \\ \text{Nr}^n \end{array} \right\} \left\{ \begin{array}{c} \text{Nt}^1 \\ \text{Nt}^2 \\ \text{Nt}^3 \\ \text{Nt}^n \end{array} \right\} \left\{ \begin{array}{c} \text{Ne}^1 \\ \text{Ne}^2 \\ \text{Ne}^3 \\ \text{Ne}^n \end{array} \right\} \right] \text{IR}$$

biographer, addressing or specifically inviting imaginative collaboration with his fictive reader.[12]

Second, the term "implied reader," representing an enlightened or knowledgeable normative reader (Booth's "ideal" reader) more or less accurately interpreting all the structures of the complete narrative transaction that the text embodies, is *also* (as a rhetorical-fictive concept generated from the text) a special form of narratee. When such an implied reader is in some manner drawn into the text (or the transaction) in a more specific way ("come, dear reader, and wander with me through a twenty years' vagary in the life of a so-and-so; help me to invent a name and a character for him"), we may have recourse to the idea of an *implicated* reader, beyond the characters (who may even be addressed by the narrator) and short of Booth's ideal implied reader outside of the narrative transaction. The term "implicated reader" (a reader figure, explicit or implicit) is here distinguished from character-narratees (even implied ones). This implicated audience, which *may* include both character-narratees and implied readers, *may* see only part of the whole even if operating on multiple levels. The implicated reader (emplotted in the text) is meant to indicate a narrative focus on the *relationship* between the author and the reader as an emphasized theme in the entire narrative transaction. Both figures are fictionalized concepts/characters. A narrative may employ a narrator who speaks on one level to a culturally determined audience of implied general readers — on another to an implied special reader who has a special status in some way deviating from the vaguely normative implied general reader — on another to an implicated reader specifically acknowledged (directly or indirectly) by the author figure — not to mention other variations. Thus to schematic 2, between implied author and simple narrator, is added in Hawthorne the author figure, in effect locating the implied author outside the narrative transaction of text per se.

The implicated reader may or may not share the values of the implied author, the narrator, the explicit narratees, or the implied narratees (including the implied general reader and the implied special reader). But however we may wish to locate author, implied author, author figure, narrator, and so forth inside or outside the textual transaction proper, the main point is that even Hawthorne's apparently simple narratives are not simple — nor are they unmediated.

In addition to author and narrator, we need to consider the relationship of narratee and (implied) reader in terms of large normative cultural values and modes of apprehending. Sometimes an implied reader is a direct narratee, sometimes not. A narratee may be most simply described as someone to whom a narrator (external or internal, explicit or implicit) speaks, to whom a story is told. The deployment of narratees is intimately connected in the narratological transaction with the effects of framing — an instance, one could say, of narratological framing. Take one of Hawthorne's provincial narrators: the seeming patriot of "The Gray Champion," who at one point seems to advocate genocide. Genocide is not something that the modern West professes to believe in, though we all know that there are persons and groups who do.[13] The question is how to mediate or negotiate among large cultural values and the multiplicity of variations upon them (including opposite values) in order to come to some concept of a normative reader. The answer for Hawthorne lies in historical knowledge and an unflagging perspectivity.

It is not my intention to lay out a comprehensive theory of narrative transaction, but rather to indicate how a brush with narratological semiotics may illuminate Hawthorne's texts. My examples of the major considerations will be brief and simplified. I offer as generally pertinent to Hawthorne's *Provincial Tales* a half-dozen paradigms (drawn from fiction in general) illustrating basic narratival strategies he employs.

Paradigm 1 [narrator to reader]. The simplest, basic paradigm involves a narrator — not a character in the narrative world — who assumes a coincidence (or a close normative approximation) of cultural and epistemological values between himself and his reader and tells an implied general reader (perhaps even addressed as "dear reader" or "you") how a character did something. In Hawthorne's "Young Goodman Brown" and "The Birthmark," the narrator at the end tells the implied general reader (however ambiguously) what to think of the protagonist and the narrative; the value judgment in general (or in ambiguous narrative, one strand of judgment) tends to parallel that of the normative implied reader representing cultural values at large (a matter not simply determined). As Ellis reminds us, however, such judgments by a narrator do not *necessarily* correspond with those of the implied author.

Paradigm 2 [first-person narrator acting as third-person chronicler]. A variation of paradigm 1 that is habitual with Hawthorne is the use of a technically first-person narrator — not a character in the narrative world — who acts as a third-person chronicler essentially in the manner of paradigm 1, but as a background author figure. This figure, while referring to himself as teller and/or author, essentially tells a third-person narrative to an implied reader (perhaps directly addressing him/her as "reader") about how a character did something. This paradigm, as we shall see in chapter three, is exemplified by Hawthorne's "Roger Malvin's Burial." (Cf. Poe's "Metzengerstein," George Eliot's *Middlemarch*, Henry James's *The Ambassadors*.) One effect is that of minimal framing of the narrative.

Paradigm 3 [narrator to "implicated reader"]. Another variation we find frequently in Hawthorne is that in which a narrator tells an implicated reader, frequently addressed in some way that suggests the narrator's attitude toward this reader is special rather than normative, how another character did something. The narrator at the end of Hawthorne's "The Gray Champion" and "Endicott and the Red Cross" tells the implied reader what to think of the characters and the narrative; but the values ascribed reveal some degree of variance between the *special* (implicated) implied reader and the normative reader, thus creating a hermeneutics of irony. In "Endicott and the Red Cross," one kind of implied reader is assumed by the narrator: that is, one who will agree with the narrator's final statement on Endicott's patriotism, heroism, and historical significance. But the events of the narrative representing Endicott's fanaticism, narrowness, rigidity, intolerance, and violence go counter to the large normative cultural values of the nineteenth-century milieu of Hawthorne, causing an ironic gap between the (patriotic, "American") implied special reader (narratee A) and the humanistic, broadly religious and moral implied general reader (narratee B). The discrepant relationship is central to Hawthorne's use of the nineteenth-century convention of the *moral*. Some of his morals he puts succinctly up front in the opening paragraphs; many are laid out in the final paragraph or two; some are explicitly multiple (as in *The Scarlet Letter*) or contradictory ("Wakefield"); most are elliptical or ambiguous ("Artist of the Beautiful," "Minister's Black Veil"); and all (I would say) are laden with irony.

Paradigm 4 [author figure as author-narrator to implicated reader]. Greater focus on authorship characterizes the paradigm of a first-person narrator, belonging to or interpenetrating the narrative world (though sometimes implied), who is especially concerned with the problems of narrative. This author-narrator may refer to himself, acting as a foregrounded author figure, and sometimes conflate himself with the putative "real" author. This kind of fictive self-reference makes the implied author a useful concept or step in separating the various fictions and avoiding the naive level of intentional fallacy cautioned against by Wimsatt and Beardsley in their classic but simplistically prescriptive and, in my view, theoretically self-defeating essay. The greater emphasis is on the author-narrator *telling* his tale ("I"), rather than simply on the narrative, usually to a heavily implicated reader. The greater such emphasis on authorship, the greater the demands on an implicated reader. Hawthorne's "Alice Doane's Appeal" (somewhat like *Tristram Shandy*) emphasizes the telling over the told: the telling becomes the told. This text has at least five narratival relationships: (1) the author-narrator telling the implicated reader a narrative of telling four narratives (one framing the other three) to an implicated reader as narratee; (2) the author-narrator's telling of three (3–5 following) narratives; (3) the alluded to "magazine story," embedded in (1) and (2) with the implied magazine readers or editors as past (insensitive) narratees; (4) the summarized magazine *story*, with two "young ladies" as immediate (insensitive) narratees; and (5) a summarized imagined *history* as story with two women as immediate narratees.

"Wakefield" illustrates a variant form highlighting a major Hawthorne theme. In a sense the narratological theme is the opposite or at least the mirror image of that of "Alice Doane's Appeal." The "Doane" story emphasizes the *struggle* between author and reader; in "Wakefield" a first-person author-narrator tells the implicated reader that he wants the "reader" to *collaborate* with him on a fiction based on a newspaper story. So also in "The Haunted Mind" a first-person author-narrator assumes a union with a reader. The reader is addressed as "you" throughout, but every "you" could be replaced with "I." The narrator is generalizing about humanity ("you speculate on the luxury of wearing out a whole existence in bed") in terms of a common bond or an *identity* of author and reader ("you seem to have surprised the personages of your dream in full convocation round your bed").

Paradigm 5 [first-person narrator-character]. An involved, centrally participating *first-person* narrator-character may tell a story, to an implied narratee as normative or generalized *reader*ship, of how the *narrator* did or observed something, as in Hawthorne's "The Celestial Railroad" or *The Blithedale Romance*. Hawthorne is less fond of this technique than Poe, or James, or Conrad — at least within the confines of a single narrative unit like a story.[14]

Paradigm 6 [first-person narrator to character-narratee]. Instead of an implied general readership, a first-person narrator may tell a narratee who is *another character*, explicit and linguistically marked, how he did something, as in Hawthorne's "The Haunted Quack." Perhaps the best-known nineteenth-century examples in English are James's *Turn of the Screw* and Conrad's *Heart of Darkness*. In the latter, the telling itself becomes a major theme emphasizing the moral-ethical import for the listener/reader. A special variation on the explicit character-narratee is the *implied* character narratee, seemingly absent but implied as in a dramatic monologue. This mode (used at times by Poe) contrasts with Hawthorne's practice, at least in individual tales. That is, Hawthorne tends to use the first-person perspective as the author convention to tell a basically third-person story, as suggested at the outset of this discussion.[15] But Hawthorne recurs to the explicit first-person narrator and character-narratee paradigm again and again in his framed-narrative cycles, *Provincial Tales* and *The Story Teller.*

These schema do not exhaust even the basic sets, nor even the variants within each (as in, say, multiple narratees and multiple levels of narratees); infinite variations can be played upon them. But, limited and simple as they are, they graphically suggest the built-in complexity of narratival relations and techniques — and the purely formal naiveté of certain critical assertions about the univocal narrators of Hawthorne's fictions and the congruence or identity of Hawthorne's early narrators with Hawthorne.

Framing: Dialogical Nature of Romantic Narratology

The pervasiveness of an authorial presence in Hawthorne's work has been frequently noted. But the ironic and double-voiced quality of this authorial presence in his early "provincial" narratives has been especially problematic for many of those most intent on claiming for Hawthorne a comprehensive and profound interpretation of the American historical experience. These critics tend to ignore the importance of Hawthorne's framed-narrative mode and underestimate the intimate connection of his authorial "voice" with the structures of narrative. Nearly all of Hawthorne's earliest narratives (over seventy from ante 1830 to 1842) are at least *twice*-told, if not also twice-*told*: their meanings radically modulate or invert, while often remaining indeterminate, in the way of his later so-called mature fictions. The reader's awareness of the double quality of these works depends on recognizing the complex narratival relations produced in part by intricate framing techniques, which to a great extent generate the multivalent or dialogical quality of Hawthorne's authorial voice. I have already noted that M. M. Bakhtin's dialogic imagination has its roots in romanticism, particularly the romantic concept of irony central to Friedrich Schlegel's theory of "new fiction." In his formulation of the dialogical and the monological, Bakhtin echoes both Schlegel and his follower Adam Müller.

Müller seems to have been the first in the romantic era specifically to have introduced the terms *monological* and *dialogical* as mutually interdependent opposite tendencies of thought and language. Summarizing in 1804 and 1806 much of the general overview of language and genre argued by Schlegel in the late 1790s, Müller emphasized the concept of mediation rather than synthesis in the dialectical doctrine of contradiction.[16] He emphasized that the dialogical aspect of ironic framing mediates without absorbing and annihilating oppositions. That is, this early romantic concept of dialectic as open-ended, expansive accommodation of dissonances was specifically dialogical rather than dialectical. Rather than dialectical synthesis of abstract ideas in which the terms disappear into unity, the dialogical recognizes language as author-narrator-speaker/reader-narratee-listener relationships. You expect someone to respond to your utterance, to hear and answer. It is a recognition that no one ever has the last word and that language is not the homogeneous and transparent medium it may appear to be on the surface. It also recognizes that language embodies generational relationships; many "time-voices" meet in any utterance and in the various responses to the utterance. Such a view describes, I believe, the philosophical stance and the narrative art of Nathaniel Hawthorne.

Central to Schlegel's concept of the "new fiction" as *Roman* is the complex idea of framing.[17] In literature, the term *frame* means more than one thing: it can mean cultural paradigms and expectations; it can mean dominant linguistic categories; it can also mean an explicit formal literary frame. In semantics and sociology, *frame* and *framing* have a slightly different (yet somewhat overlapping) meaning than in literature. But basically a frame is a context (more narrowly, a script or paradigm) for perceptions and expectations (linguistic, grammatical, rhetorical, generic, ideational, psychological, social, cultural). Different cultural expectations and generic expectations coexist. These naturally interpenetrate, and in the works of a writer like Hawthorne the existence of framing as a constituent of cognition itself (conscious or otherwise) is foregrounded.

The intricate variations of framing may be reduced for the purposes of the present argument to three basic concepts. First, *cultural* frames are present in varying degrees in all narrative. The narrative is embedded in a social and cultural context, in time, in which certain norms of behavior and belief, of attitude, of human relationship govern our understanding; this point is especially pertinent to the idea of an implicated normative reader and deviations therefrom. Second, in *explicit formal* narrative frames, we are told that we are going to hear or read (or have been hearing or reading) a tale within a tale. Third, in *implicit* narrative frames, we have to discover for ourselves, as it were, that the tale is contained. The ramifications of these modes or categories of the framing process range across Michel Foucault's *epistēmē* and M. M. Bakhtin's *dialogos* to poststructuralist reconsiderations of contextualization and intertextuality. Cultural framing, *dialogos*, and intertextuality are related to genre; and these may be in turn reconceptualized within the tradition of formal literary framing from the Middle Ages to the postmodern era. However these matters are formulated, each provides a conceptual frame for the analysis of the works of Hawthorne.

Let us take up the idea of cultural framing first as *epistēmē* and then as *dialogos*. In order to understand cultural or historical framing of a text, the reader needs to be aware of norms of cognition, perception, belief, and value — especially those of older times or "alien" cultures — like New England Puritanism. Obviously, complete recovery or encyclopedic understanding of frames peculiar to the receding past is not possible. Nonetheless, we can try to discern and identify them to the best of our limited abilities, always keeping in mind that we understand them in the context of a metaphysics of intertextuality. Moreover, we need to keep in mind the problematics of language as framed sets or lexicons of interdependent meanings.

Any pretension to a reasonably full understanding of Hawthorne's corpus of work, for example, must confront the seeming paradox of his commitment to nineteenth-century liberalism and his focus on seventeenth-century New England Puritanism and eighteenth-century American nationalism. Such concepts as liberalism, Calvinism, and nationalism must be induced from the whole of his writings, with heightened awareness of various (fictional) narrative personae and narrative voices, further framed by various concepts of audience and occasion (narratees and narratival situations). In this way, formal considerations intersect the cultural. (Some writers, like Hawthorne, call greater attention than others to such cognitive frames.) We have also to negotiate a complex of relationships from our perspectives in the twentieth (or twenty-first) century. None of these large idea sets is simple and uniform; each is a nest within a nest of often competing ideas.

Roughly like Bakhtin's dialogical "chronotope" and ideologeme, the idea of cultural framing and negotiation is also partially described by Michel Foucault's formulation of *epistēmē*, that is, with cultural "domains" that particularly identify a statement or event and that are related to past or future by disrupture as well as by continuity. Moreover, Foucault and Bakhtin, along with Jean-François Lyotard, represent the most extreme contemporary assaults on a concept of purely representational language outside of Derridean deconstruction. Bakhtin and Foucault suggest a way of understanding how cultural framing, the taxonomic process of thought and perception, the problematics of language, and concepts of genre intersect.

Foucault's concept of *epistēmē* is both simple and complex. A succinct description may be found in *Radical Reflection and the Human Sciences* (1980) by Calvin O. Schrag, who focuses first on Foucault's basic proposition of an "archaeology" of the "human sciences." Schrag notes that "this archaeology is developed along the lines of an inquiry into the epistemic domains (*epistēmēs*) that provide the framework for an understanding of the different modes of discourse which at various times have been employed in the sciences of man." Foucault attempts to identify four such epochal *epistēmēs:* late Middle Ages to late sixteenth century; seventeenth and eighteenth centuries; late eighteenth century to the early twentieth century; and the currently emerging one. Schrag remarks that "these *epistēmēs* are neither to be understood as emanations of a cosmic scheme of things, nor as serial modifications of an enduring subject of history or substance of thought, nor as stages of a quiet unfolding of a unifying *telos* of history." Instead, they are characterized as ruptures, discontinuities, and disjunctions in the history of Western consciousness. "They simply appear, if you will, alongside one another." Yet "ordering is discernible in each of them, made possible by 'discursive practice,' so we can account for these ruptures amongst the *epistēmēs* by discerning the different manners in which language confers signification upon the world." (Such a view is not dissimilar to Hawthorne's perception of American history.) For Foucault, the *epistēmēs* of the Middle Ages, the seventeenth and eighteenth centuries, the nineteenth and twentieth centuries are "distinguishable by the various uses of *representational language*," and these uses are determined by intersecting frames, each carrying an epistemological import. The "decisiveness of the emerging *epistēmē* in the middle and late twentieth century consists in its *emancipation* from the *representational model of language* that provided the ordering principle in the preceding epochs."[18] Although not strictly a "textualist," Foucault provides in the analogy of *epistēmē* and frame a useful principle for discourse analysis at a macrolevel which Bakhtin, in his own way, provides at both a large cultural level and that of text.

Bakhtin takes this idea of an emerging emancipation from the representational model of language in several new directions.[19] The basic Bakhtinian proposition is that language and culture mirror each other in intricate ways that militate against unitary conclusions and foreknown certainties.[20] The dialogical is a phenomenon of social and cultural history that inheres in language prior to any historical linguistic event. Implicit in any linguistic event is the history of prior linguistic-social events—a series of prior categorizing events. Thus the historical nature of language operates against the monological, that is, the single-voice concept of dominant cultural authoritarianism. The monological mind privileges the received standard ideas of collective society over those of the individual and of uniformity over difference.

The dialogical principle involves the recognition that all intentionary discourse has conflictual or contradictory elements competing for dominance. That is, language is never subject to the total control of a single self and its supposed unified intentions, but is instead always resistant. The idea that language is a neutral tool of a single, coherent, unitary self in the service of a carefully discriminated and categorized intention promotes the notion of a kind of self-justifying, self-sanctioning monologue. In reality, any intention has to negotiate not only with other intentions but with other contents. This negotiation constitutes dialogicity.

Bakhtin assumes that there is always someone listening (a narratee, if you like). At the other end of the communication transaction is a human being — one who will not necessarily agree with or be controlled by the sender of the communication. The dialogical is the counterforce to authoritarian constriction into illusory unity of contradictoriness, conflict, and plurality. We pretend to be free from ideological prejudice when we are not, and the monological encourages us to be blind to our confinement in the iron cage of a unitary mindset (like Puritanism). Recognition of the dialogical tends to free us from illusions of freedom, such perspectivism constituting our only true freedom. A dialogical artist, like Friedrich Schlegel, Ludwig Tieck, Fyodor Dostoevsky, or Herman Melville, deliberately incorporates and privileges a multiplicity of contesting voices in narrative.

Since the conditions that make articulation possible are manifestations of cultural forces, Bakhtin proposes two constructs to accommodate the basic historical-cultural matrix of language. His device is not *epistēmē* but the aforementioned ideologeme and chronotope: intellective and space-time embedments that must be considered in any linguistic, literary, generic event. This historical element will always operate at some level against the single-voice concept of dominant cultural authoritarianism — against the monological, which encourages insensitivity to other voices. Some literary works succeed better than others in resisting the centripetal pressures of culture to conform to monological stereotypes. When we examine the dialogical relationships embodied in romantic texts, cultural and literary framing are mutually reflective. Conventional earlier twentieth-century concepts of romantic simplicity, directness, and the single voice of the author or narrator (not to mention a single audience) gloss over the complexity of narrative.

I believe that these reconsiderations of history, language, and texts parallel Hawthorne's view of historiography and his sensitivity to the ambiguities of language, texts, and textual types. The parallels are perhaps especially close in their respective emphases on the prescriptive and limiting power of preconceptions, contexts, and frames — embedded within language itself and in the habits of traditional discursive practices. In particular, Hawthorne is aware of the power of language simultaneously to fix things in categories and to subvert by ambiguity all taxonomies. To emancipation from representational language, therefore, I would add radical reconceptualization of genre and the power of genre. That is, the genres are no longer seen as fixed by neoclassical systems or order and relation but as interpenetrating modes, much like imagination and reason or conscious and unconscious thought.

Hawthorne is not alone in this assault on fixity of genre. He is part of a tradition that includes romantic and preromantic writers, notably Sterne, Jean Paul, Tieck, Schlegel, Hoffmann, Poe, and Melville. In addition, concepts of self and others, of conscious and unconscious identity undergo a romantic shift from simpler enlightenment concepts of unity and fixity to those of flux and coherent contradiction. This shift is seen most starkly perhaps in the theoretical writings of Friedrich Schlegel, especially his concepts of the evolution of higher and higher versions or texts of the self (by the supreme transcendentalist, the Romantic Artist) to a point of "objective subjectivity" embodying indeterminacy, flux, and contradiction. As I have argued elsewhere, the implicit telos in Schlegel's thinking, however fluid and indeterminate he is along the way, marks him as romantic rather than radically contemporary or poststructuralist. Although Bakhtin is more compatible with Schlegel than Foucault may be, both Bakhtin and Foucault reject such (finally) teleological thinking as Schlegel's. Hawthorne, in my view, occupies a territory somewhere between Schlegel's sense of the dialogical and Bakhtin's.

For Bakhtin, the idea of dialogue that is disrupted, conflicted, contradictory, and without final closure does not mean that there is *no* centrality or intentionality in discourse. Just as no utterance, no discourse represents a pure authoritarian centrist position, so also no discourse can represent a purely dispersive or anticentrist position. In fact, the necessary agencies of discourse are the two basic social-linguistic forces of centrism and dispersal (or in deconstructive terminology "logocentrism" and "dissemination"). These two agencies of discourse are *mutually* interdependent (so that, for example, Bakhtin would reject the idea of continual dispersiveness argued by certain advocates of deconstruction). The *centripetal* is a unity tendency (including sanctions, homogenism, centrality, hierarchy) that seeks to suppress or control the dispersing features that make cultural dialogue possible. This dialogue includes social science, science, business, government. Morals and ethics tend to be centripetal. Even philosophy is centripetal. Certainly most historiography is centripetal, in Hawthorne's time barely recognizing its own perspectivism.[21]

The *centrifugal* is the dispersive element in discourse: those contesting strategies within an intentionary text, including irony, humor, parody. The monological foregrounds exclusivity — whereas for Bakhtin the language process is actually asymmetrical and interdependent: intersubjective, interindividual. Centrifugal acknowledgment of other voices Bakhtin calls "heteroglossia": many different languages competing for ascendancy (for monological gain or closure). This competition is the basic social phenomenon of people talking to people with multiple intentions and fluctuating control. In language, in a text, in discourse, there is an irreducible versatility that is correlative to social versatility in culture. For Bakhtin, the dialogical is the decentering counter — politically to Leninism and other Marxisms, linguistically to restrictive literary formalism and sentence linguistics, religiously to the monological Russian Orthodox Church. Like Foucault — and like Hawthorne — Bakhtin is interested in the study of *dis*continuities. That is, he is interested in the dialogical angle of style, of juxtapositions, counterpositions — in the fluctuating and dynamic, not in the static and unitary.[22]

These matters have import for concepts of genre in terms of intertextuality. Bakhtin's tendency to emphasize context over text leads him naturally enough to problems of genre, both cultural and literary. In fact, it would be no exaggeration to say that, like Schlegel, Bakhtin has a constant preoccupation with genre: not just with the stylistics of genre, but also with the social tone and the sociology of genre, and with the philosophical import of genre.[23] In this, Bakhtin's interest in cognitive taxonomies and discursive modes somewhat resembles Foucault's. Bakhtin's special theory of the novel is directly related to his general theory of genre implicating a modeling system of some reality. The philosophical import of genre is related to a concept of the organization of the world. This view, I argue, is also Hawthorne's. Unfortunately, says Bakhtin, taxonomy is usually a hierarchy, and hierarchies are authoritarian. The trick is to see *how* taxonomies embed authorization of truth. Something similar seems also to be Hawthorne's view. Taxonomies — whether generally conceptual (evil, sin, guilt; imprisonment, liberty; the conscious, the subconscious; the real, the imagined) or specifically literary (historiography, fiction; tale, essay, sketch; fantasy, realism) — are either useful or irrelevant to some angle of vision.

Bakhtin emphasizes the conceptually dialogical nature of genre itself. The origin of a generic category is defined by a space-time chronotope, representing embedments of the social-cultural complex. Genre is representative of collective memory: it lives in the present but recalls the past. There is never any pure chronotope; genre represents *intertextuality* plus *heterology*. The latter term is the English equivalent of a neologism of

Bakhtin's, by which he meant to indicate the irreducible diversity of discursive types (Bakhtin's characteristic stand against repressive unity). The term stands between "heteroglossia or diversity of languages, and . . . heterophony or diversity of (individual) voices."[24] "Framing" and "genre" are therefore taxonomic manifestations of *the heterological interplay of intertextuality*. Genre is not definitive in any way; it is more precisely the history of persistent classificatory moves, embedded in language. Genres are not the self-evident categories of classical rhetoric. Bakhtin argues that we deploy generic categories to generate readings (just as we read the world as a text) by suppressing multiplicity at the same time that we are generating new voices. *Genres have dialogical relationships with one another,* and additional perspectives result from "transgeneric" readings.

To bring the discussion more directly back to Hawthorne, we may recall once again the words of the Dublin reviewer: Hawthorne's works exhibit a "power of negative suggestion" rendered in a style that seems "easy, but which is perhaps the most difficult of all," in a genre "for which we have no definite term as yet" — namely, the "blending of the essay, sketch, and tale." A proper reading of Hawthorne's early works demands an understanding of the dialogical interplay between varieties of narrative mode and narrative presence in a continuum ranging from the more or less completely dramatized and presentational genre that Poe designated the tale proper to the heavily author-foregrounding mode of the romantic sketch.

We have noted before Poe's famous reviews (1842, 1847) of Hawthorne's *Twice-told Tales* and *Mosses from an Old Manse*. Here Poe not only provides a significant commentary on these collections, but also sets forth a distinction between the sketch and the "tale proper," the latter being what he calls the only "legitimate sphere of action" (see *E&R*, pp. 570–73). Poe values the tale as a pure genre of narrative and dramatized incident and tone pressing toward a single unified effect, usually melodramatic or sensational (both in a general sense and in the specific meaning developed in *Blackwood's Edinburgh Magazine*). The tale for Poe achieves a dramatic effect via an overall unity of many details conforming to a fully developed Freytag Triangle of carefully constructed sequence — an Aristotelian conception of exposition, complication, crisis, climax, denouement, in which every word contributes to the "preconceived" narrative-dramatic "effect." Poe criticizes Hawthorne's "repose," "quietude," and constant authorial "presence." He finds that too many of Hawthorne's narratives have the effect of a familiar "essay" in which the "absolute" and "singular" imagination of the author dominates. They are not presentational enough; instead their development is curtailed, their denouement truncated, and their fictional illusion marred by the persistent intrusion of the author's imaginative personality.[25] What Poe does not see, rather surprisingly in view of his own experimental fictions, is the dialogical interplay of genre itself in Hawthorne's narratives.

Rahmenerzählung: *Twice-told Narrative and the Reflective Self*

Critics from Poe forward have imperfectly understood Hawthorne's early experimentation with the techniques of framed narrative and of narrator mediation in both tale and sketch. Traces of the influence of the framed-narrative cycles of Chaucer, Scheherazade, and Boccaccio are evident in Hawthorne's explicitly framed-narrative sequence *The Story Teller*, and implicitly in *Provincial Tales*. I wish to reemphasize the argument of Alfred Weber that Hawthorne early mastered the techniques of a genre long practiced in Germany, the *Rahmenerzählung*. In the hands of the romantics, the *Rahmenerzählung* became a story cycle in which the narratives were related to one another in intricate ways and linked by a narrator, a series of narrators, or a series of narrators within another frame of narration.

A good American example of the *Rahmenerzählung* of explicit and formally framed narrative prior to Hawthorne's provincial tales is Washington Irving's four-part cycle *Tales of a Traveller* (1824). Irving dialogically plays against one another not only the narrator-personae but also the various modes of popular genres of narrative: the ghost story, the personal "authorial" essay-sketch, the Italian banditti tale, and the treasure-hunt or pirate adventure narrative.[26] The kind of recurrent author-narrator presence in these works is in and of itself frame-generating, and therefore almost by definition productive of the dialogical, if not of irony. Irving foregrounds *authorial* presence as such in part 2, "Buckthorne and His Friends," somewhat in the manner (though less ironic and more satiric) of Hawthorne's *Story Teller*. The relation between the frame narrative and the framed narrative in the *Rahmenerzählung* tradition sometimes tends to become the feature of central interest rather than any particular narrative itself. Despite the now legendary American folklore status of two or three of the narratives of Irving's *Sketch-Book of Geoffrey Crayon* (1819–20), the work is more impressive as an integrated arabesque than any of its components considered separately. But even in the famous "Rip Van Winkle" Irving foregrounds the narrative that is explicitly "told again." He uses frames around frames to subvert the truth claims of Rip Van Winkle, whose story the overall frame narrator, Geoffrey Crayon, says he "found" among the papers of the late Diedrich Knickerbocker, who had "found" some more or less "legal" papers "attesting" to the "testimony" of Rip, signed by him with an X and vetted by a possibly illiterate magistrate.

Explicit and implicit frames, such as those found in the works just mentioned, often blur together; and in the hands of metafictionists this interpenetration is both aggressively experimental in form and epistemologically foregrounded. Explicit formal frames in literature are basically external (around, or preceding or following another narrative, containing it). A tale that is framed externally tends to have in its simplest and most conventional form an opening commentary by a narrator (or "author") about a situation (thus culturally and historically framing the narrative at the same time) "to be told" in the "following" narrative. The narrative is normally followed by an "afterword" (and perhaps decked out with a "moral"). Sometimes the external frame appears only at one end or the other; typically, however, it appears before and after the story or stories that are framed. In narrative-cycles, the frame recurs fairly regularly in between the tales or sketches.[27]

If explicit frames can produce a double effect, implicit frames also allow for a redoubled effect. Rather than announcing overtly at the beginning of a tale that the following account was written in a madhouse, for example, the reader is allowed to find it out later, perhaps gradually, step by step, perhaps abruptly. The "dialogue" of the explicitly framed story acquires in the implicitly framed story another level of dialogicity, and the two may be combined. A good example of implicit or implied framing is Poe's "The Cask of Amontillado" (1846), a first-person narrative by a seemingly remorseless man who cold-bloodedly carries out systematic revenge upon one who has insulted him. A reference in the opening paragraph to "you" turns out not to indicate the reader but a priest. The implied circumstances of the telling of the tale some fifty years after the vengeful murder has taken place, along with a number of juxtapositions and contradictions and a strong religious motif, suggest that the terms of the apparently successful revenge plot enumerated in the first paragraph are in fact not successful, but subverted point for point. The implied narratee within the story is integral to ironic internal framing and thus the meaning of the whole. Another Poe tale provides a variant example. We do not find out until the last few sentences that the first-person narrator of "The Imp of the Perverse" (1845) is in prison awaiting execution. Hawthorne, in some contrast to Poe, tends toward explicit frames, though the design of *Twice-told Tales* contains a strong residuum of implicit framing. *Twice-told Tales*, like Melville's *Piazza Tales*, is covertly framed, implicitly suggesting the framed-tale cycle tradition.[28]

Of particular importance to the technique of the "twice-told" is the principle of contrast employed by romantic writers of narrative cycles — the effect of *chiaroscuro*, as Perry Miller observes, being much prized in America.[29] The "chiaro" (light) is played off against the "oscura" (dark). A major effect of chiaroscuro comes from the "cornice tradition" of the Renaissance novella. One mode is the contrast gained from juxtaposition of a serious or dark frame with light-hearted stories. In *The Decameron*, mostly lighter stories are told against the background of the Black Death. This effect Clements and Gibaldi call the "disaster cornice." The reverse effect is the "carnival cornice," which Poe tellingly employs in "The Cask of Amontillado," a dark story told against a lighter frame situation (literally a carnival). Among Hawthorne's provincial tales, "Alice Doane's Appeal" deploys an intricate, doubly negated version of the *Decameron* disaster cornice — inversely and obliquely contrasting the underlying moral-historical darkness of a sunny scene in the multiply framed narratives of this metafictional tale-sketch.

Common to all these framing effects is doubleness of one kind or another, whether to create verisimilitude for a fantastic sequence of narrative events or to undermine or qualify such verisimilitude. The latter was more prevalent in the romantic period, which saw the rise of a pervasive theory of irony and the dialogically twice-told.[30] More subtly, again especially in the romantic period, the principle of juxtaposition and contrast and the chiaroscuro effect is manifest in alternations between objective and subjective modes of narration or of one subjectivity with another, as in, for example, E. T. A. Hoffmann's "The Sandman" or "Mademoiselle de Scudéry," Clemens Brentano's "Story of Brave Casper and Fair Anna," Charles Maturin's *Melmoth the Wanderer*, James Hogg's *Confessions of a Justified Sinner*, Mary Shelley's *Frankenstein*, Emily Brontë's *Wuthering Heights*, Melville's *Moby-Dick*, "The Encantadas," or *Pierre*, Hawthorne's "Legends of the Province-House" or *The Marble Faun*.

John Barth, in "Tales Within Tales Within Tales" (1981), notes of narrative framing generally: ". . . framed tales — that is . . . stories within stories, which always to some degree imply stories *about* stories and even stories about story*telling* . . . appeal to us because they disturb us metaphysically. We are by them reminded, consciously or otherwise, of the next frame out: the fiction of our own lives, of which we are both the authors and the protagonists . . ." (pp. 221, 235). I believe that this is the overarching, self-reflexive theme of Hawthorne's early framed collections, *Provincial Tales* and *The Story Teller*. A major theme in *Don Quixote* and in the fiction of Borges, it is no less so in Hawthorne, as his playful sketch "Monsieur du Miroir" (1837) deftly suggests. The author-narrator begins with the observation that "than the gentleman above named" (the M. du Miroir of the title) "there is nobody, in the whole circle of my acquaintance, whom I have more attentively studied, yet of whom I have less real knowledge, beneath the surface which it pleases him to present" (2:182; *T&S*, 395). As a trope for the self, the mirror image which reveals and conceals at the same time is

especially appropriate for the authorial self. Certainly it has many resonances with the prefatorial remarks about the revealed self of the writer
quoted toward the end of the last chapter.

Hawthorne's author-narrator traces the lineage of the mirror self from
French, British, and Spanish sources. Most particularly, "some genealogists
trace his origin to Spain, and dub him a knight of the order of the CABAL-
LEROS DE LOS ESPEJOZ, one of whom was overthrown by Don Quixote"
(2:183; *T&S*, 396). He remarks that "coincidences" between himself and
the mirror self remind him of "doubtful legends" and theatrical events.
This mysterious, fictional, but real other self must be revealed to the reader
gradually; otherwise "Monsieur du Miroir might have been deemed a
shadow, and myself a person of no veracity, and this truthful history a
fabulous legend" (2:188; *T&S*, 399). Not only does M. du Miroir appear in
odd places like the bottom of wells and in glasses of liquor, but also in the
round globe of one of the brass andirons of the fireside in the author-
narrator's study while he writes. This other self comes to mock the writer
even while "writing these latter sentences" about this self-reflective self
(2:189; *T&S*, 400). The mirror self is found in dreaming as well as waking,
in fantasy as much as in everyday life: "I found him also in my dream." At
the end, the author throws a "wary glance" across the chamber, "to discern
an unbidden guest with his eyes bent on mine. . . . Still, there he sits and
returns my gaze with as much of awe and curiosity as if he, too, had spent a
solitary evening in fantastic musings and made *me* his *theme*."[31] As we shall
see, these matters are played and replayed along the theme of the interpenetration of fictive and real life in many of the *Twice-told Tales* and in the
whole of the self-reflexive *Story Teller.*

Just how contemporaneous Hawthorne's narrative aesthetics are in foregrounding the epistemological questions raised by such problematic narrative and generic relationships that we have examined in this chapter I shall
attempt in the next several chapters to demonstrate. The eight provincial
narratives identified as paradigmatic are divided into two groups of three —
"sketches" and "tales" — followed by a "hybrid" sketch and a "hybrid" tale.
Special attention is given to overall irony, ironic reversals, or possible
reversals — subversions of what Hawthorne calls the "catastrophe." One
major difference between tale and sketch is the abrupt or elliptical denouement of the sketch form. The narrative technique of both forms plays
variations on the foregrounding of the author figure, and his ambiguous relation to the narrator, as the message-bearing *hermeneut* (ironic
and otherwise) of such structures. Of course, such messages as Hermes
brings — like the two kinds of dreams described in Homer and the double
significance of the messages of the Delphic Oracle — are "twice-told."

2 Following Darkness Like a Dream: Negative Closure and Negative Epiphany in the Dreamvision Sketches

Are you sure
That we are awake? It seems to me
That yet we sleep, we dream. . . .

. . . .

Why, then, we are awake. Let's follow him,
And . . . recount our dreams.

— *A Midsummer Night's Dream* (1595)

The whole matter seems to me a sort of dreaming awake. It resembles a dream, in that the whole material is, from the first, in the dreamer's mind, though concealed at various depths below the surface; the dead appear alive, as they always do in dreams; unexpected combinations occur, as continually in dreams; the mind speaks through the various persons of the drama, and sometimes astonishes itself with its own wit, wisdom, and eloquence, as often in dreams. . . . that lurking scepticism, that sense of unreality, of which we are often conscious, amid the most vivid phantasmagoria of a dream. — *Italian Notebook*, September 1, 1858

. . . starting from a midnight slumber? By unclosing your eyes so suddenly, you seem to have surprised the personages of your dream in full convocation round your bed, and catch one broad glance at them before they can flit into obscurity. Or, to vary the metaphor, you find yourself, for a single instant, wide awake in that realm of illusions, whither sleep has been the passport, and behold its ghostly inhabitants and wondrous scenery, with a perception of their strangeness such as you never attain while the dream is undisturbed. . . . In the depths of every heart there is a tomb and a dungeon, though the lights, the music, and revelry above may cause us to forget their existence, and the buried ones, or prisoners, whom they hide. . . . Well for the wakeful one, if, riotously miserable, a fiercer tribe do not surround him, the devils of a guilty heart, that holds its hell within itself. . . . Sufficient, without such guilt, is this nightmare of the soul; this heavy, heavy sinking of the spirits; this wintry gloom about the heart; this indistinct horror of the mind, blending itself with the darkness of the chamber. . . . With an involuntary start you seize hold on consciousness, and prove yourself but half awake, by running a doubtful parallel between human life and the hour which has now elapsed. In both you emerge from mystery, pass through a vicissitude that you can but imperfectly control, and are borne onward to another mystery. — "The Haunted Mind" (1835)

However ruthlessly the "witch hysteria" was used for private ends, the supernaturalism of New England in the seventeenth and eighteenth centuries was closely bound up with the messianic zeal of religion-driven colonization. This twin process led not only to the persecution of non-Puritans, but also to the execution of their own in the Salem trials. Supernaturalism (whether as a set of beliefs or a rhetoric disguising ulterior motives) was inextricably entangled with historical "fact" in the New England experience. Hawthorne knew that as well as anyone and treats with dramatic irony different levels of hypocrisy, confusion, and madness in his provincial narratives. His treatment of the legendary and supernaturalist material destabilizes monological forms of revealed Truth, subverts the idea of exclusive possession of the unquestioned Right, problematizes perceptions of fact, and calls into question the rationality of the conscious, waking mind. Buried in layers of subjective intermediation is the whole "other" realm of unconscious experience, especially of dreams.

Although it is impossible to miss the general similarity to one another of the dream narratives of *Provincial Tales*, critics locked into a realist mode or into Poesque or Aristotelian concepts of the "tale" have variously misinterpreted, been baffled by, or simply dismissed such early supernaturalist "sketches" as "An Old Woman's Tale," "The Wives of the Dead," "The Hollow of the Three Hills," or "Alice Doane's Appeal." In this chapter, three dreamvision sketches have been placed in an order that highlights (1) the increasingly foregrounded presence of a story-telling narrator, (2) the variations on "negative closure" in the sketch form, and (3) the theme of mutual dream experience as a trope for our problematic conscious existence. Whereas "The Hollow of the Three Hills," "The Wives of the Dead," and "An Old Woman's Tale" are grouped together here, discussion of "Alice Doane's Appeal" is postponed until chapter five, after discussion of the historical romance tales, including "My Kinsman, Major Molineux," which is also treated separately as a blend of dreamvision and history.

The historical tales constitute but one part of Hawthorne's interpretation of America; coequal are these gothic sketches. Hawthorne's gothic sketches of interpenetrating waking and dreaming experience exemplify what in *A Midsummer Night's Dream* are called "shaping fantasies" that "apprehend" more than "cool reason." When Hawthorne uses gothic and visionary material from legendary New England, he is not, as the psychobiographers have insisted, retreating into an imaginative dreamworld to escape the harsh realities of the New World. The dreamvision sketches and the historical tales are complementary parts of one whole fabric of provincial experience in America. In fact, I wish to suggest that the general felt similarity of the provincial tales and sketches reflects a deliberately thematic effect and that the gothic dream sketches were probably part of a loosely contrapuntal pattern with the historical romances.[1] Certainly, we find many of the same kinds of features as in the tales: epistemological opposition and interpenetration between the supernatural and the real; blurring of the real and the imagined; imagery of the indefinite; subversion of generic conventions; irony; and resultant hermeneutical tension and textual indeterminacy.

Discourse on Dream Narrative

The indeterminate boundary between waking and dream experience, between the conscious and subconscious, the rational and irrational, the natural and supernatural, was a recurrent concern of the major nineteenth-century writers. The later nineteenth century also saw the rise of the monological theory of positivism, and even the earlier nineteenth century was always on the verge of being seduced by a concept of a possible unmediated vision of *the* reality out there — at least for the poet. Emerson wavers back and forth over the issue in *Nature* (1836). By and large, Emerson recognized (and celebrated) the role of subjectivity in the form of the special gifts of poetic insight in achieving the sense of unmediated objectivity as a return to the original Adamic ways of perceiving, uncorrupted by civilization. Nevertheless, the role of dream and of the subconscious (as opposed to the vast, benign *Un*conscious), troubled him. Even in the opening of *Nature*, the confident statement that the test of "a true theory" is that "it will explain all phenomena" is confronted with the seemingly "inexplicable; as language, sleep, madness, dreams, beasts, sex." Notice the triple emphasis on the subconscious: sleep, madness, dreams. Of the list of inexplicables, only language is directly addressed in the rest of the book. The others (all nonrational) proved problematic for an ethical metaphysics. In such essays as "Experience" (1844), Emerson associates the existence of a subconscious order of mind with epistemology in general (related especially to his growing concept of Maya) and with dream in particular: "Dream delivers us to dream, and there is no end to illusion." Poe, Melville, and Hawthorne dramatized this theme again and again in their fictions, which abound with ambiguous scenes of dream experience, dream sensation, "sleep-waking," and the like.[2]

The epistemological and ethical as well as the narratological issues of telling a tale that involves some level of dream experience (whether mythic or psychological) are thrown into high relief by Hawthorne's later contemporary Joseph Conrad. The unnamed frame narrator, the "I," of *Heart of Darkness* (1898–99), succinctly expresses a major concern of the problem of "meaning" in nineteenth-century fiction. His statements at the beginning and in the middle of the novel about the interior narrator, Marlow, sum up many of the key issues in Hawthorne. Conrad's general narrator, listening intently in the dark to Marlow's narrative of himself and Kurtz, comments that Marlow saw the significance of a narrative in its layering of narratives and narratival relationships: "The yarns of seamen have a direct simplicity, the whole meaning of which lies within the shell of a cracked nut." But to Marlow, "the meaning of an episode was not inside like a kernel but outside, enveloping the tale which brought it out only as a glow brings out a haze, in the likeness of one of these misty halos that sometimes are made visible by the spectral illumination of moonshine." How like Hawthorne this sounds, even on the surface.

But the similarities go further. For the narrator and for Marlow, the meaning of Marlow's story of Kurtz lies in the relationship of Kurtz's story to Marlow's and the relation of that double story to Marlow's four hearers in the dark on the deck of the *Nellie*. For all the more or less formal emphasis on story telling as story telling and the apparently conventional framing, this *relationship* (especially the disposition of storyteller to audience) in Conrad as in Hawthorne is ethical and moral, psychological and political — and not merely technical. Like the narrators of *Lord Jim* and *Heart of Darkness*, Hawthorne's narrators tend, even when treated ironically or possessed of ironic sensibility, to be simultaneously concerned with the act of narrative and the personal ethics of moral and political issues. Marlow as narrator reveals himself early on: " 'I had plenty of time for meditation, and now and then I would give some thought to Kurtz. I wasn't very interested in him. No. Still, I was curious to see whether this man, who had come out equipped with moral ideas of some sort, would climb to the top after all and how he would set about his work when there.' "

Marlow is of course also talking about himself, his narrative being, like other work (such as riveting together a steamboat), a " 'chance to find yourself. Your own reality — for yourself, not for others — what no other man can ever know. They can only see the mere show, and never can tell what it really means.' " Marlow does want somehow to "tell" what it "really means," and this attempt to capture meaning necessarily takes the form of narrative. For Conrad and Hawthorne, such narrative is generally framed narrative, foregrounding the interaction of narrator (or even "author") and audience (even "reader"), self and others. The complex relationship between Kurtz and Marlow and Marlow and the frame narrator, in terms of Marlow's telling a story to an audience, is especially borne in upon the frame narrator: "The others might have been asleep, but I was awake. I listened, I listened on the watch for the sentence, for the word, that would give me the clue to the faint uneasiness inspired by this narrative that seemed to shape itself without human lips. . . ." Like the shadowy Marlow of the frame who becomes corporeal, the disembodied narrator is not disembodied but flesh and blood: a human presence sits there in the dark and talks to other human beings, his monologue generating a silent dialogue.

We see a parallel between Conrad and Hawthorne in their emphasis upon the oneiric in relation to the struggle toward meaning, particularly ethical meaning. For the ethical is bound up in the psychological. The frame narrator of *Heart of Darkness* notes Marlow's anxiety over (and frustration with) his audience's perception of the "meaning" of his narrative about himself and Kurtz: " 'Do you see him? Do you see the story? Do you see anything? It seems to me I am trying to tell you *a dream* — making a vain attempt, because no *relation of a dream* can convey the *dream-sensation*, that commingling of absurdity, surprise, and bewilderment in a tremor of struggling revolt, that notion of being *captured by the incredible* which is of the *very essence of dreams*' " (my italics). Again, except for a certain aggressive bluntness, how like Hawthorne this all sounds: concern for meaning as subjectively determined, meaning as process between event and "author," narrator and audience, so that epistemologically one wonders how to sort out not only the interpenetration of interior story and frame, but also the literal and metaphoric, waking and dreaming.

The only one, possibly, who can sort it all out and keep it under control is the supreme mediator, the romantic artist. This figure, as mentioned before, Hawthorne gives the name Oberon. Hawthorne's Oberon is taken from myth, but preeminently from Shakespeare's *A Midsummer Night's Dream* (1595). As mentioned, Oberon was Hawthorne's nickname in college, meant to suggest his imaginativeness. Oberon is also a figure in Hawthorne's earliest sketches of the artist, such as "Fragments from the Journal of a Solitary Man" (pub. 1837) and "The Devil in Manuscript" (1835). Shakespeare's Oberon is prince of the imagination, king of the nightworld to which the faerie flee "following darkness like a dream" (5.1.393).

In the third act of *A Midsummer Night's Dream*, Oberon commands Puck to overcast the starry night with "drooping fog" and instill in the quarreling human rivals of the daylight world a "death-counterfeiting sleep." A strange playlike dream will come to possess their existence, and within that dream will be performed another dream-play. Then, "When they next awake, all this derision / Shall seem a dream and fruitless vision" (3.2.370–71). Indeed, in act 4, when Lysander and Demetrius are awakened from their sleep, they exclaim: "Half sleep, half waking. But as yet, I swear, / I cannot truly say how I came here" (4.1.150–52); and "Are you sure / That we are awake? It seems to me / That yet we sleep, we dream" (4.1.197–99).

Although the theme is treated seriously and even somberly in *A Midsummer Night's Dream*, there is also (as in Hawthorne) much irony and humor. The Schlegels list the play as a supreme example of one kind of romantic irony, in which the implicit fictiveness of the imaginative world explicitly frames everything. Bottom, principal player in the play within the dream within the play, awakes to find all his friends have "stolen hence," leaving him "asleep." This gives rise to Bottom's speech on visions and dreams:

> I have had a most rare vision. I have had a dream past the wit of man to say what dream it was. Man is but an ass if he go about to expound this dream. Methought I was — there is no man can tell what. Methought I was — and methought I had — but man is but a patched fool if he will offer to say what methought I had. The eye of man hath not heard, the ear of man hath not seen, man's hand is not able to taste, his tongue to conceive, nor his heart to report, what my dream was. I will get Peter Quince to write a ballad of this dream: it shall be called Bottom's Dream, because it hath no bottom. . . . (4.1.208–22)

Even in its humorous portrayal, hints of infinite indeterminacy are striking: a dream that has no "bottom" shall of course be Bottom's bottomless dream, into which we all sink, even the spectators attending the play *A Midsummer Night's Dream*. Bottom says he will sing the ballad of Bottom's Dream in "the latter end of the play." At the end of the whole play, it is Puck who gives the conventional farewell, doing so in terms of dreams, addressing the audience as if a figment of their dream:

> If we shadows have offended,
> Think but this, and all is mended,
> That you have but slumbered here
> While these visions did appear,
> And this weak and idle theme,
> No more yielding but a dream,
> Gentles, do not reprehend.
> (5.1.430–36)

The ambiguity of the line, "no more yielding but a dream," cannot be fully unraveled, any more than the teasing question the play presents: Is Puck a shadow self in some dream of ours, or are we dream-shadows in Bottom's Dream, within Puck's dream, within some other?[3]

What Joseph Conrad's interior narrator, Marlow, calls the "dream-sensation" of inquiry into "real life" is quite a different matter from retreating into moonlit dream-fantasy to escape reality, as charged against the young Hawthorne. Shakespeare's and Hawthorne's vision of literary imagination encompasses the conscious and the subconscious both, the daylight as well as the nightside. And Hawthorne displays the same kind of tough romantic irony that Friedrich Schlegel admired in Cervantes and Shakespeare, using moonlight and romance against themselves even while evoking them, undercutting historiography with history even while writing fictionalized history or historical fiction. Theseus at the beginning of act 5 of *A Midsummer Night's Dream* gives vivid sardonic expression to the relation of art and reality and the Oberonic power of the imagination. His attempt to discount the imaginative is patently ambivalent:

> More strange than true. I never may believe
> These antique fables, nor these fairy toys.
> Lovers and madmen have such seething brains,
> Such shaping fantasies, that *apprehend*
> *More than cool reason ever comprehends.*
> The lunatic, the lover, and the poet
> Are of imagination all compact.
>
> . . . .
>
> And as imagination *bodies forth*
> *The forms of things unknown*, the poet's pen
> Turns them to shapes, and gives to airy nothing
> *A local habitation and a name.*
> (5.1.2–17; my italics)

To which Hippolyta replies:

> But all the story of the night told over,
> And all their minds transfigured so together,
> More witnesseth than fancy's images,
> And grows to *something of great constancy;*
> But, howsoever, strange and admirable.
> (5.1.23–27; my italics)

This "something of great constancy" — amalgamating waking reality and dreaming, psychology and morality, history and romance, seriousness and irony, ethics and literary form — is Hawthorne's subtle art of "Oberonic" presence in the *Provincial Tales*.

Tale versus Sketch: Negative Epiphany, Narratorial Presence, and the Problem of Closure

Experimentally indeterminate as the provincial tales are, the sketches more than equal them in experimentation with narrative form and with genre and genre boundaries. They exhibit features of the tale and of the sketch, balancing and/or violating the demands of genre convention in self-conscious ironic narrative. What is the reader to make of a piece like "Alice Doane's Appeal" that subverts fictionality itself by setting up fictional conventions but not bringing them to completion, or by failing to observe distinctions between fiction and sketch? What is the reader to make of a narrator who is himself thematized in preference to the story he tells — when the story-telling "author" is as much the subject of the narrative as the putative interior tale that he tells us he tells? One might suggest, as Poe did in 1842 and 1847, that as tales proper such works are failures. But Hawthorne was consciously experimenting with narrative conventions and the limits of tale-essay-sketch. The careful reader would do well to avoid Poe's error of conceiving Hawthorne's "sphere" too narrowly.[4]

Three of the dreamvision narratives, "The Hollow of the Three Hills," "An Old Woman's Tale," and "Alice Doane's Appeal," involve such super-natural creatures as witches and wizards, apparitions and specters, and ghosts, recalling Elizabeth Manning Hawthorne's description of an early collection her brother had completed shortly after graduating from college. The fourth, "The Wives of the Dead," combining the atmosphere of the supernatural with an incident of drowning at sea, suggests the other subject besides witchcraft that Elizabeth Hawthorne remembered as part of the collection *Seven Tales of My Native Land*.[5] All four sketches are visionary in some way, each containing from two to six portentous revelations, some repeated ritualistically, some leading cumulatively to the final apocalyptic moment — which, however, is withheld or only implied.

All four of the "sketches" also foreground the dream/reality/sleeping/waking question that parallels the problem of "opposition" between imagination and actuality, romance and history, reality and fiction in other of Hawthorne's works. But the form of the "tales" of the *Provincial Tales* collection is more familiar and seems easier to deal with critically. That is, they have well-developed segments of exposition and complication and a clearly marked crisis and denouement — even if that denouement is double, ambiguous, and indeterminate if not reversible. This effect, problematized by the felt presence of an author-narrator, constitutes their overall "twice-told" quality. Hawthorne's provincial tales typically announce themselves as conforming to certain genre conventions but actually subvert them — asserting one set of thematic coherencies on the surface while insinuating alternative readings.

One particular experimental feature the dreamvision sketches have in common is what looks on a first reading to be either extraordinarily abrupt closure or no closure at all. Certainly their closure is elliptical, implying more than the reader can ever fix in the way of conventional denouement. In the introductory chapter I defined negative epiphany as a subverted, heavily qualified, or incomplete disclosure or unveiling of the overall meaning of the work. This "meaning," traditionally considered, is generated by the correlation of the parts of a work considered as a whole (incident, plot, character, theme, point of view and framing, narratological transactions, linguistic elements, and so forth). The term *epiphany* also carries the sense of sudden and transfiguring revelation.[6] As a literary term, *epiphany* is currently derived from the usage of James Joyce, who borrowed it from theology to mean a concentrated transcendent (or immanent) comprehensive understanding of a situation or the order of the text. In chapter 5 of the present study, on "Alice Doane's Appeal," the term is used in conjunction with *negative apocalypse* to suggest that — after a series of unveilings that never quite complete the pattern of disclosure they generate — the epiphany actually turns on itself. "The Hollow of the Three Hills" is a simple version of the technique complexly employed in "Alice Doane's Appeal," where meaning is recurrently offered just out of reach, always deferred. Thus, while the tales employ a conventional denouement that is subverted, the sketches employ a nonconventional denouement that seems simply to stop, leaving loose ends and disappointing reader expectations — unless one follows out the implicative logic of the narratological transaction.

In narrative technique, the most straightforward of the dreamvision sketches is the ambiguously supernatural dream revelation (done auditorially, as Poe observed, rather than visually) of "The Hollow of the Three Hills." At least it seems straightforward until we get to the end and discover that the narrative is nearly all exposition. We learn from a backgrounded narrator, who in a brief introduction sets his "story" back in the "old times" when people believed in witches, that an old crone in the forest is to act as the medium of three visions for a seemingly remorseful woman. Each vision is of a different set of abandoned loved ones. After the third brief vision, the narrative simply stops. We do not even know if the motionless woman is dead or unconscious. The piece is a sketch variation on the theme of a dream within a dream, here *approaching* the subject of a mutual, simultaneously shared dream or occult visionary experience (whether the old crone actually shares the young woman's vision is left unclarified). But the ultimate revelation anticipated at the end of the three visions is not forthcoming — the whole narrative is almost mocked by the old crone, whom we are figuratively or by implication invited to think of as the witch of the narrative itself.

The narrator of "The Wives of the Dead" is also placed in the narratival background rather than foregrounded. After a short "historical" introduction (setting the incidents of the narrative about one hundred years previous), the narrator launches immediately into his "story" of two bereaved women, which at the end does not have the effect of a story but an anecdote, for it too just stops. The narrative gives to the theme of the dream within a dream an extra turn — employing an abrupt conclusion that is actually talelike when one pays attention to its careful structure of ambiguity — providing at the end a kind of "epiphany" for the reader. But the revelation is an ambiguous one of the interpenetration of dream and reality, of dreamer and dream, and of the ontological implications of the form of a narrative. Consequently, we do not finally know what has happened.

Of the three, "An Old Woman's Tale" conveys more of a sense of a narrator as a personality — as in *The Story Teller* or the "Legends of the Province House." The title, "An Old Woman's Tale," proverbially means something untrue, a groundless superstition. It is an ambiguously supernatural narrative that is in part a portrait of a dream within a dream that is the mutual dreamvision of a young couple. It too stops abruptly as in a dream and withholds a final revelation, unless it is of dream itself. It playfully deprives the reader of conventional denouement while emphasizing in the opening frame the narrator's learning his story-telling art at the feet (literally) of an old woman, who has told him many a fireside tale (literally) when he was a boy, including the present one. The legendary tale he is about to tell us, he tells us, she learned from other storytellers, who may or may not have known the "actual" characters, or who may or may not have lived the "true" experience upon which her (or his) fiction is based. In its opening frame, the genially portentous picture of a narration within a narration subtly parallels the dream within a dream of the main narrative.

Indefinitiveness and Penultimate Revelation:
An Account of "The Hollow of the Three Hills"

As a tale, "The Hollow of the Three Hills" has no denouement. As a sketch, it portrays three dreamlike visions of a woman who may, or may not, be dead at the end. Lacking a crisis, it simply presents a three-stage revelation of the fate of the loved ones of a despairing woman, who, at the conclusion "lifted not her head" (1:233; *T&S*, 11). Through the ritualistic repetition of the separate visions,[7] we learn that the woman has broken solemn marriage vows and abandoned her parents, husband, and child. The result, whether actual or imagined, is a catalog of romantic excess: her parents are despondent, her husband is in a madhouse, her child dead. In the last sentence, the old crone (possibly a witch) who has been her medium or catalyst chuckles (like the Man in the Moon looking down on all the earthly turmoil in "My Kinsman, Major Molineux"): "Here has been a sweet hour's sport!" (1:233; *T&S*, 11).

When it is not read as a youthful adumbration of Hawthorne's major themes (such as the consequences of sin or guilt, the effects of isolation), the work is usually read as a slight but evocative tale of the supernatural. Read this way, it is seen as a technical exercise — notable for its suspension of time and place (as in the *Märchen* or fairy tale tradition), its somewhat Faustlike suggestion of demonic compact, its focus and economy of structure, or its privileging of symbolism over allegory — and for little else.[8] Michael Colacurcio, for example, calls it an "intriguing yet intellectually baffling little tale"; the "point of it all tends to elude us" (*Province*, p. 43). In the effort to "create a single, unified impression or effect" — one which Poe admired — the "tone threatens to predominate over theme, not only historical but psychological as well" (p. 42).

Poe admired the work as "an excellent example of the author's peculiar ability" to transform a subject "common-place" in romantic literature into something rich and strange. Poe writes:

> A witch subjects the Distant and the Past to the view of a mourner. It has been the fashion to describe, in such cases, a mirror in which the images of the absent appear; or a cloud of smoke is made to arise, and thence the figures are gradually unfolded. Mr. Hawthorne has wonderfully heightened his effect by making the ear, in place of the eye, the medium by which the fantasy is conveyed. The head of the mourner is enveloped in the cloak of the witch, and within its magic folds there arise sounds which have an all-sufficient intelligence. Throughout this article also, the artist is conspicuous — not more in positive than in negative merits. Not only is all done that should be done, but (what perhaps is an end with more difficulty attained) there is nothing done which should not be. Every word *tells*, and there is not a word which does *not* tell. (*E&R*, p. 575)

The narrative is indeed rather effective in its manipulation of gothic conventions to evoke an atmosphere of mystery, foreboding, and decay.

Many critics note its abstract quality, implying a separation from the historical materials of Hawthorne's other works. Colacurcio finds the work only "nominally" to have a relation to New England, either in locale or legendary tradition. It is not a particularly "American" work, he suggests, and especially lacks the "quality of moral experience in some real time past" (p. 42). Therefore, he concludes, the narrative is "considerably less sophisticated than those of the historical tales which come slightly later" (p. 42). That is, "The Hollow of the Three Hills" is for Colacurcio too purely a literary performance; it is merely *aesthetic*. "Unless we can place the action more than nominally within Hawthorne's 'native land' and follow the logic by which the moral situation is related to one or another aspect of the historic problem of 'the Devil in Massachusetts,' we seem forced to admit that Hawthorne has not yet discovered his mature historical method. . . ."[9] Even if we find Colacurcio's bias in favor of the historical and against the literary (especially the European) tradition somewhat provincial, it still may be objected that Hawthorne's description of the forest is quite like his other descriptions of the "Valley of the Connecticut" and the New England wilderness of the other provincial tales (or of *The Scarlet Letter*). And if the narrative was part of a larger narrative cycle in which the historical and the mythic were counterpointed in a serious investigation of the meaning and process of American history, then Colacurcio's judgment, even in its own terms, does not follow. For the pieces would stand in a dialogical relation to one another, negotiating the meanings of myth and history and morality.

In a brief opening frame, the narrator sets the scene at sunset in October, in "a hollow basin" formed by three hills covered with pines. The diameter of the sunken, "almost mathematically circular" depression is two to three hundred feet; the hollow is "of such depth that a stately cedar might but just be visible above the sides." Dwarf pines "partly fringed the outer verge of the intermediate hollow, within which there was nothing but the brown grass of October, and here and there a tree trunk that had fallen long ago, and lay mouldering with no green successor from its roots." One of these fallen trees, "formerly a majestic oak," rests "close beside a pool of green and sluggish water at the bottom of the basin" (a substitute for the reflecting mirror noted by Poe as "missing" from the conventions of the apparent genre). The narrator comments: "Such scenes as this (so gray tradition tells) were once the resort of the Power of Evil and his plighted subjects; and here, at midnight or on the dim verge of evening, they were said to stand round the mantling pool, disturbing its putrid waters in the performance of an impious baptismal rite."[10] As a narrative in a sequence of provincial tales, the text would suggest the "gray tradition" of New England witchcraft without sacrificing the eerie sense of being "out of time —

out of space." Rather than seeing it as flawed in its indefinitiveness,[11] we might say instead that the narrative skillfully maintains both indefinite locale *and* an American locale. (In this, it resembles, at a distance, the technique of "Alice Doane's Appeal," in which the "actual" physical spot where the narrator tells his story and where the Salem "witches" were murdered is simultaneously specific and indefinite, connecting lost local history with the rudderless ahistorical present.) To this spot of the hollow of the three hills, by prearrangement, has come "a lady, graceful in form and fair of feature, though pale and troubled, and smitten with an untimely blight in what should have been the fullest bloom of her years" to meet with "an ancient and meanly-dressed woman, of ill-favored aspect, and so with-ered, shrunken, and decrepit, that even the space since she began to decay must have exceeded the ordinary term of human existence."

Despite the skillful deployment of these gothic conventions and roman-tic clichés, the reader is uncertain whether or not the narrative is to be a traditional supernatural story. For the very question of a supernatural other realm is thematically heightened in the introductory clause of the narrator's opening sentence: "in those strange old times, when fantastic dreams and madmen's reveries were realized among the actual circumstances of life . . ." (1:228; *T&S*, 7). The opening strategy alerts the reader to the possibility that a fantastic dream or madman's reverie is about to be recounted, but it also suggests that these things have an impact on local time and space. It neither denies nor confirms a realm of the fantastic, nor does it indicate whether the reader is to accept or reject any fantastic elements in the narrative to follow. What it does, unequivocally, is to suggest the idea of indeterminacy. Even so ironical and psychologically astute a writer as Poe, who argued for the indefinitive as the essential element of poetry and who practiced a complex narrative ambiguity in fiction, may have missed the point. For he unequivocally calls the old woman a witch and places the narrative in the genre of gothic romances of magic revelation, thereby misconstruing the form and meaning of the sketch. As in the provincial "tales" we shall be examining, the element of the supernatural is ultimately (but not fully) subsumed by the psychological (or political and religious) themes of misperception, egotism, isolation, and guilt.

Under the supernaturalist surface of the narrative, these themes are hinted from the start. When the woman says that she wishes to inquire after the welfare of those with whom her "fate" is bound, the "witch" asks her: "And who is there by this green pool that can bring thee news from the ends of the earth?" As if looking for an answer, the hag peers directly into the lady's face; for the answer is none but the lady herself. The old hag remarks: "*Not from my lips* mayst thou hear these tidings . . ." (1:229; *T&S*, 8; my

italics). Gollin astutely observes that "these episodes are cast as demonia-
cally summoned auditory hallucinations; but they make sense as eruptions
of a guilty imagination. Such fantasies might torment a sinner whose will is
surrendered in dreams, the crone being the instrument of her *desire to know
the worst*."[12] Colacurcio echoes Gollin in emphasizing the psychological
potentialities of the narrative. He suggests that "the old witch's spiritualistic
power amounts to nothing more than the ability to lend a spectral reality to
the lady's *worst fears*. Perhaps her husband is not really in a madhouse, her
child not yet buried; we never really know" (pp. 43–44; my italics). She may
be in fact "both telling and hearing her own tale." Although Colacurcio
does not call it masochism, the suggestion is strong. The lady's final "humiliation," he suggests, comes in the form of a possibility: her recognition
that the (psychoanalytic/spiritual) "confessor" with whom she has sought
"privileged communication" has "plumbed the depths of her sinful heart."
That is, the old crone has made her reveal the deep buried secret desire to
hear of the misery of her "loved" ones. Thus the slight little piece may be in
part a study in sadomasochism, confirmed by the pleasure that the old
crone ("lost to ordinary human feelings") takes in the lady's suffering.
This suggestion (and that is all Colacurcio claims for it) gains plausibility
when the sadomasochistic elements of the psychology of other works from
Provincial Tales are considered: most saliently in "Alice Doane's Appeal,"
"Roger Malvin's Burial," and "The Gentle Boy," but not altogether absent
perhaps from "My Kinsman, Major Molineux." The sadomasochist theme
is manifest on both an individual and a cultural level in "The Gentle Boy";
and in "Alice Doane's Appeal" the conflicted Leonard Doane has an interview with a wizard in a scene parallel to that of "The Hollow of the Three
Hills." In any case, it seems safe to say that the sketch is a psychological
study at some level or another, but with fewer clues than even a work like
"Roger Malvin's Burial," remaining ritualistic and mysterious and preserving the aura of the supernatural in another balance of opposites.

In addition to descriptions of setting, the atmosphere of the supernatural
is maintained by descriptions of the old woman's machinations. The crone
instructs the woman to kneel down and put her forehead on the "witch's"
knees, who then covers her in her mantle. For the second time, "the
withered hag poured forth the monotonous words of a prayer that was not
meant to be acceptable in Heaven" (1:231; *T&S*, 9). When the lady hears
the old crone's first "prayer," we are told that she is "startled"; the implication is that it is a witch's prayer to Satan. But the lady is disconcerted as
much because she is afraid of those (parents, husband, child) who might
"look upon" her (thus she is mantled) as from fear of any infernal prayer.
She regains her resolve and is "still as death" (1:230; *T&S*, 8).

References to death and dying, linked to madness, increase through the rest of the tale, both literally (in the dreamvision, whether taken supernaturally or not) and metaphorically. In her second vision, for example, the noises of the madhouse are like those made by the damned in hell, suggesting an equivalency. The lady hears shrieking, groaning, rattling of chains, and roaring laughter, altogether "a ghastly confusion of terror and mourning and mirth," suggesting punishment after death (for such sinners as herself). She hears the "dreamy accent" of "love songs," which "died causelessly into funeral hymns," while "unprovoked wrath . . . blazed up like the spontaneous kindling of flame" (1:231–32; *T&S*, 9–10). Her third and last vision is of her child's funeral procession, signaled by "the knolling of a bell" that seemed to have traveled far across the earth and was now "ready to die in the air." The sound grows stronger in her mind's ear until it deepens "into the tone of a death bell" that bears tidings of "mortality and woe" to every sojourner and traveler of earth, to all that "might weep for the doom appointed in turn to them" (1:233; *T&S*, 10). The sound becomes first that of the funeral service for her own child and then "revilings and anathemas, whispered but distinct . . . breathed against the daughter who had wrung the aged hearts of her parents,—the wife who had betrayed the trusting fondness of her husband,—the mother who had sinned against natural affection, and left her child to die" (1:233; *T&S*, 11). At the end, "when the old woman stirred the kneeling lady, she lifted not her head." The implication seems to be that she is dead, but the situation is left ambiguous. The old woman's ghastly smile, mentioned several times throughout the sketch, becomes a "chuckle" over the "sport" of the last hour. So ends the sketch.

The uncertainty surrounding the woman's fate parallels the uncertainty of her visions. The use of sound rather than vision heightens not just the general effect Poe noted, but also the uncertainty of experienced reality. A more fully developed version of this technique of the indefinite is found in "Young Goodman Brown" (1835; *Mosses*, 1846). Brown first hears, not sees, the villagers that he presumes are going, like himself, to a witches' meeting in the forest.[13] As he walks beside a stranger with a writhing serpentine staff who looks just like himself, he thinks he hears the voices of Goody Cloyse, the minister, and Deacon Gookin. But try as he might, he cannot glimpse them (2:96–97; *T&S*, 280–82). Later, when he does see all his neighbors at the black sabbat, the validity of his vision is questioned by the very imagery that gives dramatic reality to the scene. The light from four blazing pines, standing like giant altar candles around a hollowed-out rock, rises and falls, flickers and fades, as the dim visages of what Brown takes to be "satanists" alternately shine forth and disappear in shadow, only to grow out of darkness again amidst the fitful illumination of red light, "peopling" the "heart" of the "solitary" woods. The fire of the pines shoots forth into an "arch" around the altar rock. In this archway a "devil" figure appears to say, "Welcome, my children . . . to the communion of your race" (2:103; *T&S*, 286). Then, "flashing forth, as it were, in a sheet of flame, the fiend worshippers were seen; the smile of welcome gleamed darkly on every visage." At least, this is what Brown thinks he sees. "Young Goodman Brown" is exemplary of the twice-told and dialogical quality of Hawthorne's tales. Once-told, it is a tale of a good young everyman's discovery of the absolute universality of evil, which he resists with all his might, whatever the cost. Twice-told, it is also the tale of an egomaniac, who loses faith in all humankind: political and religious leaders, neighbors, friends, children, wife. At the end, the narrator, with quiet irony, observes that whether or not Brown has projected the idea of universal evil (excluding himself) from his subconscious mind, the experience, whatever its source, has a disastrous effect on him — for from that hour he becomes totally isolated, a sad and distrustful man whose dying hour is gloom. Brown thus may be seen to epitomize in Hawthorne's world the extreme Calvinist world view of the Puritans, denying evil in oneself and projecting it outward where it, perhaps, does not exist. Brown walls himself off from his fellow man by drawing the ultimate circle around self, the exclusionary circle of egotism.

So too in "The Hollow of the Three Hills," the imagery of sound and of dim uncertain light suggests the mental hallucination of a disturbed ego. Initially, the lady hears a vague something, "as if other voices" were mingling with "the accents of the prayer" of the old crone (1:230; *T&S*, 8). "At first the words were faint and indistinct, not rendered so by distance, but rather resembling the dim pages of a book which we strive to read by an imperfect and gradually brightening light." The woman imagines, or sees via their voices, her aged parents. "Their voices were encompassed and reechoed by the walls of a chamber, the windows of which were rattling in the breeze; the regular vibration of a clock, the crackling of a fire, and the tinkling of the embers as they fell among the ashes, rendered the scene almost as vivid as if painted to the eye" (1:230; *T&S*, 8–9). "By a melancholy hearth sat these old people, the man calmly despondent, the woman querulous and tearful, and their words were all of sorrow" (1:230–31; *T&S*, 9), until (as in "Young Goodman Brown," "Alice Doane's Appeal," or the tales of Ludwig Tieck and E. T. A. Hoffmann) "their voices seemed to melt into the sound of the wind sweeping mournfully among the autumn leaves." Has the woman come to a witches' meeting in the forest, or has she fallen asleep and only dreamed a wild dream, objectifying her repressed guilt?

In this imagery of the indefinite, with its epistemological and ontological implications, several conventional symbols are treated unconventionally. The most important of these are the smile, the lamp, and the hearth, each associated in this sketch with demonism and flickering firelight. Although the negative connotations are here minor, they are part of an overarching ambivalent symbol pattern in Hawthorne that is of major importance, transmuting as it does the interpretation of some of his most "sentimental" tales and sketches into a rather darker vision than even his most sophisticated recent readers and critics have indicated.

In the passages just quoted, the "smile" is but one of several traditional images of positive association that undergo a transformation in this sketch (though the demonic smile is conventional in the gothic). Each time the vision becomes too intense, the lady lifts her eyes from out the mantle of darkness to find the old hag smiling, a smile that glimmers on her countenance "like lamplight on the wall of a sepulchre" (1:229; T&S, 7). The image of the lamp is associated with the smile of death on the sardonic witch-hag's face, rather than with a guiding light of hope from hearth or starlit heaven. The traditional associations of the hearth are modified in the woman's first vision of her parents. Instead of warmth and home, their hearth suggests loneliness, coldness, darkness. Even the undeveloped symbolism of the circle (major elsewhere in Hawthorne), medieval-Renaissance symbol of perfection and godliness, is darkly transmuted.[14] The "almost mathematically circular hollow" has at its greatest depth and center a stagnant green pool. The conventional reflecting mirror that Poe expected is transmuted into that which obscures rather than reflects. Yet it does retain a reflective property in one claustrophobic sense. The pool, described with the specific metaphor of "mantling waters," is associated with the mantle of the witch, in which the lady buries her head. The auditory visions that come from within the mantle "reflect" (reecho) the lady's own mind. The image of the perfect circle transforms into the circle of egotism.[15] The subversion of these traditional symbols of smile, hearth, lamp, and circle — not to mention the rainbow — in Twice-told Tales, Mosses from an Old Manse, and The Snow-Image gather force in a cumulative way in the corpus of Hawthorne's work. That is, when the individual pieces are read collectively in dialogical relation to one another (especially within each collection), the negative suggestion under the traditional symbols takes on more force.

Indeed, several critics have seen the narrative of "The Hollow of the Three Hills" as illustrating the primacy of a symbolic mode over an allegorical one in Hawthorne. Whether or not such a conclusion is valid (especially given the later twentieth-century reconsideration of the lexicon and categories of allegory), it is clear that in terms of traditional genre expectation Hawthorne has caused the reader to anticipate either a gothic legend or a fairy tale mode, in the latter of which certainly a moral is by convention in order. Hyatt Waggoner and Terence Martin take the fact that the moral of the narrative is implicit rather than spelled out to indicate a nonallegorical mode. In fact, Waggoner puts "The Hollow of the Three Hills" at the symbolic end of a continuum that leads to "The Man of Adamant" at the other, allegorical end (*Hawthorne*, p. 111). Certainly the heavily parallel repetitions of variations on the same sin of the heart suggest the generic appropriateness of an explicit moral tying everything down. But what we get is a negative epiphany. If the narrative had concluded with the fading of the light and the soughing of the wind in the forest (or some such thing), the lack of a satisfying final revelation would not be so foregrounded as in the old crone's chuckling over the sweet hour's "sport." The abruptness of non-denouement forces the reader to foreground consciousness of narrative conventions, thereby exacerbating the defeat of genre expectations. It is as if we too are the object of the old crone's laughter. In its succinct form, this "sketch," taken as a "story" by some readers but lacking full development of the features of the tale, has the same twice-told qualities of the tales — illustrating by its abrupt closure Hawthorne's subtle exploration of the indeterminate area between tale and sketch.

"The Wives of the Dead": A Tale Twice Untold

The resonantly ambiguous "Wives of the Dead," the most highly regarded of the three narratives, represents a fusion of tale and sketch, exemplifying the power of negative suggestion remarked by the *Dublin University Magazine* reviewer. Were it not for the dialogical conflation of genres and resultant temporary misdirection of the reader, enhancing both the abruptness and ambiguity of its closure, the piece would not be nearly so effective. Half-sketch, half-tale, partially defeating reader expectations for denouement, the narrative achieves indeterminacy as much as a matter of development as theme. Hawthorne makes stunning use of the implicature of the sketch form.

Although the piece has been relatively neglected critically, an extraordinarily sharp disagreement has nevertheless developed among those who have addressed the work. This disagreement highlights the central thematic issues of reality versus illusion, waking versus dreaming, along with narrative point of view and technique, that constitute the focus of the present chapter. Each of two widows ("recent brides of two brothers") receives news, *or seems to*, while the other sleeps, that her own husband is alive. (One husband has been reported killed in the Canadian war, the other lost at sea, on two successive days.) The narrative is in two symmetrical, parallel parts. (1) One woman remains awake; she receives news of her husband while her sister-in-law sleeps; she forbears to wake her with her joyous tidings. (2) The waking woman then falls asleep; the other awakes; and the events are repeated, she also forbearing to wake her sister. Neither woman wants to increase the sorrow of the other by sharing her "good news." At the end, one of them lets a sympathetic tear fall on the other's neck; suddenly "she" awakes, and the story abruptly stops.

If the "she" of the last sentence refers to the woman said to have been sleeping, as it would seem to, then there is no real denouement. She awakes to the tear of her waking companion, who is weeping for her friend's loss and her own good fortune. Readers think they have missed something. Students scratch their heads. Did we have closure? Was there some epiphany at the end that we missed?

Some readers have found in this (first, or most obvious) structure the sentimentalized Hawthorne. At the end, the second woman to awaken, Mary, feels such sisterly sympathy that she weeps; when the now sleeping sister, Margaret (who had originally remained awake), awakes to Mary's tear, they will together discover to their astonishment their mutual "good news." Mark Van Doren calls it the portrait of "a tenderness unique in story — the love of two girls not only for each other but for their husbands whom we never see." Doubleday writes that the narrative "ends in a pleasant dramatic irony as we regard Mary refraining from waking her sister in ignorance that Margaret has a happiness parallel to her own."[16] Yet if the "she" who awakes refers to the woman whom we have thought already "awake" (and about to awake the sleeping other), the text has been the narrative of the "waking" woman's dream experience.

Hans-Joachim Lang is usually given credit (or blame) for the reading of the text as dream experience because of his brief explication in a 1962 essay on Hawthorne's ambiguity.[17] But earlier readers recognized the essential ambiguity of the piece. Leland Schubert, for example, writing in 1944 on "the dream-like quality about the lights and shadows" of this as well as other of Hawthorne's early narratives, remarks casually that "Hawthorne implies, in the last word of the story, that both of these incidents are probably dreams" (p. 112). The problem with Lang's reading (which I find insightful) is that he makes some rather questionable and arbitrary assertions about the text, generating protests from critics who wish to restore a simple interpretation of the literal events. Lang claims that a writer as careful as Hawthorne would not write "an ambiguous sentence at the end of a story without meaning it to be ambiguous"; he then forces the case by asserting that "syntactically, the 'she' should refer to Mary; if it referred to Margaret, it would be a very clumsy sentence on top of being unintentionally ambiguous" (p. 88). We may wonder a little at Lang's logical ingenuity here. Having made an initial assumption in his premise about ambiguity which he then uses to prove ambiguity, he now asserts that if the pronoun unambiguously referred to Margaret it would be unintentionally ambiguous (and clumsy English) *because* it would then *not* refer to Mary.

Hawthorne's sentence is: "But her hand trembled against Margaret's neck, a tear also fell upon her cheek, and she suddenly awoke" (3:606; *T&S*, 67). There is no compelling reason why the "she" (syntactically or otherwise) "should" refer to Mary. Lang's conclusion is that the women's experience is "all a dream, and the husbands are dead. It is a story with a surprise ending. . . . the happy return was only a dream; reality is as terrible as it is."[18] That certainly is one of the implications. But the pronoun "she," rather than *having to* refer to Mary, may also in perfectly good English refer to Margaret — even while it *may* also refer to Mary.

Doubleday, while admitting that the narrative "embodies a somber recognition of the precariousness of human happiness" (p. 217), responds rather simplistically to Lang's reading of the tale "as a pair of dreams." He writes: "The objection to this reading, as it seems to me, is that we should have to assume an entirely dishonest narrator, a narrator who . . . distinctly tells us that, although Mary had been dreaming, she awakes and realizes the knocking at the door." Of course, if the third-person point of view narration is limited rather than omniscient, giving us the experience as perceived by a woman dreaming it, then Doubleday's shocked concept of a "dishonest" third-person narrator does not obtain (cf. "My Kinsman, Major Molineux"). Similarly, Doubleday's comment that the narrator elsewhere describes the effects of lantern light outside in the street, which Margaret, turning away from the window, does not see, simply ignores the point that Margaret may be a character in Mary's dream or in Margaret's own dream (or both), as described by the narrator from the same third-person limited point of view.

Colacurcio adopts, almost inexplicably, Doubleday's objections. Commenting negatively on Patricia A. Carlson's elaboration of Lang's "grammatical suspicion" into a "structural chart," he offers the opinion that "the original 'insight' remains unconvincing." The problem, he says, is not only that "this reading requires an 'entirely dishonest narrator' . . . but even more drastically that it bungles the story's management of point of view: there is simply no plausible point of transition from one dreaming consciousness to the other."[19] But such a view ignores the perfectly plausible idea that the dream experience is rendered from the beginning, that it is intentionally ambiguous throughout, and that even the literal significance of events in a narrative (as well as thematic significance and symbolic meaning) may be altered radically at any time — especially in the latter portions of a narrative, when ("surprise!") things were not what they seemed.

The real problem of the story for Colacurcio, I believe, is what I have previously indicated: it seems too purely aesthetic, a literary exercise; there is no firm historical context to work with. Indeed, the thesis of his book is in part that Hawthorne worked his way out of romanticism, the gothic, and the literary, and into the historical. The discussion of "Wives of the Dead" is the most obscurantist in his brilliant book; and one senses Colacurcio casting about for some firm place to anchor *outside* the text.[20] He writes: ". . . the tale is, on its surface, a good deal less challenging than the *richly allusive* [my italics] masterpieces in whose company it first appeared," that is, the *historical* tales of "Roger Malvin's Burial" and "My Kinsman, Major Molineux." Thus "it can doubtless be spared the laborious process of scholarly rediscovery and revaluation" that those stories "have had to undergo" (p. 100); and we can "probably be spared the troublesome (unresolvable) suspicion that everything which follows is only a dream, or a dream within a dream" (p. 103). The point is that the matter *is* unresolvable — as in a dream.

The problem once again is an *either/or* mode of thinking rather than *both/and*. Either a tale is historical and therefore worthwhile, or it is aesthetic and of lesser value. Either the women's experience in "Wives of the Dead" is real or a dream. How can it be both? But that is precisely what the narrative gives us. Both.[21] And Hawthorne clearly is counterpointing or alternating both, just as he alternates in his early body of work narratives coming from the historical side of the spectrum and narratives coming from the oneiric and psychological side. They meet in negotiations somewhere between the two: most spectacularly in "My Kinsman, Major Molineux" and "Alice Doane's Appeal."

So also Lang's insightful reading insists that there is only one reading; for him, it is all a dream, and it is Mary's. That, I suggest, is not Hawthorne's story; but it is a part of it. The suspicion that we are *enmeshed* within dream experience is a better way to think of the dynamics of the narrative — what Conrad's Marlow describes as being "captured by the incredible which is of the very essence of dreams." Thus if the pronoun reference of the last sentence is to the woman that the reader has been led to presume awake (*until* the last sentence), then we cannot know whether the good news of resurrection is true, or if one is true and the other false. In fact, we cannot know anything at all about the real experience of the "other" — that is, the "sleeping" woman in the "waking" woman's dream. If the ambiguity of the final pronoun is acknowledged, the narrative is suspended over a mystery.

What evidence is there that such ambiguity is cumulatively structured in the text, bringing us to a negative epiphany at the end? Nothing so conclusive as Lang suggests. What can be demonstrated is: that the narrative steadily insists upon dream experience; that certain positive domestic values and objects are negatively undercut; and that sentiment, hope, trust in providence, and fulfillment of desire are all subject to negative suggestion, if not reverse epiphany. The persistent pattern of doubling intensifies the innuendo of a double dream within a dream that considerably darkens the meaning of the narrative. In the course of this double reading, some traditional symbols of hope are dimmed, especially those of the lamp and the hearth (as in "The Hollow of the Three Hills"), along with, in a more oblique way, the idea of a blessing from heaven.

In this resonant ambiguity, the piece exemplifies the uncertain blending of inner and outer darkness of perception most explicitly depicted in the allegory "The Haunted Mind," a "twice-told" narrative essay (cf. St. Armand). "The Wives of the Dead" also exemplifies the variations possible in the area between what Poe called the "tale proper" and "essay" — namely, the sketch. Mediated by a subtle narratorial presence, the sketch illustrates the congruence of ontology, epistemology, form, and genre.

The narrator in fact mediates the story from the beginning. He makes his presence known in the first third of the opening paragraph, saying in his own voice that "the following story, the simple and domestic incidents of which may be deemed scarcely worth relating, after such a lapse of time, awakened some degree of interest, a hundred years ago" (3:598; *T&S*, 61). Given the involute dream structure of the narrative to follow, the narrator's comment that the "story" had formerly "awakened" interest is playful; the narrative opens and closes on variants of the word *awake*. The "only particulars to be premised," he says, calling attention to the art of story telling rather than directly to the story, are "in regard to scene and season." The time of day and the season are appropriate to dream experience: it is "the rainy twilight of an autumn day." The interpenetration of the conscious and subconscious realms of the two principal personages is immediately introduced: the "recent brides of two brothers" are "united . . . by the relationship of the living, and now more closely so by that of the dead, each felt as if whatever consolation her grief admitted were to be found in the bosom of the other." They have "joined their hearts" and feel themselves all the more to be "sisters" (3:598–99; *T&S*, 61).

While simultaneously developing parallel contrasts between them, the narrator introduces the quasi-religious motif of ambivalent "blessing," which both characterizes the differences between the two women and insinuates a dark theme. One of the sisters, Mary, is "mild" and "quiet" without being "feeble" of character. Recalling "the *precepts of resignation and endurance* which *piety* had taught her" (my italics), she suggests that they ask a blessing for that which is yet provided for them. The other, Margaret, is "of a *lively and irritable* temperament" and shrinks from Mary's words of acceptance: "There is no blessing left for me, neither will I ask it. . . ." Mary calms her, however, and persuades her to retire. The suggestion of some kind of separate but mutual dream experience (later to be connected with rather pitiable hopes of rebirth, resurrection, or an afterlife) is deftly planted. Having "slender means," the "brothers and their brides" had "confederated themselves in one household, with equal rights to the parlor, and claiming exclusive privileges in the two sleeping-rooms contiguous to it." The women retire together into their separate sleeping chambers, after first "heaping ashes upon the dying embers of their fire, and placing a lighted lamp upon the hearth" (3:599–600; *T&S*, 62).

The double imagery is striking and poignant: they heap "ashes" on a "dying" fire at the same time that they position the flame of the lamp upon the hearth. For whom is the lamp set? Is it a ritual funereal symbol associated with a candle as a prayer for the dead? Or is it a pathetic ritual propitiation, a half-hopeful half-hopeless leaving of a beacon by which those lost in the night might return home? Does the gesture symbolize hope for the resurrection of the dead, or is soteriological possibility indicated? The double gesture of heaping ashes and setting out the lamp replicates not only the ambiguous situation but also the structure of the narrative.

The first phase of the double parallel structure in fact now begins. Let us particularize it with an eye to "dream-sensation" and hints of subconscious experience. Mary falls asleep while Margaret becomes "more disturbed and feverish, in proportion as the night advanced with its deepest and stillest hours." Margaret listens to the monotonous drops of rain while a "nervous impulse" causes her again and again to "gaze into Mary's chamber and the intermediate apartment." The "cold light of the lamp threw the shadows of the furniture up against the wall, stamping them immovably there, except when they were shaken by a sudden flicker of the flame." Presumably this is the flame of the lamp, but it could as well be the dying flame of the fire in the hearth. The two armchairs on "opposite sides of the hearth," where the two brothers "had been wont to sit in young and laughing dignity," stand "vacant." Previously, the "cheerful radiance" of the fire had shone upon the "happy circle," but now is only the "dead glimmer" of the lamp.

It is at this gloomy point, redolent as it is with the wishful desire to hear that her husband is not dead, that Margaret hears a knock at the street-door. *It comes as if in a dream*: in "slow and regular strokes," muffled as though given by the "soft end of a doubled fist," accompanied by words "faintly heard through several thicknesses of wall" (3:601; *T&S*, 63). Is she truly awake? May not the rest of the third-person narrative render her sleep-waking experience or dream state from her own perspective? She looks into her sister's chamber to see her still lying in the depths of sleep. Then "seizing the lamp from the hearth," she goes to the window. A parallel light appears outside, but it is not a clear one. It blurs things, "reddening the front of the house, and melting its light in the neighboring puddles, while a deluge of darkness overwhelmed every other object."[22] Goodman Parker, the innkeeper, has brought the news that her husband is one of thirteen saved at the battle front in Canada. He is glad it is Margaret who has come to the window, he says, for he has no word of comfort for poor Mary.

Margaret's joy is immediately followed by a thought of pain; and she resolves not to waken Mary with her news, which would only sharpen Mary's sorrow. She approaches the bed quietly to see if Mary's sleep is peaceful and sees in her face "a look of motionless contentment" as if "her heart, like a deep lake, had grown calm because its dead had sunk down so far within" (3:603; *T&S*, 64). The narrator observes: "Happy is it, and strange, that the lighter sorrows are those from which dreams are chiefly fabricated." His is a highly ambiguous, if not deliberately paradoxical, remark. A couple of readings are possible. The deep sleep of Mary (as Margaret conceives it, unless, of course, it is Mary's dream) may come from her "pious" acceptance of God's will in the death of her husband, though it produces deep sorrow. The "dream" of Margaret, the less submissive and pious, comes from her more "superficial" desire to deny the situation. She does not trust in a providence that without seeming cause would destroy her husband. Her subconscious mind is more agitated than her sister's. In this way, it may be, hers is a "lighter" sorrow, generating the dream. But it is by no means clear that such is the narrator's intended meaning. Mainly, the narrator's remark functions to call into question the reader's conventional perceptions.

Hawthorne focuses more and more upon the paradox of the psychology of grief; the eros/thanatos impulse is especially highlighted. Margaret feels "as if her own better fortune had rendered her involuntarily unfaithful," but "joy could not long be repressed" even by what would otherwise cause "heavy grief." Her mind is "thronged with delightful thoughts, til sleep stole on" (3:603; *T&S*, 65). Does she now dream that she is sleeping and dreaming? Whatever the case, this sleep "transformed them" (her wishes) to "visions" yet "more delightful and more wild, like the breath of winter . . . working fantastic tracery upon a window" (3:603; *T&S*, 65). Although the narrator calls it "a cold comparison," the window is herewith associated with "fantastic tracery" embroidered upon its panes by cold winter's breath, delusive but transformative of "delightful thoughts" of wish fulfillment. That is, it is a cold, illusive medium for "resurrection" into actualized "visions" of these wishes.[23] It is the window through which come, not one, but two reprieves from death — real or imagined. At this point, the first phase of the paralleled experience concludes, as Margaret falls asleep.

The second part of the narrative duplicates the first. The other sister, Mary, awakes with a sudden start. "A vivid dream had latterly involved her in its unreal life, of which, however, she could only remember that it had been broken in upon at the most interesting point" (3:603; *T&S*, 65). This statement in fact describes the non-denouement of all three of the sketches discussed here; each narrative has the abrupt cessation of a typical dream experience. Slumber hangs awhile "about her like a morning mist, hindering her from perceiving the distinct outline of her situation." Like Margaret she hears knocking. In her midway state between dream and waking, she experiences a "pang of recollection," which seems somehow to dissipate her drowsiness: "The pall of sleep was thrown back from the face of grief" (3:603; *T&S*, 65). The passage is multiply ambiguous, working in two contrary directions. A prior implication is that sleep has covered (though with a "pall") the "face" of grief in the sense that sleep provides temporary relief from grief. But the particular sentence says that sleep is now thrown back like a veil or shroud to reveal grief. Hiding such intense grief from oneself in waking life, in sleep one metaphorically "awakens" to it. This "apocalyptic" unveiling prepares the way toward the negative epiphany at the end.

The narrator's earlier comment that dreams are "chiefly" fabricated from the "lighter sorrows" suggests, by inversion, that the dream experience about to unfold is not of the common sort but from a deeper source: the image in the subconscious of the dead loved one at the bottom of the deep lake of the woman's sorrow. The dream-wish — if that is what the rest of the narrative dramatizes — ironically reveals an existential dread in the depths of the lake of grief. This ultimate dread of the "end" masquerades as happier dream thoughts of resurrection, so that the wish fulfillment dream of the restoration of life to the dead lover intensifies the poignancy of the loss for the more pious of the two, Mary.

Another ambiguous statement describing Mary's state of mind, as she seems to hover between waking and sleeping, is that the "dim light of the chamber" (as in "The Haunted Mind") and "the objects therein revealed, had retained all her suspended ideas, and restored them as soon as she unclosed her eyes" (3:603–4; *T&S*, 65).[24] To describe what we normally consider the real world of objects as "suspended ideas" makes the "real" world seem phantasmal. When Mary opens her eyes and comes back from what she supposes to be dream, the "suspended ideas" come back to life as if resurrected — an image that Hawthorne elsewhere represents as a suspended puppet show (that is, a literally unreal imitation of life) starting up at the very point it ceased movement in some previous entertainment or existence. (Cf. "Seven Vagabonds" and "Main Street.")

The basic symbols are reintroduced in the duplication of the first half of the narrative in the second. Like her sister, Mary takes a lamp from the hearth and goes to the window, which, we remember, has been associated with fantastic tracery that transforms pleasant thoughts into visions. It translates the cold of winter reality (almost, as it were, a reliteralized metaphor) into warm thoughts. A young man in a sailor's dress, Stephen, a former "unsuccessful wooer," tells her her husband is saved. A curious misperception suggests Hawthorne's understanding of the eros/thanatos paradox. Mary has a life-affirming subconscious misapprehension that Stephen means something sexual in his statement about seeking to "comfort" her (3:604; *T&S*, 65–66), whereas, of course, he brings her comforting news of her husband.

Perhaps the darkest of the symbols is the motif of the blessing, now introduced a second time. The ship that Mary's husband was aboard is named the *Blessing*; but "the Blessing turned bottom upwards" (3:605; *T&S*, 66). As though undaunted by such potential symbolism, Mary earlier asked for a blessing and now, with the news of her husband's survival, seems to have her wish fulfilled. Margaret, the more aggressive and skeptical of the two, hurt and superstitious and all atremble, had refused to ask for a blessing; now she too has apparently got her blessing in her husband's survival. But if there is in fact a providence, it seems to have no relation to piety and belief of the traditional religious sort. Rather, after the dark irony of having the ship *Blessing* sink, the dream-wishes emerge from the subconscious depths of both widowed women. This probability is strikingly suggested by a double turn of thought. Mary watches Stephen hurry away "with a doubt of waking reality" (3:605; *T&S*, 66), especially as he alternately enters "the shade of the houses" or emerges "into the broad streaks of moonlight." To have Mary doubt her "waking reality" simultaneously calls into question what she has just learned and affirms its reality since her doubt suggests rational examination — another paradox. The narrator, emphasizing an aptly unfortunate metaphor, says: "Gradually, however, a blessed flood of conviction swelled into her heart. . . ." Putting aside the blatant pun of the "blessed flood," it is clear that this conviction of truth is so desired by her that it would have been strong enough to "overwhelm her," as the narrator says, had it come upon her more abruptly. Her "rational" state is actually deranged, and the "blessed" conviction is an *as if* proposition wrenched from subconscious desire, a wish fulfillment concretized out of dream into the objective reality of subjective dream conviction, the will to believe. But this will to believe, no matter how real the deluded think its manifestations, is not the religious will to believe in a return to life of the dead man by an alteration of providence by God. It is a will to believe in a fiction, a wish, a dream — a thoroughly convincing act of romantic imagination. The tension in Hawthorne between two forms of imagination, one religious, one romantic, is implicitly buried in the heart of this sketch.

These themes become clearer as the sketch concludes in a subtle enigma. Like Margaret's, Mary's first impulse is "to rouse her sister-in-law" (3:605; *T&S*, 66); she is about to lay her hand on "the slumberer's shoulder" but remembers that Margaret "would awake to thoughts of death and woe, rendered not the less bitter by their contrast with her own felicity." Reenacting the first part of the narrative almost point for point, the second woman lifts the lamp to look upon her sister's face, expecting it to be unquiet, but finds her "cheek rosy-tinted, and her lips half opened in a vivid smile." The peacefulness of Margaret's face parallels that of Mary's in the first movement of the narrative, but its source is different (the conviction that her husband is still alive). The narrator grotesquely describes Margaret's "expression of joy," struggling to escape through the sealed eyelids, "like incense from the whole countenance," as though the face were a *censer or a lamp*. The "joy" is an illusion, an internal fiction, sealed within the sleeper. Mary exclaims, "My poor sister! you will waken too soon from that happy dream" (3:606; *T&S*, 67). Like the first, the second part of the sketch implies that Mary too will "waken" from the delusive dream. The metaphor of the lamp suggests the possibility that the light of the lamp is delusive.[25] Mary's setting down of the lamp redoubles, gesturally and imagistically, Margaret's earlier action, as though the two women do indeed share a parallel dream. Mary's hand trembles against Margaret's neck, and a tear falls upon her cheek: "and she suddenly awoke."

Lang is half right. The pronoun reference is deliberately ambiguous. For if, as suggested by the structure and imagery of the narrative, the "she" who awakes refers to the woman we have thought awake, then she has *not* been awake and the whole sequence of the narrative has been a dream of muted wish fulfillment. By this reading, by this revelation, the piece would have a more conventionally satisfactory denouement as a "tale." But the conclusion of the sketch-tale is poised, mystifyingly inconclusive, between these two possibilities as each "story" contests for a closure forever denied. And this is the "single effect" Hawthorne sought: a twice-told, negative epiphany of both theme and form.

Telling the Dream / Dreaming the Tale:
Recounting "An Old Woman's Tale"

Although developed at somewhat greater length than "The Hollow of the Three Hills" and "The Wives of the Dead," "An Old Woman's Tale" is another experiment in severely truncated narrative, another account of dream experience cast as legend. Here the subject and the theme is that of a (possibly) mutually shared dream and the relation of dream to reality and to imagination, especially tale telling. The narrative features a much more fully developed narrator than the largely absent narrators of "The Wives of the Dead" and "The Hollow of the Three Hills" — though, in the manner of some of the provincial "tales," he quickly drops out of the sketch as an overt presence after the frame introduction.

This introduction (which we shall consider in more detail later) is proportionally a rather long one focused on the narrator's source, an old woman who used to tell the narrator "tales" when he was a boy. These tales, he says, were usually set in or around her native village, many, many years before, since she was very old when he knew her. He tells how on one occasion she evoked the legend of her entire village's simultaneously falling to sleep, for the space of an hour, every twenty-five (or fifty) years.[26] The parson would snore over his sermon; a mother's eyelids would close as she bent over her infant; the infant would be too sleepy to cry; a watcher over the mortally ill would slumber at the death-pillow; while "the dying man anticipated his sleep of ages by one as deep and dreamless" (12:110; *T&S*, 26). There was, in short, a "soporific influence" over the village "stronger than if every mother's son and daughter were reading a dull story."

The playful self-parody introduced at the beginning of the narrative is foregrounded at the end, framing the whole. The introduction to the narrative parallels the act of telling a story with sleeping and dreaming, the very subjects of the narrative to come. This wry circling back to fiction as sleep-producing is countered with truth claims by the "author" (the old woman) of the story to follow, held at arm's distance by the "narrator" who tells us her story. The following narrative, filtered through the narrator-author, is that told by the old woman as true because it is based on a "story" she heard from someone who claimed to have "lived" it. And of course it is retold to us by the narrator (from a double perspective, that of the present, and that of the boy in the past, at least as remembered by the full-grown author). After all this wry framing, concise as it is, there is hardly any surprise that the tale-sketch that follows is indeterminate. Even the setting (as in "The Hollow of the Three Hills") becomes abstract, though we know from the introduction that it is the Valley of the Connecticut in New England, vivid of memory for the young tale-teller.

On the most apparent level, the story is, however, transparent. One midsummer night's eve, a young man and a young woman sit down together in the open air in a grove of elm and walnut trees near a "spring of diamond water" bubbling into the moonlight (3:111; *T&S*, 26). The betrothed, David and Esther, are "distant relatives, sprung from a stock once wealthy, but of late years so poverty-stricken, that David had not a penny to pay the marriage fee, if Esther should consent to wed." They remark on the faery beauty of the scene. "Perhaps," says the author-narrator (12:112; *T&S*, 27) they fall asleep together. And — perhaps — the "same strange dream might have wrapped them in its shadowy arms. But they conceived, at the time, that they still remained wakeful by the spring of bubbling water. . . ." The narrator insists on making sure that we do not know if they are dreaming or awake. Although it is summer, there is "a sort of mistiness over their minds like the smoky air of an early autumn night." In a romantic dream or in some sort of devil's vision, they become "conscious that a great many people were either entering the village or already in the street, but whether they came from the meeting-house, or from a little beyond it, or *where the devil they came from*, was more than could be determined" (12:113; *T&S*, 28; my italics). A crowd of men, women, and children are yawning, rubbing their eyes, and stretching, as though all simultaneously awakened from a sound slumber. These figures later turn out to be apparitions, whether ghosts, specters, or only dream figures is never made clear.[27] But the conjunction of the vision of David and Esther — as though in a dream — of an entire village waking up from a legendary sleep — to have an ethereal existence in the dream of a young couple centuries hence — compounds the eerie evanescence of it all. If the shared vision is a shared dream, the legend of the village falling asleep in the frame underscores a double reversal: in the "dream" the villagers "wake" to a dream in which they are dream figures of dream figures — much as in *A Midsummer Night's Dream*.[28]

Among all the ghostly personages, those of two other couples draw their attention. The first pair is "a youth in a sailor's dress and a pale slender maiden, who met each other with a sweet embrace in the middle of the street" and who must have been parted from each other, David and Esther think, "fifty years at least" (12:115; *T&S*, 29). There follows in their mutual dream "(if such it were)" a procession of representative types from the old village. Several of them are described in imagery of flame, scorching heat, and "red-hot eloquence," one of whom stamps "a hole through the very earth" (12:117; *T&S*, 31). Among these figures is another couple, aged rather than young. The man is small and dressed in gold lace. The woman, dressed in spangled shoes and gold-clocked stockings, a red hoop-petticoat, and a blue damask gown, seems to be lame (cf. traditional descriptions of the devil). She carries "a sort of iron shovel" in her hand, with which she tries to dig unsuccessfully at a spot between the walnut tree and the fountain, while (as in "Alice Doane's Appeal") the moonlight shines through her (12:118; *T&S*, 31–32). For an instant, the ghostly or dream couple gazes at David and Esther "with something like kindness and affection," but it is a "dim and uncertain" look that passes away almost immediately. After some hints of a parallel between this couple and David and Esther and some description of the elderly couple in terms of cloud, color, light, and air (as though her gown were drawn from the sky, his gold trousers and scarlet waistcoat from the light of dawn), the man draws forth a watch as big as the dial on the church steeple; he and the lady disappear, as do all the other villagers, including a previously described fat man in "flaming breeches" (12:119; *T&S*, 32).

On the surface, the piece conforms to the genre of the dreamvision in which the occult world is inadvertently revealed to those still mortal— although the scene is finally grotesquely distorted in the manner of surrealism or expressionism (or of dream). The indeterminacy of events, however, is heightened to the status of a theme. On one level, the description of the clothing of the ghostly man and woman, along with the appearance of the gigantic timepiece, suggests that the lovers have slept the night away and dawn is approaching (though, culturally, that is a highly unlikely eventuality), and we remember that the young couple only "might" have shared a dream and that their perception (like each sister in "Wives of the Dead") is that they are awake. On another level, the narrative invokes the supernatural tradition of the ghostly dreamvision, in which, frequently, some message or revelation is communicated to the living. So too here, seemingly. David takes an iron shovel "bearing a singular resemblance to that which they had seen in their dreams" (12:120; *T&S*, 33), and, with images in his mind of Esther's "pretty red lips" forming "a circle" and of "a scarlet hoop-petticoat," he starts digging at a place where he thinks he saw the ghost–dream figure dig. The piece, on whatever level one reads it—folkloristic, gothic, visionary, oneiric, Freudian—abruptly concludes with an incomplete denouement that calls attention to the conventions of normal story telling that have been violated. The "soil giving way so freely to his efforts," David quickly scoops out a large hole (as "large as the basin of the spring") and pokes his head "down to the very bottom of this cavity." The epiphany comes in one last sentence: " 'Oho! — what have we here?' cried David." The failure to give the reader the anticipated revelation, the withholding of conventional denouement, the indirect assertion of ambiguity, is all so abrupt that it is disruptive and annoying — at least if we are expecting the conventions of the "tale" as Poe and others conceived it.

What shall we make of it? The critics are not much help. The narrative has been critically neglected for fairly obvious reasons: it seems slight; it is hard to connect readily with Hawthorne's grand themes, especially of moral history; its denouement seems a hastily contrived avoidance of the requirements of fictional narrative. Practically the only criticism (all of it brief) on "An Old Woman's Tale" is that by Alfred Weber (*Rahmenerzählungen*, pp. 107–12), Rita Gollin (pp. 102–3), and Michael Colacurcio (pp. 46–49). Weber connects "An Old Woman's Tale" with "Alice Doane's Appeal" as special instances of Hawthorne's experimentation with framed narrative. Gollin connects it with "Alice Doane's Appeal" and "The Hollow of the Three Hills" as examples of "the mind's entry into itself" (p. 102), which seems to me an astute observation. She suggests that "all three of these tales establish tenuous connections with ordinary reality through hints that what seems supernatural might actually be a dream," which seems a trifle understated or underdeveloped. Baym, on the other hand, remarks in passing that "the lovers . . . dream of something that really happens" (p. 27), an odd sort of offhand claim to make of a dream-within-a-dream-within-a-dream narrative. Colacurcio writes that historicity is subordinated to the mind in this work and the only thing that pulls against its "essentially anti-historical 'philosophy' " is "a faintly Romantic sense of the power of the dreaming mind itself" (p. 48). The first part of his statement seems grossly overstated. The narrative hardly features anything that could be called an antihistorical *philosophy*, though Colacurcio speculates that the repeated awakening of the village and the processional of the same generationally repeated figures *suggests* that history is not purposive, causal, or progressive. While probably an accurate general assessment of Hawthorne's view of history, this conclusion goes a considerable distance beyond the text.

Gollin emphasizes that the lovers are poor; the story for her revolves around the "charming idea" that the lovers "receive a gift from the past through a [shared] dream" (p. 103), a theme by no means so simple and clear as she maintains. Because the plot is "irresolute" and "unsatisfying" and "the shared dream . . . devoid of psychological probability," the "charming idea" is "not strong enough to redeem it." For the author of a book on the significance of dreams in Hawthorne, this analysis seems surprisingly off the mark. Colacurcio, whose tendencies are in the opposite direction, comes closer by negation or dismissal: ". . . if one's primary concern were Hawthorne's spectral or dream-like theory of the imagination, 'An Old Woman's Tale' might easily figure as a crucial and neglected document" (pp. 46–47). But he too finds the narrative unsatisfactory: "In the end we seem faced with an accomplished piece of writing that does not quite know what it wants to say" (p. 47). This sounds suspiciously like Doubleday and Baym, or Crews, when they find Hawthorne doing something different from what they think he *should* be. Colacurcio tips his historicist hand in the next sentence: "Or, if that [the judgment that the narrative does not 'know' what it is about] is too harsh," then we can say that it is "a tale concerned with 'writing about the past' which understands more about writing than about the past" — that is, "more about its Romantic procedures than its ancestral subject." (As if there were something wrong with that.) This kind of *either/or* thinking exemplifies exactly the epistemical categorization problem that Hawthorne was exploring in the mind-sets of his contemporaries; and it ignores the interpenetrating, loosely contrapuntal design (history and romance, waking and sleeping, actuality and dream) of the provincial narratives as parts of a story cycle.

Weber addresses the latter point, at least in part. He emphasizes the potential of the narrative as a parable of the origins of the storyteller's sense of the source of his own art and craft — specifically the idea of a story cycle collection. The interior story and its method of presentation serves as an "example" for the art of telling a story. He speculates biographically that the Hawthorne family told "chimney tales" (fireside tales), an activity memorialized in the frame narrative and exemplified in the interior story: thus the emphasis in the frame on the narrator's fond remembrance of the Connecticut Valley. Weber goes on to suggest that the interior story is "grotesque" in the manner of parts of "Alice Doane's Appeal": a "mix" of the monstrous, the uncanny, and the terrifying, intersecting the "normal" world, treated with "light irony" (pp. 110–11). The whole he sees as connected with folk legends of the devil, further connected to the tale-teller, who associates the old woman (the older teller) with the devil and fiction (posing as truth) as the devil's work.[29]

The most obvious implication of the abrupt or negative denouement is that the narrative is a description of a dream and ends abruptly in the manner of dreams. If so, then the description of David and Esther possibly "waking" from the ghostly vision is also a dream, and the dreamlike ghost sequence is a dream within a dream or a dream giving way to another dream. And if this double structure obtains, then what is the ontological status of the initial description of the couple walking out and simultaneously (as in a dream) falling asleep and seemingly sharing the same dream? The ontological problems of dream and reality and their epistemo-logical corollary resemble those of "The Wives of the Dead" and "The Hollow of the Three Hills." Here the structure of infinite regress and the blurring of the imagined and the real is also the structure of the introduc-tory frame. The effect, like that of "Alice Doane's Appeal," is to distance reader and narrator and source while inviting a closer sensibility of what is at stake in the narrative by foregrounding the collaborative effort of author and reader to meld (again as in "Alice Doane's Appeal") the several struc-tures into one whole. The design of the narrative coerces the reader to focus on the story-telling process, which blends imagination and reality, making the sketch somewhat self-reflexive if not metafictional. Here, then, is the structural function of the introduction.

The opening frame of the sketch emphasizes that the narrator's "mem-ory" of the old woman's "memory" of "the better part" of a hundred years is one in which she has "jumbled" her own experiences with those of tale-tellers much older than herself, embedded in tales that she had heard when she was young. She seems to the narrator to be from the era of Queen Elizabeth (12:109; *T&S*, 25). "There are a thousand of her traditions lurking in the corners and by-places of my mind," he says; and he adds, as if formulating a preface to a volume of provincial tales, there are "some more marvellous than what is to follow, some less so, and a few not marvellous in the least, all of which I should like to repeat, if I were as happy as she in having a listener."

The narrator comments further that he does "not deserve a listener half so well as that old toothless woman, whose narratives possessed an excel-lence attributable neither to herself, nor to any single individual." Hers was an oral tradition freely admitting the fantastic — a premise that informs *The Story Teller* cycle, which Hawthorne was working on at the time. Her "ground-plots, seldom within the widest scope of probability," nevertheless "were filled up with homely and natural incidents." Under these details, "fiction hid its grotesque extravagance in this garb of truth, like the Devil (an appropriate simile, for the old woman supplies it) disguising himself, cloven-foot and all, in mortal attire" (12:110; *T&S*, 25).

The demarcation between fiction and truth is blurred, and story telling is (as so often in Hawthorne) associated with the devil. In this regard, it is notable that in the opening frame we are told that the narrator's strongest visual memory of the old woman is of her "crouching all day long over the kitchen fire, with her elbows on her knees and her feet in the ashes" (12:109; *T&S*, 25). The narrator "sat on a log of wood, grasping her check-apron in both [his] hands." However realistic the details, the overall effect is somewhat odd. The scene is a bizarre "domestic" version of the sentimental cliché of the hearth from the culture of the time, with parallels to the comic-sinister hearth in "The Devil in Manuscript," in which an "author" rolls back and forth over hot coals. It compares strangely in its ambiguity with the more positive image of the hearth in other of Hawthorne's pieces (even "Fire-Worship"). Yet it conforms to the dual, even paradoxical nature of the hearth in *Provincial Tales* and in still other of Hawthorne's sketches.

Continuing the hearth and home theme, the narrator remarks that most of the old woman's tales generally referred to her birthplace, a village in the Valley of the Connecticut, a locale that is featured in *The Story Teller.* He remarks that when, "two summers since," he had ridden through her village, "one object after another rose familiarly to my eye, like successive portions of a dream becoming realized" (12:110). By this remark the stage is set for a tale within a tale of mixed dream and reality that parallels the mixing in the frame introduction of dream and reality, memory and imagination, one's own life and stories of other lives. Examining "An Old Woman's Tale" in context, as part of or a predecessor of the *Provincial Tales,* reveals it to be perfectly congruent with the other early "provincial" pieces. They all subvert straightforward conventions of tale telling by providing at least two (possibly reversible) readings in structures of dramatic irony based on an ironic theme or situation, sometimes ironically reversing on the thematic level the ironic situation. The frame of "An Old Woman's Tale" is an iconic replication of the themes and patterns of the main narrative in colloquy with itself. As a whole, the work parallels in frame and tale the structure of infinite regression: of story within a story, one narrator within another narrator, one existence within another existence, one reality within another reality, one dream within another dream.

No author . . . can conceive of the difficulty of writing a romance about a country where there is no shadow, no antiquity, no mystery, no picturesque and gloomy wrong, nor anything but a commonplace prosperity, in broad and simple daylight, as happily is the case with my dear native land. — Preface to *The Marble Faun* (1859)

As with the dreamvision "sketches," one of the more striking features of the "tales" of *Provincial Tales* is that of the "twice-told": their double narrative quality and their capacity for redoubled interpretation. These narratives are not simple patriotic or provincial tales of the "romance" of American history, but may be more properly designated historical "negative romances." A conventional (nongothic) romance tale extols the virtues of love, idealism, heroic adventure or resistance, and frequently implies the moral-spiritual correspondence and signification of nature. A negative romance employs these conventions and assumptions while turning on itself and negating, to some degree, positive romantic values. The term is meant to suggest, not an outright denial of romantic values (nor a gothic point-for-point inversion), but an indeterminate or shifting balance between the positive and the negative within an ironic form tending toward some degree of self-reflexivity. As a form of romantic irony, the negative romance entertains, incorporates, balances simultaneous affirmation and indeterminate skepticism much like the overall concept of negative romanticism.[1]

In their ambiguity, Hawthorne's negative romances in *Provincial Tales* represent a range of genre-blurring experiments with story-telling and other narrative modes: from "tale proper," to story, quasi-story, sketch, quasi-sketch, biography, history, romance. These "provincial" narratives often acquire a twice-told quality not only of theme but also of form. Like the dream sketches, they are, in different degrees, about story telling as well as the romance or history they purport to tell. The three "tales" here designated negative romances — "The Gray Champion," "Roger Malvin's

Burial," and "The Gentle Boy"—have been gathered together in this chapter because they exhibit the features of the "tale proper" defined in the preceding chapters. They follow a traditional configuration of explication, complication, crisis, and full denouement.

Hawthorne's negative romances foreground history/romance, truth/fiction relationships on what we may call an "exterior" level and an "interior" level. By the first is meant the form of the narrative as given or shaped by narrators of varying degrees of involvement and detachment—narrators whose "authorial" voices frame the story they have to tell (and in which they normally do not directly participate). By the second is meant the dramatic world of the narrative; and in Hawthorne there are at least two interior levels: a large cultural-political-religious story is paralleled with a particularized individual story in a way that suggests they are reciprocal in their causal determinism. The historical story determines the personal story, and vice versa. The "victims" of the "iron cage" of the "text" of Puritan society are also its builders and attendant jailors. In each of the three provincial tales examined here, the question of historical truth is intertwined not only with social, moral, and psychological issues but also with aesthetic issues: with the psychological and moral perceptions of individuals struggling within the abstract principles of the social system of the Puritan "New World"; and with the aesthetic and philosophical struggle of a narrator to "tell" these stories.

In "The Gray Champion" the simple question of the ontological reality of a mysterious figure that suddenly appears at a time of political crisis is entangled with at least two different moral perceptions of righteousness and political providentiality—as what initially seems a minimally characterized narrator attempts to create a patriotic legend out of dubious historiography for an implied nationalistic public. In this very activity, in the way he tells and frames his tale, his "voice" so enters the dialogue of the narrative as to become a significant aspect of its indeterminate theme. In "Roger Malvin's Burial," the reader's perception of the question gnawing the bosom of Reuben Bourne is clarified on the psychological level by the intervening narrator's gradual revelation and analysis of Reuben's egotism. On the moral-social level, the abstract chronicler-narrator's initial allusion (in a frame introduction to the "unusually minute" details preserved in historical chronicles of the incident of "Lovewell's Fight" calls attention both to the dubious morality and uncertain historiography of the numerous romancers of the event—including by playful implication himself. The tale that most prominently features a framing narrator as authorial-figure is "The Gentle Boy." The historical truth of the Puritan-Quaker conflict is entangled in moral-psychological perspectivism, emphasized by the narrator's explicit analysis of cultural pathology. The same pathology, framed less overtly by narratorial comment, is played out on the individual level in the lives of the principal personages of the tale. In Hawthorne's provincial tales any historical, psychological, or moral event is yet another text of some kind — with which a "helpful" narrator offers a reader ambiguous (or even ironic) assistance in reading ultimately as negative romance.

Of Jingoism and Genocide:
The Grayness of "The Gray Champion"

The rather slight narrative "The Gray Champion" (1835) stands as the introduction to all editions of *Twice-told Tales*. At one time the proposed title for the collection was "The Gray Champion, and Other Tales." Critics have frequently speculated on the significance of this piece as symbolic and thematic introduction to Hawthorne's first published collection (and possibly to *Seven Tales* or *Provincial Tales*). In the last thirty-five years, a debate has emerged as to how representative it is of Hawthorne's attitude not only toward American history, politics, and religion, but also toward his craft and his audience. The critical spectrum on this narrative thus itself becomes representative of the Hawthorne Question.[2]

The thesis presented here is that, as the introductory narrative of *Twice-told Tales*, "The Gray Champion," a form of the legend-tale, has the effect of a clarion call to a special form of romance — the negative. It announces not a simplistic American patriotism, but the dialogicity of the apparently monological works to follow. "The Gray Champion" exemplifies Hawthorne's ambiguous treatment of American history and provides as lead-tale a clue to the ironic perspectives of the whole of *Twice-told Tales* and the earlier *Provincial Tales*. This thesis, by no means new, is opposed by a number of critics, of whom Nina Baym is perhaps the least equivocal. The different critical perspectives of the last three decades suggest that the interpretative issue at stake in "The Gray Champion" is crucial, both to the proper reading of Hawthorne and to the critical tradition that has grown up around Hawthorne.[3] In the retrospective of intense Hawthorne criticism, it is notable that the interpretations of the lead narrative of *Twice-told Tales* vary so much as to be almost diametrically opposed, from the searingly ironic to the flag-wavingly patriotic.[4]

Some readings account better for more of what is in the text (and around it) than others. In my opinion, the two best readings of "The Gray Champion" have been those of Frederick Crews and Frederick Newberry, which, except for Crews's Freudianism, are closely congruent.[5] For Crews, "The Gray Champion" has only as its "ostensible subject" a "legend of democratic resistance" to the power of James II; its real subject is the power struggle of one authority against another in a ceaseless generational chain of competition for dominance. The figure the Gray Champion presents is not the image of the democratic spirit of "the people" (he is not dressed like an ordinary citizen), but of a "patriarch."

> The whole tale could be described as a contest of paternal figures, with various powers — including Sir Edmund Andros, Governor Bradstreet, the gathered ministers of the colony, the Gray Champion himself, and by proxy the Pope and the King of England — all vying to exploit the colonists' "filial love which had invariably secured their allegiance to the mother country" (I, 21). The Gray Champion triumphs merely through his aura of being the "chief ruler" (I, 28) on the scene. (*Sins of the Fathers*, p. 40)

Crews's insight into the patriarchal aspect proceeds from a Freudian context rather than from a social-historical analysis. Nevertheless, his deft assessment makes it clear that Hawthorne has set up a situation that throws into high relief the patriarchal structure of American society, framing it ironically (and perhaps, if one sees the childish posturing of the contesting groups as Oedipal, comically). Although the tale opens and closes with ringing pro-revolutionary phrases, continues Crews, "the intervening pages expose these attitudes as absurd." The Gray Champion who "magically arrives" to repel the representatives of the crown is "anything but an epitome of democracy," and "the people whom the Gray Champion rescues from English tyranny are . . . undermined in their pretense of standing for justice and freedom."

The irony of the tale, says Crews, is "overpowering." For example, the ministers of each parish "egotistically compete to see who can assume the most 'apostolic dignity' so as to deserve 'the crown of martyrdom' . . . while the old soldiers surviving from Cromwell's age are 'smiling grimly at the thought that their aged arms might strike another blow against the house of Stuart' " — not to mention what Hawthorne calls "veterans of King Philip's war, who had burned villages and slaughtered young and old, with pious fierceness" (see *Sins of the Fathers*, pp. 39–40). Crews sees Hawthorne's technique as similar to that in "Endicott and the Red Cross": the "opening and closing paragraphs — and no others — provide the basis of [a] straightforward reading"; the "bulk of the tale imparts a Swiftian flavor to such claims." Hawthorne "was no propagandist of the revolutionary character," but rather "an ironical observer of antagonists whose self-justifying slogans are meaningless on both sides. Power, he implies, makes a tyrant of anyone who seizes it, and history is a series of inessential reversals in which unjust rulers are supplanted by soon-to-be-unjust rebels."[6] The implications for historical teleology are enormous: the difference between purposelessness and manifest destiny.

Newberry's essay "Hawthorne's Ironic Criticism of Puritan Rebellion in 'The Gray Champion'" extends Crews's reading in a historical direction. Newberry's main point is nicely summed up by Colacurcio. Reaffirming Newberry's historicist/ironic reading, Colacurcio writes that although the ironies of the tale are "hard to detect," what Hawthorne "actually" does is to show us "how a patriotic myth is put together and, in case we care, how we might learn to escape its drastic political oversimplification." He suggests that the "patriotic rhetoric with which the sketch begins, and which rattles its saber throughout much of the tale's authorial 'talk,' is recognizable enough, and extreme enough, to make us at least suspect that Hawthorne's use of it is situational and dramatic rather than personal and didactic" (*Province*, pp. 208–9ff.). Newberry, repaying the compliment, offers a reconsidered version of his 1976 article for his booklength study *Hawthorne's Divided Loyalties*, writing that Colacurcio has "unsurpassingly demonstrated" that "Hawthorne's historiography adamantly resists a patriotic reading in any way commensurate with the democratic ideology of his time" (p. 19). According to Newberry, the closing lines of "The Gray Champion" reflect "a nineteenth-century consciousness of national typology." (This point about a dramatized "nineteenth-century consciousness" is well observed, and I return to the significance of this narratorial "voice" toward the end of my discussion of the tale.) Newberry further observes that in the opening historical frame the narrator's "rhetoric is charged with antipathy for the British, no doubt reflecting Hawthorne's deliberate though misleading appeal to the biases of his contemporary nineteenth-century audience." What "falls between the opening and closing paragraphs often stands considerably at odds with the frame. . . ."[7]

As Crews recognizes, the hermeneutical problem lies with the outspoken narrator, not only in the opening and closing paragraphs framing the rest of the story, but throughout. Crews does not, however, deal with the narrator as *obstacle* to an ironic reading—a point later made much of negatively by Baym, who suggests that the tale is unambiguously pro-Puritan (p. 72). She writes that the "first story in *Twice-told Tales* emphasizes that the author is a true American in his political and nationalist sentiments . . ." (p. 73). In fact, she claims that underlying all Hawthorne's early fictions is an unqualified nationalism. It is my contention, on the contrary, that the author-narrator figure has an ironic, double quality in the tradition of Swift's "A Modest Proposal," that a similar double narratee (implicated and implied) is tautly deployed, and that the tale has a narrative dialogicity that pervades both the *Twice-told* collection and the earlier twice-told provincial tales.

Authorial voice(s) and the text.   In "The Gray Champion" the presence of an "author" in the role of legendary tale-teller or epic bard is immediately evident; but Hawthorne's ironic use of the figure of the tale-teller under-scores the difference between the older heroic tradition and the modern (that is, romantic) treatment. As framed and interpreted by a special narra-tor persona, "The Gray Champion" does in fact at first seem a rousing patriotic story of the American fight for liberty, told by one who sides with the colonials against "oppressive" British rule. The first sentence of the frame introduction reads: "There was once a time when New England groaned under the actual pressure of heavier wrongs than those threatened ones which brought on the Revolution" (1:21; T&S, 236). Whatever this historical judgment tells us about the narrator, his initial loyalties cannot be mistaken: James II, the "bigoted successor of Charles the Voluptuous," has at the time of which he is about to write "annulled the charters of all the colonies" and "sent a harsh and unprincipled soldier" to take away "our liberties" and "endanger our religion." Because of the use of such devices as the pronoun "our" and the use of words like "liberty," many critics have been deceived into identifying the third-person narrative voice (of this and of other early provincial tales) with Hawthorne. That a separation must be made between Hawthorne (or even the "implied author") and the narrator of this tale, however, is suggested by the uncritical if not chauvinistic reference to "our religion." For one thing, the burden of Hawthorne's early stories is largely to show the tyranny of various religions (morally, politi-cally, socially, psychologically), especially that of the Puritans of New England; for another, a structure of narratological contradictions (involv-ing two narrator presences and two audiences) is carefully built up in the progress of the tale.

On the secular side, with regard to "our liberties," the difference between Hawthorne and the narrator is not so immediately evident; it develops somewhat more gradually. No particular distinction between Hawthorne as author and the narrator suggests itself in the next several sentences of the frame introduction. We are told that the administration of Sir Edmund Andros, Governor of Massachusetts (significantly called "New England" throughout), "lacked scarcely a single characteristic of tyranny." The royal governor and his council, "wholly independent of the country," made laws and levied taxes "without concurrence of the people immediate or by their representatives." The rights of private citizens were violated, the titles of landed property were declared void; dissent in the press was stifled. Andros, representing King James II, called in "the first band of mercenary troops that ever marched on our free soil." Before "these evil times," says the narrator in a doubly barbed comment that parallels in tone his opening comment, "the colonists had ruled themselves, enjoying far more freedom than is even yet the privilege of the native subjects of Great Britain" (1:21–22; T&S, 236).

The tale itself is focused on an incident that precedes (and, according to American legend, presages) the fall of both King James II and Governor Andros in the Glorious Revolution. One afternoon in April 1689, Andros, in a show of royal authority, displays his military might before the dissident colonists of Boston. Several colonialist leaders on both sides appear at the scene: Randolph, Bullivant, Dudley, along with a ship's captain, some civil officers and clergymen, and most especially "Governor Bradstreet himself, a patriarch of nearly ninety, who appeared on the elevated steps of a door, and, with characteristic mildness, besought them to submit to the constituted authorities" (1:24; *T&S*, 238). At first the confrontation is a stand-off. Then a mysterious aged man, of heroic, almost supernatural deportment, appears in King's Road and backs down the royalist troops. He announces that tomorrow James will no longer be king and Andros no longer governor. Andros recalls his soldiers. The next day the "prophecy" comes "true," and the Gray Champion disappears.

Such is the surface story. But Hawthorne covertly insinuates into one side of the conflict its equally valid opposite. Among undercutting ironies, of course, is the possibility (as in other Hawthorne stories, e.g., the *Province House* tales) that the old man is an actor or a crackbrain and the prophecy a subterfuge, a coincidence, or an announcement of something that in effect has already taken place in England — though these suggestions are not developed. What we are told is that "at length a rumor reached our shores that the Prince of Orange had ventured on an enterprise, the success of which would be the triumph of civil and religious rights and the salvation of New England" (1:22; *T&S*, 236), a rumor that provokes "bold glances" and "a subdued and silent agitation" among the colonists. The "triumph of civil and religious rights," however, does not for them mean political or religious "freedom" in the ordinary sense of the word but rather the freedom of the colonists to impose their own authority.[8]

It is on this moral-ethical point of freedom and liberty that the complexity of the narrator hangs. On the one hand, he himself seems limited, unaware of the limited if changing nature of Puritan concepts of liberty; on the other hand, the twice-told structure of the tale as a whole, told by *some* narrator, suggests a critical view of the unfortunate triumph of the Puritan political perspective. It is almost as though there were two quasi-characterized tale-tellers, one including the other, as in Irving's *Tales of a Traveller* and Poe's *Tales of the Folio Club*, in which a frame narrator presents other narrators telling particular tales. In terms of the adapted semiotic models of Chatman and Prince, the crux (or possibly ironic gap) is between a narrator and an implicated narrator (possibly an implied author figure). In this Irving-like structure, the tale suggests remnants of *The Story Teller* scheme. Whether or not it was a *Story Teller* installment, "The Gray

Champion" is, rather than an uncritical tale of the colonialist fight for American liberty, a picture of the beginnings of a new despotism. The "supernatural" figure is probably neither supernatural nor portentous of an ordained destiny. The negation of the romance of the Gray Champion is enhanced by the fact that the historical basis of the tale is in part the career of a regicide judge of unsavory reputation and questionable loyalties, William Goffe, who fled to the colonies to escape retribution.[9]

But there are more telling possibilities for this reading of an implied characterized tale-teller than coincidence or masquerade in the suspect Gray Champion's timely appearance. One is the articulated uncertainty of the seemingly omniscient narrator regarding Andros's quailing before the mysterious champion of the colonists. Andros decides not to press forward with his soldiers, but the narrator does not know "whether the oppressor were overawed by the Gray Champion's look, or perceived his peril in the threatening attitude of the people" (1:30; T&S, 242). Nor is it clear how much being warm with wine affects the governor. Another element negating the romance of righteous heroism is that the tale features a kind of "moral" that concludes only one part of the story. It is an expression by the narrator of the *colonists'* belief that the old man is the "type of New England's hereditary spirit" and that "his shadowy march, on the eve of danger, must ever be the pledge, that New England's sons will vindicate their ancestry" (1:31; T&S, 243). That this belief is perspectival—the perspective of the Puritans—is blurred by the narrator's tacit authorial adoption of it, marked by his recurrent use of the first-person plural pronoun. Nevertheless, the ambiguity of the final phrase is obvious. To what does the ancestry of New England's sons refer: their British ancestry—their Puritan ancestry—their new American "ancestry"?[10] The pertinency of this ambiguity becomes clearer as we see the two opposing groups, considered from an abstract moral point of view, blur together into one. They are equally intolerant and tyrannical, like the opposed religious and political groups in other of the *Provincial Tales*. Such is Newberry's reading, echoed by Colacurcio. Newberry goes further: Bradstreet as mediator is supplanted by the intolerant champion; in fact, says Newberry, mediators in Hawthorne are destroyed or swept away.

Although the narrator seems rather unequivocally to adopt the point of view of the colonists, our reading of his attitude is shaped by structural and referential ambiguities. A major instance is the utterance, "Satan will strike his master-stroke presently" (1:23; T&S, 237). On the surface, the statement seems to refer to the plot of the royalists, but it occurs shortly before the appearance of the colonists' Gray Champion. Then, when the narrator describes the array of colonists who have gathered in opposition to the governor's soldiers, he surveys the various types in the crowd and notes among them those aforementioned "veterans of King Philip's war, who had burned villages and slaughtered young and old, with pious fierceness, while the godly souls throughout the land were helping them with prayer" (1:23; *T&S*, 237). Satan's strokes indeed—in the very midst of the pious.

The contradictions of the Puritans are evident even in the clothing imagery of the tale. In describing the panorama of the human scene in the street, the narrator mentions among other articles of dress the patriarchal robes of Bradford and the Gray Champion and the vestments of the clergy. Newberry notes the irony of the Puritans' unconscious "obeisance to vestments, blasphemous in Puritan theology" (p. 54). The Puritans are enraged at seeing the "priestly vestments" of an Episcopal clergyman of King's Chapel accompanying the secular Loyalists and take him (or the narrator does) to be "the fitting representative of prelacy and persecution, the union of church and state, and all those abominations which had driven the Puritans to the wilderness" (1:25; *T&S*, 239). The passage contains a double irony. First, two generations of Puritan leaders themselves wanted a "union of church and state" under their own rule but regarded their governance as proper and just rather than an abomination of "prelacy and persecution." This unrecognized congeries of political and ecclesiastical power, persecution, and hypocrisy is the very thing that Hawthorne excoriates them for in other provincial tales (such as, most egregiously, "The Gentle Boy"). Second, in an unconscious "blasphemy," the Puritans regard their own ministers with "such reverence, as if there were sanctity in their very garments" (1:23; *T&S*, 237). Later, when the "ancient man" wearing "the old Puritan dress" emerges "from among the people" (1:26; *T&S*, 240), he is described as "combining the leader and the saint . . . in such an *ancient garb*" that his "stately form" could "*only* belong to some old champion of the righteous cause, whom the oppressor's drum had summoned from his grave" (1:28; *T&S*, 241; my italics). Angered at the Anglican "blasphemy" of vested power, the Puritans invest their own vestments with a mystical religious, political, providential power.[11] As Crews suggests, they are "one."

Author and audience: the "moral." If all sides are indeed one, in what ways is the hallowed Old World "ancestry" of the New World to be "vindicated"? The ancestry and the heritage are the same on both sides, for they are all sons and daughters of England. Does vindication really require blood as usual—the continuance of the tradition of pain and suffering—the imposition of a new tyranny? Such is the implication of many of the other stories of colonial history, legend, and religion of both the *Provincial Tales* and the

Twice-told Tales. The portrait of the seventeenth-century American colonists in this patriotic, provincial tale is similar to that of the eighteenth-century political activists of "My Kinsman, Major Molineux." The colonials have a rigid and one-sided view of their own rightness and the irredeemable wrongness of others. In this narrowness, they resemble Hawthorne's caricatures of religious types that represent the extremes of the Puritan world view, such as Young Goodman Brown or Richard Digby. Brown convinces himself that all his neighbors and even his bride are demonic; Richard Digby of "The Man of Adamant," rejecting his fellows, retreats to a limestone cave to live as a hermit, drinking the water that trickles down the rocks until it turns him (or he turns himself) into stone.

In the middle of "The Gray Champion" the narrator observes that, in fact, "the whole scene was a picture of the condition of New England." The irony would be obviously bilateral were it not for the seemingly unilateral second half of the statement: the "moral," he says, has to do with "the deformity of any government that does not grow out of the nature of things and the character of the people" (1:26; *T&S*, 239). The narrator sounds like a colonial apologist, an archetypal American democrat from the nineteenth century, such as the self-characterized "thorough-going democrat" of the *Province House* frame-sketches (1:329; *T&S*, 667–68), here addressing an audience of the like-minded. But such unilateral pronouncements, even "democratic" ones, are generally uncharacteristic of the overall structures of Hawthorne's works or are tongue-in-cheek parodies of moralistic fiction.[12] All the participants are the progeny of England; and what they are *does* grow out of the character of *the* people—namely, the tendency of human nature itself toward hierarchy and despotism.

Scenically, Hawthorne has arranged the "religious multitude" on one side and the civil multitude (the group of "despotic rulers") on the other; but thematically he does not attribute right to either side. Only vaguely through a *problematic* narrator does he essay an appeal to a *democratic principle not yet in effect* and one which *neither* Loyalist nor Dissenter in 1689 would have understood. The contestatory voices of dialogical fiction could hardly be more pronounced (or more ironic) in so short a piece. As other of the provincial and twice-told tales show (e.g., "The May-Pole of Merry Mount," "The Gentle Boy," "The Shaker Bridal"), the religious character of the American people is as despotic as the secular political institutions under which they operate. They seek to overthrow these institutions, nominally for justice and freedom, but really to establish what amounts to a new despotism. Especially despotic is the character of "the people" when, as the Puritans perceive in the Loyalists, religion and politics *coincide*—the lesson of the Old World and the New World both. This the nineteenth-century American democrat narrator does not appear to apprehend, as he adds his own muddled voice to the others in the tale.

Thus, combined with these problematical themes and situations, there is also the problem of interpretation of the narrator's *interpretation*. Hawthorne makes the narrator's ringing patriotic conclusion deliberately problematic; and its double effect is partly a matter of audience — both implied and implicated — a double audience like that addressed in "A Modest Proposal." The narrator, rather than living in a more democratic, more enlightened age, manifests his own nineteenth-century replications of the jingoistic, provincialist, and even genocidal sentiments of a century and a half before. His rhetoric exemplifies Bakhtin's notion of the ever-present linguistic (and thus conceptual) baggage of the past. He is presented by the author, Hawthorne, in a way (via tone, disjuncture, narrative structure) that casts him ironically and presents a "moral" of a rather different kind than the transparent one the narrator mouths. Although some critics resist the idea that Hawthorne would use an "obtuse" narrator, the narrator's statement about "our" forebears' slaughter of the Indians (especially the part about the godly Puritans urging their militia to divinely sanctioned genocide) should mediate any fundamental aesthetic problem with the gap between narrative tone (and characterization) and "Hawthorne." The narrator's seemingly naive endorsement of the colonialist cause is heavily ironic and sarcastic at some remove or another. The colonists' romanticized view of their champion accumulates negative resonances from the overall structure — and the regicide "champion" is, after all, *gray*.

In addition to a double narrator presence, the narratee of "The Gray Champion" is likewise double, standing in dialogical tension: (1) the special implicated reader who is expected to agree with the mask-narrator that regicide and genocide in certain instances (the "historical" events of the text) are necessary and acceptable; and (2) the general, normative reader who sees the moral obtuseness of the narrator and the readership his authorship represents as an agreed upon narratival device or pretense. What turns out to be a rather heavily characterized narrator (albeit by framing and implicature) tacitly assumes a provincial reader who also will give approbation at some level to jingoism and genocide — at least when the cause is "proper."

By this statement I do not mean to turn Hawthorne's narrator and his implicated reader into hopelessly obtuse moral reprobates. Instead, I see the narratival strategies and authorial presences in the tale as prototypically self-reflexive. In this case, the deft narratorial touches implicate the narrator and his assumed reader in the very moral ambiguities dialogically implicit in the tale he tells. If, moreover, we read the narrative in the context of a series of related "provincial tales" and measure the narrator against the other narrative voices, we find the "Gray Champion" narrator to be framed by the ironic overall *author*-narrator who is the complex author figure, the "Story Teller" character, dominating the sequences of early tales, who is in turn subsumed by the consciousness called Hawthorne. Hawthorne employs the ironic mask of a partially obtuse narrator, who is committed to a received version of history in the name of some other more-or-less culturally acceptable abstraction, such as religious precept, moral correctness, divinely sanctioned dominance — or economic freedom from unwanted taxation. In these ways "The Gray Champion" is subtly framed by narrative intrusion so as to suggest that the tale is not a straightforward romance of American heroism but a complex structure of author/reader levels of transactions undercutting traditional romance. "The Gray Champion" is thus an equivocal negative romance — introducing an entire volume of such twice-told tales and sketches.

"My Tale Is Not of Love"; or, How to Make a "Romance" Anyway: The Double Narrative of "Roger Malvin's Burial"

Deployment of the narrator of "Roger Malvin's Burial" (1832; collected in *Mosses*, 1846, rev. 1854) differs from that in "The Gray Champion." But the "Malvin" narrator emphasizes his presence several times, twice at length, as he enters the narrative to express an attitude or to offer a guiding interpretation of his characters' behavior. He is not treated with much irony from a perspective outside, as it were, his own — even though he provides a historical introduction as a frame for the tale to follow in which he admits to distorting for the purpose of "romance." Indeed, he himself possesses a sharp sense of irony. He seems almost to wink at the reader like a Merry Andrew. For, having claimed the province of "romance" for a tale based on "factual" historical particulars, he underscores the point that his particular story is not of love (2:393, 398; *T&S*, 97, 100); nor is it, as he makes clear in the first paragraph, of heroism.

The "moonlight of romance": history and fiction. This ironic attitude, however, is not immediately evident, even though the opening paragraph playfully elaborates the conventions of fictionalizing historical events. The narrator remarks that the tale he has to tell is based on a past event that is "one of the few incidents of Indian warfare naturally susceptible of the moonlight of romance" (2:381; *T&S*, 88). This is the "expedition" that resulted in "the well-remembered 'Lovell's Fight.'" The narrator's reference here is to the "Penobscot conflict" of Captain John Lovewell. Hawthorne subtly underscores the ironic potentialities of his name by slurring it "New England" style, giving us the local pronunciation. Lovewell had gone forth against the Pequawket Indians (in southwestern Maine, at that time part of Massachusetts) in 1725. A clue to the narrator's ironic attitude is his somewhat negative phrasing of the significance of the event. The battle, though "fatal to those who fought," was "not unfortunate" in its "consequences to the country" — for "it broke the strength of a tribe and conduced to the peace which subsisted during several ensuing years."

Emphasizing the distance between truth and what we usually call history (the memorializing of the past), and playing on the "fatal" consequences of the event and the relation of providentiality to history and of history to fiction or legend, the narrator observes that "history *and* tradition" (my italics) have in this instance been "unusually minute" in their "memorials" of the "affair." Moreover, like other twice-told stories, "some of the incidents contained in the following pages will be recognized [i.e., as history], notwithstanding the substitution of fictitious names, by such as have heard, from old men's lips [i.e., as fiction], the fate of the few combatants who were in a condition to retreat after 'Lovell's Fight' " (2:381; *T&S*, 88).

Initially, the historical introduction seems similar to that of the American democrat tale-teller of history and legend in "The Gray Champion." A careful reading suggests, however, that this narrator is both ironic and sardonic, here not only toward his characters but also toward himself as author (as in other of Hawthorne's writings). The second sentence of the tale, for example, calls attention to the problematic relation of historical statement (as truth) and fiction, but it does so in a self-reflexive way. Some past events, like that upon which his tale is based, may be *made* susceptible of the moonlight of romance by suppressing or omitting the full truth of a situation. Of course it goes without saying that a degree of selectivity and thus of some suppression of full truth is inevitable in the writing of history as well. Later in the discussion I shall return to the dialogical negotiation of the conceptual categories and literary genres of historiography and fiction, history and romance.

With regard to the historical romance of the event known as Lovewell's Fight, "imagination," says Hawthorne's narrator, "by *casting certain circumstances judicially into the shade*, may see much to admire in the *heroism* of a little band who gave battle to twice their number in the heart of the enemy's country" (2:381, my italics; *T&S*, 88). The statement takes away as much as it gives, subtly negating the romance — subtly, that is, if one does not know the "unusually minute" details of the historical circumstances of Lovewell's several encounters with the Indians. In Hawthorne's New England of 1825 to 1835, the famous fight was still being celebrated; but how many of

Hawthorne's readers a century after the event would have known the full story is unclear.

In 1724, members of Lovewell's family had been ambushed by Indians, and Lovewell made a double vow: to defend New England against the savages and to avenge his murdered kinsmen. Hawthorne was apparently attracted by the historical-moral ambiguity of this double vow, in which national and personal concerns are nicely made one. The moral heroism of this pledge is compromised by a few additional historical facts. For one thing, Lovewell's soldiers were after the bounty of one hundred pounds (an enormous sum) offered by the Massachusetts legislature for each Indian scalp brought back to Boston. For another, they had on a previous excursion scalped ten Indians they had found *sleeping*. Despite this prior atrocity, the Christian Captain Lovewell and his men were in verse and prose for a hundred years celebrated by New Englanders: Lovewell's band had (in 1725), so far as the biased European white colonialists were concerned, made a heroic stand against a superior force of (avenging) Indians. The bloody battle left many dead on both sides and also forced the abandonment of three wounded Englishmen in the wilderness. The extolling of Lovewell's stand culminated in the centennial celebrations of 1825, just prior to the composition of "Roger Malvin's Burial." It is these circumstances that are cast "into the shade" by the ironic narrator in the interests (so he says on one level) of the "moonlight" of "romance."[13] The fact/fiction problem here takes on a major cultural and historical ambiguity that underscores Hawthorne's large skeptical-epistemological theme.

But Hawthorne's narrator tells none of these details directly; he instead allows the historical context of the tale, to which he has specific implicatory reference, ironically to frame (both in the sense of abstract contextualizing and literal framing by the narrator's intrusion) the romantic elements. The technique is the same as in "The Gray Champion," where it is indirectly hinted that the figure of the Gray Champion is suspect, modeled upon the regicide of dubious morality William Goffe. Here the "heroic" figure of Lovewell is likewise questionable. The Puritan/Revolutionary cause is just as sordid — or questionable — as that of Endicott in 1634; there is no generational moral decay, just the pathos of one-sided self-righteousness. The "iron cage" of the Puritan system not only prevents historical analysis and critique, but also individual self-scrutiny. For Reuben Bourne pathetically if not tragically acts out a sacrificial drama of narcissistic guilt for a crime that was no crime, or for a failure of heroism that was no failure. These are the two narratives of the burial (literal and psychological) of Roger Malvin, who comes to symbolize the "evil wine" of eighteenth-century colonial Puritan repression and guilt: one story is that of (Reuben's belief in) a providential fate directing Reuben Bourne's entire history from the point of his "flight" in the woods; the other story is that of obsessive individual egocentricity as the double result of individual repression of guilt and of the generally repressive provincial culture. Once again (as we shall see momentarily in "The Gentle Boy") Hawthorne parallels a large historical cultural pathology with individual psychology—confounding both in the actors' sense of their moral drama, not to mention the question of historical truth.

In the historical introduction, having thus ambiguously cast his point of view and his historical narrative into doubt, the narrator is careful to point out that bravery was to be found in "both parties," not just in the colonists from Europe. Even a reader who is an American patriot interested in heroic, romantic tales of his native land should not therefore misconstrue this kind of "romance" element in any narrative to follow. Twisting the knife a little, the narrator says that the "open bravery" of both colonists and Indians was in "accordance" with "civilized ideas of valor." This double-sided statement is followed by yet another twist, a small diminution of civilized ideas of valor on both sides: "chivalry itself might not blush to record the deeds" of "*one or two* individuals" (p. 381; my italics). The final twist implicit in the introductory warning (or warning introduction) is that the tale we are in fact given, though it seems on the surface to be fraught with romantic, supernatural fatality, is not a tale of love or heroism; nor is it a providential historical romance; it is something else.

Pattern of the narrator's "intrusions." After the opening paragraph, the tale proper begins, indicated by spaced periods across the page (or in some editions white space). There are four such indications of sections in the narrative and, in different degrees, four additional main intrusions by the narrator, framing the tale symmetrically around five narrative intrusions and five episodes.

Following the hints of the historical frame, the overt themes of the tale involve concepts of fate and fatality. It is the ironic fate of Reuben Bourne to suffer excruciating guilt over something for which he is essentially blameless and to attribute to a supernatural fate his inner psychological anguish. The implied general reader (as normative narratee) is faced with a discrepancy between Reuben's view of the "commandment" laid upon him (whether perceived culturally or individually) and a commonsense assessment of the particular situation within the general situation (the problem of remaining by the side of his dying comrade in the face of the rapid approach of an Indian war party). The tale is suffused with a sense of supernatural fatality, but it is simultaneously a psychological study of obsessive guilt working on the subconscious mind. In this double structure, the two

narratives of "Roger Malvin's Burial" are rather obvious.[14] The narratological semiotics — not of the function of the narrator, but of the narratee —
constitute a major variation on those of the second half of "The Gray
Champion." At the precise mid-point of the narrative (2:393; *T&S*, 97),
after Reuben has told his gray lie to Dorcas about the burial ("I did what I
could") and equivocated ("there stands a noble tombstone above his head":
that is, the tall rock under which he had left Malvin), the narrator summarizes Reuben's feelings of guilt and hypocrisy, especially "the miserable and
humiliating torture of unmerited praise." Reuben's problem is intensified
when his neighbors all acknowledge his worthiness to "the hand of the fair
maiden to whose father he had been 'faithful unto death.' " It is here that
the narrator inserts, as though in the understated ironic mode of a Jane
Austen narrator: ". . . as my tale is not of love, it shall suffice to say that in
the space of a few months Reuben became the husband of Dorcas Malvin"
(2:393; *T&S*, 97).

Reuben's mind is at this point assaulted by what the narrator calls "an incommunicable thought," something he is self-compelled to conceal "from
her whom he most loved and trusted" (2:393–94; *T&S*, 97). "Pride, the fear
of losing her affection, the dread of universal scorn, forbade him to rectify
this falsehood." Although at this time he feels that he deserves no censure
for leaving Malvin, "concealment had imparted to a justifiable act much of
the secret effect of guilt; and Reuben, while reason told him that he had
done right, experienced in no small degree the mental horrors which
punish the perpetrator of undiscovered crime. By a certain association of
ideas, he at times almost imagined himself a murderer" (2:394; *T&S*, 98).
For years afterward, Reuben is haunted by a "torturing fancy that his
father-in-law was yet sitting at the foot of the rock, on the withered forest
leaves, alive, and awaiting his pledged assistance."

These "mental deceptions" come and go, and though he never "mistake[s] them for realities," he is yet "conscious that he had a deep vow
unredeemed, and that an unburied corpse was calling to him out of the
wilderness." Both the idea of "redemption" (in this case as the unredeemed)
and "wilderness" have taken on several meanings. For one thing, if Reuben
for a moment admits what really happened, he is truly in a wilderness. In
the narrator's opinion, then, there are two levels of delusion, ironically
related. One (Malvin sitting by the rock waiting) is a mental delusion, that
is, not literally real; the second (the moral vow to the unburied) is of
ambiguous status. The second is not one that Reuben Bourne can see as
illusory (as he can the first) or as of no legitimate moral force; instead, he is
imprisoned by or within it. The first is literally unreal; the second, as the
narrator knows, is unrealistic in another way. Reuben's wilderness experience is ontological as well as moral.

The comparison and the contrast with the habitual situations that Poe creates are striking. Poe's first-person narrators tend to be victims of psychological-perceptual delusion; Hawthorne's characters, as the chronicler-narrator makes clear, are victims less of perceptual than moral delusion. In both writers, however, the burial of matters of conscience leads to anguish and a form of insanity.[15] Reuben's struggle between the desire to make a clean breast of it and to continue to conceal his mistake is described in a way that anticipates the condition of Arthur Dimmesdale in *The Scarlet Letter*. Reuben is afraid to act; he is afraid of exposure. He cannot bring himself to ask Malvin's friends to journey into the wilderness to perform the "long-deferred sepulture," and he has not the courage to go alone because of what the narrator calls "superstitious fears, of which none were more susceptible than the people of the outward settlements." Besides, he does not "remember" the way. And yet there is "a continual impulse, a voice audible only to himself, commanding him to go forth and redeem his vow . . ." (2:395; *T&S*, 98). Year after year the summons is heard but disobeyed. "His one secret thought became like a chain binding down his spirit and like a serpent gnawing into his heart. . . ."

When Reuben finally does set out through the forest, the narrator makes his most egregious intrusion (the third one). As in Conrad's Marlow stories, *Heart of Darkness* and *Lord Jim*, or the earlier tale "Youth," the central focus is on the failure to live up to a romanticized conception of one's ideal, secret self. Having previously signaled the reader that his tale is not of love or heroism, the narrator exclaims:

> Oh, who, in the enthusiasm of a daydream, has not wished that he were a wanderer in a world of summer wilderness, with one fair and gentle being hanging lightly on his arm? In youth his free and exulting step would know no barrier but the rolling ocean or the snow-topped mountains; calmer manhood would choose a home where Nature had strewn a double wealth in the vale of some transparent stream; and when hoary age, after long, long years of that pure life, stole on and found him there, it would find him the *father* of a *race*, the *patriarch of a people, the founder of a mighty nation yet to be*. . . . Enveloped by tradition in mysterious attributes, the men of future generations would call him godlike. . . . (2:397–98; *T&S*, 100–101; my italics)

But, says the narrator, bringing the effusive flight of "romance" down to earth with a thump, and calling attention to his mediating ironic presence, "the tangled and gloomy forest through which the personages of *my* tale were wandering differed widely from the dreamer's land of fantasy" (2:397–98, my italics; *T&S*, 101).

According to the narrator, the only thing that obstructs Reuben's happiness lies in the obsessive, "gnawing cares" of his own tangled mind. Reuben has failed to live up to his secret ideal of himself, a perception heightened by cultural ideals of virtue and reinforced by Puritan religious vision. His vision of himself is also "romantic," here a code of conduct and image of self impossibly idealized and therefore negative. The "incommunicable thought" becomes the thought of incommunicability, the idea of secrecy itself. Like a Poe character who becomes more fearful *because* he knows he is fearful, Hawthorne's character is trapped by the imp of the perverse: he cannot communicate the thought because he is aware that he is afraid to do so. "Unable to penetrate to the secret place of his soul where his motives lay hidden, he believed that a supernatural voice had called him onward, and that a supernatural power had obstructed his retreat. He trusted that it was Heaven's intent to afford him an opportunity of expiating his sin . . ." (2:401–2; *T&S*, 103). The *narrator's* attitude toward his character's mental state and its causes — the social-moral codes written into his character — is made quite clear in his second intrusion early in the tale. He writes of the basic situation (Reuben's forced flight from the Indians and Malvin's resultant unburied state): "An almost superstitious regard, arising perhaps from the customs of the Indians, whose war was with the dead as well as the living, was paid by the frontier inhabitants to the rites of sepulture . . ." (2:389; *T&S*, 94). The narrator sees the causes of Reuben's torment as having no basis in reason, and he equates the Puritan world view with the "superstitions" of "savages." For such an unreal or at least unnecessary cause has Reuben Bourne suffered agonies of conscience and sacrificed happiness. Like other of Hawthorne's Puritans, his religious obsession and self-absorption have caused him to become a totally self-centered individual, one who does not deeply love his wife and who "loves" his son only for "some reflection or likeness of *his own mind*" (2:396; *T&S*, 100; my italics).

In these latter days of Freudian and neo-Freudian criticism, we have to make an effort consciously to "re-cognize" the popular genre against which Hawthorne was working his narrative, deforming the genre for psychological romance. Here Hawthorne has transformed the conventional gothic "fate" story into a double narrative, the other being a psychological study that asks if fate is not, rather than supernatural, natural, the product of our psyches.[16] The dialogicity of the tale is not merely philosophical, psychological, or moral. Hawthorne's psychological romance dialogically plays off against the conventions of the genre it deforms, exemplifying Bakhtin's notion of the heterological interplay of genre. Whatever our sympathy for the entrapped character, the conclusion of the tale is scathing in its irony. The narrator withdraws his presence completely and describes, without comment, first, the mother's joyful and then fearful anticipation of the return of the two men to the campsite, and second, the father's discovery that he has shot his son. The father's reaction makes clear the fierce irony of his name, Reuben: (in Hebrew) "Behold a Son." Crying over the body of Cyrus, Reuben is at last able to pray after many years of silence. For now his "sin was expiated, — the curse was gone from him" (2:406; *T&S*, 107). Such is a Puritan father's love for a son. And in such a manner does an American Puritan conduct sacrifice, not at the command of an ancient Semitic God, but at the promptings of his own ego. In this way does the failure of true love and heroism in the historical event of "Love-well" parallel the individual story of Reuben Bourne. Reuben's sacrifice of his son on the altar of individual egoism, subconscious though it may be, is a parable of the Puritan experience. From his personal guilt, personified by the doomed Cyrus, is psychologically born a true son of New England Calvinism: namely, himself, the deluded but pitiable egomaniac, compulsively reenacting the sacrifice of Isaac by the Abrahamic father — but with no perceived God present to stay the murdering hand.[17] The tale is not of love or heroism. It is a tale of egoism and moral cowardice.

The tale is typical of Hawthorne in many ways: in the implicit condemnation of narrow religious absolutes; in the focus on egomania and the subconscious processes, especially those stemming from religious guilt and secretiveness and isolation; in the interpenetration of the seemingly supernatural with the main naturalistic story; in the ambiguity, indeed, the indeterminacy of the real and the imagined. It is perhaps quintessentially typical in having the structure of a "tale" based on "fact," but "told again" (that is, it is a "fiction" that is "truer" than "history" as it recapitulates on the individual level cultural history). This telling again is through a recurrent narrator-author figure who develops tensions between one kind of reading of the events and ironic readings that call into question not only textual events and themes but also the stability of genre conventions. The history versus romance binary is blurred, and a major aspect of the dialogicity of the tale is generic, as several modes of perception contest with one another. Having indirectly alerted us that his subjects are not love or heroism, the narrator gives us a little romance anyway, a psychological romance that deals with the consequences of the *lack* of love and heroism.

Reuben's obsession with his own individual "morality" pits the here questionable obligation of ritual sepulture against the ambiguities of the larger morality of the vicious, mercenary, and cowardly assaults of the "Lovewell" gang upon the Indians, which were subsequently "romanticized" by the American Europeans for a century and more. (Even Thoreau comes close to romanticizing him.) And of course the question of love seems nonexistent — at least love for wife and son — only destructive love of self seems to be operative. The "iron cage" of the Puritan cultural system is manifest once again in individual pathos and tragedy — emphasizing self-guilt, and negating love. The iron cage of Reuben's individual psychological response to the morality of incomplete sepulture and his own subsequent romanticizing by his neighbors is a horrible mockery compared to the sacrifice of his son. As in "The Gray Champion," the iron cage of American "history" is manifest in the irony of a Christian culture romanticizing the aggressive slaughter of another people as heroism. So, finally, the tale that is not a romantic tale of love, or courage, turns out in fact to be one — a negative romance.

Of Sentiment and Sadomasochism: Revision and Narrative Commentary in "The Gentle Boy"

Although both widely praised and condemned, in general "The Gentle Boy" has been regarded as one of Hawthorne's most "sentimental" works (a variant of "provincial"). First published in 1831 in the *Token* (dated 1832), "The Gentle Boy" was reprinted in the 1837 *Twice-told Tales* with several deletions. Two years later the story was published by itself in a booklet as "A Thrice Told Tale" dedicated to "Miss Sophia A. Peabody," whom Hawthorne married shortly after. On the surface another tale of love, courage, and pathos in the face of adversity, it is said to have been a favorite of Mrs. Hawthorne, who was particularly moved by the death of the little Quaker child.[18] The tale is, however, somewhat more complex than "Roger Malvin's Burial" in its presentation of a double reading.

The opening frame introduction, sketching the historical context of the tale to follow, is more extensive than those of "The Gray Champion" and "Roger Malvin's Burial," though the narrator's presence is, in the revised version, hardly more pronounced. Attention to the narrative persona and the frame introduction, and especially to the revisions affecting narrative persona, clarifies the significance of its ambiguities. With special reference to the lengthy deletions from the first version, critics have given "The Gentle Boy" essentially two conflicting interpretations. The first is that the tale is a sharp indictment of Puritan intolerance, illustrated by their harsh persecution of the Quakers. The second is that Hawthorne's critique is aimed at Puritan and Quaker alike. Hawthorne's omissions from the text in its "thrice-told" version highlight this interpretative question and throw further light on the altered emphasis given to the relative presence or absence of a narrator; these revisions will be examined in some detail later. One thing is sure: the sentimental conventions and surface pathos of the tale undergo marked alteration as the narrative progresses, culminating in several fiercely ironic reversals.

Mirror images: Puritan and Quaker. The tale is certainly a condemnation of Puritan persecution and intolerance. As with "The Gray Champion," however, the story revolves around the hypocrisy of abstract righteousness represented by two opposing political-religious groups. The personal fortunes of the two central Puritan characters, the kindly Tobias Pearson and his loving wife, Dorothy, do not sustain any affirmative interpretation. They are not, as James K. Folsom reasonably but unconvincingly argues, the *via media* between two religious extremes.[19] The tender love that Dorothy bestows on the frail Quaker boy is quietly rejected, while Tobias's difficult conversion from Puritan to Quaker represents no moral gain. In this careful negation, the narrative is typical of other *Provincial Tales* that portray the sacrifice of flesh-and-blood individuals on the altar of abstraction.[20]

The opening scene immediately suggests the negative aspects of Puritanism. One autumn evening, Tobias Pearson, a Puritan, finds a little boy weeping beside the grave of his father, a Quaker, who has been hanged by Puritans because of his religious affiliation. The boy's mother, Catharine, whom they regard as fanatical, has been expelled by the Puritan majority alone into the wilderness. The basic situation would seem to constitute a severe condemnation of the Puritans, but the Puritan Pearson (though with misgivings) takes the Quaker boy, Ilbrahim, home to his wife, Dorothy, who has lost all of her own children. She resolves to be the boy's mother. Although motivated by personal needs, the Pearsons' act is still an act of Christian charity, and the portrait of the Puritans is slightly softened.

Further qualifying the situation, the boy's Quaker mother is not merely regarded as fanatical but also portrayed as such by the narrator. At one point in the narrative, Ilbrahim is held by Dorothy by one hand, by his mother by the other, and the narrator comments: "The two females . . . formed a practical allegory; it was rational piety and unbridled fanaticism contending for the empire of a young heart" (1:104; *T&S*, 122). The Puritan Dorothy Pearson is privileged by the narrator at this point over Catharine the Quaker mother, though the affirmative value of "rational piety" contending for the "empire" of a "young heart" is muted. The Pearsons seem to be exceptions to the general Puritan rule; for their Christian act costs them the friendship of their Puritan neighbors, who begin to shun them. Estrangement from their community, however, causes the Pearsons (at least, or especially, Tobias) to become more stubborn in their resistance to community pressure and even more devoted to the Quaker boy—though Hawthorne has sketched in enough of the psychological motivation to cast doubt on conventional romantic notions of courage and love. The reader is forced dialogically to negotiate among these conflicting elements rather than to side with one party or another, or even to see the two sides as evenly balanced.

The doubt becomes thematic. It is particularly evident with regard to Tobias, whose "conversion" to the Quaker cause is questionable. Tobias Pearson's conflicted character embodies the very paradoxes played out in the story on a cultural level. Indeed, in one sense, as Doubleday suggests (p. 164), the narrative is structured in four major episodes around Pearson's struggle with conversion. The irony of his situation is manifest: by practicing the "prime commandment" of Christianity, Tobias is led to reject the very religion that gives him this principle.[21] Pearson has achieved greater humanity by acknowledging in his heart a key Puritan tenet — universal sin. Pearson's acknowledgment of truly universal evil is, ironically enough (or naturally enough), the source of his Christian charity. " 'God forbid that I should leave this child to perish, though he comes of the accursed sect,' said he to himself. 'Do we not all spring from an evil root?' " (1:90; *T&S*, 112). The paradox is double-edged, however, producing a double bind.

In Hawthorne's view, the source of isolation and inhumanity is the (typical) Puritan's ultimate (even if unconscious) exemption of self from the consequences of universal sin. Charity is for Hawthorne the consequence not so much of an actual brotherhood or sisterhood of evil, but of the acknowledgment of the possibility of a community of evil. The difference is subtle and all important. It provides a major dialogical tension in his works, most obviously, I should say, in the often collapsed binary of supernatural versus psychological or metaphysical versus epistemological. The theme of the ontological status of evil is often represented in his works inversely, as in the egotistic rejection of any humanity but one's own in such figures as Young Goodman Brown or the reverend Mr. Hooper of "The Minister's Black Veil" (1836), or in the egocentric exclusion of all others from one's own center as exhibited in the Reverend Mr. Dimmesdale or Ethan Brand. Here, instead of rejecting his fellow man as his Christian neighbors do, Pearson builds a familial bond upon acknowledgment of human frailty — an action opposite that of Reuben Bourne and a host of other Hawthorne hypocrites. But on the theological level, Tobias Pearson's conversion from Puritan to Quaker represents no spiritual enlightenment (not to mention peace) and instead reflects the moral and cultural muddle of the era. The two embodiments of his religious nature are at "war" somehow, and he seems to thrive sadomasochistically on the conflict. Hawthorne's narrator describes the conflict in both the individual and the culture without siding with either; indeed, he keeps a decided critical distance.

At the center of the story of "The Gentle Boy" is a strong scene, heavily charged with ironies, portraying the double hypocrisy of the two religions. At church, while the Puritan minister delivers a warning against acting charitably (toward those outside their own faith), Ilbrahim's deranged mother interrupts with a wild speech on hypocrisy. This self-dramatizing occasion becomes a self-serving, self-revealing, and even self-reflexive act in which her "speech" serves both to indict and explain her. The dialogical effect is perhaps not totally congruent with the narrator's view of the event. In his account of her public condemnation of Puritan savagery and hypocrisy in their own meetinghouse, the narrator twice couches his own attitude toward the Quaker woman in negative if not unsympathetic terms. He introduces her speech by suggesting that her "fit of inspiration" is that of a deranged person. Her "discourse gave evidence of an imagination hopelessly entangled with her reason; it was a vague and incomprehensible rhapsody . . ." (1:99; T&S, 118). He adds further that "she was naturally a woman of mighty passions, and hatred and revenge now wrapped themselves in the garb of piety" (1:100; T&S, 119). Not only is the imagery the same as in "The Gray Champion," but also the passions of the contesting factions are represented in her tirade — made the more ironic since hatred and revenge are two cardinal sins of Quakerism. Her "denunciations [have] an almost hellish bitterness," and her convoluted, entangled speech is a possible parody of Quaker simple speech. The narrator observes that this spokeswoman for the sect of simplicity, clarity, and peace-making gives "vent to [a] flood of malignity which she mistook for inspiration" (1:101; T&S, 119–20). Yet, with the exception of the Pearsons, her charges against the Puritans are all valid. Yet again, the Quaker woman reveals herself to be as hypocrital as any Puritan. For when her son Ilbrahim goes to her, she rejects him on the spot because of her divine mission, higher than mere motherhood — or love for others. And yet again, her speech itself is a satire of her religious identity — while also being a legitimate critique of the New England Congregationalists. The dialogical claims upon the reader's impulse for unitary thematic structures and foreshadowed closure multiply. The stage has been nicely set: introducing two competing constructs, the narrative now begins to twist and revolve, the positions contesting and deconstructing both each other and each itself. The Hawthorne text may be said to emerge in the contestatory gap between opposing constructs rather than in a balanced critique of both.

Psychopathology of the "gentle" boy. The double apportionment of criticism continues. When an injured neighbor boy is cared for by the Pearsons, Ilbrahim bestows loving friendship upon the Puritan child; but when the Puritan boy is well again, he takes part in the beating of Ilbrahim by the other Puritan children.[22] The whole episode, however, is fraught with ambiguity and innuendo, augmented by narrative commentary, suggesting (and only *suggesting*) the possibility that even the "gentle" and "innocent"

Quaker boy's unconscious motivation reflects the pervasive sadomasochistic theme of the tale as a whole.

Prior to learning of the Puritan boy's "fall from a tree in the vicinity of Pearson's habitation" (1:109; *T&S*, 126), we are told that although Ilbrahim began to consider the Pearsons as his parents and to exhibit once again a happy and beautiful character, "yet the disordered imaginations" of his natural mother and father "had perhaps propagated a certain unhealthiness in the mind of the boy" (1:108; *T&S*, 125). In general, Ilbrahim's tendency in his new life is toward gaiety; but, the narrator comments, "*as the susceptibility of pleasure is also that of pain*" (my italics) so also the "exuberant cheerfulness of the boy's prevailing temper sometimes yielded to moments of deep depression." Although the narrator is careful to say that Ilbrahim is "altogether destitute" of malice, he also carefully points out that the boy has an exceptionally "sensitive" nature. The word "sensitive" is loaded. "The slightest word of real bitterness" from anyone (the Pearsons, the neighbors, other children) "seemed to sink into his heart and poison all his enjoyments"; and, the narrator pointedly adds, "malice . . . generally accompanies a superfluity of sensitiveness." Having called to our attention (by way of excepting Ilbrahim) the general linking between oversensitivity and malice, the narrator hints at the other side of the psychological equation—masochism. Acutely sensitive to the fact that the feelings of the Pearsons' neighbors remain hostile and that their children "partook of the enmity of their parents," Ilbrahim nevertheless "yearned" to bestow "a residue of unappropriated love" upon "the little ones who were taught to hate him" (1:109; *T&S*, 126).

It is in this context, then, that Ilbrahim befriends the injured Puritan boy despite what the narrator tells us in great detail is that boy's unprepossessing character. The Puritan boy's countenance, body, posture are all disagreeable, being "regular . . . in general outline" but slightly twisted or disproportionate, "faulty in almost all . . . details"; his "disposition" is "sullen and reserved" and he is "obtuse in intellect." Ilbrahim is, the narrator comments, "the unconscious possessor" of a "skill in physiognomy" that ordinarily "would have deterred him, in other circumstances, from attempting to make a friend of this boy." But in spite of the Puritan boy's "personal or moral irregularities," Ilbrahim's "heart *seized* upon" the boy, "and *clung to him*, from the moment that he was brought wounded into the cottage" (1:110; *T&S*, 126–27; my italics). Ilbrahim, says the narrator, "nested continually" by the bedside of the Puritan boy and "with a fond jealousy, endeavored to be the medium of all the cares that were bestowed upon him." Ilbrahim tells him tales of "imaginary adventures," "disjointed" and "without aim," but connected by "a vein of human tenderness which ran through them all." The Puritan child's response to Ilbrahim's story telling is to interrupt them with brief remarks "displaying shrewdness above his years, mingled with a moral obliquity" that "grated very harshly against Ilbrahim's instinctive rectitude." Despite such responses from the "dark and stubborn nature" of the Puritan boy, Ilbrahim persists in intruding his affection upon him: "Nothing . . . could arrest the progress of the latter's [Ilbrahim's] affection" (1:111; *T&S*, 127).

After the Puritan boy has recovered and gone home, Ilbrahim makes "anxious and continual inquiries respecting him" and "informed himself of the day when he was to reappear among his playmates." While on the one hand the scene emphasizes the loving, giving, and yearning nature of the gentle boy, on the other it hints of a somewhat pathological psychology, much like his natural mother's and the Quaker mentality in general. Ilbrahim *knows* (and we are told previously of his almost "street-wise" toughening before encountering the Pearsons) that the other Puritan children have adopted their parents' enmity toward him; but he places himself in their midst anyway.

At this point, the narrator significantly prefaces the actual incident of Ilbrahim's beating with an evocation of the New Testament (and specifically romantic) view of childhood — which he follows with a description of the ferocity of the "innocents" (a "heavenly little band") that rather thumpingly debunks the still Christianized but reinscripted Rousseauistic paradigm. The Puritan children have gathered on "a pleasant summer afternoon" in a "little forest-crowned amphitheatre" behind the meetinghouse. The narrator comments: "The glee of a score of untainted bosoms was heard in light and airy voices, which danced among the trees like sunshine become audible; the grown men of this weary world, as they journeyed by the spot, marvelled why life, beginning in such brightness, should proceed in gloom; and their hearts, or their imaginations, answered them and said, that the bliss of childhood gushes from its innocence" (1:111; *T&S*, 127–28). To take this statement on the pure innocence of childhood as completely straightforward, the way some readers want to take the narrative commentary in "The Gray Champion," is to misread Hawthorne badly. For immediately after, Ilbrahim, with "a look of sweet confidence on his fair and spiritual face" approaches the group of children, and "all at once, the devil of their fathers entered into the unbreeched fanatics, and sending up a fierce, shrill cry, they rushed upon the poor Quaker child. In an instant, he was the centre of a brood of baby-fiends, who lifted sticks against him, pelted him with stones, and displayed an instinct of destruction far more loathsome than the bloodthirstiness of manhood" (1:112; *T&S*, 128). Among other things, the incident suggests a devastating parody of Jesus's lesson to his disciples when he upbraided them for shooing away the children and called the children to him to teach a lesson about their innocence and peaceableness. Heightening the actual loathsomeness of childhood even more, the injured Puritan boy that Ilbrahim yearns to love calls out to him, "Fear not . . . come hither and take my hand," and then strikes Ilbrahim on the mouth with his staff, causing blood to stream forth. At this, Ilbrahim stops defending himself; "his persecutors beat him down, trampled upon him, dragged him by his long, fair locks. . . ." Indeed, left to the mercies of children, Ilbrahim would be murdered; it is the adults who save him. Had not some adult neighbors "put themselves to the trouble of rescuing the little heretic," Ilbrahim would have been "on the point of becoming as veritable a *martyr* as ever entered bleeding into heaven" (my italics). Since the narrator suggests at length that the Quakers actively seek martyrdom, the suggestion of Ilbrahim's incipient masochistic tendencies is reinforced.

Severe as his bodily injury is, the injury to Ilbrahim's spirit is greater, and he lapses into a melancholy preoccupation and despondency, punctuated by calling out in the night "Mother! Mother!" This sentimentalized, high emotional point is subject to some rather grim qualification at the conclusion of the story, which we shall look at in due course, noting at this point only that the narrator here hints of an ultimate rejection of the loving surrogate mother, Dorothy. Ilbrahim's crying out for his "mother" is "as if her place, which a stranger had supplied while Ilbrahim was happy, admitted of no substitute in his extreme affliction" (1:113; *T&S*, 129).

In the large thematic and structural pattern of the narrative, the event of Ilbrahim's beating is immediately juxtaposed to another, generally parallel, view of the masochistic tendencies of Tobias Pearson. The narrator writes: "While this melancholy change had taken place in Ilbrahim, one of an earlier origin and of different character had come to its perfection in his adopted father" (1:113–14; *T&S*, 129). The ensuing description focuses on Pearson's slow disaffection from Puritan hypocrisy and his general conversion to the Quaker cause. Despite his contempt for the Quaker belief, and for himself for lapsing into *their* hypocrisies, Pearson is driven to ally himself with them. The more he chafes under the threat of ostracism by his fellow Puritans, the more he pursues a course to insure his alienation. Meanwhile, the narrator continues to depict the rule of fanaticism on both sides. One night, a Quaker elder, after reading the Bible with Pearson, reveals that he left his own dying daughter to answer (like Ilbrahim's mother) what he considered God's summons to a divine mission. If the Puritans are portrayed as ungrateful and incapable of charity outside their own community, the Quakers are portrayed as unloving parents no less fanatical in their religious allegiances than the Puritans. Pearson's conversion would appear to be pointless.

After these revelations, the tale concludes with an appropriate ironic "balancing off" of mutual inequities. After his beating by the Puritan children, Ilbrahim becomes not only deeply melancholy but also gravely ill. His mother (somewhat improbably) returns, and the boy dies in her arms. Her grief seems a bit suspect. Or is it? The uncertainty perhaps enhances the dialogical effect. But doubtless the sentimental moment for those readers who have identified with Ilbrahim is effective. After the death of the gentle boy — and concomitant with a general but gradual historical change in New England commented upon by the narrator — the Quaker woman is, little by little, subjected to less harassment by the Puritan community and is eventually buried next to her son. Even in this general communal relenting, however, real human sympathy is denied, according to the narrator, who, unlike the narrator of "Roger Malvin's Burial," reenters the narrative (albeit somewhat surreptitiously) for some concluding remarks. "Her once bitter persecutors" follow in her funeral procession with a "decent" sadness, and with the kind of tears that are "not painful" (1:126; *T&S*, 138). The narrator's irony is patently manifest, though some readers persist in seeing only sentimentality in the tale.

Significance of the revisions. Various interpretations in the critical debate over the central target of Hawthorne's criticism make heavy use of the lengthy revisions of this tale for support of their positions. The most frequently invoked is an early passage of narratorial commentary on what Hawthorne's narrator calls the "extenuating circumstances" explaining the Puritans' actions toward the Quakers (tough times called for tough measures, the germ of the Bell thesis). In an unconscious irony that the narrator makes explicit, the Puritans have conferred "martyrdom" on two Quakers by executing them. The complete passage, omitted in later versions of the tale, reads:

> That those who were active in, or consenting to, this measure ["martyrdom" for non-Puritans], made themselves responsible for innocent blood, is not to be denied: yet the extenuating circumstances of their conduct are more numerous than can generally be pleaded by persecutors. The inhabitants of New England were a people, whose original bond of union was their peculiar religious principles. For the peaceful exercise of *their own mode of worship*, an object, the *very reverse of universal liberty of conscience*, they had hewn themselves a home in the wilderness; they had made vast sacrifices of whatever is dear to man;

they had exposed themselves to the peril of death, and to a life which rendered the accomplishment of that peril almost a blessing. They had found no city of refuge prepared for them, but, with Heaven's assistance, they had created one; and it would be hard to say whether justice did not authorize their determination, to guard its gate against all who were destitute of the prescribed title to admittance. The principle of their foundation was such, that *to destroy the unity of religion, might have been to subvert the government,* and break up the colony, especially at a period when the state of affairs in England had stopped the tide of emigration, and drawn back many of the pilgrims to their native homes. The magistrates of Massachusetts Bay were, moreover, most *imperfectly informed* respecting the *real tenets and character of the Quaker sect.* They had heard of them, from various parts of the earth, as opposers of every known opinion, and *enemies of all established governments;* they had beheld extravagances which seemed to justify these accusations; and the idea suggested by their own wisdom may be gathered from the fact, that the persons of many individuals were searched, in the expectation of discovering witch-marks. *But* after all allowances, it is to be feared that the death of the [two executed] Quakers was *principally owing to the polemic fierceness,* that distinct passion of human nature, which has so often produced *frightful guilt* in the most sincere and zealous advocates of virtue and religion. (*T&S,* 1483–84; my italics)

I have emphasized in the quotation those portions that highlight the Puritans' political views and the irony of their situation. The "extenuating circumstances" are not very extenuating. The Puritans use the word "liberty" to mean the "very reverse" of its normal meaning, restricting the idea of liberty (as noted before) to mean the "exercise of their own mode of worship." As dissenters, the Puritans themselves are subverters of established government. But the final reason attributed by the narrator as the cause of the entire situation is not restricted to the Puritans alone; the cause is "polemic fierceness" in "zealous advocates" of religion, which describes both Puritan and Quaker. Indeed, the Quakers loved to use the word "liberty."

Suggestively, the omitted passages are themselves ambiguous enough that Hawthorne's "intentions" in omitting them have been read in opposite ways: (a) he toned down the list of enormities so that the criticism of the Puritans would be more in balance with that of the Quakers; or (b) he excised the "extenuating circumstances" so that the criticism of the Puritans would be sharper, suggesting no rationalized motivation. Colacurcio rightly notes (p. 574, note 7) that Hawthorne's excisions do not really affect the rather evenly distributed criticism of Puritan and Quaker remaining in the revised tale and that the omitted key passage on the Puritans itself "imitates" the movement of the main narrative, mentioning extenuating circumstances but reciting Puritan excesses.

A third position on the motives for omitting so much in this most extensively revised of Hawthorne's tales is that he trimmed the narrative down for aesthetic reasons of economy, thematic suggestiveness, and heightened dramatic intensity — not to mention indeterminacy. Although possibly the most popular of all his tales with nineteenth-century readers, it was also criticized for being somewhat overwritten, excessive in detail, and, as mentioned, in "sentiment." Henry James, for example, called it one of the "longest, though by no means one of the most successful," of Hawthorne's tales.[23] That Hawthorne may have intended mainly to streamline the work would seem to be the point, for example, of most (or at least some) of the omitted details regarding Dorothy in her kitchen, the second of the five lengthiest deletions (T&S, 1484). Or perhaps the suggestion of a "natural" maternal instinct in a childless woman as distinguished from a feebler or nonexistent maternal instinct in the "natural" mother was for the period too sentimental on the one hand or too acerbic on the other.

It is unlikely that all the omissions have any single explanation, and a number of commonsense possibilities suggest themselves for the other (some rather insignificant) omissions. We have already looked at the first two omitted passages. The third is a description of the division of the Puritan meetinghouse into male and female. The narrator observes that those men in "martial authority," having "arrayed themselves in their embroidered buff-coats, contrasted strikingly with the remainder of the congregation, and attracted many youthful thoughts, which should have been otherwise employed" (T&S, 1484–85). This passage (it may not unreasonably be suggested) may have been exercised to suit the delicate sensibility of Sophia Peabody, or of some prudish editor. The fourth excision has to do with a preacher who seems not to have "digested" his paraded learning, as if he were "unable to amalgamate his own mind with that of the author," and whose short quotations represent "a dull man's efforts to be witty — little ripples fretting the surface of a stagnant pool" (T&S, 1485). This passage may have had a specific contemporaneous figure as its target and thus been excised for that reason. The fifth omission metaphorically describes Tobias's struggles with his conversion from Puritan to Quaker principles in terms of warfare, concluding with the idea of a "victory" precipitated by Ilbrahim's misfortune. Since Tobias is a paradoxical figure, the "victory" may have been too definitive — an important point to which I shall return later.

The last major omission[24] is, along with the long first one, the most significant. It is simply one sentence, the original concluding one. After the comment on the reabsorption, such as it is, of the Quaker fanatic into the community and the shedding of such tears as are not painful, the narrator's final comment had originally been: "My heart is glad of this triumph of our better nature; it gives me a kindlier feeling for the fathers of my native land; and with it I will close the tale."

The sentence is doubly ironic and clearly critical of the whole sad story. Why then was this concluding narrative intrusion omitted? Some "pro-Puritan" readers assume that the patriotic young Hawthorne did not want to seem openly critical of the original forebears of his "native land." James McIntosh, for example, in a textual note on "Hawthorne's Revisions of 'The Gentle Boy'" in his Norton Critical Edition of *Nathaniel Hawthorne's Tales*, suggests that Hawthorne was "evidently uncomfortable with his [*sic*] straightforward, didactic pronouncements" (p. 262). My guess is, first, that the narrator's statement is too obviously sarcastic and ironic in itself — pointed in general at the superficiality of Puritan-Quaker conversions and in particular at painless tears and trivial kindnesses. It probably seemed to Hawthorne unduly to heighten (and thus weaken the effect of) the more modulated irony of the penultimate sentence, which became the concluding sentence in the revised version.[25] Second, and possibly more important, the deleted final sentence is also problematic in that it seems to focus only on one group, one construct, and one locus of the critique — and therefore would have lessened the dialogical effect.

Hawthorne's strategy is to have the narrator reenter the narrative more overtly in the last two paragraphs (set off by spaced periods or white space) and thus complete the frame begun with the long historical introduction. The narrator comments on the political, religious, and psychological change brought by the "king's mandate to stay the New England persecutors" from "further martyrdoms." He observes that the colonial authorities, however, trusting in their provincial remoteness and "perhaps in the supposed instability of the royal government, shortly renewed their severities in all other respects." Catharine's fanaticism becomes "wilder by the sundering of all human ties"; and wherever a scourge is lifted or a dungeon opened she is (masochistically) there. "But in the process of time a more Christian spirit — a spirit of forbearance, *though not of cordiality or approbation* — began to pervade the land in regard to the persecuted sect" (1:125; *T&S*, 138; my italics). The narrator's historical summary is itself ironically cast, since the later spirit of forbearance is usually characterized by historians as more secular; thus the "more Christian spirit" is an ironic statement in implicit criticism of unchristian behavior. The narrator also suggests, duplicitously, that Ilbrahim's death has the effect of "softening" Catharine's "fierce and vindictive nature," phrasing this in terms of "as if." It is "as if Ilbrahim's sweetness yet lingered round his ashes; as if his gentle spirit came down from heaven to teach his parent a true religion"; and thus, ironically, it is as if her fierce spirit is softened "by the same griefs which had once irritated it." Is this an irony of circumstance, or a sardonic, skeptical remark by the narrator?

As Catharine becomes more "familiar" in the community (having returned to live with the Pearsons), she becomes "a subject of not deep, but general interest," a being on whom the "otherwise superfluous sympathies of all might be bestowed." The ironies are everywhere. The final sentence of the revised version is enough: "Every one spoke of her with the degree of pity which it is pleasant to experience; every one was ready to do her the little kindnesses which are not costly, yet manifest good will; and when at last she died, a long train of her once bitter persecutors followed her, with decent sadness and tears that were not painful, to her place by Ilbrahim's green and sunken grave."[26]

Psychopathology of culture: narrative pattern and frame function. Paralleling the narrative commentary at the end, the tale is preceded by a historical introduction that sets a cultural context requiring a double reading for full understanding. From a narratival perspective of exterior and interior narrative framing and commentary and non-commentary, the pattern of the narrator's intrusion into and withdrawal from the tale looks like this:

Frame
    Episode 1: [introduced by narrator's retrospective summary]
    Episode 2: [no introduction; recurrent brief comments by narrator]
    Episode 3: [narrator's introductory analysis of Ilbrahim's double nature and personal situation; narrator's concluding analysis of Pearson's double nature and the cultural situation]
    Episode 4: [no introduction; no narrative commentary]
Frame conclusion: Narrator's summary of individual, communal, and cultural situation (static, not transformed)

The Puritans and the Quakers in some way need each other to give definition and energy to their own cause; and, as we have seen, Hawthorne's narrator depicts the dehumanization that religious fanaticism promotes in both Quaker and Puritan, suggesting unconscious hypocrisy, egocentrism, and psychological complexity on both sides. Here, in the introduction, the narrator sets the psychopolitical historical context for the individual story to follow. He remarks of the Quakers that Puritan persecution was both "cause and effect" of their extremism. The tale opens:

> In the course of the year 1656, several of the people called Quakers, led, *as they professed*, by the inward movement of the spirit, made their appearance in New England. Their reputation, as holders of mystic and pernicious principles, having spread before them, the Puritans early endeavored to banish, and to prevent the further intrusion of the rising sect. But the measures by which it was intended to purge the land of heresy, though more than sufficiently vigorous, were entirely unsuccessful. The Quakers, *esteeming persecution as a divine call* to the post of danger, laid claim to a holy courage, unknown to the Puritans themselves, who had *shunned the cross*, by providing for the peaceable exercise of their religion in a distant wilderness. (1:85; *T&S*, 108; my italics)

The narrator's judgments are manifest in several overt and covert ways. In his description of the Quakers' conception of themselves as led by the inward movement of the spirit, he evinces a degree of skepticism when he inserts, "as they professed." His understated comment that the Puritans' actions against the Quakers were "more than sufficiently vigorous" results in a tone of mild sarcasm that intensifies as his comparison of the "courage" of Quaker and Puritan turns ironic. While the Quakers are drawn to danger and *self*-martyrdom, the Puritans shun such extravagant behavior; but the narrator expresses it metaphorically as shunning the cross of persecution (that is, of *being* persecuted). In the wordplay, a re-literalized allusion to Christian symbolism emerges to suggest that this is precisely what the Puritans do: they lack the central element of charity; they shun the prime commandments of the New Testament symbolized by the sacrifice upon the cross.[27] The paragraph concludes with a sentence emphasizing the double irony in which both Puritans and Quakers are implicitly condemned: the Quakers seek Massachusetts Bay *because* it is the place in the world "of greatest uneasiness and peril" to people of other religions, "and therefore, in their eyes the most eligible" of locations for them.

In the next paragraph of the introductory frame, while continuing the portrait of the masochistic attraction of New England for the Quakers, the narrator also remarks on the "fines, imprisonments, and stripes" so "liberally distributed by our pious forefathers." But the Quakers, he observes, were so enamored of persecution that they continued to flock to the place of such reputation for "nearly a hundred years after actual persecution had ceased." In fact, "every European vessel brought new cargoes of the sect, eager to *testify against* the oppression which they *hoped* to share" (my italics).

When they were barred from landing by ship, they made circuitous journeys through the Indian country and, the narrator almost comically adds, "appeared in the province as if conveyed by a supernatural power" (1:86; *T&S*, 108).

The narrator's analysis of this phenomenon amounts to a description of cultural pathology, with Puritans playing sadist to Quaker masochist needs. The Quakers' "enthusiasm, heightened almost to madness by the treatment which they received, produced actions contrary to the rules of decency, as well as of rational religion," writes the narrator, who notes the contrast with the "calm and staid deportment" of their present-day descendants. Although he is referring to the Quakers, his remark applies equally to the Puritans. But the narrator's censoriousness toward the Quakers is the main burden of the paragraph. The Quaker tenet of the "command of the spirit, inaudible except to the soul," a command "not to be controverted on grounds of human wisdom," was, the narrator comments, "made a plea for most indecorous exhibitions." These, at least "abstractly considered," says the narrator, "well deserved the moderate chastisement of the rod." Quaker "extravagances" continued to increase, giving rise to increased Puritan persecution—so that the persecution was "at once" the cause of Quaker extremism and the consequence of extremism. (Later in the tale [1:114; *T&S*, 130], the narrator remarks how the increase of the "infatuation" of the "victims" of the Puritans paralleled the increase of persecution.) The extremist result on the Puritan side was (as indicated in the discussion of the first long deletion from the text) that in 1659 the government of Massachusetts Bay "indulged" two Quakers with "the crown of martyrdom."

In the first part of the third and last paragraph of the frame introduction, the narrator turns his criticism toward the Puritan side, putting most of the blame ("an indelible stain of blood") on the provincial governor for going beyond the "chastisement of the rod" to murder. He "was a man of narrow mind and imperfect education," whose "uncompromising bigotry was made hot and mischievous by violent and hasty passions." His "whole conduct," in respect to the Quakers, "was marked by brutal cruelty." This was none other than John Endicott (unnamed in the tale), governor during the Quaker persecutions (and the subject of two other early "provincial" tales: "The May-Pole of Merry Mount" [1835, in the 1836 *Token*] and "Endicott and the Red Cross" [1837, in the 1838 *Token*]).[28]

Having indicated that moral truth or rightness lies fully neither on one side nor on the other, the narrator takes up the question of historical truth by focusing in the rest of the paragraph on "the historian" of the sect of Quakers, William Sewell.[29] This personage (also unnamed in the tale) "affirms that, by the wrath of Heaven, a blight fell upon the land in the vicinity of the 'bloody town' of Boston, so that no wheat would grow there" (1:86–87; *T&S*, 109). The narrator pictures the historian "triumphantly" recording the judgments that overtook the Puritans "in old age or at the parting hour." He notes how the historian of the sect of peace delights in the sudden and violent death in madness of the Puritans, and he is struck by the "bitter mockery" of the historian when "he records the loathsome disease, and 'death by rottenness,' of the fierce and cruel governor" at the time (1:87; *T&S*, 109). The narrator again does not quite know what to make of all the hatred and vengeance in both Puritan and Quaker.

The frame introduction does more than sketch in a "factual" historical context for the tale; it alerts us to the narrator's view of the subjectivity of history, morality, religion, and patriotism. And it also calls into question his own version — so that we need to consider a triangular incommensurability and destabilization: Quaker, Puritan, and the narrator. The "provincial" tale that follows such an introduction is, like "Roger Malvin's Burial," not likely to be a single-sided tale of patriotic romance, heroism, or love. Both sides pervert the claims of the human heart. One group only seems to be morally better than the other. The general situation parallels that of the two opposing groups of "The Gray Champion." The double irony is (or should be) quite manifest: Quaker parents abandon their children for an abstract cause, while a Puritan minister preaches against charity. Meanwhile, the narrator considers first one side and then another, coming to only tentative or elliptical conclusions.

Psychopathology of conversion. The large cultural tangle is only one aspect of the story; as previously suggested, the ironies of personal fate and the psyche are equally complex. Pearson's gradual assimilation of Quaker tenets is as double-edged psychologically as the idea of conversion is thematically. Three-quarters through the tale, the narrator offers us two paragraphs of psychological analysis and historical contextualization. "The incident with which this tale commences found Pearson in a state of religious dulness, yet mentally disquieted, and longing for a more fervid faith than he possessed" (1:114; *T&S*, 129). The "first effect" of his kindness to Ilbrahim, according to the narrator, "was to produce a softened feeling, and incipient love for the child's whole sect; but joined to this, and resulting perhaps from self-suspicion, was a proud and ostentatious contempt of all their tenets and practical extravagances." The word "extravagance" is carefully chosen (in the manner of Thoreau's usage), meaning both excessiveness and waywardness (acting out of bounds). As Pearson struggles with religious conviction, "the foolishness of the doctrine [of the Enthusiasts] began to be less evident," that is, from a Puritan point of view.

"But while he was thus becoming assimilated to the enthusiasts, his contempt, in nowise decreasing towards them, grew very fierce against himself; he imagined, also, that every face of his acquaintance wore a sneer, and that every word addressed to him was a gibe."[30] This bundle of coherently contradictory feelings in Pearson replicates in little the cultural sadomasochism in which he is mired. He loves to hate himself, loves hating others, loves being hated by others.

If this summary seems too stark, given the particulars of the text, Newberry's startling rehistoricizing of the socioeconomic, political, and religious strands of the psychology of a "historical" Tobias Pearson (pp. 44ff.) provides corroboration. As in Hawthorne's tale, the historical Pearson was one of the Puritans who had remained in England and fought in the Civil War under Cromwell, but he quitted the army of the parliament because he began to suspect the ambitions of Cromwell (which resulted in regicide and usurpation; cf. Scott's portrayal in *Woodstock*). As Hawthorne indicates, the war had come to seem to Pearson "no longer holy." Newberry suggests that in the course of Hawthorne's tale Pearson comes to recognize "that the Puritans were simply aiming to replace one form of power with another" (p. 44) both in the Old World and in the New World—the pattern of "The Gray Champion." Typically refusing to be content with simplistic one-sided portraiture, Hawthorne has his narrator cast at least some doubt on Pearson's motives for deserting to New England: there may have been a "more worldly consideration"; the New World may have presented "advantages to men of unprosperous fortunes, as well as to dissatisfied religionists" (1:94; *T&S*, 114).

More to the point, Newberry observes that Pearson is one of the elected representatives of the General Court and thus would be among those who drafted the punitive laws against the Quakers, establishing guilt as a powerful motivation for Hawthorne's Pearson to take in the "orphaned" Quaker boy, Ilbrahim. Moreover, Pearson's decision to quit the "no longer holy" Civil War, along with various other details (such as a sudden "inner light" epiphany at the graveside in the opening scene), reveals Arminian and antinomian tendencies in him that suggest that he seizes upon Ilbrahim's tragedy as an opportunity to turn away from an increasingly unsatisfactory and arbitrary Puritanism. Paralleling his perception of the English Civil War, Pearson's perception of the Puritan persecution of the Quakers in New England is that the campaign is no longer holy but something else. More unsettling is the probability that "he has discovered in himself the very narrowness of Puritanism that he had sought to escape during the English Civil War" (Newberry, p. 46). The "whole process of Pearson's shift from Puritan to Quaker," continues Newberry, is "fraught with nagging complications, aggravated by the fact that some readers have more or less accepted the Puritan point of view and argued a case for Pearson's essential weakness of character" (p. 47; cf. Crews, who sees Pearson as a "neurotic"). In any case, in "the course of his accepting the Quaker faith, Pearson becomes almost as fanatical as Ilbrahim's mother" (p. 47), while at the same time "there is reason to doubt that Pearson's 'change' in the final version reflects an unequivocal . . . [and] fully embraced conversion" (p. 48).

Not surprisingly, then, Newberry suggests that Hawthorne deleted the original passage on the "triumph" of conversion to retain a measure of "doubt" about Pearson's spiritual peace. Earlier critics, notably Seymour Gross, had suggested that "the original version indicated a spiritual peace, which is wholly absent from the final one." Colacurcio notes, however, that the first omission is ambiguous. And Newberry writes that "in neither the original nor the final version does Pearson arrive at any spiritual peace" (p. 48). Far from being a *via media* between two religious extremes, the Pearsons are as much trapped between worlds as Ilbrahim (cf. Folsom, pp. 123–25; Crews, p. 65; Newberry, pp. 48–49). Newberry reads as doubtful or ironic the apparent "easing" of the Puritan attitude noted in the historical frame by the narrator (that is, after Charles II proclaims religious toleration) and specifically suggested in the "painless" community softening toward Catharine in the final paragraph. For the children of Hawthorne's tale will become the leaders of the next epoch: "During their mature years, they will all evince 'very peculiar talents' by ruthlessly wiping out entire villages during King Philip's War and later condemning their own neighbors to die in the Salem witch trials" (Newberry, p. 50).

Equally telling, however, is the simple point that while Pearson's wife is the most humanly and genuinely charitable figure in the tale, it is not the loving Puritan foster mother who receives the love of the gentle boy. It is his irresponsible and undeserving Quaker mother (cf. 1:115; *T&S*, 130) who embraces him and receives his dying words: "I am happy now" (1:125; *T&S*, 137). If not clearly masochistic of the "gentle" Ilbrahim, its effect for Dorothy must be almost sadistic — while the Quaker mother, continuing her masochistic ways, returns, like the Puritan Hester Prynne, into the "community" to wear out her life on its fringes.

The tale is almost as classic an example of the pervasive theme of sadomasochism in Hawthorne as *The Scarlet Letter*, though hardly anything else Hawthorne wrote on the theme is quite so obvious as the love-hate relationship of Arthur Dimmesdale and Roger Chillingworth. The narrative of the "gentle" boy so beloved for its "sentiment" by Sophia Peabody and thousands of nineteenth-century readers is darkly qualified. Illustrating the ironic way in which these early pieces on America are *twice*-told, the ambiguous tale exemplifies Hawthorne's negative romance of love, courage, and truth. The seemingly sentimental "Gentle Boy" is one of the most grimly ironic of Hawthorne's historical narratives of provincial America.

The erased moral was doubtless too monological. At the end, the narrator need make no further comment beyond describing the "changed" attitudes of Dorothy and the Puritan community. And yet the narratorial tone of something like a pox on both your houses seems too elliptically presented. However antimonological on one level, such wholesale criticism seems too one-sided to bear the dialogical accommodations of the full narrative. Perhaps the narrator is at last an astute yet deficient reader of the text he presents. Can we not detect a more authorial presence than the narrator — one that is more sympathetic than the narrator — without rejecting the narrator's critiques? Perhaps that is the real reason the final sentence of the original version was omitted.

These questions are centrally pertinent to our understanding of Hawthorne's art of the negative romance. At the very least, we can say that the critical portrait of the early Hawthorne as an uncritical American patriot, seeing only "commonplace prosperity" in "the broad and simple daylight" of his "dear native land," is incredibly naive. So too are those theories of Hawthorne's artistic disintegration that point to his turning to non-American materials (culminating in *The Marble Faun* and generating the unfinished romances) in a mistaken notion of the source of his creativity. The famous passage on his "dear native land" from the preface to *The Marble Faun* has to be evaluated in the context of Hawthorne's deployment of the negative romance in the *Provincial Tales*. Otherwise, we might find ourselves suggesting that the author of "Roger Malvin's Burial" and "The Gentle Boy" saw no "shadow," "mystery," or "gloomy wrong" in the history and landscape of America. And neither did the author of *The Scarlet Letter.* Or of "My Kinsman, Major Molineux" and "Alice Doane's Appeal."

4 Story of the Night Told Over: Negative Allegory and Authorial Presence in "My Kinsman, Major Molineux"

...the mazed world,
... now knows not which is which.
And this same progeny of evils comes
From our debate, from our dissension.
We are their parents and original.
(Act 2)

When they next wake, all this derision
Shall seem a dream and fruitless vision. . . .
(Act 3)

But all the story of the night told over,
And all their minds transfigured so together,
More witnesseth than fancy's images,
And grows to something of great constancy,
But, howsoever, strange and admirable.
(Act 5)

—*A Midsummer Night's Dream* (1595)

"My Kinsman, Major Molineux" may be regarded as an eighteenth-century companion tale to "The Gray Champion." Both are political narratives of revolutionary sentiment, employing elements of romance and the supernatural that, like their colonial polemics, are subverted. "My Kinsman" also moves insistently toward an allegorical significance, but that significance is always withdrawn. More complexly ironic than "The Gray Champion," it is the most dreamlike of the four provincial "tales" considered in this study. Its insistent thematizing of dream experience forms a bridge to the dreamvision sketches that constitute the other "half" of *Provincial Tales.*

One of Hawthorne's earliest known pieces, the tale was first published in 1832, anonymously, and then forgotten. It was not acknowledged for nearly twenty years, until at last Hawthorne collected it in *The Snow-Image* in 1851. A century and a half later, the Molineux story is one of the most frequently discussed of all Hawthorne's shorter narratives. If for provincialist critics the partisan interpretation of "The Gray Champion" has been an important key to the Hawthorne Question and to Hawthorne's interpretation of America, the tale of young Robin Molineux has been seen even more generally as *the* key to understanding not only the provincial tales, but also the entire shape of Hawthorne's career as an American writer.

The critical controversies over "My Kinsman" bring into sharp focus the large issues of the Hawthorne Question: (1) the problem of Hawthorne's narrators; (2) provinciality, irony, and self-reflexivity; (3) allegory, dialogicity, and indeterminateness; (4) the semiotics of narrative structure; (5) the primacy of perspectivity and the uncertain nature of human nature; (6) the ambiguity of history and the question of America. Readers have seen this tale as so heavily laden with meanings that anyone attentive to the extended text of Hawthorne's work has to find a way through a labyrinth of commentary on its significance. In fact, the ongoing debate of critical tradition is as much the subject of this chapter as Hawthorne's tale per se.

Many critics have seen the basic interpretations of the story that have emerged as antithetical. I prefer the attitude of Frederick Crews, who, arguing that his own, heavily Freudian, psychoanalytic approach encompasses the others, writes:

> One school sees Robin's gradual emancipation from his uncle as allegorical of the American Revolution; youthful and naïve America "comes of age" by assenting to the deposition of Colonial authority (Major Molineux). Others, stressing the ceremonial violence of that deposition, see the tale in mythic terms; Major Molineux in his tarring and feathering is a ritual king, "mighty no more, but majestic still in his agony." . . . Without denying the presence of historical and mythic overtones, we would do well to ask whether Robin's own mind may not be the chief referent of Hawthorne's symbols. (*Sins of the Fathers*, p. 73)

Without necessarily agreeing that a psychological approach encompasses all the others, I do consider the tale and its many levels to be an integrated work in which the meaning of the whole is not at some "center" but in the framings, or, as Conrad's Marlow suggests, "layerings." Although one would not like to overstate the case, it is almost as if Hawthorne has anticipated or proleptically manipulated the ensuing critical debate. One wonders if he has not somehow engineered it, slyly incorporating diverse monological reader-responses into the structure of the narrative; that is, as in "Alice Doane's Appeal," implicated readership may be part of its theme.

Keeping in mind caveats about *either/or* readings, I wish to pursue

Crews's tripartite characterization of the criticism — *historical, mythic-oneiric,* and *psychoanalytic* — on to which in several stages and forms the *moral* is grafted. Accordingly, I have organized the discussion around the problems and limitations of an interlinked series of major critical positions and the interpretative readings of the tale that these ideological frames have generated.[1] After an initial discussion of the concept of negative allegory in a pair of representative Hawthorne texts, I assess the general adequacy of allegorical political readings of "My Kinsman, Major Molineux" in the context of other quasi-allegorical readings. These latter include the recurrent resonances in the tale of the dream-play tradition, represented by *A Midsummer Night's Dream,* and the many large mythic parallels readers have seen.[2] Next, I deal with the function of the formal frame introduction to the tale in terms of a counter-realism to the oneiric and mythic — and the "opposite" counter of myth and dream to historical realism. Then the related psychological readings of Simon O. Lesser, Roy R. Male, Mary Rohrberger, and Frederick Crews are explored as a prolegomenon to a reexamination of the influential and complex moral-psychological and moral-historical thesis of Roy Harvey Pearce. In turn, Pearce's combinatory readings lead to what is doubtless the most important reinterpretation of the tale since Q. D. Leavis's at midcentury — that of Michael Colacurcio.

While acknowledging Colacurcio's impressive contribution to our understanding of the narrative, I take issue with what in this instance I feel is a somewhat misdirected line of historical inquiry — one that exemplifies the problem of the historical/aesthetic binary latent in his critical method. Colacurcio takes Pearce's emphasis on moral history well beyond the natural limits of Hawthorne's text in a disquisition on history for the sake of history that displaces the aesthetic. Following the lead of *A Midsummer Night's Dream,* I suggest an aesthetic reading that I believe more adequately accounts for the tale as a whole and for its interpretations. This aesthetic reading foregrounds authorial presence and lays the foundation for the final two chapters, which argue for the importance, indeed the necessity, of reading Hawthorne's early works, his "provincial" tales, within a cosmopolitan aesthetic tradition. In this tradition, authorial presence, self-reflexivity, and romantic irony are paramount.

These matters are closely linked to the problem of the aesthetic consistency and coherence of the tale. Roy Harvey Pearce is not alone in suggesting that the unfolding symbolic action of "My Kinsman" resembles a distorted, insane performance of *A Midsummer Night's Dream* (which is itself something of an insane performance). In act 5 Theseus asks what "masques" and dances they shall have to while away the night. Rejecting the battle of the Centaurs and the "riot of the tipsy Bacchanals," Theseus notes the contradictions of "Pyramus and Thisbe." The work is both "hot" and "cold," "tedious and brief," "merry and tragical." How, he wonders, shall they "find the concord of this discord" (5.1.58–60)? In answer, Quince in fact stages the play of "Pyramus and Thisbe," which parodies the theory of the imagination articulated by Theseus and Hippolyta in act 5, but which is incorporated with all its confusion into the "constant" (coherent) aesthetic fabric of the play as a whole. "How shall we find the concord of this discord?" is the central question we shall ask of Hawthorne's text.

Hippolyta's phrase, the "story of the night told over" (5.1.23), also aptly (if ambiguously) describes Hawthorne's story. "My Kinsman" is a twice-told, dialogical story, told over again, as a story that is never quite over. If not precisely what Henry James called a "trap for the unwary" reader, the narrative yet draws the reader into various misprisionings of "what happens," including an allegorical interpretation beyond what the character, Robin, can comprehend or even imagine. But the negative allegory of Hawthorne's story resists the simple allegorical interpretations the reader is invited to provide. Thereby emerges the tale's dialogical quality — its serious invitation to consider the positive and negative aspects of the history of America, its dark yet genial humor, its romantic irony.

Negative Allegory as Negative Romance

Succinctly stated, the variously suggested allegorical "levels" of "My Kinsman, Major Molineux" are: literal-mythic-archetypal-oneiric-psychological-social-political-historical-moral-aesthetic. Granting that the allegorical innuendoes of Hawthorne's story do operate on three or four levels beyond the literal, we yet need to understand that each level incorporates the others and that the primacy or "sequence" of these levels is uncertain; exclusionary binaries do not work well with Hawthorne's texts. To distinguish, for example, a psychoanalytic reading of the tale as an allegory of Oedipal conflict from an archetypal reading of it as initiation rite is artificial. So also is a categorical separation of reading the tale as a historical allegory of America's coming of age from reading it as a personal initiation rite into adulthood, or as Oedipal conflict attendant to mature ego-identity.

These matters are further complicated by problems of romance versus realism, and allegory versus symbolism.[3] As "Roger Malvin's Burial" moves *toward* romance, so "My Kinsman, Major Molineux" moves *toward* allegory. As the realist element in "My Kinsman" is gradually subverted, so also does the romance element tend to be diffused at the end by realistic explanation. And, as romance and realism stand not in unremitting oppositional but in dialogical relation, so also is the allegorical element recurrently subverted by indeterminate symbolic suggestion. In the manner that we have used the terms *negative romanticism*, *negative romance*, and *negative closure*, we should understand *negative allegory* to mean that twice-told ambiguity in which a conventionally positive quality or unproblematic assumption in the allegorical mode is not denied but subjected to skeptical scrutiny. Negative allegory is thus narrative in which allegory is dialogically suggested and subverted. The point may be illustrated by reference to the contestatory structures of allegory and typology in two other representative tales from the Hawthorne canon. "The Minister's Black Veil" resists typological interpretation even as it evokes it; and the heavily allegorical "Rappaccini's Daughter" actually deconstructs allegory.

A casual comment on "The Minister's Black Veil" in the influential *Norton Anthology of American Literature* (1979, reprinted 1989) highlights the importance of adequate critical perspective. In a one-line note, the editor of the Hawthorne texts suggests to the student reader that Hawthorne's statement that the veil is "a type *and* a symbol" is "redundant" (1989 ed., 1:1138n.; my italics). Actually, Hawthorne's statement identifies precisely the deliberate interpretative indeterminism of his narrative. Its chief image is both a symbol and a type; its signification lies in the dialogical interaction of the indeterminate quality of the one and the determinate tendency of the other. Readers like the Norton editor want the veil to acquire a stable meaning, a one-for-one relationship between signifier and a determinate signified. The story invites the reader to take the veil typologically, as the sign of Original Sin. But the narrative as a whole resists that reductive reading, and the veil suggests several symbolically radiating meanings, some of which loop back on themselves. And just as the typological meaning yields to the symbolic meanings — which *depend* upon the typological in order to deconstruct the typological — so the form of the narrative as a whole suggests allegory while undercutting it or at least contesting it.[4] Such is also the central formal dynamic of "My Kinsman, Major Molineux."

"Rappaccini's Daughter" is an even clearer example of subverted typology/allegory than "The Minister's Black Veil." Allusions to Eden and to Dante's *Divine Comedy* imply an allegorical relationship among the four characters as they enter, or observe from the outside, Rappaccini's garden. The garden is poisoned; so there is a basic paradox, redoubled, in the "allegory," which becomes hopelessly convoluted as what first seems to be the Adam type becomes Eve, Eve becomes Adam, God becomes Satan, Satan God. Or do they? Ambiguity reigns even in what seems to be a fairly clear denouement; and what is suggested there of the tragic is undercut as the darkly parodic "allegory" resolves into ambivalent absurdity, reinforced by the self-deprecating, humorous frame introduction in which Hawthorne talks about himself as the little-known "M. de l'Aubépine."[5]

Aside from wrenching the text to make it fit, allegorically point for point, into an Oedipal paradigm, the dominant tendency of the criticism on "My Kinsman, Major Molineux" is to see the tale as so heavily typological in the political sense of "manifest destiny" as to harden into fixed allegory. Such readings ignore those aspects of Hawthorne's stories that are characterized by the ironically modulated tone the narrator takes. In "Rappaccini's Daughter" the frame introduction mocks the productions of the putative author whose tale is about to be presented in translation. In "My Kinsman, Major Molineux," the narrator takes a similarly bemused attitude toward the "shrewd" youth of the story—an attitude that is echoed (indeed, re-ified) by the "kindly" stranger, who appears as if from the outside (almost *deus ex machina*) at the end. The gentle, sympathetic mockery of the overall narrative tone and of the kindly gentleman tends to be overlooked by critics bent on claiming the work for Hawthorne's moral lessons in American history.[6]

Putting questions of tone temporarily aside, and assuming for the sake of discussion that the tale's core narrative demands some sort of allegorical interpretation, let us first consider in a general way the major contesting readings of "My Kinsman." The disorienting initiation of an eighteen-year-old youth from the country into the larger world of city and nation suggests to most readers something more than personal experience—although the nature of that experience may itself be ambiguous. One group of critics sees the experience as predominantly negative. In the urban crucible, Robin is initiated into the ambiguity, paradox, uncertainty, hypoc-risy, and guilt of the adult world; and his basic response is to retreat in egocentric defeat. Another group of more positively inclined critics sug-gests that the story actually celebrates a difficult rite of passage. In addition to the story of archetypal coming of age for an individual, the narrative is said to represent the coming of age of America—hence the special symbolic significance of the young provincial's excursion to the city. According to this reading, Hawthorne allegorically cast the American historical experi-ence in terms of intertwined mythic and psychological romance that, how-ever mundanely realistic at the end, presages the political, social, and even moral progress of America from provincial dependence on Great Britain to national independence on the world scene. In a Freudian sense of Oedipal quest for independence and separate identity (allegorically on a large cul-tural scale), the story line seems to objectify in narrative the revolutionary assumptions of "The Gray Champion"—at least as that story is read by the provincialist critics. As read by the more Jungian myth critics, the political

allegory is secondary to that of initiation and temptation ritual — the archetypal night journey and descent into the underworld self.

Both the mythic and the political are in fact immediately suggested in the
opening paragraphs of the tale, and neither is initially emphasized above
the other. After the usual frame introduction placing the individual events
to be related in a political-historical context, the tale proper begins at the
conclusion of the heretofore uneventful journey (in August, on a midsummer night's eve) of a cocksure, "shrewd" young man, named Robin. The
confident youth has come from his father's country home into town in
search of employment with his uncle, the royal colonial magistrate, Major
Molineux. Implicit and explicit allusions to classical myth and to *A Midsummer Night's Dream* begin to suggest, or half-suggest, a romance element,
some kind of dream experience or fantasy.[7] References to "a man, who, like
the Moonshine of Pyramis and Thisbe, carried a lantern" and to "The Man
in the Moon" strengthen the suggestions of the dream-within-a-dream and
play-within-a-play qualities of *A Midsummer Night's Dream*.[8] These resonances come, ironically enough, to qualify the romance elements of the
tale.

The Dream Labyrinth: Myth, Sleep, and the "Great Awakening"

If not quite a scaffolding of allegorical reference, *A Midsummer Night's
Dream* does in fact provide an important and extended gloss on Hawthorne's tale. Among the most pertinent allusions or parallels are the figures
of Oberon and Puck (known as Robin Goodfellow), and the descriptions by
Titania, Theseus, and Hippolyta of the relation of fantasy, dream, and
imagination to some waking human reality in a world of uncertainty and
confusion.[9] Enfolding these are the motifs of night and the moon — mythic
source of unsettling dreams. Titania (in some traditions identified with the
moon goddess Diana) introduces the theme of disorder. She makes an
important topical reference to the odd weather of the summer of 1594, and
her description of the dense fog and unseasonable rains also describes the
basic confusion of the play that is to follow (see 2.1.88–92), and does so in a
way that is highly suggestive regarding the events of Hawthorne's story.

The fields cannot be plowed; the corn has rotted; the sheep pens stand
empty; the crows feast on drowned and plague-stricken carcasses. Not a
very pleasant scene with which to introduce a dreamvision fairy play, or a
tale of the rising glory of a colonial America moving toward nationhood.
Moreover, the traditional amusements of the folk have been interrupted.
The squares of the Morris games are filled up with mud. The mazes in the

meadows are "undistinguishable" for "lack of tread." The implied image suggests the Molineux story: the intricate, labyrinthine paths leading to (or leading away from) a center cannot be followed. Human beings no longer bless the night with "hymn or carol." The confusion of the orderly progression of the seasons proceeds from the debate, discord, and dissension of the governing deities. Titania attributes this disorder and "lunacy" principally to the moon, "governess of floods / pale in her anger." All "is, as in mockery, set"; and "the mazed world . . . knows not which is which."[10]

The interaction of the theme of ruin, disorder, and discord with the all-pervasive dream motif is made explicit in act 3. Oberon remarks to Puck that he should "overcast the night" and put confusion in the brains of sleeping human beings. At the end of the dream labyrinth opening act 5 is Theseus's ambivalent speech on dreaming and waking, fantasy and imagination noted before in chapter two. Theseus observes initially that "these antique fables" are "more strange than true"; nevertheless, from "seething brains" may come "shaping fantasies" with their own brand of insight. These are "of imagination all compact." (See 5.1.2–8.) This same "imagination" that breeds fantasies out of seething brains may also, in the poet, give shape and particularity to the heightened emotion of lunatics and lovers—the "moon-struck" (5.1.14–17), which in Hawthorne seems also to include revolutionaries. Although such "shaping fantasies" may "apprehend / More than cool reason ever comprehends," the imagination, even when shaped and reified by the poet, may yet be delusive (5.1.18–22).

To this Hippolyta replies in a speech that, I believe, represents Hawthorne's aesthetic orientation. Elevating the shaping imagination above all other concerns, she implies that the aesthetic comprehends all it contains and dramatizes. In lines before mentioned, she observes (5.1.23–27) that however strange and wonderful the events of a fantasy-dream in the night, imagination "transfigures" the mind, so that one sees more than mere "fancy's" images, and creates something that however wild and disorderly is also consistent and whole ("something of great constancy"). From such a theme of discord in "My Kinsman, Major Molineux" dialogically emerges imaginative concord, that aesthetic embodiment that Friedrich Schlegel and August Wilhelm Schlegel, with specific reference to *A Midsummer Night's Dream*, pronounced "romantic."

The resonances with the faery world of *A Midsummer Night's Dream* from folk myth and classical mythology are a major source of imaginative concord in Hawthorne's tale. Although these allusions and parallels are primarily in a symbolic and allusive mode, their presence has suggested to some critics a definitive allegorical current to Hawthorne's tale that it cannot quite sustain, much as it evokes it. That is, a number of allusions are imported into the text from outside by scholars. But among the mythic parallels that Hawthorne's story does sustain are suggestions of abandonment in the Minoan labyrinth and a journey to the underworld.[11]

Crossing a river and paying a ferryman, Robin arrives in town at darkfall. Wandering as though "entangled" in a maze of "crooked and narrow streets" that "meander" in endless succession not far from the water-side, he stumbles into symbolically representative places: a barbershop, a tavern, a church, a spacious promenade, the back streets, the seamy part of town. He arrives at a "street of mean appearance," on either side of which is "a row of ill-built houses . . . straggling towards the harbor," in one of which dwells a prostitute in a "scarlet petticoat" (3:625; *T&S*, 74–75). The maze of streets, the darkness, the moonlight all give the town the aspect of a bewildering dream not quite yet a nightmare. His unsuccessful inquiries about his kinsman, repeated almost ritualistically, also suggest the alien sense of nightmare. He experiences in his wanderings unaccountable rebuff and ridicule from a representative procession of townspeople, who come more and more to seem almost demonic and who speak a wizard language that seems informal. One person is especially demonic of aspect, a fellow whose "forehead bulged out into a double prominence," with a long hooked nose and "deep and shaggy" eyebrows underneath which his eyes glowed "like fire in a cave" (3:621; *T&S*, 72). In the ritual three encounters with this double-faced figure (who has his hideous eye on the young man), Robin seems to confront Satan himself.[12]

Robin's first encounter is in a public place, and the impact of the man's visage is unnerving. In his second, isolated, and even more unnerving encounter, Robin is told by the double-faced, fiery-eyed fellow to wait at the intersection of two streets: his kinsman will be along in an hour. While waiting, Robin falls into a reverie — or is it sleep? He "dreams" he is back home in the forest. But suddenly he "wakes" in confusion, wondering, "Am I here, or there?" (3:633; *T&S*, 80). The question of Robin's "awakening," as in "The Wives of the Dead" or "An Old Woman's Tale," is the principal one of the narrative. To what does Robin awake? How much does he see and comprehend of either this or some other world? Has he truly awakened? Has he figuratively awakened? Where has he awakened? How lost in the dream labyrinth is he? Given the way dream and reality are typically confused, conflated, or reversed in Hawthorne, the scene is especially suggestive. As in "The Hollow of the Three Hills" and the other dreamvision sketches, conscious and subconscious perception cannot be distinguished. As with those narratives, here also two levels of the subconscious and unconscious (dream and deep reverie) cannot be distinguished. Or is it a mysterious interface between the conscious and the subconscious that cannot be distinguished from either?

In addition, as we shall see, the scene is important for the realist level of the story and any political allegory it may carry. The question of Robin's precise physical location frames the problem of the specific date of the historical events of the narrative; time and locale are important for the moral-historical interpretation (allegorical or otherwise) of these events as predictive (however ironically) of the American Revolution. Hawthorne is particularly crafty about the date (or dates) of the story, conflating events nearly half a century apart for the purposes of ironic historical typology. Yet whatever the ambiguity of literal historical event in space and time, the experience of the youth is highly charged with epistemological ambiguity and ontological anxieties that throw him back upon some basic definition of self that he cannot seem to formulate. He has previously relied upon an inconsistently formulated concept of American "self-reliance," naively assuming he goes it alone in the world. This is the supreme provincial irony of his quest for the help of his kinsman. The entire night journey experience seems symbolically to objectify his disintegrating concept of self, in which reinforcing context (home, city, nation, humankind) has played a major but heretofore unacknowledged part.

Robin's subconscious anxieties seem reified in an extended dreamlike sequence that, beginning quietly in front of an empty church, culminates in a mob scene of street violence. Amidst shouting and laughing and off-tune noises of wind instruments, a hideous torch-light procession "emptied" into the empty street—and Robin encounters the satanic figure the third time, in a combined public and private scene. It is all as though in a dream. The surreal procession is led by the fellow with the double face, now painted red on one side and black on the other, so that he looks "like war personified" (3:637; *T&S*, 84), a metaphor emphasized by critics as suggesting the American Revolution. He is followed by "wild figures" and "fantastic shapes without a model, giving the whole march a visionary air, as if *a dream had broken forth from some feverish brain*" (my italics).

At this point, then, we are given, with Robin, a revelation, the meaning of which recedes the more we contemplate it. On a cart at the center of the procession, trembling, pale as death, mouth quivering and befoamed, sits Major Molineux in "tar and feathery dignity." A not-so-shrewd country "robin," unwitting, naive, and provincial, has come to town the very night that the colonists have planned a symbolic overthrow of British royalist rule, represented by the Major. Robin's conflicted reaction is striking. All at once, "a perception of tremendous ridicule in the whole scene" affects Robin "with a sort of mental inebriety" (3:639; *T&S*, 85). The entire earth and sky seem drunken with laughter, the narrator remarks. Even the Man in the Moon seems to hear, as a disinterested observer, "the far bellow": " 'Oho,' quoth he, 'the old earth is frolicsome tonight!' " Robin realizes that

all night long the townspeople have been laughing at him, and he now sends
forth "a shout of laughter . . . the loudest there" (3:640; *T&S*, 86), though
the meaning of that laugh is less than unambiguous.[13] The realist-mythic-
oneiric-psychological themes coalesce in an "epiphany," underscored by
the question of Robin's "awakening" to some larger reality. Once again
Hawthorne has turned an ordinary incident (a young man's first journey to
town) into a romance of some kind, this time a gothic one, and an "explained gothic" at that. Never mind, finally, all the overtones of a descent
into hell and a descent into oneiric unconsciousness; the tale has a compre-
hensible everyday explanation, as in a Radcliffean romance or a detective
story. It has an Aristotelian pattern of beginning, middle, and clearly
demarcated end: a satisfying denouement that neatly, realistically accounts
for everything. Or does it?

Does the political context in which young Robin's nighttime adventures
take place account for what numerous readers feel are the multiple levels of
the text? Is the tale really at bottom a political allegory of a newly emerging
nation? Or is it primarily focused on young Molineux's subconscious and
unconscious psychological processes, capturing dream experience, and tapping the archetypal and mythic underside of human existence? Are these
frames exclusionary, and do we understand the meaning of the tale/experi-
ence any more fully, more precisely than Robin?

The explanatory conclusion really explains very little. With ironic timing, a stranger, the first "kindly" person that the country youth has met in
town, enters the narrative. He attempts to "awaken" Robin from whatever
reverie or trance state he has plunged into by asking, somewhat abruptly, if
he is "dreaming." Robin replies that he is beginning to "grow weary of a
town life" (3:641; *T&S*, 87) and wants to go back across the river. To this, in
turn, the kindly stranger offers the oblique remark that "perhaps," since he
is such a "shrewd" youth, Robin may "rise in the world, without the help"
of his kinsman, Major Molineux. This concluding moral leaves so much
unexplained, while seeming to explain everything, implicating Robin, "author," and reader all together (including critics), that we are justified in
regarding it as one of the most effective of Hawthorne's negative epiphanies. "My Kinsman, Major Molineux" pits together what seem contestatory readings of the strange events of a country youth's first, nightmarish evening in Boston: most obviously, the oneiric and mythic against
historical explanation. The "real world" clues to the "mystery" have been
there, blatantly announced in the opening historical frame, for the reader
and for Robin both, all along. But at the same time that a "normative"
political context more or less explains away young Robin Molineux's rather
gothic experiences, it also leads to an allegorical interpretation of these

"real-world" events. Moreover, the fabric of allusions to *A Midsummer Night's Dream* suggests elements of uncertainty, confusion, and sleep— actually patterns of the conflictual or the contradictory—which counter the waking and rational (or at least normative) explanation of events. The tale dialogically confronts one reading of the lunatic night with another— and another.

"Our Debate, Our Dissension":
Counter-realism in the Frame

Robin and the reader undergo a kind of parallel manipulation via the narratival structuring of the text, though the reader initially has the advantage since an "authorial" presence, one that we have seen before in the historical tales, intercedes immediately in the semi-attached or -detached frame introduction. We are presented with the voice of a chronicler- narrator, who deftly sketches in the political restiveness of the times. His tone suggests the manner of the familiar essay and the beginning of a local historical chronicle; and he is as aggressive as the narrator of "The Gray Champion" in his opening sentence.

The kings of Great Britain, he announces, had unfairly "assumed the right" of appointing the colonial governors in America, breaking with precedent and tradition (3:616; *T&S*, 68). This royal presumption, he says, actually undermined the authority of the governors with the people of the colonies, who had given greater approbation to leaders whose authority came from "the original charters." For (as in "The Gray Champion") "the people looked with jealous scrutiny to the exercise of power which did not emanate from themselves." The jealousy of the people of the rights of power is the subject of the rest of a deliberately coy and convolute sentence. The people "usually rewarded their rulers" (the colonial governors ap- pointed by the crown) with "slender gratitude for the compliances by which, in softening their instructions from beyond the sea, they had in- curred the reprehension of those who gave them." The narrator's (possibly bemused) point, in short, is that the royal governors were caught in the middle. The people of the New World gave their governors a hard time even when they tried to implement a gentle rule with due regard to colonialist sensibilities; and when the governors thus softened harsh in- structions from Britain, they incurred royal "reprehension" from the Old World.

It should be clear that, as in the other provincial tales, the introduction signals, however surreptitiously, a story that will not unquestioningly adopt one side over the other, especially not that of the American dissenters over the loyalists, nor even of the governed over the governors. Citing as his source *The History of the Colony and Province of Massachusetts Bay*, the narrator gives a list of particulars regarding the governors' treatment by the people: "The annals of Massachusetts Bay will inform us, that of six governors in the space of about forty years from the surrender of the old charter, under James II, two were imprisoned by a popular insurrection"; a third "was driven from the province by the whizzing of a musket-ball"; a fourth "was hastened to his grave by continual bickerings with the House of Representatives"; the "remaining two, as well as their successors, till the Revolution, were favored with few and brief interludes of peaceful sway." The author of the *Annals* is Thomas Hutchinson (1711–1780), last royal governor of Massachusetts (1771–1774) before the Revolution. In 1765, Hutchinson's house was ransacked by the Boston Sons of Liberty. The mob of the tale somewhat resembles the Liberty mob, which took an active part during the Stamp Act riots of 1765. But no such identification or even equivalence in Hawthorne's tale can be definitively made. Some critics have *assumed* that Hawthorne made a mistake in suggesting that his tale is set "not far from a hundred years ago" — that is (since the tale was published in 1832), in the 1730s. But Hawthorne may have been trying to generalize its pattern rather than tying it to one historical event.[14] He has built a double ambiguity into the countering of mythic or archetypal timelessness with a historical time and then purposefully conflating (literally and figuratively) two specific events not quite a half-century apart.

Whatever the precise date, Hawthorne's narrator observes that in those times of "high political excitement" even the lesser members of "the court party" (like Major Molineux) led "scarcely a more desirable life" than the magistrates. Under normal conventions, the historical frame would serve to set forth the context for a basic situation in which political instability was a major feature. In the tale that follows, political turmoil is in fact a major feature, but it is deflected from the reader's attention (actually suppressed) until the denouement. The narrator, after having set forth the normative real world context, casually *invites* the reader not to trouble too greatly about the historical situation: "These remarks may serve as a preface to the following adventures, which chanced upon a summer night, not far from a hundred years ago. The reader, in order to avoid a long and dry detail of colonial affairs, *is requested to dispense* with an account of the train of circumstances that had caused much temporary inflammation of the popular mind" (3:616–17; *T&S*, 68, my italics). The narrator has come one hundred eighty degrees from the "rights" of the "people" to the "temporary inflammation" of the "popular" mind — that is, in more direct language, the mob. He has also presumed to dismiss the historical context "temporarily" to the background as we focus on the individual story through the eyes of a green country youth unaware of any political turmoil in the prerevolutionary air.[15]

Simultaneously, then, the frame introduction with its deceptive invitation to get right down to the story sets up the ironic reversal of the real and the imagined, forcing us into a double reading along mythic-oneiric lines on the one hand and political-historical lines on the other. The political context framing Robin's experiences is placed *both* in the foreground and the background. The reader is skillfully invited by the end of the opening paragraph to forget all about the historical events of the real world and enter the naive world of young Robin's waking nightmare. The ironic technique and the general tone are rather like that of the opening frame of "Roger Malvin's Burial," where the narrator broadly hints that with a few suppressions (i.e., distortions) here and there a historical atrocity can be *made into* "romance." As in "The Gray Champion," the middle portion seems a little at odds with the frame around it: historical context is explicitly and formally framed at the beginning by "authorial" comment, then dissipated by the sense of the inexplicable in the dreamlike movement of the body of the narrative, until vividly dramatized at the end.

As the gothic quality of the tale threatens to dissolve into the normative political explanation that all the mysteries and demons of the night are part of an insurrectionist masquerade, Robin seems to perceive what a fool he has been. The allusion to the fools' play-within-a-dream-within-a-play in *A Midsummer Night's Dream* becomes even more pertinent. Rather than a good fellow, he seems to realize, at bottom he has been a pompous ass; and, a bit shamefaced and certainly rather egocentric, seeming not to care much for the fate of his kinsman, he decides he had best return home. The kindly stranger (possibly also laughing at him to a degree) suggests that he stay awhile, remarking somewhat puckishly on his shrewdness (3:641; *T&S*, 87). Given the mild irony of the narrator's use of "shrewd" prior to this point, the word has, if not a mocking, a bemused tone, so that the narrator and the stranger are paralleled. A symmetrical if elliptical completion of the introductory frame is implied.

It is largely on the final personal statement by the enigmatic kindly stranger, combined with the narrator's historical commentary in the opening frame, that the reading of the tale as political allegory turns. But as usual in Hawthorne the allegory is unstable, the denouement reversible, the tale twice-told. As a moral romance of America, the tale contests the very provincial quality that critics like Baym and Doubleday see as embarrassing in Hawthorne. For, as in "The Gray Champion," the side apparently favored by the narrator (or his assumed American readers) reverses — or at least balances off against others. Not only are the American colonists described as demonic and their leader as satanic; their opponent, the Major, for them the emblem of despotism, is favorably described (despite his terror). He is large and majestic, with "strong, square features, betokening a steady soul"; his "pride strove to quell" his fear "even in those circumstances of overwhelming humiliation" (3:638–39; *T&S*, 85). Around this human figure of combined dignity and ridicule, the colonists cavort "like fiends that throng in mockery around some dead potentate, mighty no more, but majestic still in his agony. On they went, in counterfeited pomp, in senseless uproar, in frenzied merriment, trampling all on an old man's heart" (3:640; *T&S*, 86).

At this point, then, we hear Robin's equivocal laugh. On the one hand, with his laugh of "recognition," suddenly everything (the odd reactions, the unaccountable rebuffs, the secret meanings, the coded language) seems to fall into place for the reader. It is as if epiphany for the reader is meant to coincide, *despite* the historical frame introduction explaining the political situation, with Robin's concluding epiphany. "My Kinsman, Major Molineux" illustrates Hawthorne's experiment with the convention of the historical tale-teller who withdraws to tell his story implicitly from a completely interior perspective focused on one character. But the historical introduction in the opening paragraphs provides, formally, an open-ended frame for a reversal of the interior psychological drama of the perspectival character. A reader inattentive to elements of the opening framing by the tale-teller will tend to misread the entire structure by focusing only on one side of the story, namely, the events as misinterpreted by the protagonist. (This effect is a variation on what Hawthorne does with the reader-narrator relationship in "The Gray Champion.") To this extent, the reader's experience parallels that of the main character.

But one of the triumphs of the tale is that it draws the reader into Robin's increasingly nightmarish disorientation while maintaining an ironic distance. We see both through his eyes and through the eyes of a narrator who is separate from him—a distance reflected in the narrator's sudden comment on the Man in the Moon, bemusedly, ironically watching the "lunacy" below. Although it cannot be fully clear on a first reading (indeed, the structure of the tale is carefully designed to prevent it), the historical context prepares for the denouement of young Robin's "dream" experience in two contrary but complementary ways. First, it sets up a historical explanation for the seemingly inexplicable behavior of the townspeople; second, it temporarily takes that explanation away. In effect, the technique parallels that of the multiple allegorical innuendoes of the tale as a whole, the large movement of which is to evoke a specific historical time, confuse it, dismiss it, conflate it, supplant it with the mythic and allegorical, reassert it, and finally leave it ambiguous.

To privilege a realist political reading would be to give the tale a one-sided reading — a double reading in its way, but not a dialogical reading. The dialogical does not cancel out its constituent, conflicting elements. The political-realist understanding does not take away the mythic-oneiric or psychological levels of the tale. The very misinterpretations (made by Robin, by the normative reader, by the critics) give rise to the mythic and psychological levels of the story. The tale incorporates conflicting elements into its structure, foregrounding and framing the ambiguity of the text and the experience it renders. The conclusion is indeterminate, another version of elliptical closure. Presenting meaningfully conflicting claims for mean-ingful closure, it modifies and even undercuts as many meanings as it suggests, requiring the reader dialogically to negotiate among them.

The structure of the tale itself and the critical tradition surrounding it suggest that the *problematic reading* of an event (or a text) and its context is central to what the tale is about. The romance element, as well as the suggestion of negative romance, turns within the text on a *mis*reading of a political event in one direction by an ignorant wilderness youth. And ironically enough, outside the text it turns on *mis*reading in another direc-tion by the critics, as though they themselves were as shrewd as Robin. The shameful conduct of the Major's kinsmen (including Robin) is hardly an appropriate affirming symbol or allegorical sign for the new independent nation in the family of nations. Like "The Gray Champion," the text will not bear the meaning of a positive, pro-colonial allegory in which America is instructed to repudiate her old home. So seductive has the allegorical complexity of this provincialist reading become, however, that it has not only persisted through all the problems attendant to it but has in fact become the dominant reading in one or another of its phases.

"More Than Cool Reason Ever Apprehends":
The Psychoanalytical Frame

A moral-historical reading of Hawthorne's fiction as an investigation of the American past has repeatedly been put forward as suggestive of the whole shape of his career. The most elaborate of these historical interpretations, based largely on "My Kinsman, Major Molineux," is that of Roy Harvey Pearce. His is a tortured but provocative attempt to reconcile Hawthorne's negative portrait of the colonists with the critical reading of the tale as an allegory of America's "moral" history and its political "progress" toward independence — its coming of age.[16] This positive reading, in which America must somehow assume both "guilt" and "responsibility" for its history in order to achieve adult nationhood, is ambivalently dependent on Freudian psychoanalytic constructs.

In "Robin Molineux on the Analyst's Couch: A Note on the Limits of Psychoanalytic Criticism," Pearce offers a mild critique of Simon O. Lesser's analysis in *Fiction and the Unconscious*. Pearce argues that a pure "psychological" analysis of the character Robin Molineux does not do justice to the literary work, the *story* that Hawthorne wrote.[17] He suggests that at one level (but only one level) Lesser is correct: we "inevitably" come to look upon the narrative "through the eyes of psychoanalytic criticism" because the "tale itself seems to be explicitly a version of what is for psychoanalysis the crucial segment of man's struggle for adulthood, the Oedipal situation" (p. 96). Pearce insists that "even the merest amateur of psychoanalysis" cannot but discover "the fact that Robin Molineux . . . is searching for a father-figure" (p. 97) and that in this search his "difficulties [are] of his own unconscious creating" (p. 99). It is evident that Robin's "search is charged with a sense of dream-work," that he finds his father surrogate "under deeply traumatic conditions," and that "without quite meaning to . . . he *helps destroy him* even as he finds him" (pp. 96–97; my italics). Robin's uncle, Major Molineux, stands for the father who is "at once the loved and the hated, a teacher of the ways of independence and a lord who denies the very goal he reveals."[18]

Although several of the points he grants Lesser are powerfully suggestive, Pearce is perhaps overly generous. For one thing, it is nowhere clear that Robin has *made* difficulties for himself — in fact, almost the reverse; he accidentally finds himself in an unfamiliar and tense situation which he misreads. The only real difficulty that Robin makes for himself comes from his youthful overconfidence, his belief in the efficacy of his strength of body and his "shrewdness" of mind. These rather typical traits of youth conveniently gloss over for him his belief in a protector and drive him on in an adolescent machismo mood of misled self-sufficiency — at least for a time. It is also untrue that Robin pursues his search, as Lesser and Pearce say, without any "ardor." He is gradually worn down. The "obvious conclusion" that Robin will have to submit to the "authority" he "seems" to seek to escape is based on an a priori assumption that he in fact is seeking to *escape* "authority" (the unconscious Oedipal struggle) rather than seeking its benevolent protection (the stated, conscious premise of Robin's journey). Since, in the text, Robin never expresses any "hatred" (Lesser's word) or even jealousy of the family back home in the forest, or of his "kinsman" in the city, these tensions and ambivalences, *if* they exist, *must* be subconscious; and this analysis of subconscious tension is specifically dependent on a somewhat questionable (or at least frequently misapplied) Freudian theory, not to mention a much misused Freudian premise.

In reductive literary-critical understandings of the Freudian model of the mind, a pair of symbolic binaries are always operative. Conscious motives are regarded as divergent from the "real" ones; subconscious motivation is taken to be the real motivation. That is, conscious thoughts are mere subterfuge and self-deception. This mix of conscious and subconscious motivation is most easily and conventionally formulated as *opposites*: real versus apparent. Pearce offers an unconsciously parodic capsule statement of psychoanalytic premises. He sees Robin as "confused over what he really wants" — that is, "what he unconsciously, therefore really, wants" (p. 99).

Certainly the idea that subconscious motivation is the real motivation may be the assumption of some texts. It is one of the major themes of Hawthorne's story of Reuben Bourne. But even if this simplistic concept were always and completely true, Pearce's psychoanalytic interpretation of "My Kinsman, Major Molineux" still depends on the assumption that Robin is acting out yet a second psychoanalytic construct, invented by the brilliant but somewhat bizarre Freud: Oedipal conflict. In literary criticism, Freud's many followers (until the revisionism of current neo-Freudians) heavy-handedly applied the Oedipus "complex" like a cookie-cutter to any and all texts indiscriminately. Is Reuben Bourne acting out an Oedipal conflict? Is all rebellion against authority Oedipal? Is Tobias Pearson's rebellion against Puritan authority Oedipal? Should "The Gray Champion" be read as Oedipal?[19] In "My Kinsman, Major Molineux," the most concrete instance of such an idea comes at the end when the kindly stranger suggests that Robin may rise in the world without the help of his kinsman; and it is not at all clear what Robin thinks of this almost irrelevant (or potentially sarcastic) comment. The psychoanalysis of the dynamics of the tale seems, to a degree, imposed from outside (and, as we shall see, the significance of the kindly stranger episode that concludes the tale is ambiguously resonant with symbolic suggestion of a different kind).

Crews and Rohrberger, synthesizing the psychoanalytic criticism of the tale as of 1966, put the paradoxes of the case succinctly and cogently. Rohrberger writes that Hawthorne uses a "typical dream structure" to "objectify psychological states"; each "incident and character become[s] a symbolic representation of the youth's inner conflict"; and the story is like an anxiety dream of "isolation and rejection." The "crossing of the river in the moonlight is highly suggestive of the passage from consciousness to sleep." The "boy's movements up and down the streets of the city, the apparent inconsistencies and incongruities in the appearances of the people he meets and the situations he finds, the use of light and dark, the tonal effects — the tapping of the cane, the sounds of voices, the tinkling of bells, the laughter — all combine to create the aura of the dream."[20] After a series of dreamlike (increasingly nightmarish) encounters and turnings in the labyrinthine streets of the city, Robin falls into a drowsy reverie, imagining to himself his forest home, his father, his mother, his sister, and an absent relation.[21] In his reverie, he tries to follow his family into the door of "his father's household," but "the latch tinkled into its place, and he was excluded from his home" (3:632; *T&S*, 80). This dream detail is supposed to reveal what Rohrberger calls "the essential motivation for Robin's behavior":

> It is clear that the *figures of authority* whom Robin meets *reflect* his feelings for *his father, the first authority*, and that these feelings are *essentially hostile*. In the story the situations involving the father-figure are all variations on one pattern. The *father rejects the son*, and the son, seeking to establish his own identity, is ridiculed by male by-standers. These circumstances are repeated until the kinsman with whom the boy seeks to make identity and so establish his own ego-ideal [*sic*] is shown ridiculed by the attending crowds. Robin's anger and hostility toward the father who has rejected him are expressed symbolically in the tarring and feathering of another father, Major Molineux. . . . seized by the spirit of the crowd, Robin joins in ridiculing the Major, and Robin's laugh is the loudest of all. His *hostility* is thus *released*. . . . The townspeople have acted out in violence the *anger* Robin subconsciously harbored. . . . (pp. 38–39; my italics)

Crews, writing in the same year, starts from the same *a priori* assumption as Lesser and Rohrberger that (somehow) it is clear that Robin's relation with his father — and *thus* other figures of authority — is "essentially hostile." Crews goes to the extreme of claiming that Robin merges himself with a "jealous, jostling democracy of father-haters." The experience is cathartic, says Crews, purging Robin of "both filial dependence and filial resentment" (*Sins of the Fathers*, p. 78). He praises the story for its "modern" appeal: it is ambiguous and ironic; it is a symbolic narrative in a mode opposite to that of "The Gentle Boy"; it is taut and economic, with no narrative commentary after the introductory paragraph; its meaning inheres "not in its outward events but in the anxiety they provoke in Robin" (p. 73). He observes that "even critics who denounce literary Freudianism have recognized that Robin's real search is for an idealized father" (p. 74), and in this search "anxiety is the keynote" (p. 76), not only in Robin's frustrating experiences but also in the imagery that attends them, such as the "primitive phallic reference" in all the "uncertainty over the size and efficacy of long wooden objects" (cudgel, cane, and so forth). Hawthorne has "given an exact symbolic account of filial ambivalence — an account which *must* be symbolic because the struggle it renders is unconscious" (pp. 75–76; my italics).

Further evidence of Oedipal struggle is the scene with the prostitute, which Crews outlines symbolically. Robin as the son of a New England clergyman is "motivated both by a powerful sexual curiosity and by a spirit of accusation" (p. 77). The "fantasy" of the father or father-surrogate (Molineux) living with a prostitute is, according to Freud (according to Crews), "a common one." So too is the reaction—when "an adolescent [boy] can no longer believe that his parents are exempt from sexuality"—of seeing the mother as no better than a whore. Moreover, the incident dramatizes "revived Oedipal longing," for the image of the father-surrogate cohabiting with the prostitute is "a thinly disguised representative of himself" (p. 77). Robin is "secretly eager to see his kinsman degraded" (p. 75); thus, at the end, Robin, who has been "led . . . through a series of initiations in which other adults have shown contempt for the Major," laughs the loudest laugh of all there at his kinsman. Because of all these ordeals, he "will now be free" (p. 78); but it is "only" in the "combined company" of the crowd with himself that he "can laugh at deposed majesty." The precise logic of this assertion is unclear; but clearly, for Crews, Robin's experience is definitively cathartic, a symbolic account of "the crisis of late adolescence and its resolution in favor of a healthy independence from the paternal image" (pp. 74–75).

The overall interpretation to which Rohrberger comes, however, is the opposite: (1) "simultaneously, Robin's strivings toward self-identity are destroyed, as he joins in the mockery"; and (2) Robin also assumes "the responsibility and blame"—in "guilt and defeat." Both (or all three) are highly questionable assertions, one going beyond the text, the other reading more into a statement in the text than is warranted. The text does not tell us that Robin assumes responsibility and blame any more than it indicates "freedom"; and even if the text did so indicate, to assume "responsibility" is not necessarily to feel guilt or to go down to defeat. (One can, for example, assume "responsibility" for one's children and yet not be held "guilty" for their individual actions.) But perhaps Rohrberger's vision of Robin's "defeat" is less unsupported textually than that of critics who see in Robin's (and the crowd's) "release" of subconscious anger against authority a "triumph." Otherwise, her commentary neatly summarizes a somewhat tortured consensus on the psychoanalytic reading of the tale.

Rohrberger concludes with a variation on the interpretation of Roy R. Male, writing that Robin "abandons his initial quest for identity and submits instead to the control of another guardian, the kindly gentleman, the embodiment of the perfect father image" (p. 39). The signification of the kindly stranger has considerable importance for the argument of the present study. Michael Colacurcio gives a good deal of emphasis to countering the psychoanalytic critics in an effort to suggest what he believes a more likely historical identification of this figure; and I in turn wish to modify Colacurcio's historical analysis. Therefore it is important to lay out clearly the genealogy and the particular terms of the critical debate on the symbolic identification of the kindly gentleman as the "perfect father image" as set forth in Male's seminal analysis.[22]

Male suggests that "clues to the meaning of [Robin's] nightmarish evening are supplied by the Freudian theory of dream interpretation, which asserts that visions of the father figure may commonly split into two or more images" (p. 49). These images manifest themselves in the various figures of male authority that Robin encounters: the elderly gentleman who repeatedly utters "two successive hems," the watchman who frightens Robin away from the whore in the scarlet petticoat, and so on, including the satanic figure of the "double-faced fellow," whose "infernal visage" symbolizes the "dual aspect of this psychic conflict," namely, the "young man's yearnings for freedom from authority and for a worldly patrimony."[23] Male claims that the "grotesque fusion" of the two sides of the man's face "is a distorted father image in which *youthful misrepresentation* of both the real father and the real uncle are combined" (pp. 50–51; my italics). That is, Robin's imputed hostility to his father is at some level a distortion.

At this point in Male's reading a countercurrent is established: "As the evening wears on, the bewildering shades of the false father are gradually counterbalanced by more reliable visions" (p. 51). "Robin imagines," continues Male, "how this evening has been spent in his own household" (i.e., his father's household); Robin's reminiscence is of "the real father, the man who gave his son half the remnant of last year's salary so that the youth could seek his fortune in the city." But after this dreamy reverie, Robin is "again beset by ambiguities" until he is "awakened" by "another image of the true father"; this gentleman Hawthorne describes as "in his prime, of open, intelligent, cheerful, and altogether prepossessing countenance." The "fatherly" stranger becomes a "kindly guide," who offers "a clue to the bewildering shapes of the town" when he suggests that a man may "have several voices, Robin, as well as two complexions." Basically, then, Male's reading is, like Crews's and Pearce's, positive. Robin finds in the shadowy stranger his symbolic ego model, a true father-figure, one who seems to be in calm control of the ambiguities of the world.

Male accepts the idea of hostility to the father but modifies that to include the idea of adolescent distortion. I would go a bit further. The idea of actual "hostility" to the "real father" is *nowhere* indicated in the text. Male's provocative idea that the first "authority" figure Robin meets in the town (the elderly gentleman) "grotesquely personifies the youth's rebellion against pietistic parental authority" (p. 49) is based solely on the fact that Robin's father was a minister and the idea that "in the past Robin had listened *wearily* to his father's homilies" (my italics). Left out is the fact that Robin now regards his father's homilies as "among his dear remembrances" (3:632; *T&S*, 80). Does being bored by sermons and platitudes from one's elders indicate "hostility"? Rohrberger, we remember, characterizes Robin's attitude as "essentially hostile"; but Hawthorne's actual text says that Robin thought of his father as a "good man" (3:682; *T&S*, 80). Robin also associates his father's sermons with "golden light" shining in the western clouds, in marked contrast with the pervasive obfuscating moonlight of Robin's nightmare adventure away from home. Whatever the framing irony, Robin pictures his father tenderly at "domestic worship" and sentimentally as having a "slight inequality" in his voice when he came to speak of the absent family member. When the door-latch clinks down and Robin feels "excluded from his home" (Hawthorne's words), is it because he has been "rejected" by his father or because Robin feels isolated, lonely, insecure, and confused on this strange evening away from the hearth?[24] Is Robin's reverie not instead an image of home as benevolent and protective? When, under the benevolence of his uncle's favorable intentions, Robin thinks it "high time to begin the world," his father generously gives him "*half* the remnant of his last year's salary" (3:635; *T&S*, 82; my italics). Is this "rejection," Oedipal hostility? Would that we all were sent by our parents out into the world to make our own way with such provision.

Nevertheless, the Oedipal "allegory" or dream pattern is as powerfully *suggestive* as the mythic night journey and dream patterns and the political allegory in the rest of the tale. It is obvious that Robin does encounter a series of authority figures, themselves in rebellion against other authority figures, and that Robin is in quest (however ambivalent) of some kind of paternalistic assistance. And the behavior of the kindly gentleman toward Robin (however ironic) may certainly be described on one level as "fatherly." Pearce, while assuming a psychoanalytic (Oedipal) basis for understanding the tale, seeks what he considers a larger meaning — beyond the psychological but based upon it, in historical symbolization of a social-moral content.

"In Adam's Fall": From Psychoanalysis to Moral Historicism; or, Myth, Regeneration, and Progress Reconsidered

Pearce observes that the psychoanalytic approach is too restricted: "Hawthorne's Robin is Mr. Lesser's and a good deal more. For Hawthorne's Robin is not merely freed to become an adult (perhaps he will, perhaps he won't; we aren't told at the end)." Hawthorne's tale also "projects a created world—not just a single figure" (*Historicism*, pp. 100–102). The larger meaning intended by the author, says Pearce, is "historical," not merely psychological. At the very least, the "pseudo-historicity of the tale" must be "taken into account" (p. 100), for "every red-blooded American should recognize . . . something like the Boston Tea Party"; that is, American readers will recognize in Robin's adventure something like a mythologized historical context. So far, so good. But then Pearce says: "*Hence*, Robin in achieving his maturity is, unconsciously, an agent of *progress*" (my italics). Pearce writes: "The concern of the story is not just Robin's struggles to free himself from authority, but also the implications of that struggle—with all its ambiguous, fearful, nightmarish quality and its hesitating doubt—for his future as a member of the society for whom he is surrogate and/or icon, and thus of the future of that society itself" (p. 101).

So "history" for Pearce is a special kind of history—at least American history is, for it implies teleological social "progress." To get to the "moral" level of that "progress," we have to recover the "history" embedded in the tale. Pearce's first critical move is to identify two historical personages in the tale. One is William Molineux of Boston, leader of *anti*-Loyalist mobs. The other is another "celebrated mob-leader," one "Joyce, Jr." (an assumed name of one of the organizers of anti-Loyalist dissension). But there are some major problems with this assuringly solid, and seemingly innocent, opening historical maneuver.[25] Most obviously, one might wonder how an *anti*-Loyalist historical Molineux becomes the victimized *Loyalist* Molineux of Hawthorne's story.

This "inversion" Pearce accounts for as follows: (1) there were at least *two* Molineux figures known in Boston history; and (2) William Molineux was interpreted in *two* different ways by his contemporaries depending on whether they were dissenters sympathetic to his anti-Loyalist cause or were Tories antagonistic to him. For Pearce, the fact that William Molineux was known as a rebel is not a problem; Hawthorne simply "transformed" him into a Loyalist for the tale. But Pearce fails to explain clearly why a writer would use a little-known historical figure "backwards" and not care whether his readers caught the inversion. Surely a writer as historically careful as Pearce claims Hawthorne is would have a reason for inverting the allusion. Pearce's oblique answer is that Hawthorne was deliberately alluding to what Pearce "ventures" to "posit" was an existing "Molineux legend." Hawthorne's purpose was to invert the political orientation of the historical Molineux for purposes of symbolic conjunction of Loyalist and anti-Loyalist causes. This three-step critical maneuver is ingenious if logically suspect, especially since there are almost no indications of a "Molineux legend."[26]

Hawthorne was specifically historical, says Pearce, not only in his naming of the Major, but also in the description of the satanic, double-faced figure; even his "parti-color face" is a specific reference to "Joyce, Jr." Pearce fails, however, to tell us why "Joyce, Jr." is *not* also transformed, like Molineux, to stand for the reverse of *his* historical representation — or how we are to know that one allusion is inverted and another to be taken straight. I would in fact welcome evidence of dialogical conflation in this figure — especially as the personification of generalized Jacksonian Era mob violence — but it is hard to see its patterning in the tale. Rather it is the critic who is in this instance providing the dialogical from outside the text. Nevertheless, the large point of Pearce's major stratagem is clear: the two Molineuxes are *symbolically one* (p. 141); their oneness represents the positive and the negative sides of the conflict. Thus Robin comes to know his oneness with his kinsman. How such symbolism actually functions in the figure of the tarred and feathered Molineux of Hawthorne's tale Pearce does not precisely say, nor how the nondissenting youth comes to know his dual nature through his nondissenting uncle (except by the assertion of extratextual implication). Pearce's concerns are, again, larger: we are informed that the "Molineux theme" was a "primary interest, perhaps *the* primary interest, of the young Hawthorne" (p. 146).

If this "Molineux theme" is a bit vague and shape-shifting, one fairly clear statement of it involves the "imputation" of simultaneous right and wrong (or simultaneous "guilt and righteousness") "through history." That is, a moral rightness-and-wrongness on both sides of an issue is revealed by history, or is discovered through historical investigation and interpretation, dramatized in Hawthorne's fiction. Pearce writes: "Something like Original Sin becomes the prime fact of our political and social history. Adam's Fall and the Idea of Progress become not two myths but one" (p. 141). With this part of his thesis (however labeled) I have no quarrel. Indeed, the implication that the Fall is *re*enacted in episodes of "progress" underscores Hawthorne's skeptical perspective.

But Pearce's explanation for the simultaneous emplotment of the myths of fall and progress takes a direction not justified by the text (nor, I would say, by the corpus of Hawthorne's work). It is once again a little obliquely put: "the argument of the tale" is that if we are "to become more than we are, we must destroy something in ourselves, then we cannot forget what it is we destroy. The tale exists to tell us. The two Molineuxes are one" (p. 141). All this is a complicated way of indicating the *Felix Culpa* theme. Pearce even calls it this, once, later on (p. 157); and it is a governing theme in his essay on *The Marble Faun* and the "twilight of romance." But Pearce seemingly forgets that the sculptor, Kenyon, puts the idea of the Fortunate Fall as a "perplexity": "Here comes my perplexity. . . . Is sin, then, — which we deem such a dreadful blackness in the universe, — is it, like sorrow, merely an element of human education, through which we struggle to a higher and purer state than we could otherwise have attained? Did Adam fall, that we might ultimately rise to a far loftier paradise than his?"[27] It should be superfluous to observe that the idea is put as a question. Perhaps it is not superfluous to note that the question is not answered.[28]

Pearce, however, is fully committed to the ultimately positive and didactic view of the great myth of Fortunate Fall for both self and world (or at least American) history. Because the theme of a fall is "central in all of Hawthorne's fiction," one's "coming into the world is coming into evil," and "knowledge of the world is knowledge of evil"; but "knowledge is life," and "life is good," if "tragic" (*Historicism*, p. 182). Pearce's interpretation, then, is that the story centrally enacts the symbolic drama of Robin Molineux's coming to self-knowledge by "inevitably" destroying and driving away "himself, or part of himself." But such exorcism is "not as a means of categorizing and putting away . . . incidents out of our past, but rather as a means of knowing, identifying with, and accepting those incidents and that past" (p. 140). The didacticism is self-evident: Hawthorne's use of history in his fiction (somehow) instructs us how to be better people by (somehow) facing up to our past and our obligations to the future.

Stemming from the idea of the American Adam and the burden of Original Sin, the key to Pearce's analysis is moral and philosophical "guilt." Mob violence, reenacting Original Sin, symbolizes mob guilt. Against universal guilt Hawthorne pits individual freedom. That is, a major part of the chain of argument has to do with the symbolic (or even unconscious) relationship of Robin and the crowd of American townsmen "patriots." Pearce tries to accommodate Lesser's view that Robin unconsciously senses the crowd wants to free itself of the authority that "old man Molineux" represents. (As Rohrberger puts it, the crowd symbolizes and acts out the youth's repressed impulses to assert his freedom from the father.) Pearce takes the link between Robin and the crowd in a slightly different direction: the crowd represents the new (emerging, rebellious) nation, as Q. D. Leavis argues. But Molineux, says Pearce, "for all that we and Robin know, is totally innocent of the things for which he is tormented and destroyed." (Pearce is in the habit of speaking of the "destruction" of Molineux and even at times of Robin.) "The crowd is thus guilty. Robin shares their guilt" (p. 101). Guilt is the "price" Robin must pay for his "freedom."

Obviously, there are a number of jumps, gaps, and historical dislocations in all this, the most pertinent of which is perhaps the idea of freedom (or liberty). What freedom? In a passage already quoted, Pearce tells us that Robin is "not freed" to become an adult: "perhaps he will, perhaps he won't; *we aren't told.*" (my italics). Pearce's astute observation in this is more textually precise than those of either the "triumph" critics or the "defeat" critics. The tale is dialogical on this point; perhaps Robin (and his people) will, or will not, come to understand and experience liberty. And yet the main point remains for Pearce that "guilt is explicitly the fundamental aspect of Robin's relation to his world" (p. 100), which, for Pearce, constitutes mature, adult responsibility for both the individual self and the about-to-be-born American nation.

The didacticism of such a positive, allegorical, historical concept of moral romance may be questioned on grounds other than logical consistency. Rohrberger's analysis, for example, leads her to conclude that Hawthorne considered the "unprincipled and violent" colonists "hardly fit for the exercise of self-government." The townspeople and Robin symbolically mirror each other: "through analogy with Robin, the colonists are revealed as being inept, insecure, and unready for self-regulation." Although Robin calls himself a shrewd youth, "he shows little shrewdness in his dealings with the townspeople. He is the country boy who is, by turns, ill at ease and suspicious." Moreover, his "inability to make his own way, and, by analogy, the colonists' unreadiness to govern themselves are shown by Robin's ready acceptance of another guardian, the kindly gentleman, who, at the end of the story, directs and controls Robin's behavior" (p. 33). It is not clear to what extent the kindly gentleman actually controls Robin's behavior or on what level. Nevertheless, her basic position that the colonials come in for heavy criticism in the structure of the tale, and that the kindly stranger plays *some* kind of interpretative, mediating role, seems hardly open to question. But her sense of Robin's (and the emerging nation's) new dependence is the opposite of Pearce's sense of individual and national maturity.

Pearce's attempt to merge binaries (characters, allusions, structures, themes, moral-historicism and psychoanalysis) into "one" would seem to reflect a New-Critical impulse to reconcile the contesting elements of the implicit dialogicity of Hawthorne's tale. Except possibly for the desire for final resolution, the general impulse to see conflictual or contradictory aspects as part of one whole seems to me to be aesthetically right. In a note appended in 1968 to "Robin Molineux on the Analyst's Couch," Pearce takes cognizance of various psychoanalytic readings other than Lesser's and cites that of Frederick Crews as the "most sensitive and subtle" of them (p. 106). Yet, Pearce complains, even "he too" is "committed to the psychoanalytic critic's either/or as regards a 'psychological' as against a moral-historical interpretation of the story." With a few differences, this is a point I should like to emphasize in the next phase of the discussion, where implicit binarial thinking takes a new turn. Without accepting or rejecting uncritically the psychoanalytic readings, or Pearce's moral-historical reading, we need not fall into thinking in categories of exclusivity — concluding that the story is *either* this *or* that.[29]

"A Local Habitation and a Name": A Rehistoricized Detective Story; or, the Roman à Clef Revisited

In a sense, this *either/or* critical conflict is the starting point as well as the conclusion of Michael Colacurcio's entire study, *The Province of Piety*. One-half of Colacurcio's framing thesis would seem to derive directly from Pearce: the "moral historicism" of Hawthorne's tales presents righteousness and guilt simultaneously. But he comes to a conclusion opposite that of Pearce. Rather than dramatizing, within duality, the "moral" of historical social progress, Colacurcio's Hawthorne presents a doubly ironic "deconstruction" of the emerging religio-national mythos.

Yet in his own way, Colacurcio also takes what appears to be an almost absolutist *either/or* stand, the oppositional terms of which are the moral-historical reading (in the singular) and the mythic-oneiric readings of "My Kinsman, Major Molineux." Essentially rejecting the latter as incompetent, irrelevant, or distortive, he takes the historical aspect of the moral-historical analysis a good deal further than Pearce does. What Pearce calls the "pseudo-history" of the tale Colacurcio is at pains to demonstrate is careful historiography. It is, for him, very specific and accurate fictionalized historiography — which forms an almost one-to-one allegory of fictional character, event, and place with historical characters, events, places. In effect, Colacurcio's analysis makes the tale a rehistoricized literary detective story. In trying to identify the "real world" historical counterparts of every event and every person in the tale, he reduces (at least in this instance) the chief interest of the narrative to that of a roman à clef. Crucial to the argument is his identification of the exact time and place of the narrative events and of the "kindly stranger."

Colacurcio observes that the "historical locus" of "My Kinsman, Major Molineux" is "unarguably more obvious" than that, say, of "Roger Malvin's Burial." The Molineux narrative has a "proleptic" relation to the American Revolution, an event that at "its fifty-year anniversary celebration in 1826" was "altogether more famous than the original doings (or memorial sayings) at Lovewell's Rock." On the other hand, the distinctively literary aspect of the tale has generated a critical history that can "fairly be described as the dialogue created by a series of more or less elegant attempts to set it free from its historical moorings" (pp. 130–31). Most critics, Colacurcio suggests, have mistakenly felt that the meaning of the story is somehow totally self-contained in an archetypal reenactment of a rite of passage. He writes that to them "the sequence of Robin's night-time confrontations . . . seems regulated by some absolutely universal law of growing up. It is as if the entire genre of *bildungsroman* could be epitomized in the single evening of ambiguity and weariness of some Provincial Everyman . . ." (p. 131). But the "problem of 'Molineux,' " he says, is different from that of "Roger Malvin's Burial." Whereas with "Malvin" it seems that "*only* some fairly sophisticated form of historicism can fairly comprehend all the tales' arcane references and adequately unify its fictional logic," with "Molineux" the critical "problem is evidently to show that *any* form of historicism is supple enough to avoid reduction."

Nevertheless, the historical setting does "very intensely matter," and "even the staunchest 'myth critic' " has to acknowledge that "Molineux" is "pointedly" historical and particular. "To be sure," he adds, "Hawthorne's prosy headnote seems to call us off from too detailed an investigation of the local history of Boston in the earlier eighteenth century," but "surely the anti-historical signal may be entirely ironic, as are the similar gestures at the beginning of 'Malvin.' " Perhaps, "as Roy Harvey Pearce long ago suggested . . . Hawthorne means to alert the reader to the sort of language or habits of perception that have erased all real ugliness from the historical memory" (pp. 131–33). Colacurcio then goes on to suggest the ways in which the tale deconstructs the emergent national mythos, represented by Fourth of July patriotic rhetoric, which, by thrusting certain particulars into the shadows, makes the revolutionary history of America into a popular romance.

He does, in fact, overwhelmingly demonstrate that the historical level of the tale does, as he says, "mean *something*." He recapitulates the historical basis of "Molineux" identified by previous critics and accepts (rather uncritically) Pearce's thesis of a Molineux legend and the identification of the mob leader with the double face as Joyce, Jr. Although this impulse to identify the personages of the tale with historical persons leads to some questionable interpretative judgments, Colacurcio also makes some especially cogent interpretative observations about the date of the events of the story. Building on the discoveries of some neglected critics, he constructs an argument that reveals the precise date to be surprisingly important. The events *seem* to be those of the Stamp Act riots immediately prior to the Revolution; but, as we have seen, Hawthorne's narrator specifically states that "the following adventures . . . chanced upon a summer night, not far from a hundred years ago." Part of Colacurcio's overarching thesis is that Hawthorne does not alter historical events to suit his tales; and to the extent that Colacurcio avoids restricting Hawthorne's tale to the *either/or* proposition of myth or dream versus history, his critical approach is refreshing. He simply asks: why not accept Hawthorne's dating? Assuming that Hawthorne does in fact mean to set the tale some forty-five years before the Revolution, what evidence for this date is there in the tale and what is its significance?

Among other things, the currency that Robin and the ferryman exchange suggests the "rum riot" years of the 1730s, generated by the Molasses Act of 1733.[30] Colacurcio suggests that the economic history of the Revolution might well begin with the Molasses Act, which was renewed and made "perpetual" in 1764. This event was on the eve of the extension of the British Stamp Act to the American colonies in 1765, the coincidence of which resulted in the formation of the Sons of Liberty and the intensification of those activities that led to the Boston Massacre and the Boston Tea Party. The Molasses Act, which compelled rum distillers and dealers to buy molasses from British colonies in the West Indies, was met by popular protests in a foretaste of the Stamp Act violence. In particular, Colacurcio points out, it accelerated the depreciation of paper money (lamented by Governor Hutchinson); Hawthorne is thus making a "learned" connection between the "sexangular piece of parchment" that Robin receives "as change from the ferryman and the tavern cheer he cannot afford to purchase" (p. 565n.). Hawthorne makes it quite specific that this "tavern cheer" is a bowl of rum punch, brewed from materials to be associated for the next half-century with the Molasses Act. In Hawthorne's story, the tavern goers are "draining as many bowls of punch, which the [great] West India trade had long since made a familiar drink in the colony" (3:621; *T&S*, 71). The narrator adds that "nearly all, in short, evinced a predilection for the Good Creature in some of its various shapes" and suggests that this predilection is a vice to which Americans "have a long hereditary claim." Insisting once again on the precise date, Hawthorne's narrator says that this "claim" is testified to by the Fast Day sermons "of a hundred years ago."

For Colacurcio, Hawthorne's depiction of a 1730s rum riot as if predictive or "proleptic" of the famous Boston Tea Party of 1773 and the American Revolution of 1776 constitutes a subtle but thorough debunking of the romantically heightened typological significance of the events.[31] Rather than a glorious fulfillment of Protestant Destiny in the New World, this turning point in American history is typologically symbolized in Hawthorne's story by a neutral depiction of an unruly people in a partially debased cause. Even Robin's dreamlike reverie in which he asks himself the question "Am I here, or there?" becomes indicative of the debunkery of patriotic symbolism. Is the country youth "here," witnessing a forgettable rum riot in the 1730s, or is the representative youth "there," witnessing the same pattern of behavior just preceding the glorious American Revolution? Colacurcio extends this ambiguity to the reader: ". . . surely one major effect of the story is to leave the reader wondering, uncertainly, whether he is 'here' in a minor episode of provincial unruliness or 'there' in the glory and chaos of full revolt" (p. 134). Perhaps, he says, "this cardinal ambiguity of setting" is "somehow the clue" to a more proper interpretation than that of Leavis or Pearce. "What if," Colacurcio asks, "Hawthorne were perceiving that the American Revolution were *not*, or did not *necessarily* enfigure itself as, some inevitable rite of national passage? If so, then the tale of Robin Molineux is more ironic than we have yet supposed, its patriotism more bitter . . ." (p. 134).

Like others before him, Colacurcio suggests that the "Hutchinson Mob" episode from *The Whole History of Grandfather's Chair* glosses the political situation of "Kinsman." He refers us to the child Laurence's reaction in the "Boston Massacre" section (part 3, ch. 5), which reads: " 'The Revolution,' observed Laurence, who had said but little during the evening, 'was not such a calm, majestic movement as I supposed. I do not love to hear of mobs and broils in the street. These things were unworthy of the people when they had such a great object to accomplish' " (4:595). What Colacurcio does not point out is that the passage contrasts Laurence's romanticism with a disappointing historical reality, even though that romanticism, in this instance, constitutes the subjective moral-ethical basis of judgment, and the ugly reality its presumably objective referent. Romanticizing the typological destiny of America leads to the sacrifice of individual living beings upon the altar of abstraction.

Colacurcio presses the contrast between the romanticized version of American destiny and some more complex Hawthornesque reality. Stressing the word *majestic* in Laurence's speech, he writes that "nowhere . . . have the convulsive events of the American 1760's and 1770's" been made to appear "more simply and calmly majestic than in the public oratory which marked the semi-centennial celebrations of 1826" (p. 135). But the events were recorded in a much different way in Hutchinson's *History of Massachusetts Bay*, the work referred to in the opening paragraph of Hawthorne's tale. Colacurcio perceives Hutchinson as perceiving a "slow but perceptible drift toward criminal violence" in America, which in effect became a "fatal constitutional error" of democracy. No one wanted to hear of mobocracy; everyone wanted to hear "that the Revolution had been a major event in Holy History." In "the Cosmic Progress toward a Universal Salvation in Holy Liberty, it figured only slightly less important than the Birth of Christ and the Protestant Reformation, whose libertarian meaning it essentially

fulfilled" (p. 136). But Hawthorne was "striking back at the flagrant idola-
tries of America's pseudo-Puritan civil religion: in the face of a nearly
overwhelming national consensus in favor of the holy-historical significance of 1776, Hawthorne is studying the majestic Revolution in terms of a
minor outbreak of provincial unruliness, a mob scene" (p. 136). Was the
Revolution the "completion of the Divine Plot so long preparing, the final
unveiling of God's own historico-literary *majestas?* Or just another local
anxiety, one more utterly 'temporary inflammation of the popular mind' —
predictably violent and relentlessly ordinary?" Such, says Colacurcio, is the
"irony and insult" of the historical headnote. If the "epistemology of the
tale" is "remotely 'typological,'" it is so "only in some negative or ironic
mode."[32]

After this persuasive reading of the historical events (Hawthorne "relentlessly reduces Apocalypse to rum riot"), Colacurcio becomes highly
speculative, even as he appears to become more factual. Having firmly
associated the literal events of the tale with a 1730s rum riot, Colacurcio
wants also thematically to tie the tale more tightly to Hutchinson and the
1770s. Hutchinson saw the colony as having "the wrong sense" of its
relation to England: the colonists mistakenly saw the legitimate laws and
restrictions imposed upon them from the mother country as an invasion of
their rights, liberties, and properties. Although Hutchinson thought these
restrictions unwise (because imposed without representation of the colonies in Parliament), he favored strict enforcement of the law. His legalistic
attitude made him unpopular, leading to the aforementioned ransacking of
his house by a mob in 1765 after the extension of the Stamp Act. His
punctilious adherence to the letter of the law did little to mitigate the
increasing dissension that resulted (in 1770) in the Boston Massacre and,
during his term as colonial governor (1771–1774), the Boston Tea Party
(1773). But Hutchinson was inclined to be generous in his appraisal of his
contemporaries, and he looked to the similar situation of Ireland for extenuating circumstances. He observed that the Americans were not alone in
their erroneous understanding of their governmental relations, for Ireland
presented the examples of the coalescence of political views of John Locke
and a "Mr. Molineux." Colacurcio develops at some length (cf. Doubleday,
Abernathy, Franzosa) the possible relevance of this Irish William Molineux
in a way that is almost as confusing (vis-à-vis Hawthorne's tale) as that of
Pearce. The American Molineux, like and unlike the Irish Molineux, like
and unlike Pearce's Molineux, somehow is and somehow is not a loyalist, is
and is not in some way involved in conspiracy. (Would that these ironic and
dialogic conflations were so *in* the text.)

Having identified the name "Molineux" to his satisfaction, Colacurcio

addresses the name "Robin," which, he asserts, "itself is scarcely an innocent name in the lexicon of eighteenth-century political conspiracy"
(p. 140), for it suggests "Robinocracy," a term associated with Lord Bolingbroke and a so-called "Robin" Walpole. Historically, the *Robinarch* is a false
priest or minister who has usurped power.[33] Just how young Robin of
Hawthorne's tale stands for or is to be associated with such a cluster of
political ideas Colacurcio never makes fully clear, and the critical confusion
is much like that around the significance of the name "Molineux." What is
clear, however, is that Robin is, as Colacurcio says, painfully initiated into
the politics of conspiracy.

Other more pertinent identifications of place and person follow, although some interpretive confusion remains. Colacurcio observes that
the gentleman of the "two sepulchral hems" inaugurates the *"political
irony"* of Robin's reference to the man with "authority" as "some country
representative" (p. 142). "Almost certainly," writes Colacurcio, betraying
the uncertainty, "the authoritative gentleman" that Robin encounters is "a
'Representative' in the intransigent local 'Parliament,'" who stands for
"the values and interests of the resistance, the 'Country Party.'" "Quite
probably," he adds, the authoritative gentleman "is the Speaker of the
Massachusetts House of Representatives." The evidence is perhaps a bit
soft: the "hem-hem" attribute suggests the man is clearing his throat as if
about to make a speech. The absurdity is appealing but hardly conclusive—
although the point gains force from being a necessary part of a chain of
systematic identifications, which depend one upon the other. For "only that
position," Colacurcio argues, "would seem to justify" the reappearance of
the figure "at the climax of Robin's political initiation" (p. 142) on the
balcony of the building where the House of Representatives deliberated
(and apparently slept).

This interpretation sounds as if it is based on the solid ground of textual
and historical fact: that is, the building *is* the legislative house and not, as it
is usually taken to be, the Province House of the royal magistrates. This
identification, however, is part of an aggressive hermeneutic. The identification of the figure depends in part on the identification of the building,
which depends in part on the identification of the figure—all within a
specific, historical *interpretation* of the story.[34] I do not object to the possibility of such an interpretation (it is rather proleptically brilliant), but it is
misleadingly presented as not only historical but factual; and it generates
questions Colacurcio leaves unanswered. What, for instance, in the heated
atmosphere of the tale, is the political connection of the country youth and
his family to the aristocratic town-dwelling loyalist, Major Molineux? Why,
if the major is courtly and anti-country (Colacurcio says the Speaker of the

House is his "deepest official enemy"), does the country father send his country son to seek their urban and courtly kinsman, *especially* if times they are a'changin'? Do Molineux's ambiguous country connections make him even *more* the victim of irrational mobocracy? If the gentleman of the two hems represents the "country" resistance, why does he rebuff the "country" youth so rudely? He responds "in a tone of excessive anger and annoyance" (3:619; *T&S*, 70) to Robin's admittedly ill-timed query about the dwelling of his kinsman, Major Molineux, even though he could clearly see that Robin is from the "country." The first words of the innkeeper to Robin, after all, are: "From the country, I presume, sir?" (3:622; *T&S*, 72).

When the gentleman of the sepulchral hems angrily tells Robin, "I have authority, I have — hem, hem — authority" (3:619; *T&S*, 70), it is not at all clear by *what* authority he threatens Robin with the stocks for the poor "respect" that Robin shows "his betters." His statement sounds more like urban elitism than country — or colonialist — democracy. (But if we accept Colacurcio's identification, the authoritarian attitude gives the scene one more ironic turn.) It is also important to note that it is the "shrewd" Robin who *guesses* that the man is "some country representative" (3:619; *T&S*, 70). He may not be that at all; the text shrewdly does not tell us. Thus Colacurcio is on shaky ground in accepting (of all people) *Robin's* designation, especially in a narrative as heavily ironic as Colacurcio takes it to be. Robin's possibly "wrong" guess may have the effect of leading the accompanying reader down a wrong street in the maze. As to the clinching evidence of the gentleman's appearing on the balcony of the building across from the church later, it is by no means clear what building Robin faces. All is left deliberately confused in this "evening of ambiguity" (3:632; *T&S*, 80).

Let us explore further the problem of specificity of topography in Hawthorne's tale. For Colacurcio, the secret historical identities of the characters and thus their symbolic meanings are interwoven with the symbolic function of place (especially of buildings); and these identifications lead to an unusual identification of the "kindly stranger" at the end.

Using the "Bonner Map" of 1722, printed as the frontispiece in Warden's *Boston*, Colacurcio plots the likely route of "the Molineux procession." Colacurcio is not the first critic to map out the final action of the story; and in fact he pointedly disagrees with Julian Smith's identification of the spot where Robin is waiting with the kindly stranger. Smith suggests the steps of the Old South Church, across from the Province House, the royal governor's mansion from 1717 until the Revolution. But Smith, Colacurcio says, is "all-too-certain" about his facts.[35] Colacurcio offers instead another corner as "equally consistent" (but which becomes an all-too-certain identification as well). He puts the scene of the Molineuxes' humiliation at a preceding intersection: ". . . the Molineux procession advances down King Street, from the Long Wharf, turns a corner where the First Church and the Town House face each other, and sweeps on down Cornhill Street to a meeting at the Old South" (p. 569 n.100). The symbolic significance of the buildings between which Robin finds himself is thereby different from what Smith proposes. *Rather than* the conservative Old South, we have First Church, stronghold of colonialist sympathies; *rather than* the royal Province House, we have the dissident legislative Town House.

But it seems to me that the ambiguity of the thematically "equally consistent" corners works with fine irony both ways. Robin in both instances is caught in a complex conflict between church and state, mother country and emergent nation, that transcends his understanding. The ambiguous setting spatially as well as temporally symbolizes the "mazed world" in which one "knows not which is which." In the one instance, Robin appears to be between Old South Church and the governor's mansion, representing Anglican-Tory loyalty and the authority of the king; in the other, he appears to be between First Church and the legislative building of democratically elected representatives of the people. Thus Robin's question "Am I here, or there?" is central — as is the whole question of his "awakening." The uncertainty of whether Robin is facing the Province House or the Legislative House suggests more than the uncertainty of his own potential political orientation. It forcibly suggests his huge unawareness of the political issues swirling about him and his naive ignorance of the very nature of the "actuality" through which he wanders. Is human actuality in any sense objective? Is it all subjectively constituted? In a sense, the specific place does not matter to the dynamics of the tale. In another sense, the uncertainty even of *a physical spot* (as in "Alice Doane's Appeal," as we shall see) is almost the symbolic perfection of the "evening of ambiguity."

That is why Colacurcio's tacit assumption that his corner is *more* than "equally consistent," and his consequent identification of the kindly stranger *as a minister of First Church*, goes against his astute critical premise of the importance of identifying the *essential ambiguity* of the historical foundations of the tale. What Hawthorne does is to play one thing off against another, evoking "a local habitation and a name" and subverting them simultaneously. Perhaps it is in this sense that the conflicting historical associations of the name "Molineux" make aesthetic sense. Is it this Molineux, or some other Molineux? Are the dissidents tormenting the enemy, or one of their own? Can one tell the difference? What we *can* assent to without much qualification is Colacurcio's interpretation that Robin has "blundered his way" into the center of an action entirely independent of his personal anxieties and with which he has only accidentally to do — and that therefore the elaborate interpretations of the psychoanalytic-moral-historical-progressivist allegory of the narrative are "all-too-certain" regarding Robin's (and America's) midsummer night's eve.

At the least it should be clear that whatever the mythic resonances of the ritualistic frenzied dance around the "dead potentate," the picture is hardly a "patriotic" endorsement of the American Revolution. If anything, it is a picture of those emotional "awakenings," both political and religious, of the 1730s and 1740s that erupted into erratic, half-insane public conversions and mob violence, replicated later at the time of the American Revolution. In this context, then, the tale is also a dubious pseudoallegory of America's Great Awakening, with all the ironies attendant to that association. A paradoxical mixture of personal and political motives, of the psychological and the sociological, is presented from the inner perspective of a naive youth's first encounter with the reality of the outside world. And its arrogance, mendaciousness, and violence are also mirrored, in one degree or another, inside the young man himself. In that sense, the narrative is not a mythic underworld journey *versus* a psychoanalytic coming of age *versus* a moral-historical political allegory. Robin's experience is a symbolic descent into an inner and outer hell, where mythic night-journey, psychological self-confrontation, and absurd political reality fuse into one, generating Robin's self-mocking, self-defensive laugh of quasi-recognition and the reader's recognition of the "mazed" world of life and literary texts. As Colacurcio writes, "the procession of political events simply moves on, as unconcerned about Robin's maturity as it is unthreatened by his politics" (p. 144). The predictive independence theme is debunked ("proleptically"), and the progressivist historical-allegory reading comes tumbling down even as it is erected. The tale is a negative allegory.

The "Concord of this Discord": Narrative of the Kindly Stranger

The question is not *whether* Hawthorne is a historical writer but to what extent historical events, persons, and places are employed and to what end. As Frederick Crews says in defense of his own method (and in criticism of the historicist and mythic critics), "the pertinent question for criticism is *how far* outside the literal plot of this tale we must go in order to make sense of it" (p. 73). Colacurcio finally displaces the literary significations of the story, or at least marginalizes them to an unacceptable degree. He tends to privilege a certain kind of narrow, literary historicism, deconstructing the aesthetic.[36] By Colacurcio's own announced principles and amply demonstrated critical insights, the historical and the aesthetic are not mutually exclusive; but he recurrently makes them so even while acknowledging the deliberate ambiguity of the story. The tale invites historical allegorical interpretation but also resists it, just as it invites and resists mythic and psychological allegory. Colacurcio sees this dialogical effect until he finds his own allegorical "key."

On such topographical and political "evidence" as detailed above, Colacurcio's final speculation is that the stranger is not only *a* minister but in fact one of two historical personages: Jonathan Mayhew, who died in 1766, or, more likely, Charles Chauncey, pastor of First Church (Congregational) for sixty years from 1727 to 1787, a staunch supporter of the American "patriot" cause, leader of the dissident ministers opposed to imposition of bishops in America by the British. Thus, in Colacurcio's symbolic tableau we find the following. On the balcony of the building across the street stands the Speaker of the House of Representatives, the leader of the dissident "Country Party," laughing at a young Robin also from the country. Leading the tar-and-feather brigade is Joyce, Jr., well-known dissident mob leader, who also laughs at the ignorance of a country youth. Frightened but dignified in his agony is a William Molineux, urban Tory representative of the king, who yet has kinship ties with the country, whose name also suggests a merchant of Boston, who is a political dissident, with an Irish kinsman of the same name who is a dissident theorist-activist employing the governmental arguments of John Locke. Beside Robin on the steps of First Church is its minister, Charles Chauncey, leader of the rationalist dissident ministers (who, I may add, were opposed to the harsher doctrines of Calvinism and the emotionalism of the Great Awakening represented by Jonathan Edwards); bemusedly, if inwardly, the minister laughs at the country bumpkin. This interpretation is simultaneously provocative, contradictory, and a little reductive, adding perhaps (in its own way) to what Colacurcio calls the "intolerable critical confusion" surrounding the tale.[37]

Nevertheless, Colacurcio's fundamental reading of the ironies of the tale seems (as usual) essentially correct, and I regard his position (minus the absolute historical identifications and the dismissals of mythic and psychological readings) as the soundest of the various critical readings. In fact, emboldened by the speculative flights of so thoroughly historicist a critic, I offer my own, literary, identification of the kindly stranger — one, I think, no more unlikely or remote than some already proposed. Given the theme of authorial presence in the *Provincial Tales*, it is as if the unnamed kindly stranger were an embodiment of the "third-person" narrator of the tale, when, at this point, he steps into the story to watch, and watch with, Robin.[38] The mysterious "stranger" offers a sympathetic but bemused comment: Robin could pick himself up, recover his shaken self-confidence, and continue on in the world; the experience is perhaps not quite so portentous and shattering as the youth (or the typical critic) thinks it is. The stranger is, *not Hawthorne*, but a symbolic figuration of, a substitute agent for, a Hawthorne: that is, an *author figure*, symbolically present in the narrative.

By a sure identification of the stranger as Chauncey, Colacurcio makes him a co-conspirator in the night's festivities, rather than just an inhabitant of Boston who knows what is "in the air." The text allows one so to speculate, but it does not definitively support that idea. Notice the dialogical and ironic resonances of the conclusion if the stranger is taken to be (as he is literally in the text) a friendly but knowledgeable observer standing to one side of events — and a symbolic figuration of the author. The stranger is described as a gentleman "of open, intelligent, cheerful, and altogether prepossessing countenance" (3:633; *T&S*, 81). He accosts Robin "in a tone of real kindness, which had become strange to Robin's ears." When Robin asks him about his kinsman, the stranger replies, smiling, "The name is not altogether strange to me." Robin rehearses briefly his personal history, concluding that he has "the name of being a shrewd youth" (3:634; *T&S*, 82). "Good-naturedly," the "friend" replies: "I doubt not you deserve it." When Robin asks if he knows the satanic figure who directed him to wait at the intersection, the stranger replies: "Not intimately . . . but I chanced to meet him a little time previous. . . . In the mean time, as I have a singular curiosity to witness your meeting, I will sit down here upon the steps, and bear you company" (3:635; *T&S*, 82). They hear the noise of shouting growing nearer. When Robin asks what may be "the meaning of this uproar," the stranger says, "Why, indeed, friend Robin, there do appear to be three or four riotous fellows abroad to-night. . . ." The tone is that of the ironic detachment of the Man in the Moon: Oho, Robin, aren't the fellows frolicsome tonight? When Robin observes that what sounds like "one shout" must be composed of "at least a thousand voices," the stranger makes the one statement that comes closest to an authorial "moral," and he puts it in the form of a question: "May not a man have several voices, Robin, as well as two complexions?" (3:636; *T&S*, 83). When Robin tries to leave the scene, the stranger lays hold of the skirt of his gray coat and says: "You forget that we *must* wait here for your kinsman" (my italics). The stranger then asks, pointedly, "Will you recognize your kinsman, if he passes in this crowd?" (3:637; *T&S*, 84). The crowd rolls past. After Robin's "epiphany," the stranger inquires, "Well, Robin, are you dreaming?" (3:640; *T&S*, 86). To Robin's request for directions to the ferry, he responds "with a smile": "You have, then, adopted a new subject of inquiry?" (3:641; *T&S*, 86). And finally, the stranger denies Robin the right to leave town and return home, just yet, and offers the concluding, ironically simple comment: ". . . perhaps, as you are a shrewd youth, you may rise in the world without the help of your kinsman, Major Molineux" (3:641; *T&S*, 87). The point of view of the kindly stranger is, while not at all unsympathetic, rather detached, above all the lunacy, while he yet participates in the drama in an observer's role, throwing in a few "authorial observations" for good effect.

The narratological paradigm would resemble those of the other provincial tales we have been looking at, but with a significant variation. The implied narrative intrusion, wherein the author-narrator is literally absent but figuratively present (paralleling the historical introduction which is then put under erasure), makes explicit the several levels of Robin's experience or "initiation." The presence of the kindly stranger as a symbolic, closing frame-device coalesces at least five hermeneutical levels of figuration for Robin. (That is, the stranger as ironic mediator is the vehicle for the vexed "epiphany" at the end of the tale: for Robin, for the stranger, for the reader.) Robin is simultaneously an overconfident youth initiated into the world's complexities; the naive misperceiver of events, suffering from an oneiric disorientation; a mythic pilgrim to an archetypal underworld; an allegorical initiate into political/historical process; and a partial initiate who when he sees the "political explanation" may or may not see his own foolish confidence and his indeterminate, ambiguous or ambivalent feelings for his "kinsman." Like young Goodman Brown, he may or may not have some comprehension of the final indeterminacy of the whole experience of his Great Awakening to the larger world.

The historical frame introduction, left formally (explicitly) incomplete or open-ended, is by implication reasserted not only in the political "explanation" provided by the tarring and feathering of the major, but also by the presence of the authorial figure. The double framing reveals the reversal of the interior drama of the central perspectival character, Robin. The ending of "My Kinsman" is thereby, on one level, a reversal of the O. Henry type that Hemingway said he could not write. Yet the reader is made to feel an ironic authorial or narrative presence at the end (in the implied closing of the frame), when all is wrapped up in a suspect "moral." It is this twice-told, archetypal, yet personal psychological experience of the initiation of youth into the doubleness of the world that constitutes the main burden of the tale, not some chauvinistic allegory of American independence. The political-allegorical interpretation, taken straight, leads to a woefully inadequate "moral" to the experience rendered in the narrative, much like the parodic moral of "Wakefield" or the romantic-ironic ones of *The Scarlet Letter*. (Cf. Janssen.)

"Molineux" gives us simultaneously both an inside and an outside vision, explicitly at the beginning and implicitly at the end. As in German romantic metafiction and metadrama (any of Jean Paul's novels; Tieck's *The Topsy-turvy World*, 1799; Brentano's *Godwi*, 1801; Hoffmann's "The Sandman," 1816–17), or other of Hawthorne's own works ("The Devil in Manuscript," 1835; "Main Street," 1849; *The Marble Faun*, 1860), the external narrator of "Molineux" seems to step into his story and sit down beside his character to offer an enigmatic comment on the meaning of it all. At the same time that such a strategy heightens the dislocatedness and the dream-effect of the whole tale, it connects "Molineux" to the dream sketches that make up other of the narratives of *Provincial Tales* and recalls the narrator-story-audience relation of "Alice Doane's Appeal." The "shaping" fantasy, the "bodying" imagination, gives to "all the story of the night told over" its "great constancy" howsoever "strange and admirable." The aesthetic level "comprehends" all the other concerns (from mythic to psychological to historical), producing "the concord of this discord."

The suggestion of the symbolic figuration of the storyteller in the kindly stranger becomes more compelling when "My Kinsman, Major Molineux" is seen in the context of other such figurations and literal author presences in Hawthorne's earliest narratives. In the next chapter, we shall look at that most obvious embodiment of authorial presence in the *Provincial Tales*, the tale-within-a-sketch or sketch-surrounding-a-tale, "Alice Doane's Appeal." Authorial presence is in fact the *theme* of "Alice Doane's Appeal," which features a literal storyteller, telling his combined gothic, dreamvision, historical, romance story, over, and over again, to an ambiguous audience. The narrative gives us, deceptively, both full and abrupt closure, depending on whether the reader takes the recounting of a gothic story or the attempt of the storyteller to affect his audience to be the central focus. The ultimate audience is symbolically figured by two "young ladies," whose attention, sympathy, and empathy the storyteller seeks rather desperately to capture. As the author is literally in the text, they, of course, are literalized figures of Hawthorne's reader.

5 The Power of Negative Suggestion: *Alēthēa* and *Apokalypsis* in "Alice Doane's Appeal"

Moonlight, in a familiar room, falling so white upon the carpet, and showing all its figures so distinctly, — making every object so minutely visible, yet so unlike a morning of noontide visibility, — is a medium the most suitable for a romance-writer to get acquainted with his illusive guests. . . . details, so completely seen, are so spiritualized by the unusual light, that they seem to lose their actual substance, and become things of intellect. . . . Thus, therefore, the floor of our familiar room has become a neutral territory, somewhere between the real world and fairyland, where the Actual and the Imaginary may meet, and each imbue itself with the nature of the other. — "The Custom-House" (1850)

Hypocrite lecteur . . .

— Charles Baudelaire, "To the Reader," Preface to *Flowers of Evil* (1857)

The reader will remember that in the opening chapters we had reference to the assessment of Hawthorne's "power of negative suggestion" in the 1855 *Dublin University Magazine*. The reviewer praised Hawthorne's quiet humor and subversion of allegory. He remarked that Hawthorne excelled in a genre or mode "for which we have no definite term as yet": that "most difficult" mode, the "blending of essay, sketch, and tale." In this chapter, I wish to pursue the power of negative suggestion as "negative apocalypse" in the metafictional blending of essay, sketch, and tale in "Alice Doane's Appeal." We find in this narrative an unsettling, nontraditional concept of *apokalypsis*, which, like that of negative allegory, is not only romantic and ironic, but also anticipatory of current deconstructionist views of revelation. Once as critically neglected as "My Kinsman, Major Molineux," the slight but complex "Doane" narrative appeals to current readers precisely because of its ambiguity, its self-reflexive indeterminacy, and its foregrounding of the problems of authorship. Considered for years to be incoherent and embarrassingly revelatory of the artist's own disturbed psyche, the narrative is in fact a remarkable nineteenth-century metafictional treatment, part tale, part sketch, of authorship and the relation between the created fictive world and the historical record of the "real" world. In its simultaneous evocation and subversion of revelation, the narrative brings together the problematized themes of the supernatural, the legendary, providentiality, dreamvision, imagination, fiction, history, truth, provincialism, literature, and historiography that we have seen throughout our exploration of the *Provincial Tales*.

Like *The Story Teller* cycle, "Alice Doane's Appeal" embodies what is one of the most exaggerated effects of authorial presence in Hawthorne's early provincial narratives. Everything bears the stamp of an authorial persona and his concentrated writerly concern with the tension between and interpenetration of fiction and history and the veil of appearances over "truth." The narrative foregrounds the old philosophical problem of inside and outside, the contained and its containing frame. As in other of the *Provincial Tales*, traditionally discrete realms of "reality," such as dreaming and waking, imagination and actuality, blur one into the other—as do conventionally discrete modes of narrative and other discourse.

In part, the problem is an interpreter's insistence on treating a certain order of appearances as truth. We shall with Hawthorne be exploring the relation represented between the Greek words for revelation (*apokalypsis*) and truth (*alēthēa*). Metaphorically, the latter means that which is unfolded (like a warrior's skirt), spread out, without concealing wrinkles or hidden folds in itself. The overall structure of Hawthorne's tale causes two orders of veiled truth to contest each other, not only in the folding but also in the unfolding. The first articulation of the veiling theme in the frame foreshadows the cumulative apocalyptic movement of the whole work. Although the word *apocalypse* generally means in English a prophetic disclosure or revelation, it has been taken by most speakers to mean the "final" revelation, the "end" of the world. The word has come to have this meaning of the last word or of an end-time blueprint from the interpretation of the Millerites and other nineteenth-century millennialists of the Revelation of Saint John in the New Testament. For Hawthorne, the etymological roots are more pertinent: Greek *apokaluptein* = to uncover, unveil, with the hint of a reversal (*apo-*). It is in this sense of a "final" revelation in the narrative as a "reverse veiling" that I use the word, that is, as "negative" revelation in which discovery is always deferred—or the deferral turns out to be the discovery.

Throughout the course of the last chapter I both contested the criticism on "My Kinsman, Major Molineux" and tried to make the critical readings dialogically self-contesting. In this chapter I shall frame "Alice Doane's Appeal" in an initial, separate section on traditional criticism. Critics have had major problems with the gothic elements of the inner narrative and with what they take to be the biographical-psychological implications of the "personalized" historical frame. These misreadings, in fact, uncover for the reader the skillful dialogical structure of the narrative.

While an overview of the interior tale and interpenetrating frame (or vice versa) highlights the dialogicity and metafictional ambiance of the whole work, the opening frame segment especially illustrates the significance and insistence of authorial presence. The first frame also introduces, immediately, the themes of delusion, illusion, and unveiling or unfolding. These themes are constituted in the perceptions of the narrator as an ever-present persona, whose central concerns as a literal "author" are in fact with the interrelated themes of history versus fiction, the conventions of narrative, the veil of appearances, and the "true" meaning of dis/closure.

These themes are cumulatively disclosed in the structural relationships of metafictional interaction and the ironic deployment of narrative conventions in the unfolding sections of the whole. The effect is a moving backwards and forwards simultaneously while progressing toward an apocalyptic vision that both unveils and veils, reveals and conceals. The movement of the narrative is both in and out of the frame/tale and forward toward a combined negative epiphany. Hawthorne's narrative gains a cumulative thematic unity as it moves from an initial act of imaginative vision (inaugurated by the author-narrator) in the opening frame to a fictional dreamvision scene in the interior gothic tale to three sequential, increasingly climactic visionary sections toward the end of the narrative. In these "visions," past, present, and future, imagination and actuality, fiction and history, tale and frame, truth and appearance are all melded together in a final *ellipsis*.

In the interests of concision, I forgo a detailed examination of the elided and ironically manipulated conventions of author-reader collaboration in the interior gothic tale (parallel with the metafictional strategies of the frame). Instead, the coalescence and cumulative import of various visions and epiphanies in both frame and gothic tale are explored in terms of a permanently penultimate *apokalypsis*. One more narrative turn brings to light these themes as they are folded within authorial presence in the work and as they enfold the themes of literature and historiography. That is, *apokalypsis*, *phantasie*, and *alēthēa* reveal the simultaneous (im)permanence of the "monument" of written text and its requisite conventional "moral."[1]

Gothic Discard; or Autobiography of the Forbidden?

The reader will not find it hard to uncover the reason earlier critics tended to dismiss "Alice Doane's Appeal" as a youthful botch. Its seeming incompleteness suggested that Hawthorne thought the "central" gothic story a dead-end and abandoned it, acknowledging his failure in a weak "historical" gesture toward proper denouement. Nothing, it seems to me, could be further from the truth. Such readings mistakenly take the center of the narrative to be an awkwardly summarized gothic tale embedded in the frame narrative for merely conventional gothic effect. Critics assume that Hawthorne so little valued the "original" tale that he half-heartedly summarized it within a biographical frame that only loosely contains it. These assessments entirely miss the significance of the insistent interpenetration of frame and interior tale and the radical continuity that results from disruption of convention and deliberate intergeneric blurring: from the frame narrator's summary of his manuscript tale (containing within it Leonard Doane's summary of his summary narrative to a wizard), to his account of the circumstances of his reading of his tale to two women, to his recounting of these two curiously simultaneous events to us as a problem in narrative mode and time.

Nina Baym, for example, concludes that frame and tale "cannot be considered as parts of a cumulative effect"; the "contrast" between the turbulent agitation of the tale and the calm commentary of the frame is simply too great.[2] She suggests that the "pure rant" of the sections of the gothic tale narrated by Leonard Doane infiltrates the frame narrative until "there is no sign of the measured, reserved, balancing, and ironic speaker who is now reading his early effort to us, and the contrast in prose styles within the revised version is instructive." She argues that Hawthorne's text "solves the problem" of "creating an American Gothic" (or, rather, it attempts to solve it) by "producing an extreme and *extremely conventional* example of the wildest of the species. This is in a sense no solution at all all. . . . And, because it is *so conventional*, it is no less flat than *Fanshawe*," another early "gothic discard" (p. 112; my italics). For her, the only originality of "Alice Doane's Appeal" lies in the attempt in the frame to use the witch-hunting Cotton Mather as a surrogate for the "gothic hero-villain" and to substitute "real and particular" historical events for conventional fictive ones in the genre of the gothic. Certain events of American history "correspond exactly to the requirements of the gothic but with infinitely more urgency and meaning to his audience" (p. 113).

Baym's treatment is itself conventional, reflecting the dominant critical reception of the work as a failed youthful experiment — what Van Doren, for example, calls "a confused rewriting of something done more simply before, perhaps in college."[3] Critics assume, without hard evidence, the existence of an earlier "Alice Doane" text, relegating both versions to Hawthorne's "juvenilia."[4] In the bulk of criticism before the 1980s, there is either no mention of "Alice Doane's Appeal" at all or merely the barest of glancing references. Even those books that attempt to deal with the nature of Hawthorne's artistry and his concept of the artist tend to neglect the work.[5] Fewer than a dozen articles do more than touch on the intertwined concerns of history, romance, realism, and metafiction; and of these less than half take the metafictional structure to be more than an annoying convention.[6]

One of the most misleading approaches to "Alice Doane's Appeal" has also been the most popular: the psychobiographical. Hyatt Waggoner claims that Hawthorne's text *demands* a psychoanalytic interpretation. He notes "contradictions" in "Alice Doane's Appeal" but mistakenly takes them to be part of the text's overall incoherence (*Tales and Sketches*, pp. vii–viii; *Hawthorne: A Critical Study*, pp. 48–56). I particularly disagree with his claims that the "fragmented" and "incoherent" nature of "Alice Doane's Appeal" reveals the "forbidden" aspects of Hawthorne's distressed psyche: his Oedipal and incestuous obsessions. Waggoner writes that "nearly all of Hawthorne's later themes are implicit in the work." It contains "strands from which many of Hawthorne's finest and most typical tales were later woven": secret guilt, the haunted mind, fate, universal sin, the curse from the past — and deeper and deeper guilt, obscure shame and obscure dread, compulsion by some nameless force, a feeling of being bewitched, seeing a world that is essentially "cold and unreal, frozen and lifeless." But "the strands are not woven in this tale, they are loosely tangled." Hawthorne has "not achieved the distance between himself and his symbols necessary for a good story" (*Critical Study*, p. 50). The "world" of "Alice Doane's Appeal," he says elsewhere, "is not only — as in some sense much of Hawthorne's most impressive work is — a world of dream." It is also "a world of nightmare from which the awakening is compulsive because the dream-fantasy has become at once too transparent and too close to the forbidden." It "foreshadows the breakdown in control so evident in the late romances he could never finish" (*Tales and Sketches*, pp. vii–viii).

We have seen this kind of misprisioning of authorial presence and distanciation before. Much of the narrative is decidedly dreamlike; but dream experience is a major focus of much romantic literature. And Waggoner knows as well as any other nineteenth-century scholar that incest is a prominent theme of romanticism, employed not only for its lurid shock value, but also for its potential as an attack on smug bourgeois family values (reinforcing the allure of the dark "outsider" hero) and as a master gothic trope for the problematic nature of identity.[7] It is closely associated with the figure of the doppelgänger and the phenomenon of split personality, figuring in scores of gothic tales. Yet Waggoner writes that "the incest motif, though of course a common enough theme in the Romantic movement, here seems to be more personal and compulsive than a literary borrowing." But he does not tell us why; it is an arbitrary judgment. He merely suggests that the story "means more to the modern reader than Hawthorne consciously intended it should" (*Tales and Sketches*, p. viii).

Frederick Crews obliges Waggoner's call for a full-scale psychoanalytic reading with a Freudian analysis of what is for him a key work. He projects "Alice Doane's Appeal" as a fantasy revealing Hawthorne's psychology, instead of seeing the tale in its context of literary convention and genre. He too takes the focus of the narrative to be the interior gothic tale and makes the central interest of the entire narrative incest and Oedipal conflict. His misplaced critical emphasis on the psychoanalytic text within the text is, like that of Waggoner and others, transferred to Nathaniel Hawthorne as one who in Crews's view struggled all his life with a half-acknowledged, raging Oedipus complex. The "vile and ineradicable weed of incestuous obsession has done its utmost to choke off every rival theme in Hawthorne's tale," he declares.

> No wonder, then, that Hawthorne's narrator hesitates to begin his story, backs away in disgust from his own descriptions, and vacillates between erotic insinuation, sarcasm, and apology. *Hawthorne himself,* we must suppose, shares his narrator's "dread of renewing my acquaintance with fantasies that had lost their charm in the ceaseless flux of mind". . . . Hawthorne's own sense of guilt, rooted in the twin theme of incest and patricide, *informs his idea of history* and *sabotages* his efforts at moral *objectivity.* (*Sins,* p. 59; my italics)

Crews adds that for Hawthorne "the sense of the past" is "*nothing other than the sense of symbolic family conflict writ large.*"[8] But Hawthorne's sense of "moral history" is far from being informed by personal psychological obsession. It is all rather like assuming that Poe was a dope addict because he wrote tales involving opium, despite the fact that opium was a literary motif that (as M. H. Abrams and Alethea Hayter have shown) was a master convention of the romantic era. Or like assuming that Hannah Foster, Susanna H. Rowson, Louisa May Alcott, or Sarah S. B. K. Wood were seducers and rapists or had perverse designs upon their brothers, fathers, and male cousins — instead of playing off the popular literary conventions of the day.

These older (and still predominating) psychobiographical critical estimates show clearly what is at stake.[9] My contrary claim here is that the major concern of the *whole* narrative of "Alice Doane's Appeal" is the problematic relationship of fictive "author" to text, audience, and genre and that its particular form/content focus is upon the problem of *conventions* of fictional and historical narrative. In a way, Baym is right to stress that "Alice Doane's Appeal" is "extremely conventional." That is part of its point. It is also highly nonconventional, as Hawthorne manipulates negative suggestion to question the conventions of both literary and historical narrative. Such a reading takes Hawthorne at his own word. For, in one of the "relinquished" prefaces to *The Story Teller* cycle, the author-narrator suggests that the interconnection of the cycle of works and their frames is what is most important to him and that the frame-sketches may be more valuable than the tales themselves.

The rather blatant self-reflexive pun in the title of the "Alice" narrative (which is scarcely about Alice Doane at all) has not gone unnoticed by critics. The general "appeal" lies in the effect of the surrounding narrative that tells two, and then three, interrelated stories; and the presence of an I-narrator as "author" is emphasized from the first. He appeals in various ways for attention and understanding from an audience — an audience literally in the frame tale present-time, allusively in the past, and gesturally in the future in its address to us as readers.

A "Wild" and "Grotesque" Tale: Metafictional Interaction and the "Spot of Time"

The reader may remember that Hawthorne characterized some of the works in his *Provincial Tales* manuscript to Samuel Goodrich as "wild" and "grotesque." The gothic story of Leonard and Alice Doane may certainly be described by these words. Indeed, the author-narrator applies the word "grotesque" to the Doane story at the end of the narrative. Traditionally the grotesque is a fusion or blurring of normally discrete realms (see *Romantic Arabesque*, pp. 163–70). Going beyond conventional grotesque, Hawthorne's narrative embodies a primary proposition parallel to his formal radicalism: the recurrence in almost all his work of "fact" and "fiction" existing disconcertingly side by side in the same continuum. The imaginary and the real fuse or blur in a "ghostland" or a "dreamland" or (more aesthetically) a "neutral territory" of perception and cognition that *almost* suggests the mystical or the visionary. We have pursued this theme in various forms (including the philosophical problem of inside/outside) throughout the *Provincial Tales*. In "Alice Doane's Appeal" it is heightened. Both the "real" world of the author and the women and the "imagined" world of the story are rendered with a dreamy innuendo that simultaneously suggests the reality and fictiveness of each (and both). The questions of the actual and the imaginary, of history and romance, are played out along epistemological and aesthetic lines. These are not monologically abstract, but involve negotiations of author and reader. Hawthorne rarely lets the reader forget the collaborative act of imagination in which author and reader are engaged or the uncertainty of that enterprise and its relationship to a presumed real world, which is itself perceived through fictive constructs, the conventions of which themselves veil what is presumably uncovered.

Thus the tale-teller and his audience are the focus of the work at least as much as, if not more than, the gothic tale is. The interior story is told in retrospective summary to the reader by an author recounting how he tried to affect his audience by repeating the story verbally—as it had been written earlier as one of a series published in the *Token*—to hearers (two "fair auditors") who are resistant to its force. We are told in the frame introduction that the narrator takes a walk up a hill with two young women to the site of a "death tree" and a "grave yard," or some *approximation* of such a "spot." These are in his imagination physical links with the past (or should be). But the significance of the past is problematic. He especially notes the ignorance of the present generation of villagers regarding the significance of their own rituals, indeed, their very history. He then muses on the problems of fiction and authorship. His own tales have brought him little fame, he says, causing him to burn other of his compositions. By the congruence of geography and history and authorial presence, the themes of fiction and truth, romance and history, past and present are, however ambiguously, conjoined from the start—in a negative "Spot of Time."

From the first the twin themes of historical and literary authorship are intertwined around the key role of the *imagination*. The author-narrator asks the women to imagine the town and the forest as they might have existed about one hundred fifty years before; his audience is to exercise some historical imagination in preparation for his work of fiction—a gothic tale of doubles, incest, and murder. This almost matter-of-fact introduction of the mysterious commodity of the imagination initiates a sequence of "visions" (historical, fictive, and otherwise) leading to highly imaginative scenes, each problematically apocalyptic. These include:

(A) a protovisionary imaginative scene of Salem and environs a hundred and fifty years before from the prospect of Gallows Hill at the end of the frame introduction and beginning section 1;

(B) the dreamvision in the gothic tale of Leonard Doane of his dead father in section 5;

(C) a vision of the world as frozen in section 7;

(D) a vision of specters in a graveyard in section 9;

(E) an imaginative "vision" (foregrounded fictive re-creation) of the execution of the witches of Salem in the concluding frame of section 10;

(F) an implied double "epiphany" (one overt and false, one covert and "true") relating to the whole narrative in terms of fiction/truth, romance/history, also in section 10.

These strategically placed visionary scenes mesh with the other overt structures of the tale and will be loci for the present discussion.

The "problematic structure" of "Alice Doane's Appeal" is lucidly analyzed by Charles Swann, who suggests a four-part division that he knows somewhat falsifies the text: "(a) an introduction which establishes a context for what follows; (b) the edited version of Alice Doane's tale; (c) the narrator's portrait of Salem witchcraft; and (d) finally, a conclusion."[10] This clear description is a good starting point but does not, as Swann admits, give a precise sense of the structuration of the narrative and blurs the technique of the "conclusion." For Hawthorne carefully places what are Swann's parts (c) and (d) together in the last section for powerful negative closure. Swann's four-part paradigm obscures the important point that throughout the narrative as a whole a pattern of alternation of telling the interior gothic story of the "past" and recounting the present-time situation (of the author-narrator of the story and his audience of two female listeners) shapes an interpenetrating double story. The frame presents (or purports to present in the first two-thirds and more of the narrative) the "real" and the "present," the here and now, as it were. But it does so mixed with commentary on the gothic story of Leonard and Alice Doane that becomes, in the frame's own temporal and physical location, confused with the gothic story. The discrete realms of the gothic fiction and the present reality (not to mention historical reality or romance) bleed one into another throughout the narrative.

The opening gambit of the first section after the introductory frame is to situate the gothic tale about to be related both historically and geographically, though both time and space are deliberately left a bit indefinite. "Nearly" one hundred fifty years have elapsed between the time of the frame and the discovery of the body of a murdered man "at about the distance of three miles" — from Salem presumably, because it is "on the old road to Boston." The method of expression emphasizes the point of reference as the present-time of the frame, the time of the interior story being historically coincident with the Salem Witch Trials. A point three miles out of town on the old Boston road is both specific and not. The season, in contrast, is specific; it is December, the diametrically opposite time of the year of the frame, which is June (ironically, the month of the witches' executions).

This dating is one of many oppositions carefully maintained and then blurred between the frame narrative present and the gothic narrative of the past. Thus the present-time of the frame is the progress of a summer afternoon through sunset into night; but as sunset approaches and passes, while the author-narrator reads from his manuscript, the precise time frame becomes unclear. It darkens towards midnight in the tale. Is it also midnight in the frame? Has the narrator truly kept the young women out that long? It is not until the end of the work that the ambiguity is at all resolved. Despite (or because of) these long maintained ambiguities of time and place, the contents of the manuscript, the circumstances of its reading, and the subsequent double result (aborting one tale and telling another) constitute the parameters of present and past in the narrative as a whole.

In the frame, as in the gothic story, dreaming and waking, conscious and unconscious states, and the literal and the symbolic are blurred in an acknowledgment of the subjective warping of place, time, and mode. As we have noted, Hawthorne's author-narrator locates their physical position at a certain "spot" that is not precisely certain (somewhat as in "My Kinsman, Major Molineux"). By only approximating the historical spot, the author-narrator simultaneously evokes and breaks the sense of historical continuity. The motif of the geographical "spot" — in New England "near" Boston — becomes a major symbol of the human ability — or *lack* thereof — to link empathetically with the past of a town, region, province, nation, or people. Likewise, the temporal locus is left somewhat ambiguous but is more or less specifically somewhere past the first quarter of the nineteenth century, possibly 1834, the publication date of the narrative (*Token*, dated 1835). The gothic tale he tells is located geographically in the same "spot" as the frame narrative — suggesting some sense of the continuity of "reality" — and temporally sometime in the 1690s. As he begins, the author-narrator of the frame specifically asks the two women to imagine Salem as it might have been in 1692.

The structural divisions of the narrative as a whole are marked by white spaces (or in some editions, spaced periods or lines across the page) indicating ten breaks in the text for a total of eleven sections — rather a lot for so short a narrative.[11] Indeed, these narrative interruptions — paradoxically serving as progressive transitions while simultaneously deferring the development of the interior gothic tale — constitute an important part of the meaning of the whole narrative. The introduction is given over wholly to the frame situation. The frame is also foregrounded in the telling of the

Doane story in sections 1, 2, 4, 6, 8, and 10; Leonard Doane (Alice's "brother") tells his own story in 3 and 5; in 7 and 9, despite the employment of third-person point of view, interior narrative and frame are blurred, as they are in the concluding portion of 8, which acts as a transition into the indeterminacy of 9. Section 10 contains a deliberately abrupt summary of the conclusion of the gothic tale, making clear the unimportance of its conventional gothic ending. That is, the foreshortening of the denouement of the Doane story (a technique we have examined in the dreamvision sketches) emphasizes the irrelevancy of the gothic conventions to the real concerns of the author-narrator: the authorial problem of audience and the epistemological problems of historical/fictional narrative modes.

Whereas it is principally in the frame narrative that both the present and the past are presented, and where tale and tale telling meet, the interior gothic tale (in apparent contrast to the frame) presents the "marvellous" and the legendary past. The legendary past is represented as having taken place in the very region inhabited by the author-narrator and the women, indeed, at the very "spot" where they are now sitting (or *somewhere* thereabouts). The tale is not represented as, or based on, actual history, but as a fictional story following certain literary conventions and formulae of the day. The author-narrator begins his story in (and from the distanced point of view of) the present-time frame with a summary of how the interior tale began — both as originally intended for publication and as now read to the two women. He devotes sections 1 and 2 to this summary, keeping our attention on the situation of author reading his tale to an audience.

The interior gothic story is told from the personal *retrospect* of the disappointed author interruptively commenting on this "second" (or third) attempt at the same tale. He begins in section 1 with a picture of a dead man's body frozen at the edge of a small lake. "*I read on,*" he writes, "and identified the body as that of a young man, a stranger" (12:284; *T&S,* 208; my italics). This technique produces the curious effect of closeness to the narrator and distance from the story — identification with the author's concern for telling his story and for its audience — rather than interest in the interior story itself. "*The story described,*" the author-narrator continues, "the excitement caused by the murder" and "other commonplace matters" (my italics).

Bringing the frame and fictional gothic narrative closer together, the author-narrator says that the "stranger" had been "resident during several of the preceding months in the town which lay at our feet" (12:284; *T&S,* 208). This reference to the town at their "feet" is to the narrator and the women high up on Gallows Hill, circa 1830; the "tale" he tells "took place" as it were at this very "spot," in this world, in the "actual" past. Then, ironically, after carefully preparing the women in the frame for the "actuality" of setting for the wild and grotesque tale he is about to read, the narrator again deliberately insists on distance between us as readers and those story events, sacrificing the sense of immediacy and actuality. The "excitement caused by the murder" is presented, not directly, but in the following manner: "The story described, at some length, the excitement . . . , the unavailing quest after the perpetrator, the funeral ceremonies, and other commonplace matters, in the course of which, I brought forward the personages who were to move among the succeeding events." By this summary, the narrator not only achieves a separation between those events and us as readers, but he also has it both ways. He hints at the immediacy of the tale and keeps the armchair reader at some distance, while eventually, in the metafictional realm, merging it all in one imaginative act.

This statement ("in the course of which, I brought forward the personages who were to move among the succeeding events") is to become surprisingly important. For these personages are *said* to be but three — Leonard Doane, his sister Alice, and a wizard — but the identities and number of the characters become ambiguous as the tale develops. In accordance with well-established gothic conventions, Doane has conceived a passion for his sister and a murderous jealousy of a rival, a fourth character, Walter Brome, whom he suspects of having deprived Alice of her innocence. But Doane sees that Alice "must inevitably love" Brome because he is Doane's "very counterpart," literally his counter-double, in whom all his own virtues are reversed. Brome is his mirror image. (The reverse parallelism of the mirror image is apparent in the overall structure of the text as well: the personages of the frame are a man and two women, while in the tale, two men and a woman are the center of attention; and, as previously noted, in the frame it is summer, in the tale winter.)

The gothic story progresses rapidly in sections 3, 4, and 5, with Leonard Doane telling his own tale in sections 3 and 5. This first-person narration is 'quoted,' as if the frame narrator were giving us representative selections from his manuscript exactly as read to the two women (rather than summarized). As a transition to this quoted material, the author-narrator says at the end of section 2, "In the following passage, I threw a glimmering light on the mystery of the tale" (12:284; *T&S*, 209) — a permutation of which he repeats six sections later. Thus a double narrative perspective is employed as the narrator goes on to describe how his character, Leonard Doane, "went on to describe" his own character, that is, as it had been described in the narrator's earlier version.

One of the striking elements of Doane's self-told story is a "dreamvision" or mad "fancy" in section 5. When Doane kills Brome, as in madness or a dream, he fancies that his victim's face "wore a likeness of my Father" (12:287; *T&S*, 211), so that now we have at least three doubles and a kind of double incest in the forbidden act of symbolic parricide. The author-narrator then takes over the narrative in section 6, summarizes Brome's state of mind, and in section 7 describes the moonlit sky by which the people of "this living world" all seem like frozen apparitions in a province of ice, suggesting the lowest regions of hell in Dante. But it is uncertain whether this generalized or universalized description is part of the interior fictional story of the past (the story of Doane) or a description of the sky and landscape around the narrator and the two women listening to his tale (whose "hearts" we discover later are somewhat frozen). "Fictive" and "real" worlds blur together. The narrator at the opening of section 8 observes that "by this fantastic *piece of description*, and more in the *same style*, I *intended to throw a ghostly glimmer round the reader* . . ." (12:288–89; *T&S*, 212; my italics). This phrasing not only parallels the end of section 2, but also subtly relocates the "ghostly glimmer" from the tale to its reader. The statement also describes what he is trying to do for us (his present readers) in his summary re-narration of his story. The past audience of prospective *Token* readers, the "present audience of the two young ladies," and the implied reader of the present text of the "ladies" and the past readers — like the seventeenth century and the nineteenth, the historical incidents and the fictional — all merge.

Thus, buried in the middle of "Alice Doane's Appeal," lie Leonard Doane's own words, presumably the exact manuscript being read to the women; but Doane's own narrative is interrupted by the author-narrator just as, in a sense, the author-narrator's retrospective narrative is "interrupted" by Doane. In between Leonard Doane's sections (in section 4) the action of the gothic tale is again summarized by the author-narrator of the frame. The Doane tale is continued in sections 6 through 10 but in an alternating mode wherein, in section 6, for example, the author-narrator of the frame takes over the narration from Leonard Doane but adopts the third-person limited point of view (the logical effect of having quoted portions of Leonard's first-person narrative). The author-narrator combines this technique with conjured visionary scenes from a possibly omniscient point of view (in sections 7 and 9) of ambiguous (literally double) provenance that apply to either tale or frame or to both. This strategy generates an in-between realm (or neutral territory) of past and present, fiction and reality, that comprehends both frame and interior tale.

The very brief eighth section has aspects of all these modes. The story-teller progresses to a third-person omniscient summary of the journey of Leonard and Alice Doane to a graveyard, and then shifts back to his own situation of trying to affect his listeners and to the relation of the fictive to the historical. The author-narrator observes the faces of the women to check the effect of his story so far, to see if he should proceed with his tale. Taking "courage," he leads a "fated pair" to "a new made grave." But "suddenly" there seems to be a "multitude of people among the graves" (12:289; *T&S*, 212). This is, apparently, in imagination. But whose? Is it the author in reverie as he pauses in his reading of the tale? Or is it a scene in the interior tale? Or is it a shared hallucination or vision? Or is it, in fact, an infernal spectral manifestation of all the damned of the past? Not only is it not clear at this point whether the graveyard apparitions are those of the Doane story or those of the frame scenes or some universalized abstract vision, but also the storyteller does not make it clear until later who this "fated pair" is that he has "led" to the burial site: Leonard and Alice (literally in an imagined story), or the two young women (figuratively, in imagination). Hawthorne has deliberately blurred the frame reality with the interior fiction in a manner reminiscent of "An Old Woman's Tale" and "The Wives of the Dead."

Section 9 then is given over to evocation of a ghostly scene of the graveyard, in which delusion and moral enormity and ambiguity are paramount. The generalized description of the graveyard vision leads in section 10 to a waveringly maintained third-person omniscient point of view. The narrator abruptly comments that "in the course of the tale, *the reader had been permitted* to discover that all the incidents were results of the machinations of the wizard" (12:291; *T&S*, 214; my italics). The "explanation" of causation and motive in the tale is that Brome is Doane's twin brother and Alice thus Brome's sister. Like a half-comprehending victim of nature and fate in one of Ludwig Tieck's gothic *Märchen*, Leonard Doane discovers he is guilty of incestuous jealousy, symbolic parricide, and apparent fratricide.[12] Even more abruptly, we are told that "the story concluded with the Appeal of Alice to the spectre of Walter Brome," and this "spectre" replies by "absolving" Alice Doane "from every stain" (12:292; *T&S*, 214).

Bringing the interior fiction into the frame once more, though by more conventional means, the narrator comments that the peculiar vegetation of the hill on which they are sitting has sprung from the bones of the wizard. The young women start, then laugh. Piqued that his tale has not had the desired effect, the narrator again (as at the beginning of the narrative) appeals to their sense of the historical past. He now tells another story, based, apparently, on historical truth rather than on legend or composed entirely of imaginative fiction. But carefully juxtaposed with the truncated and merely reported denouement of the gothic tale, this other story is also, in its way, gothic, conjuring up in not very factual language the ghosts or specters (there is an important difference) of Puritan persecutors and their executed victims. Employing his fictional abilities, the author-narrator creates a figure on horseback at the rear of the death procession: one so "darkly conspicuous, so sternly triumphant, that my hearers mistook him for the visible presence of the fiend himself" rather than the witch-hunting Puritan minister, Cotton Mather (12:294; *T&S*, 216). The "blood-thirsty" minister triumphantly oversees the procession of the victims of the "witch-craft delusion" to the "spot" of their execution just outside Salem, Massachusetts. Although purporting to be a historic rather than a fictional depiction, its provenance as fiction or history is, as we shall see, highly problematic. Nevertheless, this historical narrative affects the imaginations of the women more profoundly than the fictional narrative; they tremble at the word-monument of the fictive re-creation of the factual historical past. "Alice Doane's Appeal" seems to conclude with the triumph of historically based narrative over more purely fictional narrative. But the author-narrator's words describing his intent are carefully chosen: ". . . I detained them a while longer . . . and made a *trial* whether truth were more powerful than fiction" (12:292; *T&S*, 215; my italics).

If the Doane story is brought to an abrupt stop, the "author's" frame narrative is given a slightly more conventional denouement; but, to him, it has to be an unsatisfactory one. For his audience, in their dependence on historical-factual imagination (which, however, is also an act of fiction, with its own set of generic and epistemological conventions), exhibits a deficient understanding of fictive imagination. As baldly described in the summary here, the potential for ironic undercutting, for negative suggestion, is rather obvious. It is less obvious as one reads Hawthorne's narrative. These issues, so clear in the abstract, are, like the phenomena of Tieck's *Märchen*, veiled and indefinite, simultaneously masking and revealing a metaphysical crisis. The conclusion of the whole remains, like the dreamvision sketches, ambiguously poised. Rather than posing simple *either/or* questions, "Alice Doane's Appeal" encompasses such questions in a *both/and* frame.

The metastructure of the narrative — that is to say, the large patterning of the complex interaction of framed narrative and frame narrative — conforms to the general patterning of narrative intrusion that we have examined in the other *Provincial Tales*, though here the term "authorial presence" is particularly apt. Counting sections 7 and 9 as equally tale and frame, we find that the narrative is by bulk exactly balanced until section 10, where the interior tale gets one paragraph of about one-third of a page and the frame two and one-half pages. Of course, nearly one-half of the "frame" here is taken up by the fictive-historical re-creation of Salem in 1692 and the imaginative portrayal of Cotton Mather — for a rather remarkable narratival balance that suggests the artistic deliberation of the form of the work.[13] The "circumstances in which the story was told" are described in such a way as to suggest the embedment of the authorial perspective in the epistemological problem of perception, description, and narration. Even the initial convention of the narrator's having taken two young women for a walk undergoes immediate metamorphosis into a problematic narratorial situation. Throughout the entire narrative, the storyteller is ambivalently portrayed in his struggles to tell at least three interconnected stories, the poles of which are fact and fancy, audience and author, tale and sketch, romance and history, truth and delusion.

The "Author" in the Frame: Perspectivism, the Veil of Appearances, Historiography

The reader will find that a close reading of the opening frame reveals not only the prominence of the apocalyptic theme of the deceptiveness of appearances, but also just how deceptive the narrative mode is as the text moves back and forth across time frames, ontological realms, and generic modes, especially those of fiction and history.

The narrative, as we know, tells a dark and fetid gothic tale in the middle and concludes on an even darker, if muted, note. But it begins in a lightsome mode as if it were to be a sunny *jeu d'esprit* centered on a young man's fancy (love, romance, sexual interest, flirtation), something we might expect to encounter in *Godey's Ladies' Book* or *Burton's Gentleman's Magazine*. The narrator says in the first paragraph that he has not led the two young women to any of the apparently usual places for a stroll—such as Legge's Hill, Cold Spring, or the shores of the Neck—nor yet to "Paradise." This last seems to be a casually suggestive innuendo, a bit of ironic sexual humor turned into a gentlemanly compliment: ". . . if the latter place were rightly named, my fair friends would have been at home there" (12:279; *T&S*, 205). Thus the first sentences ironically deploy certain genre conventions that misdirect the reader's expectations. By the end of the narrative, this play on a place name redeemed into a decorous compliment (that they are angels) comes to have a more sinister meaning (like the Hebrew word '*Salem*). The technique is like other of Hawthorne's subversions of the word *home*. Indeed, in the very next sentence, the narrative begins to darken: the narrator remarks that just before they actually begin their country walk, just as they leave the outskirts of town, he and the young women turn away from the street of tanners' and curriers' shops. The overall progress of the narrative is to become steadily darker, and "Paradise" as an otherworld concept is ambiguously undercut by the later "visionary" graveyard scenes.

Vaguely implying some sort of Dantesque journey, the narrator describes their ascending a hill, its "dark slope and the even line of its summit" suggesting to the narrator a "rampart" along the road. Although this "eminence formed part of an extensive tract of pasture land" and though ("strange to tell") the whole slope and summit are of a "peculiarly" deep green, scarcely a blade of grass grows from the base upward; and what does grow there he calls a "deceitful verdure." The author-narrator lavishes some detail on this deceitful vegetation, which, he tells us, is a plentiful crop of wood-wax. It wears the same glossy green throughout the summer, except when it suddenly, for a short period, puts forth a profusion of yellow blossoms as though overlaid with gold or sunshine. In this period the scene is also overlaid with the illusion of gold in the glory of sunshine beneath a cloudy sky. The irony of this description may not be immediately apparent: how is the earth sunny if the skies are cloudy, veiling the sun in the real sky above? Thus does the wood-wax give an illusory appearance to things. The imagery sets up a series of permutations on the theme of veiling, including that of apocalypse, associated later in the narrative with the appearance of light on and through ice. The casual description symbolically replicates the truth and appearance theme of the whole narrative on more than one level, one of which is the self-reflexive aesthetic-philosophical question of narrative itself, whether fictional or historical. Does fiction reveal or veil actuality in its wood-wax illusion, its simulacrum of the real? Does fiction or history reveal the truth? Do our notions of historical narrative veil the truth that historical narrative has a fictional component — indeed, may be fiction? The structure of "Alice Doane's Appeal," rather than abruptly shifting from fiction to history at the end (supposedly suggesting the triumph of history over romance), carefully prepares us in the opening frame for a historical denouement that we shall see to be deliberately subjective.

The illusory wood-wax underscores this theme. The narrator suggests that in actuality the true vegetation (green grass meant to "nourish man or beast") has been destroyed; but this devastation is veiled by the wood-wax. Destruction and deceit, it is implied, like this "vile and ineradicable weed," lie before them almost as if a curse had been pronounced upon the spot. We have come a long way, just in one paragraph, from the first faint promise of a story of an afternoon's dalliance. There is some dark mystery associated with the vague history of this spot of land. The suggestion of a blight, laid upon the spot like a supernatural curse, suggests a specific historical point in time. And a specific *historic* event, connected with this particular "spot" of earth, promises somehow to clarify the *mystery* associated with it.

The narrator identifies himself (and presumably his readers) by the reference to "our" fathers, constituting among other things an assertion by the narrator of some sort of factual basis as opposed to any superstitious, legendary, purely imaginative basis for the narrative (or parts of the narrative) that follow. Hereby the "gothic tale" is grounded in a "real world" frame. At the same time, the real and the fictional, the romantic and the historical, are problematized. What seems to be a clear-cut distinction between real and imaginary is both maintained *and* subverted throughout the narrative (that is, the double narrative of both frame and interior tale). Seeming clarity may be a deceitful clarity, just like the vegetation that veils the hill with false green and gold.

Nevertheless, the narrator here interjects the following "historical" judgment that initially seems to clarify matters: ". . . a physical curse may be said to have blasted the spot, where guilt and frenzy consummated the most execrable scene, that our history blushes to record" (12:280; *T&S*, 205). For "this was the field where superstition won her darkest triumph; the high place where our fathers set up their shame, to the mournful gaze of generations far remote." Indeed, the "dust of martyrs was beneath our feet. We stood on Gallows Hill."

With this historical-topological reference, several matters are identified by local allusion, including a not as yet fully specified reference to the Puritan Witch Trials of 1691–92. But Gallows Hill is just outside Salem, Massachusetts; the point could hardly be much clearer to an American reader. The opening paragraph thus functions, though in a much more personalized and specific way, like the other "historical" frames in the *Provincial Tales*. This introductory frame (extending for six paragraphs) contextualizes the personal story or stories about to be related in terms of New England history, to which is attached a moral interpretation of some kind or another.

Although the real and the fictional, the romantic and the historical are clouded in the narratives to follow, the narrator presents himself as actively courting the historical influence of the spot. But in describing their walk up Gallows Hill, he also uses the word "pilgrimage," as though their journey were to a shrine or monument of some sort, though unmarked. He comments on how few make a pilgrimage to this "famous" (or notorious) hill, noting instead "how many spend their lives almost at its base" and "never once obey the summons of the shadowy past, as it beckons them to the summit" (12:280; *T&S*, 205–6), where there may lie some sort of veiled revelation. The narrator's implicit criticism of the fact that so few people obey the summons of history to meditate on the meaning of the past for the present is made more explicit in the rest of the paragraph and is developed further in the introductory frame, as the motif of written history merges with tale writing or telling.

Foreshadowing the conclusion of the whole narrative, the storyteller comments on the relative lack of written history to commemorate the witch trials: "Till a year or two since, this portion of our history had been imperfectly written" (12:280; *T&S*, 206); we are "not a people of legend or tradition," he adds, in a example typical of Hawthorne's double irony. For one thing, he is about to tell a legend connected with the region (as he does in other provincial tales, like "The Hollow of the Three Hills" and "An Old Woman's Tale"). For another, New Englanders are a people insistently historical; but they are provincially so in the negative sense. Their provincialism causes them to edit history according to the present prevailing view of their place and destiny. Like other *merely* provincial peoples, they omit the unpleasant or retrograde side of their history.

As we have seen in the other *Provincial Tales*, most notably perhaps in "Roger Malvin's Burial" and "My Kinsman, Major Molineux," Hawthorne is particularly ironic about the historical editing out of the provincial record of "errors" against humanity (moral errors, sins against Christianity itself). That is, the provincials erase history which does not fit the religious, political, and historical theory of Protestant manifest destiny in North America. The muted negative phrasing that follows suggests a wearily sarcastic tone: "it was not every citizen of our ancient town" who could "tell, within half a century, so much as the date of the witchcraft delusion" (12:280; *T&S*, 206). This statement confirms reference to the events of Salem in 1692 and reveals an attitude toward these events that regards the charges of the crime of witchcraft as false or at best deluded. The author-narrator's judgment is to provide an ironic contrast with the gothic narrative (purportedly about the "machinations" of a male witch) that he is to read to the two women. Moreover, the specific reference to historical delusion emphasizes the theme of what is real and not real, making quite explicit what is to be an insistent blurring of real and unreal throughout the narrative(s) of intertwined romance and history that follow.

The tone of the rest of the paragraph is ambiguous, hovering between seriousness and sarcasm, and may be set down as another example of romantic irony, here concerned with the problematics of historical truth. As with "Roger Malvin's Burial," "The Gentle Boy," and "My Kinsman, Major Molineux," the narrator refers to historiography. "Recently," he observes, "an historian" has "treated the subject" in a manner that "will keep his name alive" in the "only desirable" way that one could be connected with "the errors of our ancestry." That is, the historian has converted "the hill of their disgrace" into "an honorable monument of his own antiquarian lore." What Hawthorne's narrator calls the erroneous judgments of the Puritan ancestors become the building blocks for a "monument" to the author of supposed objective history. The monument motif is one that opens and closes the entire narrative of "Alice Doane's Appeal." (Cf. "The Ambitious Guest.") The lack of a marker, a stone, a sign, or a cross at the spot of the executions of the supposed witches on Gallows Hill merges with the idea of written narrative (fictional or otherwise) as the only important monument to past events, whatever their reality. The ironic innuendo about historiography and the relation of history to truth and to legend and superstition is that the historian's principal purpose has been to treat the subject in a manner calculated to give himself popular fame as the chronicler of provincial (and "politically correct") history. Fame is the very thing as yet denied to the author-narrator of "Alice Doane's Appeal."

The ambiguity of history is further developed at the end of the paragraph: ". . . we are a people of the present and have no heartfelt interest in the olden time," says the narrator. The absence of "heartfelt interest" in the past is the result of ignorance and the failure of sympathy. The narrator observes that the young men "scare the town with bonfires on this haunted height" every fifth of November (Guy Fawkes Day) in "commemoration of they know not what." They are "without an idea beyond the momentary blaze," much like the rioters in "Molineux." In merely commemorating the commemoration ceremony, the substance of which has been forgotten, it never occurs to them, says the author-narrator, to pay "funeral honors to those who died so wrongfully" and who, "without a coffin or a prayer, were buried here" (12:281; *T&S*, 206). The ahistorical aspects of the emerging American mentality are clearly suggested. The semi-veiled Guy Fawkes allusion suggests the Catholic/Protestant tension, though the Catholic threat in England was hardly ever as serious as that of Puritan to Anglican rule. Since the New Englanders no longer remember this historical "fact" one way or the other, their loss of a sense of their Old World history is insinuated, along with the growing negative provinciality of an "American" history.

This idea of the loss of cultural connection with the Old World is Frederick Newberry's framing suggestion regarding the unifying thematic principle in Hawthorne; and some readers have argued that an Old World/ New World conflict is symbolized or allegorized in "Alice Doane's Appeal." But I would argue that here the real, the important history is concerned with that delusion (both past and present) which causes human beings to abandon sympathy and empathy — and with the difficulty of a true history itself — rather than with the theme of the Old World versus the New World. This theme of delusion is epistemologically and morally connected with the theme of subjectivity, the broad theme of the *Provincial Tales* and of Hawthorne's fiction in general. The subjective or perspectival informs Hawthorne's theory of history and historiography; and the tensions between legend and history, objectivity and subjectivity, fiction and reality, permeate both the dreamvision sketches and the historical tales. The next development in the introductory frame, for example, has to do with the *mood* of both the narrator and the two young women, subtly bringing to the fore the importance of subjectivity, both positive and negative.

Our narrator turns from the recent historian of the Salem Witch Trials back to his two female companions, who with "feminine susceptibility" (that is, sensitivity) "caught all the melancholy associations of the scene." They feel this melancholy atmosphere without, apparently, any particular historical knowledge; they have a "feminine" intuition of something "wrong." Yet the "gayety of girlish spirits" is not totally overcome by such sensitivity. The narrator's own "more sombre mood" contrasts with theirs but yet is "tinged by theirs." Their emotions come and go "with quick vicissitude, and sometimes combined to form a peculiar and delicious excitement." Their "mirth" brightens the "gloom" that he feels in the spot (the one he is leading them to by conscious choice) into a "sunny shower of feeling" like a "rainbow in the mind." At least their initial lighter spirits affect his heavier one, to a degree.[14] Although the narrator's mood is tinged by theirs, his efforts by the end of the narrative will darkly affect theirs, at least temporarily.

Once again he recurs to himself as the basic point of reference as he describes how with words both "merry" and "sad" they tread "among tangled weeds" almost hoping that their feet will "sink into the hollow of a witch's grave" (recalling allusively the scene of "The Hollow of the Three Hills"). This apparent fancy, however, has a basis in a kind of "reality" as they approach nearer the graveyard of the "witches" hanged in 1692. The two themes of subjective mood and the existence of *some* kind of history subtly merge. There is a *historical* reality that human beings were executed at this very spot only a century and a half before. But what does it mean that people were executed for a delusion, and how is any fact different? Hawthorne manages to get around this kind of poststructuralist circularity without quite denying it. The narrator simply continues: "Such vestiges [of memory and history] . . . have vanished now, and with them, I believe, all traces of the precise spot of the executions" (12:281; *T&S*, 206). The vanishing of the exact location of the deed weakens the sense of local history, of connection with the past.

The meaning of history is to be recaptured by the imagination, by the fictive reconstruction of events — always, however, with the caveat of the *as if*, the constant remembrance that narrative is an interpretative lens. Having just said that the "precise spot" has been lost, the narrator mentions the prospect of town and village from "this unhappy spot" whither he has led them. The lost spot and a specific spot are merged, simultaneously identified — the specific spot simply being whither the author has led his unsuspecting audience. The spot to which he brings them figuratively substitutes for the actual historical spot, as he indulges in a little fiction: from this spot, then, from the prospect on the hill, we are afforded a prospect of the past, and its future (the present moment), from the retrospective prospect of which a version of the past emerges. Another poststructuralist conundrum.

At first, the author-narrator's description suggests a pleasant and rich scene. But he observes, as if in some wonderment, that "no blight" has fallen on Essex County as a whole. It is as if *he*, who rejects the "superstition" of witchcraft, were yet somehow expecting God's avenging hand to have touched the spot. He notices in particular that thrusting out of the "close assemblage of wooden roofs" is many a spire — ironic icon of the betrayal of Christian charity in the witchcraft trials. The scene is recapitulated by the narrator as though gazing directly on the past from the prospect of Gallows Hill: "The idea thus gained of its former aspect, its quaint edifices standing far apart, with peaked roofs and projecting stories," leads to the imaginative vision of a single "tall spire in the midst," when the town was but a seventeenth-century wilderness village. The single spire would seem to suggest the monolithic quality of the Puritan oligarchy; certainly the single spire of the Puritans is no spiritually truer (in fact less so, if the essence of Truth is perspectivism) than the multiplicity of contemporary spires. Indeed, it seems that "time and human toil" have wrought "no change" on a country unmarked by strong natural features.

Nevertheless (or therefore), as the sun begins to set, the three of them "threw, *in imagination,* a *veil* of deep forest over the land, and pictured a few scattered villages, and this old town itself a village" (12:282; *T&S*, 207; my italics). Driving the point home, the narrator adds: "as when the prince of hell bore sway there." Historically, the Puritans thought it was they who held sway against the forces of darkness; but they were assaulted by the *idea* of Satan, and they acted like devils themselves in the witch trials. Thus from the humane perspective of rational, Christian charity some one hundred and fifty years in the future, the satanic *did* hold sway then, when it veiled the minds of the Puritan ancestors with an evil idea (a point implicated in the specters of the visionary scenes later).

Sunset gives rise to imagination: that dusky area between two realms. By means of imagination, the narrator and his companions gain a "vision, in short, of the town in 1692." The imagined vision here is not in itself apocalyptic; but this event initiates the sequence of increasingly powerful (but delusive) apocalyptic visions structuring the narrative. This imaginative historical vision, he says, will serve "to introduce a wondrous tale of those old times" (12:282; *T&S*, 207). Since the "wondrous" tale of "old times," however, is not a historical narrative but a fictive one of the most highly romantic sort, a series of literary motifs succeeds the historical.

In telling us about himself as an author, the narrator adopts (who knows with how much tongue-in-cheek?) a Byronic world-weariness. "I had brought the manuscript in my pocket," he says; it was written "when my pen, now sluggish and perhaps feeble, because I have not much to hope or fear, was driven by stronger external motives, and a more passionate impulse within, than I am fated to feel again" (12:282; *T&S*, 207). The self-consciously literary formulaics of Byronism are clear. One may compare this motif in "Alice Doane's Appeal," for example, with the motifs of burning manuscripts and authorial world-weariness in the story of the author Oberon in "The Devil in Manuscript" and in the accounts of the Story Teller's journey out and weary return home in "Passages from a Relinquished Work" and "Fragments from the Journal of a Solitary Man," where one author figure merges with the other, Story Teller with Oberon. The "Alice" narrator writes:

> Three or four of these tales had appeared in the "Token," after a long time and various adventures, but had encumbered me with no troublesome notoriety, even in my birthplace. One great heap had met a brighter destiny: they had fed the flames; thoughts meant to delight the world and endure for ages had perished in a moment, and stirred not a single heart but mine. The story now to be introduced, and another, chanced to be in kinder custody at the time, and thus, by no conspicuous merits of their own, escaped destruction. (12:282; *T&S*, 207)

What we tend to forget about Byronism, however, is its dual nature: sorrow and disenchantment blended with humor and romantic fantasy and idealism. The humor and irony of *Don Juan* is in one sense a sardonic quixoticism, though resisting the loftily sentimental idealism of Cervantes's hero.

Subtly, with mild self-deprecating irony, the "author" of "Alice Doane's Appeal" suggests his modest stature as a man of letters (in contrast to the recent historian of the province). He comments that he has never *before* intruded his performances on an audience by any but the "legitimate medium," that is, the press. It must be this consideration, he thinks, that persuades the young women to consent to hear him read. He has them sit on a mossy rock, close by the very spot where the three of them "chose to believe" that the death tree had stood in 1692. Even here the power of the imagination is emphasized; for they do not "know" precisely the spot, or the tree, historically speaking.

With "a little hesitation" caused by "dread of renewing my acquaintance with fantasies that had lost their charm, in the ceaseless flux of mind" (12:283; *T&S*, 207–8), he begins the interior narrative. By his looking again at an imaginative fantasy of prior composition, he fears he may find that what charm of invention and the remote past may have had in his personal past as author-creator-chronicler will have changed in the ceaseless flux of time and thought. The frame introduction, then, ends with a statement that emphasizes the creative process, the vicissitudes of time, and authorial anxiety. The concluding strategy of the "introduction" also includes a summary retrospect of the *strategy* of the opening of the interior fictive tale: "*I began the tale*, which opened darkly with the discovery of a murder" (my italics). The playfulness of it all is obvious, but the epistemological theme is nevertheless heightened, linking the story thematically with the other provincial tales examined here. The technique of authorial retrospective summary and comment will persist throughout the entire narrative and come to dominate it.

Technique of Penultimate Apocalypse

The reader will have remarked in the foregoing the importance of metanarrative and self-reflexivity to the ambiguities and lacunae of the "interior" gothic tale of the Doanes (essentially sections 1–6, bleeding through sections 7–9 to the beginning of 10). These in turn are important to the analysis of the *Rahmenerzählungseffekt* of the whole narrative. Especially pertinent in the gothic tale is the insistent doppelgänger motif, in which at least three (possibly four or five) identities merge, a matter left mysterious even at the end. It is so mysterious, in fact, that the truncated and elliptical denouement of the gothic story leaves the frame author's audience unmoved. Throughout the Doane story the author figure repeatedly remarks that he can throw only a "glimmering light" on the events of the tale. This metaphoric narrative light is combined with literal light in both interior tale and exterior frames. The literal light is highly delusive in both the frame (wood-wax and cloud, sunset, and the coming on of night) and the interior tale (ice light and night glare). Such glimmering and dim vision is not only part of the deliberately unsuccessful mystification of the narrative. It is also an essential effect (in its very lack of success) of the text as a whole. For it is attendant to a series of quasi-apocalyptic visions and dreamvisions that prove to be a structure of negative *apokalypsis*.

The first vision: the enemy-father. Counting the picture of Salem in 1692 conjured up (in the opening frame) by the imaginations of the storyteller and the two women as a protovisionary scene of less intensity, the first apocalyptic vision may be said to occur in section 5. At the edge of the ice along a lonely road around a lake, Leonard Doane stands over the body of the murdered Walter Brome. The face of the corpse seems to Leonard to change into another's. And at this point we are told that a wizard, to whom Leonard is telling his story, smiles and utters an occasional word that has the effect of "mysteriously filling up some void in the narrative." The gaps in the story, in fact, demonstrate Hawthorne's mastery of the gothic conventions he subverts, as he foregrounds the ambiguity of author-text-reader relationships and genre expectations.

The author-narrator is careful to note that Doane's narrative is interrupted by the eerie laughter of the wizard. Or is it merely the wind? Whichever it is, Doane "pursued his fearful story" again, telling of the dream sensation surrounding his visionary experience — an experience set in motion by the wind at the lake of ice. At first exulting over the dead man, Doane's glee was dissipated by (in his words, in single quotation marks) a 'torpor' and by a 'dimness' before his eyes, giving him the 'sensation of one who struggles through a dream' (12:286; *T&S*, 210). Someone other than Walter Brome seemed to lie dead before his eyes, as Doane experienced a transporting reverie of childhood horror — the slaughter by Indians of his parents. The face of the corpse was that of Doane's own father.

The time frame seems abruptly to shift and yet does not: as the dream-vision began to pass, Doane was to find himself again by the body of Walter Brome. For as he gazed in reverie at the face of the dead man, a 'cold wind whistled by, and waved my father's hair. Immediately, I stood again in the lonesome road . . . a man of blood, whose tears were falling fast over the face of his dead enemy.' The juxtaposition and the phrase "dead enemy" further link Brome and the father, making, as it were, the father an "enemy" too (as remarked by Waggoner and Crews). 'I bore the body' [of Walter Brome] 'to the lake, and would have buried it there.' But 'before his icy sepulchre was hewn, I heard the voices of two travellers and fled.' Thus ends Leonard Doane's internal narrative; and we again return to Doane speaking in the dark to the wizard.

Doane has "sought this interview with the wizard" because he is troubled by dark impulses and dreams regarding his sister, Alice. But does the wizard exist, or is he too a vision as "in madness or a dream"? The text is indeterminate, except that the author-narrator remarks that the wizard "on certain conditions, had no power to withhold his aid in unravelling the mystery." With this vague promise that the mysteries will, in fact, be explained, the storyteller observes: "the tale drew near its close." But the explanation of the gothic mysteries is deferred once again. Hawthorne's technique at the end of section 6 is to shift our attention from Doane's telling the wizard his dark story on a winter's night in the seventeenth century to a young "author" telling us a story of a certain midsummer night's eve in the nineteenth century.

The tale drew *near* — but does not quite reach its close. Doane's vision of his dead father parallels three others to follow in the double narrative, but sections 7 through 9 do not progress the Doane story directly. We have to wander with brother and sister (and maybe a wizard) to a graveyard, share a couple of incomplete visions, and wait until section 10 to find out what happened. Then, as in jest, from a metafictional point of view, the narrator begins the final section by saying, "I dare not give the remainder of the scene" except in "a very brief epitome" (12:291; *T&S*, 214). "In the course of the tale," he says, "the reader had been permitted to discover that all the incidents were results of the machinations of the wizard. . . ." By this hypertrophy of the summary technique of narration (after all the delayed build-up of reader expectations) the reader is let down flat. As before, the author-narrator gives a description of how he continues to manipulate his narrative, how he has allowed the reader to "discover" the "truth." Or was it Leonard Doane, the narrator of the manuscript, whose reliability is suspect, who has permitted the reader to "discover" whatever is to be discovered?

There is too much "void in the narrative" for the reader reasonably to fill up. The scene in the graveyard is ambiguous and indeterminate: there may or may not be a troup of "fiends" witnessing the scene. The author-narrator continues: "I described the glee of the fiends at this hideous conception" (that is, the "revelation" about the wizard). The fiends are said to be eager to know if the design "were consummated"; and the narrator next tells *us*, as though we ourselves (readers) were fiends eager for a properly horrible denouement to a dark tale: "the story concluded with the Appeal of Alice to the spectre of Walter Brome." One statement is all we get of the climactic event: we are told that Walter Brome's "reply" to the appeal of Alice Doane, "absolving her from every stain," prompts the dissolution of the apparitions of ghosts and devils in the graveyard. The effect is rather like that of the truncated end of "An Old Woman's Tale." One senses the smile of the author as the conventions play out, are subverted, yet remain elliptically insistent. The denouement of the frame narrative will also be deliberately abrupt and problematic, though perhaps more satisfyingly inclusive. Inside and out, the framed and the frame, mirror each other.

Harold Beaver's suggestive title for his essay on "Roger Malvin's

Burial" — "Towards Romance" — applies also to the major cumulative movement of the narrative of "Alice Doane's Appeal." It moves *toward* something; the narrative unfolds toward an apocalyptic revelation, which is never finally fully unveiled. Its movement is toward one vision after another, each one penultimate. From the series of negative apocalypses there emerges for the reader, as the meaning of the narrative as narrative, a concluding negative epiphany. The "final" revelation that we are offered in section 10 of "Alice Doane's Appeal" is a complicated interlineation of: (a) the author-narrator's imaginative re-creation of the historical witch trials of 1692 and the figure of Cotton Mather; (b) the gothic tale and the gothic villain; (c) an author-to-reader revelation about the relative power of literary and historical imagination. This revelation, however, undergoes at least two turns before the indeterminacy of the entire structure is negatively revealed. Along the way are two other negated apocalyptic visions. These two subsequent visions, which appear in sections 7 and 9, are applicable to the historical event of the witch trials of 1692, to the fictional gothic tale of the same time, and to the narrative present of the 1830s.

The second vision: ice light and frigid "glory." When we come to section 7 from the agitated turmoil of the Doane story rehearsed for us in sections 1 through 6, it is striking how unclear it is whether we are still with Leonard and Alice in the "tale" or back in the "real world" with the author-narrator speaking to the two women on Gallows Hill or whether we are being addressed by yet another, omniscient, narratorial voice in universalized terms on the human condition. We read, as the first sentence of section 7, that "the moon was bright on high." It was night on the lonely road when Leonard Doane killed Walter Brome; it was night during his interview with the wizard. Night has also been coming on in the frame narrative as the storyteller reads his manuscript to his companions. Whether "the moon was bright on high" applies to the narrative present or the past gothic fiction is left ambiguous. The observations on the "inherent brightness" of the glowing blue firmament, the burning of the "greater stars," and the "mysterious glare" of the northern lights are without specific temporal reference. This blurring or blending of the interior story with the frame story of the author-narrator telling his tale calls into question the actuality of the historic scene where witches and wizards were executed. According to the logic of the narrative, what is "real" is the recognition of the omnipresence of fiction, if not delusion. Such *anagnorisis* applies to fictional time, to (a more "ignorant") time past, and to the here and now — the here and now including all the others, as it were, even if in ignorance of time past.

The scene is said to be the "creation of wizard power," a phrase suggestive of the whole narrative as well as of the dreamvision of the section. The deceptive summer sunlight on the deceitful wood-wax vegetation in the frame introduction is now winter ice light. Both kinds of light veil as they illumine. The rest of section 7 develops the motifs of coldness and deceptive light as symbols of the failure of sympathy and empathy, suggesting the human distance among people and between past people and events and present ones. The imagery of ice and its reflected and translucent light projects a false "glory" around all things. The "frigid glory" of this icy glare creates an optical illusion, etymologically a "halo," rather like that of the pale lunar rainbow that appears elsewhere in Hawthorne's early tales.[15] The sky itself, we are told, with its variety of lights, is (or was) scarcely so brilliant as the earth, its "ice" illumined by the play of the northern lights on the horizon. The trees are first said to be hung with diamonds and many-colored gems; the houses were (or are) overladen with silver, the streets paved with "slippery" brightness. The frigid halo "flung over all familiar things" reaches from cottage chimneys "to the steeple of the meeting-house, that gleamed upward to the sky." Once again, as in the frame introduction, the image of that steeple among the cottages is suggestively linked with a light that veils. (As we shall see, the delusion that building a steeple can substitute for true Christian charity is the real horror.) The real witches or fiends are not supernatural agents of the devil, but ordinary people, pious but hard of heart, encased in ice:

> This living world, where we sit by our firesides, or go forth to meet beings like ourselves, seemed rather the creation of wizard power, with so much of resemblance to known objects that a man might shudder at the ghostly shape of his old beloved dwelling, and the shadow of a ghostly tree before his door. One looked to behold inhabitants suited to such a town, glittering in icy garments, with motionless features, cold, sparkling eyes, and just sensation enough in their frozen hearts to shiver at each other's presence. (12:288; *T&S*, 211–12)

It is a description of New Englanders, those provincial Americans who would become witch-hunters, violating the sanctity of the human heart because of their cold belief in a pure and pernicious idea. It also describes those around us, now, in the "living world." With this description, section 7 concludes.

As the creation of wizard power, the visionary scene of ice light is linked to both the gothic legend of a wizard and the 1692 delusion of wizardry and witchcraft. Since there are no quotation marks around the paragraph that constitutes section 7, presumably all this has been addressed to us by the frame narrator, giving us a generalized description of the icy world we live in (the narrator, the two women, ourselves). But clearly, since it is summer in the frame narrative, the ice-light vision (however generalized a description it may be) has to be taken as part of the manuscript tale of Leonard Doane as well. Indeed, the narrator opens the next section with the comment that "by *this* fantastic piece of description, and more in the same style, I intended to throw a ghostly glimmer round the reader . . ." (12:288–89; *T&S*, 212; my italics). The phrasing parallels the "glimmering light" of the end of section 2 (12:284; *T&S*, 209), linking the whole, particularly the imagery of the physical scene of the gothic tale and the narratival metaphors of the author-narrator. The "reader" mentioned both times includes the *Token* readers, the surrogate audience of the narrator's "two fair auditors," and us in our armchair world. That is, the author-narrator includes us, as the implicated readers of the double narrative of "Alice Doane's Appeal," in the cold veil of appearances described as pertaining to the Doane story and to human existence in general. But the shift of reference from text to reader also suggests another meaning of the symbol of narrative glimmering.

The second part of the opening sentence of section 8 suggests the typical Hawthornesque concept of the relation of the actual and the imaginary as the province of romance. The author-narrator attempts the "ghostly glimmer" so that the reader's "*imagination* might view the town through a *medium* that should take off its every-day aspect" (my italics). The imaginative description provides a new lens. The sentence continues to underscore the literary: the imagination might make "it," the town presumably, "a proper theatre for so wild a scene as the final one." Or perhaps the ambiguity of the antecedent means that the imagination itself is the "proper theatre," as in so many other of Hawthorne's works.

The technique of narrative retrospective summary is taken up again — briefly. The "wretched brother and sister," Leonard and Alice Doane, "were *represented* as setting forth, at midnight, through the gleaming streets" (my italics). Along the way, Leonard and Alice "seemed" to see the wizard accompanying them. All the "gleaming" of that frigid halo of the pervasive ice light is conducive to *some* kind of visionary experience, whether transcendental or psychological.

Alice and Leonard were led, says the author-narrator, to the town cemetery, where "all the dead" have been laid, including the murdered man buried three days earlier. The author-narrator has told the young women that the spot whither *he* has led *them* is a place of unhallowed burial — a witches' "grave yard" on Gallows Hill. Abruptly, the author-narrator writes: "I paused, and gazed into the faces of my two fair auditors, to judge whether, even on the hill where *so many had been brought to death by wilder tales than this*, I might venture to proceed" (12:289; *T&S*, 212; my italics). With this comment, history and fiction are conflated in a new, almost literal way. Fictions have consequences for the lives of people.

This point looks forward to the denouement of the narrative as a whole, which hangs upon the reaction of the storyteller's audience. Their reaction is in two main phases. The first is their double response to the climactic scene of the frame author's gothic tale; the second is their reaction to his substitution of Cotton Mather and the Salem Witch Trials for the wizard and the gothic tale.

The frame author describes the first reaction of the "ladies" in ambiguous and self-reflexively ironic terms. "Their bright eyes were fixed on me; their lips apart. I took courage, and led the fated pair to a new made grave, where for a few moments, in the bright and silent midnight, they stood alone." Once again, deliberate ambiguity of reference becomes the vehicle for blurring fiction and reality. The pronoun *their* seems in the immediate local context to refer to the two listeners. But does it? After the first reference (to "their" bright eyes), the shift is abruptly (or seemingly) back to the tale: the "fated pair" surely must be Leonard and Alice in the communal graveyard, standing in the bright and silent moonlight by a new-made grave. Yet, as suggested earlier, figuratively the "fated pair" may also refer to the literal listeners, led in imagination by the author-narrator, to a newly made grave at midnight in the 1690s, as he has led them to a literal grave site on Gallows Hill.

Suddenly, "there was a multitude of people among the graves." What graves? Those in the graveyard of the Doane tale? Those of "the spot" on Gallows Hill where the pair of listeners are sitting? Is the sentence to be taken as literal, imaginative, then, now, in the future? The scene is as indefinite as the vision or dreamvision experienced by Young Goodman Brown. Suggestively, the detail of the bright eyes of the women fixed on the narrator parallels the sparkling eyes of the townsmen with frozen hearts in the visionary scene of the preceding section, just as the "author's" gazing into the women's faces links him with his narrator, Leonard Doane, gazing into the face(s) of the dead by the lake of ice. Section 8 ends with this intimation of the penultimate apocalypse, preceded by another, described at length in the next section.

The third vision: imagination and the "forge of villainy." Section 9 continues the generalized description of the "multitude among the graves" begun in section 8. Imperceptibly the focus shifts gradually but insistently back to the present time of the frame as the next apocalyptic vision is uncovered:

"Each family tomb had given up its inhabitants, who, one by one, through distant years, had been borne to its dark chamber, but now came forth and stood in a pale group together" (12:289; *T&S*, 212). The emphasis on "each family," on their emerging "through distant years," and on their forming a pale group "together" is more significant than it appears on the surface. Individuals and families and representatives of the community as a whole emerge out of the past. But do they emerge *out of* superstition (imagination) or *in* supernatural reality? *in* legend or history? *in* this tale of Leonard and Alice Doane, or *in* the frame narrative?

The author-narrator gives us a description that constitutes a static processional, foreshadowing that described in section 10. But is it from an omniscient point of view or does it reflect Leonard Doane's? Or both? The tableau includes representative types: the gray ancestor, the aged mother, the descendants, some aged, some in their prime, and the children "who went prattling to the tomb." There is (or was) the maiden who died before "passion" had "polluted" her beauty. Husbands and wives arose (or are arising) from their graves, along with young mothers who had forgotten to kiss their first babes, so long pillowed on their bosoms. Some wear "their ancient garb"; some are dressed as "old defenders of the infant colony, and gleamed forth in their steel-caps and bright breast-plates, as if starting up at an Indian war-cry." Others had been pastors of the church. There are the illustrious early settlers and the "heroes of tradition and *fireside legends*" and "men of *history* whose features had been so long beneath the sod that few alive would have remembered them" (12:290; *T&S*, 212–13; my italics). There were also the "faces of former towns-people, dimly recollected" from the childhood of Leonard and Alice, and "others, whom Leonard and Alice had wept in later years." These last "now" were (or are) "most terrible of all, by their ghastly smile of recognition." One at first wonders what this smile of recognition signifies. It is quickly "clarified" by an important generalization that actually further complicates the scene. "*All*, in short, were there; the dead of other generations. . . . Yet *none* but *souls accursed* were there, and *fiends* counterfeiting the likeness of departed saints" (my italics).

The indeterminacy (and interdeterminacy) of the scene derives from more than the merging together of the past and present of the historical graveyard and the present time of the frame narrative. Our uncertainty is not just the result of our not knowing what the ontological basis of this description is. It is not even that we are unsure whether this is Leonard Doane's perception, or his lack of such a perception, or the author-narrator's. Are the mingled accursed souls and fiends diabolically conjured to confuse Leonard and Alice? Especially perplexing, the statement that *all* were there, yet *none* but the accursed, seems to constitute either a wholesale condemnation of human kind, amounting to a proposition of universal evil like the devil's in "Young Goodman Brown," or to be a flat contradiction. Are *all* the deceased Puritans of Salem accursed? That, after all, is Goodman Brown's error: projecting the idea of universal depravity and condemnation on to others. And why are "fiends" among the departed Puritans of Salem, "counterfeiting" their likenesses?[16]

Here the case made by a handful of critics for Hawthorne's deliberate evocation in various works of the controversy over specters and "specter evidence" that attended the Salem Witch Trials illuminates both Hawthorne's precise use of historiography and his careful construction of literary effect.[17] In essence, the problem of specter evidence is this: since the devil has the power to put images into the mind of a prospective sinner in order to trap the unwary, how can one be sure that testimony as to witchcraft is valid? At the Salem Witch Trials, several people were convicted on the testimony that they had been *seen by those they afflicted.* Twenty persons were executed. The theological question examined later was: how does one know if he saw, say, John Proctor, afflicting him or the *specter* of John Proctor? Satan may have conjured up the image of John Proctor in order to ensnare a previously innocent soul; and the devil, they knew, would willingly send to early death twenty innocent souls to entrap just one for hell. The concept of specter evidence seems to clear up the problems in the graveyard vision of "Alice Doane's Appeal" — though not completely.

Specter evidence is linked in intricate ways to seventeenth-century concepts of the mental faculties and Puritan convictions regarding truth and delusion. One of the most important faculties (partly because it seemed so equivocal) is the great subject of the romantic era and the subject of much of Hawthorne's work — the imagination. As Perry Miller observes, the imagination in the Puritan model of the mind "had never been bound to the senses and could form images beyond and in excess of nature."[18] Miller explains the precarious or suspect position of the imagination: ". . . once [the imagination] is depraved it becomes utterly lawless, and will throw up *phantasms* of *unnatural lusts to seduce* the will and affections; it can lead enfeebled reason in its train, or if the reason objects, cut short the arc of the reflex and present its *perverted images* directly to the will or immediately to the *passions*" (p. 257; my italics). This analysis describes Leonard Doane's condition: we are told early in his story that he has a "diseased imagination" and "morbid feelings" and that he feels unnatural lust for his sister and is not in control of his passions. Leonard Doane's first vision (of the face of Walter Brome merging with the face of his father) and the graveyard vision here described (*as if* Doane's) may be the products of a depraved imagination. The interior gothic tale is thus another psychological romance carefully crafted by Hawthorne, rather than an unintentional revelation of forbidden desires in the psyche of the author.

But the concept of specter evidence is even more ominous in its political and historical import than mere individual insanity. Miller writes that the Puritans regarded imagination as especially "dangerous" because "Satan, retaining his angelic incorporeality, can insert images into it without any agency of the senses, thus tempting the will with imaginations of such vices as could never have been conceived merely from experience." The devil thus has no need of "speaking with an audible voice" or "representing things to our bodily eyes" but has "a closer and more secret way of access to our Imaginations" whereby he can "represent" the *images* of things.

Darrel Abel, making use of the same elucidation of the Puritan model of the mind or soul (*Moral Picturesque*, pp. 135–36), implies that Hawthorne probably was among those readers of Richard Sibbes's *The Souls Conflict*, a widely read book on what Miller calls "the imagination and its crimes." Abel's point is that "Hawthorne does not merely admit the epistemological uncertainty arising from confusions of the subjective self and the world; he deliberately exposes and artfully exploits it in his tales. If there is such a thing as 'certainty,' it is in subjective conviction, not in objective certification" (pp. 136–37). But there is a further point to be made, also suggested by Miller. Sibbes's "most significant charge" against imagination as "sinful fancy" is that it "forms images either of happiness and delight, or of horror and terror, which are unreal, which are not in accordance with the nature of things," so that the lives of many persons are (in Sibbes's words) "almost nothing else but a fancy" (Miller, p. 258). This condition is, in fact, a central subject of gothic fiction (as in almost any of Poe's tales, for example), and is, I believe, one of the main points not only of the Doane part of Hawthorne's narrative, but of the entire narrative.

Miller observes that passages of this sort make clear why to Puritans what we might call " 'romantic' poetry, visions of supernal and unearthly loveliness . . . were not only nonsense, but sinful." By the same token, "romances" were dangerous because they are "adorned" with "Fictions," with "representations" of (in the words of the Puritan Samuel Willard) "things according as we fancy they should be, not regarding what they are indeed" (quoted in Miller, p. 258). The New England Puritans thought they had a tight grip on Reality: "Things are good or evil in the Puritan view," writes Miller, "not according to our opinion but *as they are in themselves*" (my italics). He goes on to say:

> The New England divines rephrased Sibbes on countless occasions, as for example Hooker in *The Application of Redemption:*

> A mans imaginations are the forge of villainy, where it's al framed, the Warehouse of wickedness, the Magazine of al mischief and iniquity, whence the sinner is furnished to the commission of al evil, in his ordinary course. . . . The Imagination of our mind is the great Wheel that carries al with it.
>
> Consequently, the first act of regeneration must be a cleansing of the imagination, an enforcement of strict conformity between the mental image and the thing. . . . (*New England Mind*, pp. 258–59)

It is precisely this "certainty" that Hawthorne calls into question in the confrontation in "Alice Doane's Appeal" between two kinds of narrative (the historical and the literary), two kinds of fiction (extraordinary and ordinary), and two kinds of interpretative imagination (theological-historical and romantic-fictional). "Alice Doane's Appeal" demonstrates the difference between the puritanical sense of the imagination and Hawthorne's romantic concept of imagination. Clear-cut separations, definitive categories, neat compartmentalizations into what is real and unreal, are, like the phases and segments of the narrative of "Alice Doane's Appeal," illusory.[19]

The apocalyptic revelation in the graveyard in section 9 of "Alice Doane's Appeal" may be "real" (*all* the Salem Puritans were "souls accursed"); or it may be "unreal" (the delusion of Leonard Doane's diseased imagination); or again it may be "real" (a vision conjured up by Satan), in which case it is "unreal" (not true). One of the deft ironies of Hawthorne's narrative is the way in which it confronts delusions one with another in an almost unending succession of negative *apokalypsis*. The inherent dialogical quality of the narrative is suggested by these interpenetrating alternatives. The reader is faced with the possibility that (as in gothic romance) Leonard Doane's vision in the graveyard (if it is his alone) is the product of a "diseased imagination"; and the possibility that the vision in the graveyard (whosoever it is) is the product of Satanic machination. If the vision proceeds from the imagination, it may be literally "unreal" but figuratively "true" as art portraying the human heart. If it proceeds from the devil, it is "real" but an "illusion." The dialogical confrontation of seventeenth- and nineteenth-century *epistēmēs* constitutes the framed romantic irony of an arabesque.[20]

As the description of the graveyard vision continues, the language seems to confirm the demonic, spectral nature of the vision. The "countenances" of what seemed venerable men are now contorted by pain or "hellish passion" alternating with "unearthly and derisive merriment" (12:290; *T&S*, 213). And had the "pastors" prayed, "all saintlike as they seemed," it had been "blasphemy." The "whole miserable multitude, both sinful souls and false spectres of good men, groaned horribly and gnashed their teeth, as they looked upward to the calm loveliness of the midnight sky, and beheld those homes of bliss where they must never dwell" (12:291; *T&S*, 213–14).

The vision is highly Dantesque. Among the "miserable multitude" of the sensual and the passionate are chaste matrons and maidens with untasted lips who had slept in virgin graves "apart from all other dust," whose faces now wore a look from which the "two trembling mortals" shrank (presumably Alice and Leonard, though the two young women of the frame are not out of the question). It was "as if the unimaginable sin of twenty worlds were collected there." The phrase "twenty worlds" is especially suggestive, not only alluding to the twenty victims of the Salem Witch Trials, but also implying that each consciousness thus lost were a "world" in itself. The use of the word "passion" throughout the narrative is clarified by the comment that the faces of once fond lovers were now bent on one another "with glances of hatred and smiles of bitter scorn," exhibiting "passions that are to devils what love is to the blest." But again we must question whether this is the distinctive voice of the frame narrator or Leonard Doane, whose psychological nature is twisted round "passion." In either case, Doane, inhabiting the icy world, consumed with passion and lacking love, is in league with devils.

The apocalypse climaxes in dissolution. As in "An Old Woman's Tale," the moonbeams on the ice of the graveyard glitter through seemingly palpable objects: a warrior's breastplate or the letters of a tombstone or the form that stands before the marker. The breeze sweeps "all the unreal throng" into "one indistinguishable cloud together." Rather than just the spectral multitude before Leonard and Alice Doane, all the past, all the present, all fictional characters, all historical characters are melded together; and the penultimate section ends. Just before the vision is swept away, the narrator exclaims: "Such was the apparition, though too shadowy for language to portray." Of course, as the author-narrator well knows, his language has done just that: portrayed an apparition.

"Whether Truth Were More Powerful Than Fiction": *A Trial, a Moral, and a Monument*

The reader will recall that the "fiends" are eager to know if the wizard's designs upon Alice and Leonard (and apparently Walter) "were consummated." But the interior gothic tale concludes with the absolution pronounced by Walter, dispersing the "apparitions" in an abrupt denouement that is no denouement. A new throng of ghosts and devils is immediately to rise up — different yet similar — real yet imaginary — literal and metaphoric — historical but fictional.

The author-narrator writes: "The sun had gone down. While I held my page of wonders in the fading light, and read how Alice and her brother were left alone among the graves, my voice mingled with the sigh of a summer wind." This apparitional effect is like the wizard's laugh blending with a gust of wind in Leonard's narrative in section 4. The initial reaction of the storyteller's audience is not clear. "Not a word was spoken till I added that the wizard's grave was close beside us. . . ." Indeed, the wood-wax "had sprouted originally" from the wizard's "unhallowed bones." At this, the "ladies started." But then, like the wizard, they laugh.

Our author, however, maintains "an awful solemnity of visage." His gothic tale is based on historical legend associated with the spot; and he is, therefore a "little piqued" that a narrative that "would have brought even a church deacon to Gallows Hill, in old witch times, should now be considered too grotesque and extravagant for timid maids to tremble at" (12:292; T&S, 214–15). Confirming that the midnight vision in the graveyard described in the previous section (despite the blurring of time and place) was indeed that of Leonard and Alice Doane, the storyteller decides to detain his friends "a while longer on the hill" even though "it was past supper time." For he wants to make "a trial whether truth were more powerful than fiction."

We have come full circle in the frame narrative. Images and motifs from the opening frame begin to recur, as the narrator describes how "we looked again towards the town," which is "no longer" (now, in the frame narrative present) "arrayed in that icy splendor" that he has described "beneath the glow of a wintry midnight" in sections 7–9. The phrase "no longer" suggests that the fictive imagination has indeed clothed or veiled the "actual" scene before them with icy light. At the same time, the author-narrator emphasizes the "unreal" realness of the fictive midnight vision, which, he says, had been "shining afar through the gloom of a century," and had made "it" (the town? the story? the vision?) "appear the very home of visions in visionary streets." Having said this, he hints at the indistinct boundary between his seventeenth-century fiction and the scene of the nineteenth-century town below. "An indistinctness had begun to creep over the mass of buildings and blend them with the intermingled tree-tops" of the surrounding wilderness "except where the roof of a statelier mansion, and the steeples and brick towers of churches, caught the brightness of some cloud that yet floated in the sunshine." Once again the prospect of the skyline of the seventeenth century is, by association and suggestion, blended with that of the nineteenth — with the spires of churches (catching both light and shadow) prominently featured. "Twilight over the land-scape," the storyteller observes, "was congenial to the obscurity of time."

The fourth vision: hoar antiquity. Therefore, "with such eloquence as my share of feelings and fancy could supply, I called back hoar antiquity. . . ." The precise locale and the history supposedly attending it are specifically evoked, paralleling the introductory section of the narrative, as he bids his "companions imagine an ancient multitude of people, congregated on the hillside" and at any other place that a glimpse of "this spot" might be obtained. The irony of the word "congregate" is obvious; and by the use of "multitude," he links this re-created vision of the historical inhabitants of Salem Village with the "multitude" of accursed souls and fiends of the second graveyard vision. The fourth vision begins.

Summarizing in the manner of section 1, the storyteller writes: "I strove to realize and faintly communicate the deep, unutterable loathing and horror, the indignation, the affrighted wonder, that wrinkled on every brow, and filled the universal heart." At first indefinite, the point, we realize, is the horror the *villagers* felt at having discovered real witches among them. Shifting to the present tense (emphasizing the presence of the past), the narrator observes that the "whole crowd turns pale and shrinks within itself," when the accused "emerge from yonder street." These accused witches, however, he now calls the "virtuous," inverting the judgment of the Puritans upon themselves and the witches.

Casting himself into his historical narrative as an observer among the crowd, the storyteller writes: "Keeping pace with that devoted company [the "virtuous" accused], I described them one by one." Continuing the motif of gazing into faces, he gives a generalized description of representative types in a processional inversely parallel to that of the specters in section 9 and the beginning of 10: "here tottered a woman in her dotage, knowing neither the crime imputed her, nor its punishment"; "there another, distracted by the universal madness" of the witchcraft delusion, "till *feverish dreams were remembered as realities,* and she almost believed her guilt" (my italics); a once proud man, "broken down by the intolerable hatred heaped upon him" (somewhat like Major Molineux), seems to hasten his steps as if "eager to hide himself in the grave hastily dug at the foot of the gallows"; a mother looking back at her peaceful dwelling, "cast her eyes elsewhere, and groaned inwardly yet with bitterest anguish, for there was her little son among the accusers"; an "ordained pastor, who walked onward to the same death," his lips moving in prayer, but not in a "narrow petition for himself alone, but embracing all his fellow-sufferers and the frenzied multitude."

As he called the accused the "virtuous," so now the storyteller describes the accusers as the "afflicted." The wordplay, of course, suggests that rather than having been afflicted by witchcraft, they are afflicted in mind — the devil's triumph over them. A "guilty and miserable band," he calls the accusers rather than the accused: "villains who thus avenged themselves on their enemies"; "viler wretches, whose cowardice had destroyed their friends"; "lunatics, whose ravings had chimed in with the madness of the land"; and "children, who had played a game that the imps of darkness might have envied them" because it "disgraced an age, and dipped a people's hands in blood" (12:294; *T&S*, 216). The adjectives "miserable" and "guilty" joined with the word "multitude" reinforce the linguistic link to the specter apparitions of section 9, suggesting that the Puritan townspeople are, after all, "souls accursed," "fiends damned," and "counterfeits." The "historical" description is highly "literary" and "gothic."

Those of us who have lived through the middle years of the twentieth century will be forcibly reminded of Arthur Miller's *The Crucible* (1952) and the implicit allegory of the "witch-hunt" of the McCarthy era. Miller takes the historical incidents in Salem and gives us a historical interpretation of that history in terms of psychological perversion and desire for power that parallels the political oppression of the 1950s. Hawthorne, I dare say, had he lived through these years would have done the same — though with greater subtlety and complexity. The McCarthy figure of "Alice Doane's Appeal" is Cotton Mather, but Hawthorne's "villain" is much more enigmatic than Miller's. In the same paragraph as the description of the afflicted — the penultimate paragraph of the narrative — we read: "In the rear of the procession rode a figure on horseback, so darkly conspicuous, so sternly triumphant, that my hearers mistook him for the visible presence of the fiend himself. . . ." The situation is very much like that of the satanic, double-faced figure riding a horse in the witch-hunt procession of "My Kinsman, Major Molineux." The storyteller continues, sarcastically, "but it was only his good friend, Cotton Mather, proud of his well-won dignity, as representative of all the hateful features of his time. . . ." The judgment, the irony, the sarcasm, are all very clear. But the rest of the sentence turns ambiguous: Cotton Mather is described as "the *one blood-thirsty man*, in whom were concentrated those vices of spirit and errors of opinion that sufficed to madden the whole surrounding multitude" (my italics). Such a generalization (concentrating all the blame in a single figure) is quite unlike Hawthorne, and another twist in the narrative is in the offing.

And "thus I marshalled them onward," proclaims the storyteller, both the innocent and the guilty, "till their shadowy visages had circled round the hill-top, *where we stood*" (my italics). Seeking even greater effect, the author-narrator says, "I plunged into my imagination for a blacker horror, and a deeper woe, and pictured the scaffold. . . ." But at this point his two "companions seized an arm on each side," their nerves "trembling." At last he has touched them: "sweeter victory still, I had reached the seldom trodden places of their hearts, and found the well-spring of their tears."

The narrator's "trodden" metaphor suggests the literal situation of their walk up Gallows Hill and into the past (both literary and historical); and, of course, it recurs to the statement in the introductory frame about his townspeople's lack of "heartfelt interest" in history. By his fictional abilities, the storyteller has brought into vivid imagining for his audience a history of the scene. The power of his imagination has affected their imaginations, creating a fanciful phantasm in their minds which will affect the emotions — though they think it is reality and truth that so affect them. The storyteller says at this point, significantly: "And now the past had done all it could." They slowly descend the hill, watching the lights as they twinkle "gradually through the town" (as in Dante's *Inferno*). Minor ironies are noted as they return (cf. "Young Goodman Brown") from their visionary experiences to the quotidian world of their town and their time. They hear the "distant mirth" of boys at play and the voice of a young girl "warbling somewhere in the dusk," a pleasant sound to "wanderers from old witch times."

The fifth epiphany: moral historiography and monumental imagination. The narrative concludes with the monument motif, introduced in the introductory frame, and a final comment on the meaning of the word *appeal*, constituting the apparent "moral" of the work. These wanderers from the past, ere they leave the hill, "could not but regret that there is nothing on its barren summit, no relic of old, nor lettered stone of later days, to assist the imagination in appealing to the heart." The author-narrator comments that we build memorial columns at battlefields, on heights "our fathers made sacred with their blood," which we commemorate as though "poured out in a holy cause." The provincial memory celebrates selected events in the holy war against both the oppression of Satan and his wild half-human minions in the New World wilderness and the oppression of misguided Old World religions. We celebrate the establishment of white, European, Puritan colonial power in the new hemisphere, romanticizing it with ballads to Lovell's Fight, legends of a Gray Champion, memorial columns to the Revolution, and conveniently forget the extenuated circumstances of these events, not to mention other, more negative events. The battlegrounds made "sacred" with the blood of heroes also cost the blood of others — those who are sacrificed along the way to someone else's purpose — blood which is soaked into the ground of Gallows Hill and perhaps has generated its odd vegetation of deceit and delusion. There should also be a monument to that: "here, in dark, funereal stone, should rise another monument, sadly commemorative of the errors of an earlier race," a monument not to be cast down so long as the "human heart has one infirmity that may result in crime." The irony is patient and patent: the "crime" to be memorialized is not witchcraft. Hawthorne's narrative of "Alice Doane's Appeal" is the dubious monument to our enduring propensity to error, egoism, and failure of sympathy.

Thus the concluding sentence would seem to constitute the "moral" of the piece. The appeal for a monument to assist imaginative remembrance of the bad as well as the good is in one sense the ultimate appeal of the narrative, but that appeal is as deceptive and ironic as the narrative itself. It is as deceptive as the author-narrator's comment that the graveyard scene is too "apparitional" for language to portray. Clearly, our "author" has no need of any monument other than the hill itself, his historical knowledge, and his knowledge of the deceptiveness and uncertainty of knowledge. Appealing for inclusion of the negative as well as the positive in our history (and the concomitant recognition of the fictional in history), the storyteller has all along suggested that final knowledge of good and evil is uncertain, as uncertain as the difference between legend and history, truth and fiction. His radical skepticism is built into the narrative from start to finish, culminating in the negative epiphany of the "final" vision.

But the culminating *apokalypsis* only seems to be the "true" vision of the historical. Is it historically accurate to cast Cotton Mather as the "one blood-thirsty man" responsible for all evil — whether as the symbolic surrogate of either the infernal wizard or the demonic protagonist of the gothic tale — or as the demonic incarnation of the spirit of Puritan vigilance and persecution? The storyteller's representative audience *appears* to be affected not by the storyteller's gothic romance playing out all those dreary literary conventions, but by the "tragic romance" of "true" history. The "tragedy" and "romance" of history are, however, re-created by a storyteller. The storyteller's surface moral is once again penultimate. The audience is unaware of the role of imagination and convention in "real," historical narrative.

To clarify this point, and to emphasize its narratival significance, let us return to the historiographical passage of the frame introduction. The storyteller says of the "historian," with measured irony, that he has the "better wisdom" that "draws the moral while it tells the tale." This is an especially interesting comment, tonally and semantically, in view of Hawthorne's habit of drawing morals. (Colacurcio, p. 552, believes that the tone here is "undoubtedly" ironic.) The suggestion seems to be that the moralizing of the historian to whom Hawthorne refers is embedded in the narrative, permeating it without conscious reflection, and may be the more suspect or even pernicious for that reason. The "while," then, implies a high degree of subjective bias to the historical account. And the question remains, "better wisdom" than what? Or a wisdom "better" than what? Than unvarnished history — whatever that might be? Better wisdom than that of other historical accounts? We remember that Hawthorne's author-narrator comments that the historian in question has tried to "keep his name alive" by converting the hill of the forefathers' "disgrace" into "an honorable monument of his own antiquarian lore." Following the lead of historicist critics, we may suggest that the precise identity of this historian makes a difference.

Indeed, the historian has been rather conclusively identified as Charles Wentworth Upham, author of *Lectures upon Witchcraft*, published in Boston in 1831, a book critical of the witchcraft delusions of seventeenth-century New Englanders and of Cotton Mather in particular.[21] Now one would not ordinarily think that Hawthorne would be critical of a book critical of past egocentrism, arrogance, and inhumanity in the cause of a delusion. But, as we have seen throughout the *Provincial Tales*, Hawthorne is critical of one-sided arrogance, of monological pronouncement, of assurance that one possesses the Truth. Therefore, Upham, profoundly influencing as he did our notions of the historical truth of what happened in Salem, is worth special notice. The supposedly correct recovery of a past and the moral presentation of such history by historians like Upham is important to the concluding interpretation of "Alice Doane's Appeal." That is to say, this version of the past in which Cotton Mather serves as cultural scapegoat is likely a misreading of the past.

Chadwick Hansen in *Witchcraft at Salem* (1969) gives an account of what he calls the "distortions" of the historical record and the "malicious" portrait of the Mathers as power-crazed witch hunters. The villain of Hansen's revisionary history is Robert Calef, whose caustic "reply" to Cotton Mather's *Wonders of the Invisible World* (1693) is titled *More Wonders of the Invisible World* (1700), a book he had to have printed in England because the Mathers prevented its publication in America. It was Calef's version of the witch trials, and of the Mathers' role in it all, that Charles Upham followed in both his 1831 *Lectures upon Witchcraft* and his later *Salem Witchcraft* (Boston, 1867). Hansen defends the Mathers and charges Calef with lying, laying at his door the historical distortions of the next two and a half centuries. He writes (p. 191): "I realize that in calling Calef a liar I differ from virtually every other person who has written about him since his own time. But the charge is not made recklessly." After presenting his evidence (such as it is) that Calef indulged in malicious innuendo and half-truths, Hansen puts the historiographical situation succinctly:

> History has not been fair to Cotton Mather. Indeed the majority of historians have, in complete defiance of the facts, presented him as a man who instigated witchcraft trials to satisfy his own lust for fame and power. This view owes much to Robert Calef, but the historian *chiefly responsible* for perpetuating it is the Reverend Charles Wentworth Upham, whose . . . [books on witchcraft] made him the standard authority in the field. Upham, who was a mayor of Salem as well as its minister, was Hawthorne's model for Judge Pyncheon in *The House of the Seven Gables*, and Upham's books display both the malice and the defective moral perceptions of his fictional counterpart. It is Upham who perpetuated the warped image of Cotton Mather which remains his popular image, despite the efforts of more conscientious historians to correct it.[22]

If one accepts the identification of Upham as the model for the pious hypocrite Judge Pyncheon, it would seem to provide substantial corroboration of Hawthorne's ironic attitude toward Upham as Salem minister, local Salem official, and Salem "historian." If Hawthorne is referring to Upham in this story, the aim of the "historian" alluded to in "Alice Doane's Appeal" should be cause not for fame but for shame; for he is keeping his name alive via calumniation of the dead. The "historian's" laying the blame for the witch trials at the door of the family of one man, Cotton Mather, is implicitly criticized, even as the witchcraft craze itself is lamented. The literary-historical monument is comprised more of *negative apokalypsis* than of *alēthēa*.

If the text referred to is Upham's witchcraft treatise of 1831, the timing suggests that what we have is in fact an original version of Hawthorne's story and not necessarily an actual revision of an Ur-text written in the 1820s. Or, if not the original text, could we not, in some fundamental way, have the originary intention? For the point of "Alice Doane's Appeal," as we have it, has to do with the author telling his tale — and probably always did. It is a specifically author-foregrounding work, representative of other such pieces in Hawthorne; and it does not stand in isolation in the *Provincial Tales* but instead culminates a major thematic narrative strand. The "Alice Doane's Appeal" that we have is contemporaneous with the metafictional, highly self-reflexive framed story cycle *The Story Teller*.

It cannot be definitively determined that the author figure of the narrative is the Story Teller of *The Story Teller* any more than the literal Hawthorne. But he is *a* storyteller, one of many complex tropes of authorial presence in Hawthorne's works. Just as the interior gothic tale cannot be said to represent Hawthorne's psyche, so the critical point of the frame is not that Hawthorne himself burned some of his early works in disappointment or frustration (he may have), but that the author figure of "Alice Doane's Appeal" says *he* has. In both framed tale and frame narrative, the "author" is following romantic literary convention.[23] Hawthorne's author figure takes a certain ironic attitude toward his tales, the craft of authorship, and himself as author. When the final question of truth or fiction is presented in "Alice Doane's Appeal," the historical is dialogically played off against the literary with the same ironic sensibility. And in *The Story Teller*, these matters are treated semiparodically, with romantic irony, *in extenso*.

If Hawthorne thought Upham's nineteenth-century judgments were based on a "simplistic moralism," as Colacurcio suggests (p. 552), then the "denouement" of "Alice Doane's Appeal" ironically gives yet *one more fold* to the central theme of truth and fiction, history and romance, in the *Provincial Tales*. Certainly Hawthorne's depiction of Cotton Mather elsewhere, as in *Grandfather's Chair*, is less critical. Complicating the portrait in the Doane narrative is the foregrounded qualification of the historical by the dreamlike, the visionary, the imaginative, and the fictive. The two women's epiphany is delusive. What they think is the pure fact of history is mediated. The apparent parallel epiphany for the reader that truth is more powerful than fiction is, likewise, delusive. Any epiphany built into the text is this: the concluding "historical" narrative, with its revelation of the Truth at last, which so affects the audience as "real," is a *fiction* from start to finish. And this the Story Teller figure of the narrative has known from the start.

6 The Oberonic Self

"I jest to Oberon, and make him smile. . . ." —*A Midsummer Night's Dream*

The paradigmatic sketches and tales we have examined make it clear that the *Provincial Tales*, rather than being merely sentimentalized or purely patriotic pieces, were instead negative romances framing a counterpoised tension of positive and negative attributes of the American forebears. Central to each is the framing authorial presence of the narrator. Given the original metafictional interconnections of the early narratives, especially clear in *The Story Teller* scheme, it is evident that the full effect of narrative intrusion or narrator/author presence has been effectually lost. By disassembling the *Provincial Tales* and *The Story Teller*, Hawthorne's editors did Hawthorne (and us) a major disservice. When, however, the surviving tales are read in conjunction with even the dream sketches of *Provincial Tales*, Hawthorne's themes of the interpenetration of times, perspectives, realities, and modes become linked more tightly to the indeterminate "location" of the story-telling "I" as third-person narrator.

In this chapter, I attempt to recapitulate the large argument of the entire book in the context of the erased (or unobserved) generic boundaries of tale and sketch as Hawthorne developed them. The implications of this generic blurring are reified by the frequent occurrence of more or less satiric (certainly ironic) narratorial intervention in the works of Hawthorne, including the many prefaces and occasional epilogues (such as the whimsical, ironically serious "second" conclusion of *The Marble Faun*). The satiric artist-fable "The Devil in Manuscript" (1835), serves as an introduction to the "Oberonic" nature of the storyteller in *The Story Teller*. The self-reflexive framework of *The Story Teller* itself has both a visionary motif and, as its principal structural line, the theme of imagination in conflict with New England provincialism. This conflict is embodied in the westward journey of a young would-be writer, fleeing from the oppressive Puritan atmosphere of New England. As he travels the northwestern frontier (the

Great Lakes), the story-telling youth "performs" his works along the route of the Erie Canal to different audiences. Featuring the native scene, foregrounding authorial presence via author tropes, combining and interlineating tale and sketch, *The Story Teller* is an especially appropriate work with which to conclude this study of Hawthorne's provincial narratives.

From Tale to Sketch: The Strange
Art of "Authorial" Presence

Hawthorne's self-reflexive irony is more obvious in the sketches of *Provincial Tales* than in the tales, particularly when they conclude abruptly with such reader-frustrating interjections as "Oho! What have we here?" Principally with this effect in mind has the paradigmatic set of dreamvision sketches been ranged as examples of non-denouement, or nonconventional denouement. In these, the full effect depends on recognizing that the narratives are not in the genre of the "tale proper" as Poe conceived it but are sketches (or something between tale and sketch). These sketches feature play with narrative conventions, often directly by a narrator, in tension yet in collaboration with conventional reader expectations.

As we have seen, "The Hollow of the Three Hills" is nearly all exposition: a "witch" is the medium for three "visions" of the abandoned loved ones of an apparently remorseful woman. After the third brief vision, instead of the completed complication or crisis which we would normally expect at this point, the narrative simply breaks off. The piece shares the ironies and ambiguities of the provincial tales, however, making it more resonant in context than it is in isolation. The supernaturalism of the piece may be only apparent or apparitional; and the apparent interior consciousness, the old woman through whose "magic" we see the psychological events of the moral life of a distressed woman, may not in literal textual fact be the supernatural medium of the woman's consciousness but the projected icon of her repressed subconscious. The most subtle of the sketches is "The Wives of the Dead," in which the narrator is not foregrounded. After a very brief historical introduction setting the incidents of the narrative about one hundred years previous, the narrator launches immediately into his story of two bereaved women, which, at the conclusion, does not have the effect of a fully developed story. On the surface, it is left anecdotal. But when the sketch is seen in the context of the variety of experiments with ambiguity found in Hawthorne's provincial narratives in general, its indeterminate doubleness of crisis and denouement (one structure dependent on the conventions of the sketch, the other on those of the tale) is clearly congruent with Hawthorne's other early radical explorations of theme, form, and genre. The whole hermeneutical problem illustrates, like the interpretative problem of "The Gray Champion," the necessity of recovering the historical and generic conventions of Hawthorne's time as Hawthorne deformed and deployed them. "An Old Woman's Tale" deprives the reader of denouement while emphasizing in the opening frame the narrator as a storyteller who learned his art at the feet of an old woman who has told him many a tale (including the one being told again), which she has learned from other storytellers, who may or may not have known the actual characters, or who may or may not have lived the actual experience upon which her (or his) fiction is based. The male narrator (who was the boy of the retrospective introduction) wishes he had an audience as attentive as the one the old woman had—that is, himself, the storyteller. Symbolically, the ideal audience for an author is an author—a circularity carrying problematized philosophical and aesthetic import that Hawthorne addresses directly in "Alice Doane's Appeal."

"Alice Doane's Appeal" is in this regard the least subtle of the sketches: it is the most highly metafictional and aggressively author-foregrounding narrative of the *Provincial Tales* narratives we have examined. Although it tells an interior gothic story, it is, in its framing by a recurrently manifest author-narrator, more centrally a treatment of authorship and audience in terms of the relation between the created fictive world and the historical record of the "real" world. It is literally a "twice-told" story, a tale-sketch of multiple signification. As we have seen, the author-narrator pointedly observes that by a "fantastic piece of description" of ambiguous place and time he had intended to "throw a ghastly glimmer around the reader"—a parallel to what he is trying to do to a second and third audience as he summarily renarrates his story. The abrupt denouement, wherein the author's second audience is affected only by evocation of the historical past— by what they conceive to be "truth" rather than mere "imagination"— emphasizes the all-encompassing importance of the figure of the author in a metafictional tale-sketch that is central to a full understanding of the *Provincial Tales* project. The next step for Hawthorne was to be the full-scale characterization and involvement of the author figure in the intricate framed-narrative cycle *The Story Teller*.

Throughout this study, I have argued that the literary (or the fictional) and the historical are counterpointed yet conflated in Hawthorne's early writings—indeed, throughout his career. The sketches are played off against tales. Although focused on an American region and its legends, history, politics, religion, and character, the tales of *Provincial Tales* are not "provincial" in the other sense of the word. The twice-told quality of the tales goes counter to the connotations of crudity and naive simplicity suggested by the word *provincial*.

The variations of narratorial presence and the manipulations of minimal framing techniques represent a high degree of sophistication. We have seen that "The Gray Champion" is not a one-sided patriotic evocation of an American legend but a double-edged presentation of excesses on both loyalist and revolutionary republican sides, the revolutionaries in this instance representing the religious interest of the colonies, as those of "My Kinsman, Major Molineux" represent the secular and burgher interests. An incipient American allegory (again as in the more fully developed "My Kinsman, Major Molineux") is cut short; and the narrator is a curious mixture of earnestness and obtuseness. "Roger Malvin's Burial," rather than a tale of expiation, is a psychological portrayal of a disturbed personality, suggesting an ambiguous psychodrama of Puritan culture. It also illustrates the tension between a seemingly supernatural tale of fate and a psychologically realistic tale of repression and compulsion, employing a minimally intrusive narrator, who, after a historical frame introduction and one relatively lengthy interior expletive passage, essentially bows out to leave the tale almost totally dramatized. The idealist, Reuben, his head filled with dreams of heroism and patriarchal glory, wanders in his eighteen-year psychotic state as though in some never-ending nightmare, unaware of being entrapped in a personal and cultural labyrinth. The structures of contradiction at the end are so patent that there is no necessity for further comment by the narrator. "The Gentle Boy" features a similar configuration, though the narrator is more intrusive and judgmental. Rather than a sentimental tear-jerking romance, the tale is a grim portrayal of the operations of symbiotic sadomasochism in individuals and the American (New England) culture at large. Although the narrator offers an oblique sarcastic comment at the end ("her once bitter prosecutors followed her, with decent sadness and tears that were not painful"), it is understated enough to have the effect of dramatic irony.

"My Kinsman, Major Molineux" illustrates Hawthorne's experiment with the convention of the historical tale-teller who withdraws to dramatize his story implicitly from a completely interior perspective focused on one character, but whose historical introduction in the opening paragraphs forms an open-ended frame for a final reversal of the interior psychological drama of the principal perspectival character. A reader inattentive to the opening framing by the tale-teller will tend to misread the entire structure by focusing only on one half of the story. That is, the events as misinterpreted by the protagonist. The same kind of structural and hermeneutical relationship of narrator and reader as found in Poe's "Ligeia" and "Usher," foregrounding indeterminacy, is central to Hawthorne's third-person narratives, though it is achieved differently. Poe essentially never interposes an external narrator into his fictions. Hawthorne almost habitually does.

When Poe objected to this feature in his 1842 reviews of *Twice-told Tales*, he observed that Hawthorne possessed an absolute "singularity" of high "imagination" but disapproved of Hawthorne's narrative persona constantly intruding upon the dramatized events of story. For Hawthorne thereby emphasized the essaylike aspects of his prose rather than the "legitimate" sphere of the fictional. The Hawthorne persona, Poe observed in 1847, after the publication of *Mosses from an Old Manse*, is *"self impelled to touch everything"* and impelled to give "its own hue, its own character to everything it touches" (*E&R*, p. 579). Poe foregrounds the first-person narrator as a less than fully self-conscious character in a drama. Hawthorne foregrounds the author-narrator as a self-conscious figure both in and out of the dramatized world of the text. This author persona is emphasized in the sketches, an effect especially evident if the sketches are examined as a genre sequence slightly different in form and character from the tales, but bearing intricate relationship to them.

It was to be Poe's influence, however, that became the most pervasive on the formal development of the so-called short story in America for the next hundred and thirty years. A line representing the dominant tradition from 1830 to 1960 can be drawn from Poe through Henry James to Hemingway and beyond in the conception of the short story as dramatized and presentational, with strongly reduced author-narrator presence. Given the legacy from Poe of a cleavage between the short story and the sketch (or any other "impure" form of the short story or tale proper), the dividing line between the narrative that is told by a teller and the completely dramatized narrative is clear.[1]

The conceptual bifurcation between the more traditional mode of Hawthorne and the more "modernist" mode of Poe is by no means a judgment on the modernity of Hawthorne, who is in other ways more new and experimental than Poe. Hawthorne's foregrounding of perspectivism and the "teller" is closer to the practice of Jorge Luis Borges, John Barth, Thomas Pynchon, and other postmodern metafictionists, who celebrate the tradition of *Tristram Shandy*. Likewise Hawthorne's narrative cycles are studies in authorship, in story telling and the act of story telling (whether fictional or historical), and in the art of observation as the act of finding materials for prose narrative. The tales and sketches are products of the strong presence of the "author" at the reader's elbow.

In the light of the insistent metafiction of "Alice Doane's Appeal" and the varying levels of self-reflexivity and authorial foregrounding in the other paradigmatic provincial tales, the suspicion articulated at the end of chapter four acquires a certain extratextual probability: that we have a symbolic "author" figuration in the personage of the "kindly stranger" of "My

Kinsman, Major Molineux." In fact, the theme of authorship and authorial presence is, I would say, obsessive in Hawthorne, as suggested by works like "Seven Vagabonds" (1833), "The Canterbury Pilgrims" (1833), "Little Annie's Ramble" (1835), "Wakefield" (1835), "The Ambitious Guest" (1835), "The Vision of the Fountain" (1835), "The Devil in Manuscript" (1835), "Monsieur du Miroir" (1837), "Fancy's Show Box" (1837), "The Toll-Gatherer's Day" (1837), "Chippings with a Chisel" (1838) — or the frames of the "Legends of the Province House" (1838–39) and the frame of "Rappaccini's Daughter" (1844) — or pieces like "A Virtuoso's Collection" (1842), "The Hall of Fantasy" (1843), "P.'s Correspondence" (1845), and "Main Street" (1849). Not to mention the frame-narratives of *Grandfather's Chair* (1841), *A Wonder-Book* (1852), and *Tanglewood Tales* (1853), or the prefaces to various other narrative collections and the novels.

In some of these, Hawthorne employs the characteristically romantic technique of the "projected ego" of the artist, perhaps most graphically exemplified in Walt Whitman's *Song of Myself* (1855). In Whitman's poem, the poet persona projects himself out into the landscape of America, in a series of individual and panoramic scenes, and enters the minds of representative characters as both observer and as empath in fusion with the character. We find variants of this device recurrently in Hawthorne. In "Sights from a Steeple" (1831), the author-narrator wishes for "the Limping Devil of Le Sage" or "a spiritualized Paul Pry" to uncover roofs and hover invisibly around man and woman, merging with them even to the point of "retaining no emotion peculiar to himself" (1:220; *T&S*, 43). We have seen the empathizing artist figure in "Alice Doane's Appeal," not only implicitly throughout, but also in such touches as the narrator's conjuring up the Salem Witch Trials and then walking with the accused in imagination, peering into their faces. It is in fact the overarching theme of "Wakefield," and a similar mix of putative objective authorial distance and subjective fusion with character is emphasized at the end of "The Old Apple-Dealer." In "Little Annie's Ramble," the author-narrator imaginatively walks alongside a little girl exploring the day. The few critics who have commented on the sketch have generally assumed that the black-coated male figure literally takes Annie for a walk; but the town crier's alarm about the lost girl and the mother's panicky reaction confirm that Annie has wandered off by herself and that the account we are given is the imagined one of the speculative, ego-projective narrator: that is, the author figure has not been literally walking along with the little girl, but with such a child in imaginative projection.

In "The Toll-Gatherer's Day" the author figure, "while lounging on a bench at the door" of the toll house at a river bridge, says "I amuse myself with a conception, illustrated by numerous pencil sketches in the air, of the toll-gatherer's day" (1:234–35; *T&S*, 508). That is, it is the imaginative projection of what such a day *would* be like (a processional typifying the traffic of such a day in such a locale, and typifying at another remove "life's" procession through morn, noon, and eve) as it might be perceived by a meditative old toll gatherer (as though a projection or figuration of the narrator himself) watching the procession of life from sunrise to sunset. In "Night Sketches" the "I" narrator leaves his chamber (where he has been reading exotic adventures of romance and faraway travel) as himself. Yet once again it is possible that this sally forth into the night is only in his own imagination. As in "The Toll-Gatherer's Day," in his procession he sees a procession of life. "Monsieur du Miroir" (a sort of "Borges y yo") presents the mirror image of the narrator as an imagined character who is the author figure imagining the author imagining the mirror figure in an implied infinite regress of mirror images. The author-narrator writes reflectively of the mirror character: "Still there he sits and returns my gaze with as much of awe and curiosity as if he, too, had spent a solitary evening in fantastic musings and made me his theme" (2:195; *T&S*, 404).

With regard to "historical" writing, a narratorial/authorial persona is a foregrounded subject in such self-reflexively satiric works as "Main Street." In this work, a showman narrator (manager of a paper and canvas stage show) traces in summary fashion (with the "turn of a crank") the changes over two centuries that the main street (running symbolically east-west) of the Indian province of Naumkeag undergoes as it grows into a native village and then the town of Salem. In addition to the showman, there is another framing narratorial/authorial presence; both delight in taking ironic jabs at the inexorability of "Anglo-Saxon energy." Along with several minor breaks in dramatic illusion, there are six major interruptions of the historical panorama within a beginning and ending frame emphasizing the relationship of an implied author, the separate showman-narrator, and a double audience.

And then there is the matter of persona and voice in the long "authorial" introductions to *Mosses from an Old Manse* (1846) and the second edition of *The Scarlet Letter*, and the chapter of "Conclusion" to *The Marble Faun*.[2] The appended final chapter of *The Marble Faun* is especially pertinent; for the "author" conducts an "interview" with two of his characters in an effort to find out what happened to the others. The scene is equally suggestive of the romantic-ironic tone of "My Kinsman, Major Molineux" and "Alice Doane's Appeal" and the whimsical yet benevolent and serious tone of portions of the "Rappaccini" frame or "Monsieur du Miroir," or the fragments that remain from *The Story Teller* cycle. The narrator writes, once again foregrounding the author-reader relationship: "There comes to the author, from many readers of the foregoing pages, a demand for further elucidations respecting the mysteries of the story" (6:522). A "new edition" affords an opportunity "to explain such incidents and passages as may have been left too much in the dark." The author is sorry if he has but imperfectly succeeded in giving his "Romance" the kind of atmosphere "essential to the effect" at which he has aimed. He had hoped "to mystify this anomalous creature [the Faun] between the Real and the Fantastic, in such a manner that the reader's sympathies might be excited . . . without impelling him to ask how Cuvier would have classified poor Donatello, or to insist on being told, in so many words, whether he had furry ears or no." For those who do ask such questions "the book is, to that extent, a failure" (6:522–23)—which is a gentlemanly way of saying that such readers have failed to read it properly.

And yet, "to confess the truth," the author has been "himself troubled with a curiosity similar to that which he has just deprecated on the part of his readers, and once took occasion to cross-examine his friends, Hilda and the sculptor, and to pry into several dark recesses of the story, with which they had heretofore imperfectly acquainted him" (6:523). While on the surface this passage says that the characters of the "romance" are "real" (and the story thus "true," as per eighteenth- and nineteenth-century fictional convention), the literary convention behind the literary convention also is clear. With the ironic smile of the Merry Andrew, the "author" has fictionalized himself, inserting himself into the world of *The Marble Faun* (without ever until this point becoming a character in that world) to inquire into the mysteries of a story he has himself concocted. "We three had climbed to the top of St. Peter's," he writes, "and were looking down upon the Rome we were soon to leave, but which (having already sinned sufficiently in that way) it is not my purpose further to describe." At the end, the author playfully insists on himself both as observer-character in the real world and as author-character of/in the fictional romance that is "real" though imagined.

The slightly whimsical quality of the romantic irony is patent. The author asks Hilda about a certain "mysterious packet," to which query Hilda replies that she did not know what was in it, nor did she feel she had any right to be curious about it. Kenyon comments that it is impossible to speak of its contents. The first authorial inquiry produces few results. Kenyon instead speculates vaguely about Miriam's family connections with someone in the "papal government" from whose "irksome scrutiny" she doubtless wanted to "withdraw." Upon this, the author figure remarks: "Yes, it is clear as a London fog" (6:524). Kenyon rambles on, and after a bit the author figure says, "Ah, quite a matter of course, as you say. . . . How excessively stupid in me not to have seen it sooner!" (6:525). Yet, says the "author," there are "other riddles" which he would like to have explained. Receiving the same kind of elucidation as before, he observes that "the atmosphere is getting delightfully lucid" and yet "there are one or two things that still puzzle me . . ." (6:526). Getting the usual garrulous non-answer from his characters, he asks, in a final authorial irony, whether Donatello *did in fact have pointed and furry ears* like "the Faun of Praxiteles." And the character gives the appropriate answer to his "author," at this point standing for obtuse readers: "I know, but may not tell," says Kenyon (6:527). The final gesture of a somber and tragic romance is a mild authorial raspberry.

Enter Oberon: The Authorial Devil in the Manuscript

As the whole enterprise of writing historical narrative is dramatized in all of its grand seriousness and absurdity in such a work as "Main Street," so the specifically literary is also given satiric or romantic-ironic treatment in other works. An especially revealing treatment of "authorship" and the character of the author persona is "The Devil in Manuscript" (1835; *Snow-Image*, 1851). The piece illustrates the midway position of many of Hawthorne's compositions, somewhere between story and sketch, and provides a thematic introduction to *The Story Teller*. "The Devil in Manuscript" offers a concise parody of the concerns of an author over publication, publishers, the public, and a public "name." One of the ironies of Hawthorne's early career is that after having published the equivalent of a volume of tales and sketches and dominating the pages of two important magazines, he yet had no name as an author. His sardonic bemusement is suggested by the redoubled irony in "The Devil in Manuscript" of two mutually reflective authors discussing the favorite subject of authors — authorship. It also provides a suggestive conjunction of the devil figure (whatever his metaphysical status for Hawthorne) with the "demon" that resides in the manuscript sheet or in the brain of the author figure under the rubric of the magical but problematical "Oberon."

"The Devil in Manuscript" begins comically in the mode of light grotesque and darkens into a presentation of what seems a bizarre mental aberration. On a cold December night, the narrator spreads his cloak to the wind and sails along the street at ten knots, knocking one person down. He is on his way to meet his friend, Oberon, a fellow author. In front of a blazing hearth, he feels an impulse to roll among the hot coals, while Oberon tells him that there is (or he could *believe* there is) a "devil" in his pile of "blotted" manuscripts: "Oh, I have a horror of what was created in my own brain, and shudder at the manuscripts in which I gave that dark idea a sort of material existence!" (3:575; *T&S*, 330–31). Thus early in the tale the problematic relationship of the "real" and "fictive" worlds is hinted at. When the narrator mentions his desire to be a successful novelist, Oberon, "half seriously" exclaims, "Then, indeed, my devil has his claw upon you!"

Oberon explains that he purposes this night to burn his manuscripts and destroy the devil that resides in them, for he is now a defeated author, "careless" of a "reputation." The fictive shadows with which he has surrounded himself in his writings mimic the realities of life in such a confusing interpenetration that he has bewildered himself and withdrawn into a life of solitude. When the narrator expresses surprise, Oberon ironically observes that the "sacrifice" of his manuscripts is "less than you may suppose, since nobody will publish them." "That does make a difference," is the narrator's dead-pan reply (3:576; *T&S*, 331). Oberon then recounts his various rejection notices in a passage that constitutes a satire on American publishing conditions. He has sent his tales to seventeen booksellers, whose rejection letters he has also burned "as fast as they arrived."

The narrator — in some contrast to the more melancholy Oberon — has a sarcastic turn of mind. He does not, for example, oppose the burning of the tales; for they would probably "make a more brilliant appearance in the fire than anywhere else" (3:577–78; *T&S*, 332–33). Then, picking up the manuscripts with a mixture of affection and disgust, Oberon describes some of the tales in such a way that objective and subjective are inverted, illustrating how the author has become the "victim" of his "own enchantments." When he throws the manuscripts into the flames, Oberon has an epiphany that is immediately given a negative cast. He describes objects that "he appeared to discern" in the fire: lovers clasping each other in their arms while "flame . . . bursts from their glowing hearts"; the "features of a villain writhing in the fire that shall torment him to eternity"; holy men and angelic women burning like martyrs. "A city is on fire," he shouts (3:581; *T&S*, 335). Just as the tales are nearly consumed, a broad "sheet" of flame seems to flicker "as with laughter" and roars up the chimney; Oberon thinks he sees the "demon" in that last sheet of flame. Suddenly, outside in the cold, alarm bells sound, and the cry of fire goes up. Oberon leaps up in exultation: "My tales! . . . The chimney! . . . The Fiend has gone forth by night. . . . Here I stand, — a triumphant author! Huzza! Huzza! My brain has set the town on fire! Huzza!" he shouts like a devil himself (3:583; *T&S*, 337).

This grotesque metafictional comedy has several perspectives playing over it. For one thing, it shows the artist in a hostile but possibly self-deluded relationship to society. It illustrates the ironically self-deprecating attitude in Hawthorne's works toward authorship. The "story teller" is somewhat to one side of normal life, one who has almost bartered life in a Faustian contract. The figure of Oberon and the narrator seem ironic projections of one "author," wherein the melancholy fantasist-artist side (Oberon) attempts to elicit sympathy from the more jest-prone social side (the narrator from the world outside Oberon's chamber). Both are devilish or possessed by devils — as suggested by Oberon's early comment about his devil's claw and the narrator's desire to roll in the hot coals. Since the narrator, the audience for Oberon's self-reflections, is also an author, the audience is the author too, in that solipsistic author-reader circularity we have noted before in Hawthorne's works.

As to the events of the tale, the naturalized or normative world explanation is that the sparks from the manuscripts go up the chimney and set the town ablaze. But the mad writer thinks (or says he does) that the "fiend" in his brain has escaped the subjective manuscript world and that he himself is the triumphant "author" of the destruction of the objective real world. Conventionally, it is mad to think like this, but throughout the tale it is suggested that the real world is as much a fiction of the brain as is the manuscript world and vice versa, for the manuscript is a real world to its author. As the "fictional" world burns, so too do the "real" world's pages apparently begin to curl in flame, in an ironic literalization of metaphor. Or do they? Here again is another facet of Hawthorne's double dramatization of the critical problem; it is a comic version of the author's recurrent addressing of the inside/outside problem of metaphysical, cultural, and egoistic self-containment.

The piece blurs the distinction between real and fictive and between tale and sketch. Its peculiar and abrupt denouement (if it can be called that, for there is no complication, no crisis) enhances its earnest playfulness and the melancholy irony. The tale-sketch is representative of the developing image of the "author" that pervades the earlier collections. The doubled representation of the Oberon figure as he emerges in the dismantled *Story Teller* is a major theme in Hawthorne: the ironic, self-reflexive portrayal and embodiment of the author figure.

The Story Teller *in* The Story Teller

The configuration of this persona called "author" and his double-edged mode of portrayal is developed in the third cycle of early tales and sketches, a much more elaborate and comically framed sequence than the two preceding collections. Reflecting the focus of certain earlier works on the author in quest of history and legend (more than on history or legend itself), this work, largely inclusive of the preceding collections, Hawthorne called simply, and revealingly, *The Story Teller*. It was planned as early as 1832 and submitted as a two-volume manuscript in 1834 to Park Benjamin, whom Hawthorne hoped might aid him in securing a publisher for the pieces as an integrated work. Both in and of themselves and in the way they modify the interior patterns of individual tales, the frame sequences of *The Story Teller* and its interior sketches foreground with playful yet serious humor the struggles of the author and his treatment by the world.

The overall scheme was a species of picaresque, modeled directly upon, among other works, Cervantes's *Don Quixote*, Le Sage's *Gil Blas*, and Irving's *Tales of a Traveller*. As Samuel Goodrich had done with Hawthorne's *Provincial Tales* manuscript, Benjamin, failing to find a publisher, printed several of the *Story Teller* pieces out of sequence and without Hawthorne's name in his *New-England Magazine*; he also published some of the frames as separate sketches. As with *Provincial Tales*, any reconstruction of the "relinquished work" of *The Story Teller* is at best only speculative. Each piece was to be framed by travel narratives and by descriptions of how the stories were told by the Story Teller and how they were received by the various audiences he met along the way. The main theme is announced in the title: the tales and sketches are concerned with story telling, the modes of story telling, the audience for story telling, the gathering of materials for story telling, and the character and vocation of the Story Teller himself.

A "relinquished" work. The general outline of *The Story Teller* emerges if one weaves back and forth among the first two published volumes of shorter narratives, *Twice-told Tales* and *Mosses from an Old Manse*, and several uncollected pieces. A number of cross-references, allusions, and thematic, scenic, and temporal connections, when juxtaposed, suggest a continuous frame narrative. A series collected in *Mosses* under the title "Passages from a Relinquished Work" provides both the basic schema and an indication of how some of the tales of *The Story Teller* were to have been placed in context.[3] "Passages from a Relinquished Work" itself exists in a somewhat dismantled form. Along with the four parts in the "Passages" series proper is a related (indeed, overlapping) lengthy story-sketch, "Seven Vagabonds," published separately and then collected in *Twice-told Tales*—so that there are five parts in all.

The "Passages" as published in *Mosses from an Old Manse* is composed of four sketches: "At Home," "A Flight in the Fog," "A Fellow-Traveller," "The Village Theatre." These frame-sketches are pervaded by self-reflexive ironic humor varying from lightly comic to serious, in which story telling as a dynamic of "author" and "audience" is made a central subject by conjoining story telling with acting on the stage (for which there is an immediate audience response). Hawthorne thereby produces a double disruption of that dramatic illusion sought and superbly achieved by Poe in his narrative fiction. Hawthorne draws attention to the act of story telling, emphasized by acting the part of the Story Teller for an audience, so that part of the text is the context of the author as "Showman" in the act of acting.

The overarching theme of the conflict between culturally institutionalized religion (specifically New England Puritanism) and the artistic imagination (specifically romantic and literary) is comically announced from the outset, in the prologue, "At Home." Echoing Fielding's *Joseph Andrews* (1742) and a host of other novels in the comic biographic or autobiographic mode of picaresque that eventually leads to *Huckleberry Finn*, Hawthorne's green narrator (not far past his eighteenth year) reveals that his restless spirit is chafing under the repressiveness of his puritanic guardian. As we learn later in *The Story Teller*, the narrator's quest in part is for the glory of a "name," and there is no indication in what survives of the manuscript that he could, in the manner of some *Bildungsroman*, ultimately be content with bourgeois life. His guardian does have something of a name; in fact it is of such "considerable eminence" that it is "fitter for the place it occupies in ecclesiastic history than for so frivolous a page as mine." Of course, in the local vicinity, and among the "lighter part of his hearers," his guardian has another name: old Parson Thumpcushion, called so "from the very forcible gestures with which he illustrated his doctrines." One could even estimate his powers as a preacher "by the damage done to his pulpit furniture" from the "pounding and expounding" when he grew warm, slapping his open palm, thumping with his first, and banging with the "whole weight of the great Bible." The narrator is convinced by these demonstrations that the parson has at bay Old Nick himself or "some Unitarian infidel" (2:457–58; *T&S*, 174).

The narrator describes himself as "a youth of gay and happy temperament, with an incorrigible levity of spirit, of no vicious propensities, sensible enough, but wayward and fanciful. What a character was this to be brought in contact with the stern old Pilgrim spirit of my guardian!" (2:459; *T&S*, 175). The parson is insistent on the narrator's adopting a profession; but the narrator, having a moderate inheritance, avows his "purpose of keeping aloof from the regular business of life." This purpose, he says, "would have been a dangerous resolution anywhere in the world; it was fatal in New England. There is a grossness in the conceptions of my countrymen; they will not be convinced that any good thing may consist with what they call idleness . . ." (2:459; *T&S*, 175). The consequence of these conflicting attitudes is, as in the opening of *Walden,* "a piece of light-hearted desperation." "My readers," the narrator suggests, must be aware of "my notoriety" and "must have heard of me in the wild way of life which I adopted." This "wild way of life" is that of the writer; and what we learn of him is wild only by conventional bourgeois New England standards.

The young man has conceived the "idea of becoming a wandering story teller" from "an encounter with several merry vagabonds in a showman's wagon" (2:460; *T&S,* 176) about "a year or two before." For this encounter, we must go to the 1833 sketch "Seven Vagabonds," where a full description is given of the narrator's experience with a traveling tent-theater troupe of "performers" of various kinds, led by an old showman. It is this encounter that suggests to the narrator that he could recite his own works on stage.[4] Composing and "performing" stories will be his vocation, his calling.

If, at this point, we go to the end of the third section of "A Relinquished Work" ("A Fellow-Traveller"), we find the unremitting "fictionality" of story telling implicitly affirmed. The narrator tells us that each of his stories is modified to suit each particular taste; he even provides two or more beginnings and "catastrophes" or endings for many of the stories, depending on what the occasion or audience seemed to require (2:470; *T&S,* 183–84). The passage provides a succinct statement, with framing irony, of the plan of *The Story Teller.*

In "Seven Vagabonds," meanwhile, we find the narrator (presumably the Story Teller) staring in awe at another young man, a member of the tent-theater troupe who is the "author" of an actual printed piece (a pamphlet with blue covers). The narrator casts himself into the fictive role of this published author. The narrator imagines the "author" figure as himself (or vice versa): "Thus . . . would he traverse the land . . . sometimes walking arm in arm with awful Literature; and reaping everywhere a harvest of real and sensible popularity . . ." (1:398; *T&S,* 143). " 'If ever I meddle with literature,' " thinks the narrator, " 'it shall be as a travelling bookseller.' "

Here again, as in the example of "The Devil in Manuscript," is Hawthorne's double figuration of the author. He presents us with the acknowledged author of a published book and another, would-be author, our narrator. Moreover, just as in "The Devil in Manuscript," there is a devil motif, though here in "Seven Vagabonds" it is shifted to a degree from the young author(s) to an old confidence-man who enters the theatrical tent. The double motif is redoubled. This con-artist figure provides a counter to the showman-leader of the troupe; and the two older con-artists provide a parallel to the two complementary young "authors," so that the two pairs of authors and con-artists symbolically represent the doubleness of authorship as "entertainment."

The master of the traveling show (himself earlier called a "magician" by the story-telling narrator) asks the new "conjurer" his destination. Like that of the other vagabonds, the con-artist's destination is Stamford, where a camp meeting is to be held. The narrator then sets to work imagining what "enjoyments" the old "Straggler" would have as he wandered the country; and a series of allusions to the devil, pertinent as well to the character of the author-narrator, suddenly tumble out. "As he pretended to familiarity with the Devil, so I fancied that he was fitted to pursue and take delight in his way of life, by possessing some of the mental and moral characteristics, the lighter and more comic ones, of the Devil in popular stories." Among these "might have been reckoned a love of deception for its own sake, a shrewd eye and keen relish for human weakness and ridiculous infirmity, and the talent of petty fraud. Thus to this old man there would be pleasure even in the consciousness so unsupportable to some minds, that his whole life was a cheat upon the world. . . ." In this regard, "every day would furnish him with a succession of minute and pungent triumphs" (1:405; *T&S*, 148–49). These triumphs would include bilking misers, causing ostentatious gentlemen less rich than himself to throw him coin, telling fortunes to would-be novelists, and even living in true poverty among the poor, "though he would not always be so decidedly diabolical" as that. The old con-man's "pretensions to prophetic knowledge" (such as just practiced on the narrator) would provide "an inexhaustible field of enjoyment, both as enabling him to discern so much folly and to achieve such quantities of minor mischief," activities congenial with his "sneering spirit." The double nature of the narrator finds in "all this . . . a sort of happiness which I could conceive of, though I had little sympathy with it" (1:406; *T&S*, 149), a comment that provides a special gloss on the double character of the Story Teller figure: simultaneously idealistic and satanic, empathetic with the diabolical yet distant.

The first-person narrator of "Seven Vagabonds" seems to be the narrator of the first section of "Passages from a Relinquished Work" ("At Home") and "The Devil in Manuscript." The clues to the latter, however, are indirect and complicated, whereas the connections between "Seven Vagabonds" and the opening of "Relinquished Work" are quite clear. Among other things, the narrator of "Relinquished Work," like the youth of "Seven Vagabonds," has a double nature of lightheartedness and melancholy, earnestness and irony; he is both distinct of personality and at times in his role of observer something of a chameleon. Although his dominant feature is a "gay and happy temperament," his neighbors regard his story-telling inclination as a species of "idleness," so that he feels the previously mentioned "light-hearted desperation" about life in New England (2:459; *T&S*, 176).

After mentioning his encounter with the vagabonds in a showman's

wagon during a summer shower, the "Relinquished Work" narrator comments that his project of becoming a wandering storyteller has "prototypes
in the East," as well as in "wandering orators and poets whom my own ears
have heard." There is, moreover, the example of "one illustrious itinerant
in the other hemisphere, — of Goldsmith, who planned and performed his
travels through France and Italy on a less promising scheme than mine"
(2:460; *T&S*, 176).[5] But it is chiefly because of his "bitter grudge" against
Parson Thumpcushion, who "would rather have laid me in my father's
tomb than see me either a novelist or actor," that he pursues his idea of
uniting the two professions of actor and writer in a mutually reflective way.
"After all it was not half so foolish as if I had written romances instead of
reciting them."

But he does, in fact, write. The pages that follow, he tells us, will "contain
a picture of my vagrant life, intermixed with specimens, generally brief and
slight, of that great mass of fiction to which I gave existence, and which has
vanished like cloud shapes" (2:460; *T&S*, 176). With each story he will also
give "a sketch of the circumstances in which the story was told. Thus my
airdrawn pictures will be set in frames perhaps more valuable than the
pictures themselves" (2:461; *T&S*, 177). The prologue concludes with a
partially tongue-in-cheek statement that he is writing the book "for the
sake of its moral." Elsewhere, as in "Wakefield" or "Night Sketches,"
Hawthorne's narrator-author mocks the idea of the moral, which may not
logically follow from the text or exist at all, even though the reader is
supplied with one (or more). From these moral pieces, the narrator says,
"many a dreaming youth may profit," even though they are only the
experiences of a mere "wandering story teller." These remarks set the stage
for the merging of the "real" world of the frame narrative in which the
Story Teller lives and the "fictive" world of the Story Teller's stories.
Moreover, the incipient imagery of visions in the clouds and airdrawn
pictures is congruent with the growing insistence on indistinct imagery of
mist and fog in the frame narrative.

Indeed, the metaphor of cloud-and-air pictures undergoes a partial literalization in the next section of "Passages from a Relinquished Work," titled
"A Flight in the Fog." The scene is as suggestive of negative epiphany as the
ice light and night glare of "Alice Doane's Appeal." The literal fog and the
imagery of fog become a symbol of the uncertain relation between fantasy
and reality, fiction and fact — in other words the world of the Story Teller's
habitual imagination. In June, the Story Teller sets out from his village in a
"heavy mist," pauses on a hill, and gazes into a "gray cloud" that suddenly
seems "to have taken the aspect of a small white town." The vapor trailing
from the cloud forms "wreathes and pillors," but the "visionary" scene is so

indistinct that he cannot tell whether these structures are "hung in air" or "based on earth" — a succinct formulation of the obsessive apprehension of the visionary artist figure, repeated in various forms throughout Hawthorne's works. The deep concern that it is all an unreal illusion is apparent just under the surface of even the innocuous statement that "it was singular that such an unromantic scene should look so visionary" (2:462; *T&S*, 177).

In the cloud formation, the Story Teller has two major interpenetrating visions, each one employing a master convention of romanticism and embodying the tension of provincialism and cosmopolitanism. One such convention is the evocation of "home" — his humble, provincial village — as both starting point and terminus of his archetypal journey out and back again. The other is of the great "archway," formed by an awesome providential "rainbow," beckoning him with shining promises of discovery, adventure, and fame down the road that disappears into the distance.[6] He sees (like Oberon in the fire) an entire city, which is a mixture of the village he has grown up in and of the worlds created in his tales (or *to be* created in his unwritten tales, which, we recall, are to vanish like cloud shapes). "Half of the parson's dwelling was a dingy white house, and half of it was a cloud. . . ." Whereas Squire Moody's grand mansion is "wholly visible," the brick bank building is in clouds. Only two red chimneys of his paternal residence can be seen above the mist, and he has no memories of anyone there. The "foundations of what was to be a great block of buildings had vanished, ominously, as it proved. . . ." The "dry goods store of Mr. Nightingale seemed a doubtful concern" and "Dominicus Pike's tobacco manufactory an affair of smoke." The last reference applies to a surviving tale of *The Story Teller* manuscript, "Mr. Higginbotham's Catastrophe," in which Pike, here a character from the Story Teller's village, tells a story of having heard a story as he journeys possibly the same road as the Story Teller.

In this cloud vision of future, present, or past reality, the Story Teller also notes "the white spire of the meetinghouse" as it "ascended out of the densest heap of vapor, as if that shadowy base were its only support." The metaphoric application of this vapory vision to institutionalized religion is obvious, much like that of the icicle steeple in "Main Street" and the snow-blasted steeple used as a witch-divining rod in "Alice Doane's Appeal." The Story Teller adds a "qualification" to the seeming harsh criticism: ". . . to give a truer interpretation, the steeple was the emblem of Religion, enveloped in mystery below, yet pointing to a cloudless atmosphere, and catching the brightness of the east on its gilded vane." That the steeple points upward to a region beyond the fog on earth does not suggest advocacy of any particular religion; it only indicates that true religious sentiment may point toward some kind of light beyond the darkness and obscurity of earthly institutions below. But what that light may illuminate in the "cloudless atmosphere" (since visions are made of cloud stuff) is not specified; and the possibility that it illuminates nothing at all is fairly strong, as suggested in other "steeple" sketches like "Sights from a Steeple" (1831) and "Sunday at Home" (1837). In these *Twice-told* sketches, imagery of cloudscape and sunlight similar to the opening of "Alice Doane's Appeal" and the second section of "Passages from a Relinquished Work" will be found to suggest the conflict between religious imagination (bound down to earth, mud, and murk) and the romantic imagination (of airy cloud creatures from myth). Both imaginative constructs are suspect, dialogically contesting each other: the romantic paralleling and contesting the religious — or the religiohistorical — the latter for the American writer being preeminently the Puritan imagination. The tension of these two complementary kinds of imaginative acts or structuring is a central theme of *The Story Teller, Twice-told Tales,* and *Provincial Tales.* Hawthorne's contrastive "opposition" of the Puritan and the romantic imagination, however, includes recognition that both are imaginative constructs, *as if.*

Amidst this misty blurring of the real and the imagined in "Passages from a Relinquished Work," another fusion and inversion occurs. The vision of the birthplace as beginning and end fuses with the image of the great arched portal through which the narrator must travel. The portal is of time as well as of space; future and past are collapsed in the archway. If there is providence ("destiny," "fate"), then it is all one; past and future are contained in time present — a version of the transcendentalists' "present moment." In its pale way, the scene, whatever its ironic-satiric elements in the manner of Byron, is another Wordsworthian "Spot of Time" subverted: a negative epiphany. The Story Teller seems to see the village (both the "imagined" one and the "real" one, each interpenetrating the other) from the future. It is as though he has always already journeyed down the long road and returned years later and is now remembering the past. This visionary "memory" then constitutes his "future." He sees (or thinks he sees) a rainbow in the fog forming the "misty archway of futurity" through which he must advance. "The sun, then just above the horizon, shone faintly through the fog, and formed a species of rainbow in the west, bestriding my intended road like a gigantic portal" (2:463; *T&S,* 178–79). He had "never known before that a bow could be generated between the sunshine and the morning mist."

The picture of the visionary archway is more important than it may appear, isolated and briefly developed, in this frame-sketch. For the artist it is the archway to his future, his preordained destiny, as he thinks, thus constituting also his past as seen from the visionary predestined future. Versions of this archway of imagination recur throughout Hawthorne's works as a major symbol. Among these are doorways, portals, interlaced forest boughs, windows — each capable of producing (especially in fog or the glare of ice or fire) a nimbus of light, such as the rainbow. We have already seen (e.g., in "Wives of the Dead") the special use of the window as imaginative arch; although it has strong religious connotations, it principally suggests intuitive or imaginative (or visionary) "revelation." On other windows too (high, gothic, arched), Hawthorne remarks a "fantastic tracery" of frost more closely associated with romantic visions than with religious. All such apocalypses are quietly negated. Giovanni's multiply delusive "vision" of Rappaccini's garden, for example, is initially through a gothic (arched) window.

Hawthorne counters the high romantic archway vision in "A Flight in the Fog" with a series of qualifications of imagery and allusion. He has the Story Teller describe the archway in a manner that emphasizes its doubleness. The arch of the "rainbow" of mist, unlike the rainbow colors of "Mirth's" attire in "Seven Vagabonds," has "no brilliancy . . . but was a mere unpainted framework, as white and ghostlike as the lunar rainbow, which is deemed ominous of evil" (2:463; T&S, 179). The unpainted white and ghostlike moon's "rainbow" is the opposite of the "solar" rainbow, sunlight symbol of hope and covenantal providence. The archway of moon and moonlight, so often associated with Hawthorne's concept of "romance," is also associated with uncertainty and ill fortune. We may remember in this context that it is in an "archway" of fire in "Young Goodman Brown" that the devil appears to make his wonderfully ambiguous remark regarding human "destiny": "Welcome, my children . . . to the communion of your race!" He is the arch-liar, but it may yet be true that the forest gatherers have come to the communion of the human race in the sense of fulfilling the propensity to an interior evil vision.

Like the gates of dreams in Homer (Odyssey, 19.600–606) to which Hawthorne specifically alludes in, for example, the "Legends of the Province House," the great traditional symbol of the rainbow as Hawthorne uses it is double. In Homer, dreams are said to come to human beings through one or another of the two gates. Those that come through ivory are false; those that come through the gates of horn are said to be true.[7] In Hawthorne, such dreams and visions are both untrue and true, both ivory and horn at the same time, just as the Delphic Oracle's interpretation of all messages from the gods is double. In the long tradition of the auguration of the "speaker from beneath the mask," Hawthorne makes the rainbow "message from the gods" both positive and negative. The hermeneutical reading of "omens" and "auguries" in Hawthorne parallels the ambiguity of the Delphic Oracle and reinforces the classical caveats—as if horn and ivory were the key (as they are in Conrad's *Heart of Darkness*) to the great romantic drama of interpretation that Hawthorne recurrently portrays.

To hold two contrastive views simultaneously, consciously, and accommodatively is a species of romantic irony, exemplified for the romantics by *Don Quixote*.[8] That such is the key to the Story Teller in *The Story Teller* is in fact made clear in the context around the archway vision in the mist and cloud. References to Don Quixote and Sancho Panza in relation to the problem of reading "auguries" is another way in which Hawthorne qualifies the Story Teller's vision of the archway of his destiny. An "augury" may mean either the act of divination or the sign interpreted. The word has Latin roots suggesting "shining" and Greek roots suggesting a "ray" of light—thus the traditional religious iconography of the radiant light of a halo or of the rainbow. Whereas in English the word *augury* is usually favorable and the word *omen* usually suggests evil, Hawthorne gives *augury* an ambivalent connotation, foregrounding the epistemological uncertainty of negative epiphany.

Before the private Pisgah vision, the Story Teller, having heard the prophetical call to leave his native village, remarks that in renouncing middleclass expectations of a provincial life he "had never felt such a delicious excitement, nor known what freedom was, till that moment when I gave up my home and took the whole world in exchange . . ." (2:463; *T&S*, 178). The language is specifically religious (though ironically inverted), setting up a further irony in the portrayal of the romantic artist discovering his vocation. Rather than experiencing Byronic melancholy over the necessity of leaving home, he feels joy at leaving New England sternness and commitment to religious duty: "Never was Childe Harold's sentiment adopted in a spirit more unlike his own." Therefore, "naturally enough, I thought of Don Quixote." Recollecting "how the knight and Sancho had watched for auguries when they took the road to Toboso," the young Story Teller begins, with a feeling "between jest and earnest," to experience "a similar anxiety." This anxiety for augury is "gratified, and by a more poetical phenomenon than the braying of the dappled ass or the neigh of Rosinante"—namely, the gigantic rainbow portal. This vision may be more poetical than the braying of an ass, but it is less unequivocal.

The importance to the character of the Story Teller of this complex set of attitudes should not be underestimated. It is a key to his character and the narrative tone of *The Story Teller* that he feels a "similar anxiety" to what the two Spanish adventurers together felt (the mixed feelings somewhere "between jest and earnest") and that at last he sets out desperately with a light heart. In such confusion he is yet purposive, determined to put both physical distance and the distance of a fictitious name (appropriately enough for a story teller) between himself and Parson Thumpcushion, lest the old man "put an untimely catastrophe to my story" (2:464; *T&S*, 179). Although obvious, it is yet worthwhile to emphasize that the metaphor is ironically apt: the Parson might apply a fictive convention (catastrophe) to the author's life (story).

Another pair of doppelgängers. In the third of the four sections of the "Relinquished Work," titled "A Fellow-Traveller," the Story Teller encounters a very odd version of Quixote's Sancho. This is a young man about his own age carrying a volume, whose realism is framed by his own version of the imaginative, in this case, the Puritan imagination. The Story Teller encounters him after passing a much reduced "real-world" version of the great romantic archway: a brook runs under the road "through a little arch of stone" (2:464; *T&S*, 179). The young man is an itinerant student for whom the world is (as for the Story Teller) a text. For the student (one Eliakim Abbott, unnamed for several pages), the world is conventionally or allegorically the exemplification of a specific text: the Bible, the volume he carries with him. Thus we have a literal figuration of author and reader or interpreter, each bringing a different perceptual frame to bear on their texts. The Story Teller wishes the young preacher could read a different text and were "a merrier companion; such, for instance, as the comedian with whom Gil Blas shared his dinner beside a fountain in Spain" (2:465; *T&S*, 180). The young religious reciprocates the feeling that his companion lacks an important trait. The "story teller" and the "abbott" are linked by seriousness and comedy, each wishing the other had more of one or the other.

The two contrasting young men are to travel along for a week, discussing such things as providence and purpose, as they do on the first day they break bread together. They remark, each in his own way, on the differing natures of the "pilgrim" and the "wanderer," though Abbott does not ever seem to understand that artistic wandering may be as much of a pilgrimage as a religious journey is. (In his conception of the artistic pilgrimage as providential, Hawthorne's artist is typical of the romantic paradigm laid out by Wieland and Goethe and continued in famous narratives by Tieck, Novalis, Jean Paul, and others.) The pilgrim, of course, journeys toward a goal as a matter of belief; the wanderer (here the artist, the Story Teller) has no specific goal other than the journey itself, which he will recount. That is, the goal is the recounting of the journey, itself a pilgrimage to the shrine of fiction. The journey and its recounting also become the artistic pilgrimage of high romanticism. The two travelers, like Don Quixote and Sancho Panza, are not merely contrastive but complementary, and not finally separable into romantic and realist, or religious and secular.

Their provincialist conversation on home exemplifies their different but complementary natures, that of the artist being more comprehensive than that of the religious devotee. After sharing Abbott's food, the Story Teller invites him to a future supper.

> "Where? At your home?" asked he.
>
> "Yes," said I, smiling.
>
> "Perhaps our roads are not the same," observed he.
>
> "Oh, I can take any road but one [the one directly back "home"], and yet not miss my way," answered I. "This morning I breakfasted at home; I shall sup at home to-night; and a moment ago I dined at home . . . but I have resolved not to see it again till I have been quite round the globe and enter the street on the east as I left it on the west. In the mean time, I have a home everywhere or nowhere, just as you please to take it."
>
> "Nowhere, then; for this transitory world is not our home," said the young man, with solemnity. "We are all pilgrims and wanderers; but it is strange that we two should meet." (2:466–67; *T&S*, 181)

The conversation then turns to providentiality and purpose. When the Story Teller asks the young man where he is going, Abbott says, "I do not know . . . but God knows." That Abbott should not know if God knows, the Story Teller finds strange. "And how is your road to be pointed out?" asks the Story Teller, recurring to the idea of auguries. "Perhaps by an inward conviction . . . perhaps by an outward sign." To this, the Story Teller replies that Abbott has a sign already, himself, the Story Teller. "We are told of pious men in old times who committed themselves to the care of Providence, and saw the manifestation of its will in the slightest circumstances, as in the shooting of a star, the flight of a bird, or the course taken by some brute animal. Sometimes even a stupid ass was their guide. May not I be as good a one?"

The stupid ass of a storyteller and the rather inept would-be abbot do "follow the same road" for a while, literally, and the Story Teller observes that they are lucky not to be overtaken by "the keepers of any lunatic asylum in pursuit of a stray patient" (2:468; *T&S*, 182). He speculates that "perhaps the stranger felt as much doubt of my sanity as I did of his." But in a statement that casually glosses the (romantic) primacy of aesthetic perception, the artist remarks it seems to him that the religious could doubt "with less justice, since I was fully aware of my own extravagances, while he acted as wildly and deemed it heavenly wisdom." Equally important is the Story Teller's judgment that "we were a singular couple, strikingly contrasted, yet curiously assimilated, each of us remarkable enough by himself, and doubly so in the other's company." So it is, then, that "without any formal compact, we kept together day after day till our union appeared permanent." The two journey together as a composite doppelgänger, as arch-companions (in both senses of the word), a romantic version of a Don Quixote and Sancho Panza not so much romantic and realist as artistic and religious, for whatever imaginative reality the combination of these poles may represent.

The genially negative romantic quality of their relationship is developed through the Story Teller's fledgling "performances" on the road. About a week after the two travelers have joined together, the Story Teller gives an improvised reading "to an audience of nine persons, seven of whom hissed me in a very disagreeable manner, and not without good cause" (2:468; T&S, 182). The Story Teller decides to refund their money (as in "Main Street") and is at last "gratified with the round of applause," an event that forces him to realize that he has "immensely underrated the difficulties" of his "idle trade." He must concentrate all his powers on his craft: wide observation, varied knowledge, deep thoughts and sparkling thoughts, "lofty imagination, veiling itself in the garb of common life," and "pathos and levity, and a mixture of both, like sunshine in a raindrop" (2:469; T&S, 183) — once again, the complementary combination of opposites.

The section concludes with a straight-faced parody of slap-dash writers that reads almost like a direct counterstatement to Poe's doctrines of "preconceived effect" and "unity of impact" *and* makes a genial mockery of the idea of the "twice-told" tale. The Story Teller begins seriously enough by giving us his thoughts on "practised art," noting the impossibility of ever achieving in actuality his artistic vision. But he continues on, like Don Quixote, doing his best to overcome his own recognition of the impossible. In fact, one of the "few sources of pride" to him is that, "ridiculous as the object" of artistic perfection is, he follows the ideal with "firmness and energy." Not much of this is easily recognized as parody. But he continues by saying that to the end of achieving artistic perfection, he has "manufactured a great variety of plots and skeletons of tales, and kept them ready for use, leaving the filling up to the inspiration of the moment." This technique of on-the-spot "extemporaneous" performance (plugging in prefabricated sections as needed) works very well for him most of the time, he says, blithely unaware of the light which it casts on his artistry. He says that he "cannot remember ever to have told a tale which did not vary considerably from my preconceived idea." As a performer for the crowd, he observes that, "oddly enough, my success was generally in proportion to the difference between the conception and the accomplishment. I provided two or more commencements and catastrophes to many of the tales, — a happy expedient, suggested by the double sets of sleeves and trimmings which diversified the suits in Sir Piercy Shafton's wardrobe" (2:470; *T&S*, 183–84).

The irony underneath the naiveté constitutes another of Hawthorne's sardonic remarks on art, audience, and authorship, a characterization that also applies to the Story Teller's baffled conclusion: "my best efforts had a unity, a wholeness, and a separate character that did not admit of this sort of mechanism." The passage is a good example of romantic irony that portrays an artist figure who is often the fool but is yet to be taken seriously. The passage makes fun of organic unity while advocating the unity of the well-told narrative; it criticizes while seeming to praise the "double story" that is superficial merely. If the centrality of the "twice-told" is as multiform as the argument of the present study suggests, it is a fine stroke of irony that Hawthorne should make fun, in the guise of the absurd but serious artist, of a key tenet of his art by diminishing it to the incompetency of a hack vaudeville act. And yet the Story Teller's "best efforts" somehow had a "wholeness" that did not employ such "mechanism." The passage on the Story Teller's aesthetic practice is itself twice-told.

The last section of the "Passages from a Relinquished Work" is titled "The Village Theatre," which again reifies, in the fictive frame-scene, the stage/acting analogy. On the first of September the Story Teller (preceded by playbill notices of "an Unprecedented Attraction!") is to "recite his famous tale of Mr. Higginbotham's Catastrophe." In the older editions of Hawthorne's works, this tale is omitted from the "Relinquished Work" of *Mosses from an Old Manse* because, after the dismantling of *The Story Teller* by Park Benjamin, the tale was collected in *Twice-told Tales*.

In the context of the wandering Story Teller's telling the story of the traveling pedlar's story telling, a parallel between the conditions of the Higginbotham narrative and the frame narrative emerges. Both narratives are centrally concerned with story telling (the narrator three times hears and three times tells the story of Higginbotham before the final "explanation"). The parallels have the effect of blurring the distinction between the "fictive" and the "real" in the frame fiction (in addition to the blurring of these in the tale proper), an effect that is lost when "Mr. Higginbotham's Catastrophe" is printed separate from the frame. The Story Teller observes in the frame (in conformity to the specious "twice-told" technique explained in the previous section) that the tale of Higginbotham "could hardly have been applauded by rapturous audiences," as the play-bills claimed, because it was "as yet an unfilled plot; nor even when I stepped upon the stage was it decided whether Mr. Higginbotham should live or die" (2:471; *T&S*, 184). Thus even the detail of the play-bills' lie about the Story Teller's fame and the celebrity of his tale deepens the theme of fiction (lying play-bill) about a fiction (the fame) about a fiction ("Mr. Higginbotham's Catastrophe").[9]

The negative doppelgänger relation complements the romantic irony of the Story Teller's situation. Taking a walk before his upcoming performance, "to quicken my ideas by active motion," the narrator passes by the school-house, where Eliakim Abbott has "collected about fifteen hearers, mostly females" (2:471; *T&S*, 185). Abbott speaks with such "agonizing diffidence" that "several of the little audience" leave and the Story Teller steals out to spare him further embarrassment. This incident presages the embarrassment the Story Teller is about to experience. He goes to the barroom of the tavern for a glass of wine before his own performance, where the "feeble" tragedy of *Douglas* is being concluded before an eager and overflowing house. He remarks that his own tale was "originally more dramatic" and "afforded good scope for mimicry and buffoonery." But he had not known the "magic of a name" until his "performance" of "Higginbotham": for as often as he repeated the name "Higginbotham" there were "louder bursts of merriment than those which responded to what, in my opinion, were more legitimate strokes of humor" (2:473; *T&S*, 186).

The relation between the Story Teller's intentions and his audience's reactions is an uncertain one. What the Story Teller does not know is that an attractive "young person of doubtful sex" (a theatrical person who has been playing both male and female parts), with whom he had his glass of wine, has fastened to his collar a stiff cue of horse hair: ". . . unknown to me, it kept making the queerest gestures of its own in correspondence with all mine. The audience, supposing that some enormous joke was appended to this long tail behind, were ineffably delighted, and gave way to such a tumult of approbation that, just as the story closed, the benches broke beneath them and left one whole row of my admirers on the floor. Even in that predicament they continued their applause" (2:473; *T&S*, 186). Although a satiric scene, it seriously embodies the problematic relation of author and audience and the question of authorial intent — and thus should be placed with "Alice Doane's Appeal" as a complementary comic dramatization of these issues.

Such then is the manner in which a superficially somber tale like "Mr. Higginbotham's Catastrophe" was to have been framed in *The Story Teller.* Even the title points to the story-telling motif. As the narrator remarks, "In after times, when I had grown a bitter moralizer, I took this scene for an example of how much of fame is humbug. . . . From the pit and boxes there was now a universal call for the Story Teller" (2:473–74; *T&S*, 186). Although the Story Teller asserts that "fame" is humbug, the implication is that authorship, story telling, is a humbug of some kind too. Obviously, reading "Mr. Higginbotham's Catastrophe" separated from its humorous context of author and audience will not produce the double perspective it was to have had in *The Story Teller.* Although the "gothic" riddle is self-contained within the tale, much of the self-reflexive irony is lost without the frame-sketch containing it.

In the concluding paragraphs of "Passages from a Relinquished Work," the overarching theme of a performative religious versus a literary-theatrical "vocation" returns in the guise of a genial parody of the conventions of the eighteenth-century novel. The narrator receives a letter in the hand of Parson Thumpcushion. "Doubtless he had heard of the rising renown of the Story Teller, and conjectured at once that such a nondescript luminary could be no other than his lost ward" (2:474; *T&S*, 187). Hawthorne now has the Story Teller wrestle with the affections that this letter generates. "His epistle, though I never read it, affected me most painfully. . . . I hastened with the letter to my chamber and held it unopened in my hand while the applause of my buffoonery yet sounded through the theater." The "applause" of his "buffoonery" is so beguiling compared to New England guilt (think only of Roger Malvin, Tobias Pearson, or Young Goodman Brown) that he begins to see his guardian in a new light: "Another train of thought came over me. The stern old man appeared again, but now with the gentleness of sorrow, softening his authority with love as a father might, and even bending his venerable head, as if to say that my errors had an apology in his own mistaken discipline." So thinking (a nicely self-serving version of the rationalization that the artist must resist the temptations of "love" and "reconciliation"), the Story Teller burns the letter. He has made his grand choice to "risk" the "trial" of the wide world; and the burning of the unread (doubtless, loving and forgiving) letter is in retrospect, he thinks, an augury of the "irrevocable choice between good and evil fate" (2:475; *T&S*, 187). His buffoonery is complete.

Whether or not we wish, eventually, to take the final step after we have read these surviving fragments of *The Story Teller* and conclude that the dying Oberon of the end and the narrator of the beginning are one and the same figure — or complementary versions of the same figure — it will be well to remember that amidst all the heavy romanticism of the artist and his (melo)dramatic posturing are jokes, parodies, comic deflations, incompletely worked out, but worthy of the applause of Schlegelian "buffoonery" nevertheless.[10] The final ironic absurdity of "Passages from a Relinquished Work" is deft. Despite the "liberal offers of the manager" and "a laudatory critique in the newspaper," which is precisely what the young author-performer desires, he leaves town to avoid the pursuit of the Bible-thumping parson. But he sets out in the company of the Bible-carrying Eliakim Abbott, each young man "following the same road," but "on two such different errands." Seeking to elude the "type" of the Puritan parson, the Story Teller journeys as with his Puritan shadow self, a young evangelist who "groaned in spirit, and labored with tears to convince me of the guilt and madness of my life."[11]

The return of Oberon: "fragments from the journal of a solitary man." The concluding frame segment of *The Story Teller* seems to be the work titled "Fragments from the Journal of a Solitary Man," first published, in two parts, in the *American Monthly* in 1837 (uncollected). "Fragments" is a sentimentalized yet mildly mocking lament—from a first-person point of view acting in effect as a third-person frame—for the early death of an "author" named Oberon. The Oberon of "Fragments" is much in the Wertherian and Byronic mode, while his doppelgänger, the first-person narrator who describes Oberon to us, is more shadowy. The ambiguity of narrative persona and frame foregrounds the issues of authorship and authorial presence in *The Story Teller* and *Provincial Tales*; and the *Story Teller* version of Oberon and the narrator, like the Oberon and narrator of "The Devil in Manuscript," tend to merge into one symbolic authorial figure.

But these claims cannot be maintained with absolute assurance. Just as we cannot be certain that the Oberon of "Fragments" and the Oberon of "The Devil in Manuscript" are the same, so we cannot even be sure that "Fragments" was the original conclusion to *The Story Teller.* We do not know if the unnamed narrator is the Story Teller, the author-narrator of "The Devil in Manuscript," or some other author figure; nor is it clear if this later Oberon is an older version of the youthful Story Teller of "Relinquished Work" or "Seven Vagabonds," or if the narrator is yet another figure. Moreover, in between "Relinquished Work" and "Passages from the Journal of a Solitary Man" stand the two series of travel narratives, titled "Sketches from Memory, I & II"; and by the time we get to these middle sequences of *The Story Teller,* it is no longer clear that we are still listening to the same Story Teller we have followed in his flight from Parson Thumpcushion into the White Mountains.

Nevertheless, simultaneously with the increasing ambiguity of narrative provenance, we are led step by step to the assumption of a single narrative identity by the congruence of incident, character, scene, imagery, and theme between the relinquished passages and the journal fragments. The natural conclusion of the themes introduced in "Passages" is the master romantic convention of the great circular journey, which is completed in "Fragments." The romantic-ironic tonality of the earlier depictions of the youthful peripatetic artist and his companion, the young would-be divine, continues in the portrait of the older artist and older narrator. If not all full of tears and flapdoodle, as Huck Finn would say, Hawthorne's *Künstlerroman* is certainly full of both *Weltschmerz* and satire. The "Fragments" sequence provides an appropriate conclusion to Hawthorne's most elaborate *Rahmenerzählung*, and its complex irony of melancholy and genial humor is worthy of Schlegel's designations, *arabesque* and *Roman*. Certainly the ironic portrait of the antagonistical but complementary sides of the author figure suggests a continuous provenance with "The Devil in Manuscript." If the "Fragments" was, as it seems to be, part of the original manuscript, "The Devil" in some version or another would fit nicely somewhere after the middle and before the conclusion of the *Story Teller.*

More importantly, the question of the narrator and Oberon brings to a head the matter of the personae of these works, of "Seven Vagabonds," of "The Devil in Manuscript," and of *The Story Teller* at large. What exactly is the connection or separation of Oberon and the Story Teller? Or of Oberon and the narrator of "The Devil in Manuscript"? Or of the Story Teller and any of the other author figures of *The Story Teller*? Or *Provincial Tales*? The ambiguity is perfectly consistent with the indeterminacy of the narratives that we have been examining; and it is hard not to believe that this effect is in part a deliberate figuration — especially with the recurrent fusions of dream experience with some sort of waking reality.

Certainly the similarities between the two Oberons and the two narrators are striking. In the untitled first section of "Fragments," Oberon has given the narrator his journal to keep, but he has instructed him to burn the remainder of his tales and other narratives. The unnamed narrator's initial portrait of Oberon is as a recluse who has had a sadness on his spirit that, "added to the shrinking sensitiveness of his nature, rendered him not misanthropic, but singularly averse to social intercourse" (12:24; *T&S*, 487–88). In his journal, Oberon settles on dying young and has a striking dream of walking down Broadway, "with some singularity of dress or aspect which made me look ridiculous." When passersby seems first startled and then horrified, Oberon checks himself in a mirror in a shop window and awakes from his dream with "a horrible sensation of self-terror and self-loathing" (12:29–30; *T&S*, 492). He had been promenading Broadway in his shroud. Such is his double epiphany. His mind is haunted by a twin vision, both waking and dreaming, of death and of absurdity.

This kind of doubleness, here incorporated in a single character, not only recapitulates "The Devil in Manuscript"; it is also an extension of the symbiotic doubleness of the two pilgrims of the "Fellow-Traveller" and "Village Theatre" sections of "A Relinquished Work." Moreover, it will be recalled, the youth of "A Relinquished Work" had prided himself on seeing the desirable characteristics of all humankind even in an obscure and sad world. Although he had set out to leave the judgmental provinciality of New England behind him in order to discover the possibilities of the cosmopolitan world, he was apprehensive about leaving his familiar "home." Upon setting forth on the great journey, he described his complicated feelings as "light-hearted desperation." Thus the double ambivalence of Hawthorne's characteristic author figure seems, symmetrically, to have been also foregrounded at the beginning and end of *The Story Teller* remnants.

A brief look at the second, concluding segment of the "Fragments" ("My Home Return") will illustrate these points, especially the likelihood that it is indeed the original conclusion to *The Story Teller.* The narrative is a description of Oberon's final journey home — to die. The "author's lament" is voiced both by the narrator (who, like the narrator-author of "The Devil in Manuscript," is Oberon's one close friend) and by Oberon himself (as recorded in his journal). Oberon remarks the alterations in people and the village. Yet the past and the present (which had been the foreseen future) fuse to become one entity. Although there is change, the artist's history (particularly as conceived at the beginning by the young would-be author) is almost static, paralleling in individual terms Hawthorne's skeptical observations on the progress of cultural history. This second Oberon becomes a new author-narrator figure, part separate from, yet part of, the frame-narrator author. His retrospective description of the scene at the beginning of *his* youthful journey is essentially the same as the initiation of the journey by the Story Teller in "Relinquished Work." *Oberon* remarks how when he left home years before he had stood on a hill and looked "forward to the pale mist-bow that overarched my path, and was the omen of my fortunes," but had "misinterpreted that augury" (12:36; *T&S*, 496). This recapitulated scene thus connects the pieces as parts of the same "relinquished" work. By the coincidence of the vision of the "mist-bow" with its heavy freight of romantic (and here partially ironic) symbolism, the narratives of Oberon and the Story Teller of "Relinquished Work" finally merge into coherent unity.

This coincidence also tends to confirm the suggestion that the two authors of "The Devil in Manuscript" are two aspects of one identity. One is lighter hearted and given to genially sarcastic jest; the other is sentimental and melancholy — the same combination that the Story Teller describes in himself. The narrative voice of the author figure who descends from the

White Mountains and undertakes the long-level canal journey to the Great Lakes is also both melancholy and sarcastic. The melodramatic lament for self in "Devil in Manuscript" connects tonally and thematically with the "Dream of Oberon" in his shroud on Broadway and with the vision of the artistic self, dying, unappreciated, but aware (whether in his own person or in that of his author-friend-narrator-doppelgänger) of his absurdity. Once again the double, if not paradoxical, nature of the Story Teller is emphasized. The two sides together constitute the ironic, self-conscious, romantic "author" that is the persistent voice behind, in, around, and at a distance from the volumes of sketches and tales by Hawthorne.

Hawthorne and Oberon

To make some concession to the biographical, we may recall that the self-reference of the Oberon of "The Devil in Manuscript" is in part privately symbolic. Like one of his pseudosatanic authors in this piece, Hawthorne is supposed to have burned whole quires of his manuscripts; and we remember that his nickname at college, in reference to the highly imaginative tone of his conversation, was Oberon; and he signed the name Oberon to letters to Henry Wadsworth Longfellow and Horatio Bridge. One can hardly avoid making the leap from story to life and back again, like one of Hoffmann's or Hawthorne's devilish characters.

But we must not be overly simplistic about the "Hawthorne Question" and ignore the high degree of literary convention and fictionality involved in the creation of an artistic persona. Although the characterization of Oberon conforms to the traditional picture of Hawthorne's own temperament in his early years, we should not be misled by biographical resonances into overlooking the specifically Byronic quality in the author-persona of the Story Teller. Byronism was in large measure the creation of a myth of the self—a romantic literary self. And Byronism, like Quixotism, is both positive and negative, sardonic and idealistic, serious and humorous. When Oberon observes that now he must pay the price for stepping to one side of life and relinquishing his claim upon what he calls "human sympathy" (a recurrent apprehension of the vocation of authorship in Hawthorne), we need to remember that for Hawthorne *sympathia*, along with *caritas* and *perspectiva*, is one of the principal requisites of the artist. Oberon, however much he is a symbol of authorship, is also an ironically dramatized character and does not stand for the whole complex of "authorial" attributes. Oberon is as much the subject of *perspectiva* as any nonauthorial character.

Nevertheless, our formulation of the trope of the authorial self or the technique of authorial presence need not be unnecessarily complex. We need not have recourse to certain poststructuralist distinctions between the written self and the writing self in order to clarify the embodiment of the Story Teller in Oberon as complementary fictional doppelgänger; nor need we invoke the Geneva school of phenomenological structuralists to see the Story Teller/Oberon figure as an icon of the *cogito* of Nathaniel Hawthorne himself. We may simply observe, with Millicent Bell, that Oberon is not Hawthorne: he "is merely the first of Hawthorne's significant masks, the 'I'-character who is only another of the writer's creations." As Bell says, "even the narrating 'I' of the early tales or sketches is identified with Hawthorne at our peril. If he is psychologically true to Hawthorne at all, he is true in the sense of being a self he proposed to himself, a self he tested and considered as a possibility of himself, even a self he sentimentally liked to pretend that he was when depicting himself to others."[12] But as in Jane Austen, in Hawthorne sentiment is qualified by irony. Oberon is a carefully built up persona, a romantic-ironic portrait of the artist, reified and con- tested by another authorial presence, the unnamed narrator, who may or may not be the story-telling youth—just as Oberon is or is not the original Oberon. In any case, the authorial name of Oberon, once highly significant in literary tradition, is a clue to the duality of Hawthorne's author figure and the dialogicity of his narratives.

As mentioned in the early portions of this book, the name Oberon is rich in association. He is the fairy prince of night who presides over such creatures as fauns, satyrs, and elves in the realm of creative fantasy. The usual identification of Oberon Hawthorne scholars make is that of the fairy king in Shakespeare's *A Midsummer Night's Dream*, an identification pa- tently present in Hawthorne's mind as the allusions in "My Kinsman, Major Molineux" corroborate. But another important work glossing the figure of Oberon is Ben Jonson's *Oberon, The Fairy Prince* (1611). Jonson's *Oberon* is written in a mode that was highly attractive to Hawthorne: the tradition of the masque. The double tradition of the masque provides another, equally important, dimension to the authorial trope of Oberon.

Employing emblematizations and ritual elements from legendary history and religious myth, the masque typically dealt with an enchanted other world, with such subjects as the gods of Olympus, idealized ladies of romance, the world of faery, and other such "imaginative" creations from the unconscious or inhabiting the borders between waking and sleeping. Its vogue, however, gave rise in the Renaissance to the counterdevelopment of the antimasque. The manifestly dialogical subgenre of the antimasque intrudes, into the benign world of faery, elements contesting the domi- nant genre. These contestatory or counter-elements included not just hags, witches, and demons, but also deliberate structural and thematic dissonances. Indeed, the contestatory quality of the antimasque came to seem to many Renaissance critics to pose a threat to prevailing concepts of unity. By 1634 Thomas Carew's *Coelum Britannicum* had as many as eight anti-masques, producing what contemporaries regarded a chaotic effect. In between the masque proper and the extravagance of Carew's sometimes extraneous antimasques stands Ben Jonson's *Oberon*. Jonson had sought to blend masque and antimasque into a new unity accommodative of antag-onistical elements.[13] Seen in this literary-historical frame, Hawthorne's adoption of the name Oberon is even more resonantly suggestive of the profoundly dialogical nature of his literary tradition. In our discussion of the dreamvision sketches and "My Kinsman, Major Molineux" we have seen that *A Midsummer Night's Dream* in itself suggests aesthetic "concord" emerging from "discord." As interpreted by the Schlegels and other ro-mantic writers, the "authorial" figure of Oberon — ruler of the world of the imagination, creator of and character in his own enchanted world, mediator between that world and a quotidian "real" world — embodies a romantic irony of harmonized dissonances.

Thus it is that Hawthorne's authorial figures or presences display a heightened awareness of the dislocations of factual events in the fictive process of time and its interpretations: a supersensitivity to the inter-penetration of the fictive imagination and any factual perception of the world. Hawthorne's author figure deliberately problematizes the relation-ship of history and romance, fiction and fact, in conjunction with that of multiple audiences and foregrounded author-narrators. Like Oberon, Hawthorne's conflicted, self-conscious Story Teller ends up a character in his own sequence of stories and sketches, both in the tales proper and in their connecting frame-sketches. Hawthorne's author does and does not, simultaneously, take the vocation of writing seriously. He sees the absurdity of the world and of himself but is compelled to write. His complex concern for the authorship of an author — for the writing self — also embodies the attendant ontological problems of history and literature as fact and fiction, the epistemological problems of reality and imagination, the aesthetic problems of form and genre, and the impossible problems of romance and realism.

The icon of the Romantic Artist as Oberon or Oberlus embodies Frie-drich Schlegel's concept of "objective subjectivity." Schlegel's sense of the pervasive irony both in the text and in its author (beyond textual double voicing) integrates the many strands we have found in Hawthorne's concept of the artist persona bound up in the great romantic icon of Oberon. By recognizing the necessary incompleteness of truth and the partialness of one's own perceptions, Schlegel argued, one takes the first step toward a "transcendental" higher view. The higher view is never complete but always evolving; and it requires the interpenetration of the artist's subjectivity with his texts to achieve a higher objectivity.[14]

The corollary for Schlegel and Hawthorne is that those people who earnestly believe that they have the one and only truth in the form of *the* answer are misguided. They are the victims of egotism; they deny other perspectives; they eschew the dialogical. Thereby they deny the humanity of others. For Hawthorne — as we have seen in the *Provincial Tales* — these monologists could include not only self-absorbed egomaniacs, psychologically disturbed dreamers and visionaries, but also the American Puritans, the Quakers, the Tories, the anti-Loyalists, the mobs, the patriotic legend mongers — even the historians of the American experience. It is not that such people are always unremittingly wrong; it is that they do not recognize their own partiality, their own subjectivity. From inside his own culture, Hawthorne demonstrates that the Puritan provincials and their descendants do not see that they see "New Englandly." Constrained in their ethics, religion, politics, and historiography, they do not or will not see their own provinciality. Certainly, at a fundamental level, such monologists are antiliterary, just as are writers of didactic fiction who draw simplistic morals.

For Schlegel and for Hawthorne — and in congruence with romantic theory in general — it is the heightened *aesthetic* frame or perspective that most nearly approaches the ideal mode of objectifying subjectivity. For Schlegel and Hawthorne, the literary stands at the apex of the aesthetic hierarchy. Within the literary, Schlegel's privileged genre, as it is for Hawthorne (as it is for Bakhtin), is not the poem but the double-voiced genre of fictional narrative — *Rahmenerzählung, Novelle, Roman.*[15] Fiction generates a "higher subjectivity" by its aesthetic incorporation of paradox, contradiction, ambiguity — by its dramatization of the inconsistencies of the human condition — by its deliberate intermixture of irony and earnestness, humor and pathos. The romantic artist objectifies through simultaneous aesthetic distance and presence, constantly resubjectivizing at a higher and higher level. In this way, Hawthorne is thoroughly romantic.

Throughout this study, we have again and again noted what Poe called the "fortuitous combination" of "antagonistical elements." We have seen this combination both in the authorial presences of Hawthorne's narratives and in the narratives themselves considered as narrative structures and transactions. Most simply these elements can be binarily labeled positive and negative, optimistic and pessimistic. In the *Story Teller* manuscript, the combination of both gaiety and gloom (with telling reference to the ancient symbol of the rainbow) is directly attributed to the Story Teller himself. As we have seen, when he starts out on the road with his companion, the young Puritan preacher, Hawthorne's narrator lists the requisites of the fictive artist, invoking both Cervantes and Byron: "wide observation, varied knowledge, deep thoughts, and sparkling ones; pathos and levity, and a mixture of both, like sunshine in a raindrop; lofty imagination, veiling itself in the garb of common life," along with "practised art" ("Passages from a Relinquished Work," 2:469; *T&S*, 183). They (the Story Teller and the Preacher) must look, the Story Teller thinks, like Sancho Panza and Don Quixote. Not only is the entire romantic/realist conflict between appearance and reality evoked; so also is that interpenetration of these seeming opposites in Sancho and Quixote that anti-neoclassic critics like Friedrich Schlegel thought was the paradigmatic representation of the romantic self and the romantic author.

This quality is particularly clear in the involutions and ironies offered us by the author figure of the most problematized and highly foregrounded metafictional work of the *Provincial Tales*. I mean, of course, that conjunction of seventeenth-century Puritan "history," eighteenth-century "gothic romance," and nineteenth-century "realism," the tale/sketch "Alice Doane's Appeal." The reader will recall that, in the frame, a bemused attitude toward the figure of the authorial self (though by no means so extreme as that in the "Aubépine" frame of "Rappaccini's Daughter") structures a subsequent fictional meditation on authorship, both literary and historical, and the ever-present goal of "fame." The writings of the Salem historian in "Alice Doane's Appeal" were cheaply aimed at contemporary fame, while the narrator remarks that his stories and sketches in the *Token* brought him no fame as an author. Something is missing. And that something is an interpenetrating sense of the absolute necessity of perspectivity and the uncertainty of right, wrong, fame, shame, fact, fiction, and all such falsifying binaries.

The paradoxical centrality of perspectivism needs to be recognized in any consideration of fact and fiction, romance and history, the actual and the imaginary. An essential step toward an approximation of objectivity is the fundamental romantic recognition of subjectivity that Schlegel, Tieck, Hoffmann, Brown, Irving, Poe, Melville, and Hawthorne acknowledged. For Hawthorne, legends, historical events, stories, stories of historical events — or even "facts" themselves — are all texts. A text is a transaction and a negotiation, a process that we have seen to be multiply framed and mediated from author to reader. The "complete" text of an event includes interpretative texts upon that text.

Fiction and history differ presumably in the ontological reality of the initiating event (itself one of a quantum series of events). But how does one get back to the real historical event when it is constituted by a series of texts? For Hawthorne the fictional construct truth is always an *as if* proposition. Rather than monologically presenting one side (one interpretation, e.g., of historical process), Hawthorne dialogically dramatizes doubleness, multiplicity, and contradictoriness. In this way romantic fiction is realistic and true. That is, true romance is historically faithful *and* faithfully fictional. A true romantic fiction would be faithful to both the facts and the romantic myths *and* to the subjective interpretations that accrete around those historical facts and those myths, becoming part of them. Such romance is truer than mere factual recounting, truer than free-floating romance cut loose from local legendary history. The true romance of history is acknowledged to be factual and fictional, framed by the recognition of the ineradicable intertwining of fact and fiction in the human imagination.

The embodiment of these matters, as found in Hawthorne's written self, we may term (though it is perhaps a less than fortunate fall into jargon) the Oberonic self. It is this complex, self-ironic persona of the Story Teller as Oberon—the Oberonic self—that is the authorial presence we should attend to, not some presumed biographical Hawthorne. We must, as he says, "make quite another kind of inquest, and look through the whole range of his fictitious characters," including those of the "authorial self."[16]

Poe fretted about the pervasive impress of an absolute "singularity" of imagination in Hawthorne's tales and sketches; but this writing self is much more complex than the monotonal melancholy that Poe thought was its central characteristic. Acutely aware of itself as posing as writer, the Oberonic persona is indeed self-impelled to touch all and to give its peculiar hue to all it touches. But it is bemused at and by itself for doing so. And, like a Merry Andrew, the Oberonic self nods and winks—whether at two versions of the authorial self on the road from Connecticut to Toboso—or at those other archcompanions—author and reader.

We must reconceive Hawthorne's tradition and the shape of his career. At the very least, we must acknowledge that Hawthorne's complex and ironic manipulation of romantic conventions of narrative is manifestly evident in the deliberate authorial presence of his earliest tales. But Hawthorne's art of authorial presence also has important implications for the history of the American short story. That is, as suggested earlier, the Poesque line of authorial suppression leads to the postromantic style of realism represented by Hemingway, whereas the Hawthorne mode of figured authorial foregrounding leads to metafiction and postmodernism. In any case, attention to embedded and foregrounded author-reader relationships, given so much careful attention by Hawthorne, enriches our understanding of the central features of his art: his deployment of negative romance, his concomitant dialogical understanding of the psychology of individuals and cultures, his focus on and through the lenses of egoism and provincialism, his interpretation of the interpretation of American history — in sum, his comprehensive romantic irony and his mastery of romantic narratology.

Notes

Introduction: Romantic Context of the "Hawthorne Question"

1 The title of Agnes McNeill Donohue's collection, *A Casebook on the Hawthorne Question*, highlights the issue. Donohue pursues the theme in her collected essays on Hawthorne, the title of which neatly catches one aspect of the problem: *Calvin's Ironic Stepchild*. Cf. Green.

2 Dryden, pp. 9–10. Dryden undertakes a phenomenological analysis of the mind of "Hawthorne" rather than interpreting Hawthorne's works per se; he has a useful discussion of the writer's persona in the prefaces and elsewhere (pp. 132–42); these formulations figure in his definition of "form" in his *Form of American Romance*.

3 Easy generalizations about Hawthorne and Puritanism or Hawthorne and history (or for that matter Hawthorne and ancestral guilt or the Oedipal syndrome) continue to be made despite the powerful and subtle literary-historical analyses of Michael Colacurcio and Frederick Newberry. These two historicist critics, both of whom recognize Hawthorne's aesthetic distance, will be touchstones throughout the discussion. But historicism has its limits, and I attempt to restore the balance somewhat more toward the aesthetic. With regard to Colacurcio, however, I wish to say at the beginning that whatever demurrals I make (and I make a number of them), there is simply nothing in Hawthorne studies that can compare with his work.

   Several promising new books focused on or dealing extensively with Hawthorne's early fiction appeared after the present manuscript was first submitted for publication. (Some titles therefore do not appear in the bibliography, though essays by certain of the authors do.) These include: Monika M. Ebert, *Encoding the Letter "A": Gender and Authority in Hawthorne's Early Fiction* (New York: Haag & Herchen, 1990); Melinda M. Ponder, *Hawthorne's Early Narrative Art* (Queenston, Ontario: Edwin Mellen Press, 1990); Charles Swann, *Nathaniel Hawthorne: Tradition and Revolution* (New York: Cambridge University Press, 1991); Lauren Berlant, *The Anatomy of National Fantasy: Hawthorne, Utopia, and Everyday Life* (Chicago: University of Chicago Press, 1991); Richard H. Millington, *Practicing Romance: Narrative Form and Cultural Engagement in Hawthorne's Fiction* (Princeton, N.J.: Princeton University Press, 1992). Additionally, a monograph by J. Hillis Miller, one of the titles of which is *Hawthorne and History*, has appeared (Oxford: Basil Blackwell, 1991); focused on "The Minister's Black Veil," the volume contains various supplementary materials: an introduction to the critical theories of Miller by Martin Heusser and Harold Schweitzer, a bibliography of Miller's writings, and a forty-page interview with Miller on the "authority of reading."

4   The concept of the "extended text" in Hawthorne's works is the foregrounded subject of a work in progress on the interpretation of Hawthorne's interpretation of America. The extended text becomes a central issue in chapter 4 on "My Kinsman, Major Molineux."

5   The phrase "provincial tales" generally designates Hawthorne's early stories and sketches of America; it derives from the titles of the first two collections just named and the subject matter of all three. After graduating from Bowdoin College in 1825, and before the publication of the first edition of *Twice-told Tales* in 1837, Hawthorne tried repeatedly to publish integrated narrative cycles; the history of his lack of success and the dismantlement of these early collections by the editors of *The Token* and the *New-England Magazine* is briefly recounted in chapter 1. The foregrounding of authorial presence in *The Story Teller* is the main subject of chapter 6.

6   I have in mind a handful of specific critics who in my judgment have authored important "position papers" on how to read Hawthorne and assess his career. Doubleday and Baym, for example, represent similar biographical, professional, and psychological orientations that I find rather too narrowly and conventionally conceived. Doubleday also represents a more historicist approach (in some ways Baym is antihistoricist). M. D. Bell presents a sophisticated historicist approach that argues (mistakenly in my opinion) the "declension theme" in Hawthorne's view of Puritan history. Crews argues from a combined psychological and historical position, deriving in part from the mid-century "debates" of Pearce, Lesser, and Leavis (see chapter 4). Colacurcio, Newberry, Dekker, and McWilliams represent a critically enlightened historicist position which I find congenial in general, but aspects of which I critique.

7   The opinion, for example, of James, Van Doren, Wagenknecht, Fairbanks, Becker, Doubleday, Baym, and even M. D. Bell. Baym suggests that Hawthorne's main literary concern in his early works was to "pacify" an audience "distrustful" of "imagination," surely an extreme reading of the shape of his career. Baym also sees the early Hawthorne as "unambiguously pro-Puritan." I use her studies of Hawthorne as a touchstone for this critical point of view, which she is by no means alone in holding. See L. B. V. Newman (hereinafter LBVN) on "The Gray Champion" (pp. 142ff.) for an overview of the dominant nationalistic, pro-Puritan reading; cf. chapter 3 of the present study. Also see Ruland for discussion of "provincial" America as seen by James through Hawthorne.

8   Such is the underlying assumption shaping Baym's *Shape of Hawthorne's Career*, though it is so much a literary-biographical convention (cf. Arvin, Mellow, Stewart, Turner, Van Doren, Von Abele, etc.) that she does not see it as posing any problem. Cf. Colacurcio's reformulation of this problem in his first chapter.

9   Pearce, *Historicism*, pp. 169ff. Pearce's thesis is much more complicated than the brief synopsis just given. It involves a two-stage "solution" to the Hawthorne Question around what he calls the "Molineux theme" centrally informing Hawthorne's works; this thesis is discussed in more detail in chapter 4.

10 Hollinger, pp. vii–viii. Hollinger's last sentence implicitly suggests that the doctrine of American "exceptionalism" has been a two-edged sword — a nationalist affirmation, yet a self-deflating one on the question of provincialism. Exceptionalist thinking, as Hollinger implies, has created a historiographical problem. It has produced inconsistency among historians who see the American European heritage as crucial, yet who somehow do not see that heritage really at work in the province. This problem is evident in literary history as well; cf. the notation on resistance to the concepts of "negative romanticism" and "romantic irony" below. Turning the usual presumption upside down, Oswald Spengler (reflecting attenuated notions of romantic primitivism and naturalness) regards the pro-

vincial as the apex of a cyclical rise before a decline toward megalopolis. Spengler turns out to be highly useful for contextualizing concepts of the American frontier. For suggestive comments on provincialism in a broad context, see Slotkin, Sundquist, Von Frank.

11   Poe was more one-sidedly against provincialism, whether that of the South, New England, or America at large. He spoke out against nationalism in literature, which he (rightly) understood as implying exceptionalism and therefore provincialism in a narrow sense. In "Exordium to Critical Notices" (1842), he condemned literary nationalism as a "political" rather than a "literary" idea. See *Essays & Reviews* (hereinafter cited as *E&R*), p. 506; cf. pp. 1027–28ff. See *Native Muse*.

12   *Dublin University Magazine* 46 (October 1855): 463–69; reprinted in *Recognition of Hawthorne*, pp. 71–78; quotations pp. 73–74; italics mine. As with other reviewers of the time, the Dublin reviewer notes with implicit approval what F. O. Matthiessen was later to call Hawthorne's technique of multiple choice.

13   The problem is related to the logic of *either/or*, of the inclusive binary: here, either inside *or* outside language and culture. A fundamental critique of naive binarial thinking pervades Hawthorne's writings. Curiously, many of his critics fall into the very trap of which he is so wary, discussing him as American *or* European, provincial *or* cosmopolitan, local *or* universal, immature *or* mature, historical *or* aesthetic, etc. Cf. Pearce. One of the best practical discussions of "containment" in culture, language, and history — the inside/outside problem — for an American artist is Neufeldt on Thoreau, esp. the preface, pp. viii–x, and the afterword. See Kloppenburg's critique of Hollinger and LaCapra. M. D. Bell loops around the issue of being caged within a culture, its history, and one's own perceptions, which Hawthorne foregrounds in the sketch "Main Street" (1849). Taking the narrative as a prime example of his main thesis, Bell points to a passage where a "Showman" narrator traces in summary fashion the changes that over two centuries the Indian village of Naumkeag undergoes as it grows into the town of Salem. Slightly misreading the text, Bell uses it to evidence Hawthorne's "theory" of historical-moral decline from the first generation of Puritans. (Cf. Perry Miller on Puritanism in general.) But in fact Hawthorne observes that the first generation was able to transmit only a general "gloom" and a "counterfeit" vision. Even this counterfeit vision grew dimmer "and then it might be seen how hard, cold, and *confined was their system, — how like an iron cage* was that which they called Liberty" (3:449; *T&S*, 1031; my italics). I would argue that Hawthorne uses the paradigm of historical "progress" ironically against the familiar notion of "decline," by which he calls into question both nineteenth-century theories of progress *and* the competing theory of decline from a presumably superior past age.

14   Despite certain claims to the contrary, Hawthorne's distinction between the novel and the romance in the preface to *The House of the Seven Gables* and elsewhere reflects the dominant understanding of the time:

When a writer calls his work a Romance, it need hardly be observed that he wishes to claim a certain latitude, both as to its fashion and material, which he would not have felt himself entitled to assume had he professed to be writing a Novel. The latter form of composition is presumed to aim at a very minute fidelity, not merely to the possible, but to the probable and ordinary course of man's experience. The former — while, as a work of art, it must rigidly subject itself to laws, and while it sins unpardonably so far as it may swerve aside from the truth of the human heart — has fairly a right to present that truth under circumstances, to a great extent, of the writer's own choosing or creation. (*Works*, 3:13)

Without directly saying it, Dekker makes clear that Baym is incorrect in her claim that Hawthorne essentially invented the distinction between novel and romance and that the "Chase thesis" is in fact a distortion along Hawthorne lines ("Genealogy of American Romance"). In "Concepts of the Romance in Hawthorne's America," Baym notes some terminological confusion in a few nineteenth-century American reviews; taking these as the norm, Baym in effect reverses the historical situation. For it was not Hawthorne who was confused or deliberately manipulative in this matter—as a glance at the famous British discussions will instantly confirm. See, for example, Samuel Johnson, *Rambler* No. 4 (1750), Bishop Richard Hurd, *Letters on Chivalry and Romance* (1762), James Beattie, "On Fable and Romance," in *Dissertations Moral and Critical* (1783), Clara Reeve, *The Progress of Romance* (1785), Walter Scott, *On Romance* (1824), or the *Britannica* entries for 1817 or 1824. Cf. *Novel and Romance* and *Scott on Novelists and Fiction*; see T. Martin, *Instructed Vision*; for Hawthorne, see Bier, Broadhead, H. H. Clark, B. Jones, Levy (1973), Stubbs.

15 See Blackall, Garber, Handwerk, Kiely, Lyons, Miyoshi, Porte, Ringe (1950, 1977, 1982), St. Armand, Steele. The romantic matrix of both Jungian and Freudian psychology becomes clear through historical investigation of the development of the "field" of psychology. See Whyte, Ellenberger, and my own discussions in "The Nightside," chapter 6 of *Poe's Fiction*, and in "Gothic Fiction of the Romantic Age." Cf. Holmes and Fogle (1981). I shall observe distinctions among the provinces of "subconscious" personal motivation, "unconscious" enculturation of perspectives on race, class, gender, ontology, etc., and the "Unconscious" romantically conceived as containing the archetypal, the mythic, sometimes the providential. Cf. Bickman; also see B. Jones on Hawthorne's "faery land." For studies integrating the broad metaphysical speculations of the time on the nature of mind with the analysis of individual subconscious motivation, see D. B. Davis, *Homicide*, and Lloyd Smith, *Motives*. Recent psychological studies of the themes of hypocrisy and secrets (and their means of disclosure) include Harris and Hutner. Also see note 33 below.

16 Relevant standard studies of the development of "romance" from the Middle Ages to the end of the eighteenth century—against which the new romance form of "arabesque" may be measured—include Lang, Ker, Saintsbury, James (preface to *The American*), Griffin, Lewis, Pettet, Tuve, Vinaver. Special status, of course, has to be accorded to Frye's *Anatomy of Criticism* and *The Secular Scripture*. Also see Beer, Hamilton, Jameson, McDermott, P. Miller, Post, I. Williams, A. Wilson. Cf. Eigner and G. Levine. For an approach through popular literature and formula fiction, see Cawelti; see Mathews, Reynolds on popular literature and Hawthorne. See notes 18 and 19 below.

17 The configuration of "romance" as conceived in the 1790s and early 1800s by Friedrich Schlegel is a main subject of *Romantic Arabesque*. It is not my intention in this book to plunge headlong into the debate on "novel" versus "romance," though such debate is impossible to avoid completely. (See *Novel and Romance*, ed. Williams.) The question of the "American Romance Tradition" arose in the nineteenth century, particularly in response to Nathaniel Hawthorne. See, for example, several reviews in *The Recognition of Hawthorne* and *Hawthorne: The Critical Heritage*, esp. pp. 453–60, 476–86, 486–503, 513–22. The issue was given strong scholarly-critical impetus in this century by Trilling, Pearce ("Twilight of Romance"), and Chase. Chase adopts Hawthorne's basic distinction and then proceeds to extend it in provocative but somewhat blurred ways. Cf. Mills's rejection of the Chase thesis. Also see Pearce's "Romance and the Study of History" and Perry Miller's "The Romance and the Novel." Among earlier studies Orians, Gerould,

and Cowie are especially useful. Two psychoanalytically oriented studies are Fiedler and Porte. Spengemann begins with a useful distinction between the "poetics of adventure" (ch. 1) and the "poetics of domesticity" (ch. 2), both of which subjects have been given political interpretations by a number of critics in the 1980s. Further studies of the American romance tradition are noted below.

18   The word *deconstruct* has now come into general use in practical criticism as meaning something (textual sign, voice, an ideological construct, or a process) counter to the privileged idea in a culture or discourse, or a destabilizing reconsideration, or a simultaneous embodiment (somehow) of that which subverts the asserted or generally accepted statement, value, construct. As used in this broad sense, the specific deconstruction of Jacques Derrida is not intended; the endless "play of signifiers" is not necessarily implied. The 1980s saw "discoveries" of a subversive dialectic in response to what Bercovitch called a pressing need for *re*-assessment of classic American texts as "works of *ideological mimesis*, at once implicated in the society they resist . . . , nourished by the culture they seem to subvert" (p. 642). M. J. Hoffman anticipates this subversive dialectic concept by at least fifteen years. McWilliams offers a subversive, ironic reading of Hawthorne's reading of American history and nationality. Carton attempts to disassociate his ironic dialectic from my own formulation of Poe's romantic irony, but it seems to me largely a distinction without a difference — except that "dialectic" is the wrong word; see *Romantic Arabesque*, chs. 1 and 3. Reynolds does not really address the "subversive imagination" of his subtitle so much as set up a binary of affirmative and nonaffirmative works; and despite references to the "dialogical" theory of M. M. Bakhtin, he does not really delineate either dialogic or dialectic in texts, but rather suggests some tension between "high culture" texts (the canonized works) and popular literature.

Recent studies of the historical romance in America (shaped by Chase's still essential distinction between novel and romance) provide permutations of a subversive dialectic. Several are lucidly surveyed by Dekker (1989), who usefully and gracefully locates his own *American Historical Romance* in the debate of the 1980s among M. D. Bell, Carton, Dryden, Budick, and R. S. Levine. For studies of the problems of historical fiction, the relation of history, ideology, and literature, see books by Becker, M. D. Bell (1971), Buell, R. Clark, Dale, Gilmore, Henderson, D. Levin (1959, 1967), Pease, H. Shaw, Simonson, Strout, White (1973, 1987), and essays by Allen, M. D. Bell (1985), Berlant, Bronstein, Kermode (1977), Krieger, Pearce, Weinstein, White (1976). Also see essays in *Ideology and Classic American Literature* and *Literature of Fact*. For general studies (with reference to Hawthorne) of the romanticism and novel/romance problem, see books by Coale, Cowie, Eigner, Elder, Gilmore, Girgus, T. Gross, Perosa, Stubbs; and essays by Charvat, Cowie, Dickstein, Foster, Holmes, P. Miller. (See notes 15–17 above, 19 below; cf. W. Ellis, Greenwald.)

19   See Peckham, "Toward a Theory of Romanticism." There are (at least) two romanticisms. I am reluctant to use the currently popular terminology of Theodor Adorno (*Negative Dialectics*), partially because of the confusing history of the term *dialectic* (discussed further in chapter 1) and partially because Adorno means something special by the term. Basically "negative dialectic" indicates recognition that every proposition carries within itself its own negation, on which it is dependent for any "real" positivity. But Adorno is particularly concerned about the increasing split in the modern world between subjectivity and objectivity, even in self-conscious modern art. Art, he argues, must sustain a living subjectivity, an ongoing process of intense self-scrutiny (negative criticism), to prevent itself from either simplistically asserting positive meanings or (equally

bad) simplistically asserting meaninglessness. Adorno's conclusions in *Aesthetische Theorie* bear parallels to the concepts employed here of negative romance, negative allegory, negative closure; and Adorno owes perhaps as much to Friedrich Schlegel and romantic aesthetics as M. M. Bakhtin does for his formulation of "dialogic" (q.v. below and chapter 1). Bakhtin privileges aesthetic containment or embodiment. Keats's famous but truncated formulation of "negative capability" is closer to Schlegel's idea of simultaneous "objectivity/subjectivity." Related is Ricoeur's concept of the distanciation of the artist figure. Such distanciation combined with involvement lies at the heart of romantic irony, wherein one is simultaneously in earnest and not. See Behler.

For my previous formulations of romantic irony in America, see in addition to *Poe's Fiction* two subsequent essays on irony and indeterminacy in American gothic fiction: "The Apparition of This World" and "The Development of Romantic Irony in the United States." Buell argues that it is a mistake to claim an *American* romantic irony, that it is really a German or strictly Continental idea. For the counter position, see, in addition to "Romantic Irony in the United States," my reply in *Romantic Arabesque*. Cf. Behler, de Man, Garber.

20   Related critical studies focused on the subject of indeterminacy have recently appeared. For a general narratological consideration, see Iser (1977). Sutherland offers a summation of previous critical speculations on indeterminacy in Poe and Hawthorne; her exhibits are *The Narrative of Arthur Gordon Pym* and *The Marble Faun*, to which she adds James's *The Sacred Fount*. The "poststructuralist" effort by Pahl is often terminologically substitutive of an older critical tradition. J. Auerbach argues a rather odd pseudo-psychoanalytic thesis that touches on problems of indeterminacy. See Budick's subsection titled "Indeterminacy and the Tradition of American Romance," pp. 81–83, and Keller's examination of ambiguity in typology. Among the many studies of indeterminacy in the gothic tradition, I would single out A. G. Lloyd-Smith's *Uncanny American Fiction* for its anatomy of seven varieties of the uncanny; but also see Newlin and Haggerty; cf. Ringe, *American Gothic*.

21   The main target for Hawthorne is the oppressiveness of an authoritarian (and specifically patriarchal) society, in religion, morality, politics, and gender issues. (See Fliegelman, esp. with regard to my discussion of "Molineux" in chapter 4.) To call Hawthorne a negative romantic or a romantic ironist is thus to affirm that what happens to Hester in *The Scarlet Letter* or to Zenobia in *The Blithedale Romance* is a conscious dramatization of gender issues rather than an unconscious revelation of latent misogyny. This is not to say that there are *no* latent unconscious elements in texts. The gender question is peripheral in the present study of the early provincial narratives but central to Hawthorne's later work; and occasional reference to the critical debates on Hawthorne and gender will be made *passim*. Like Bakhtin and Ricoeur, I am privileging largely conscious artistry as a kind of distancing. But there are caveats. Of the principal forms of distanciation that Ricoeur suggests, we may (following Henrietta Moore) specify four: (1) persistence of meaning suggests transcendence of the passing moment; (2) overlapping differences between text and authorial intention suggest that texts often mean more than the author meant to say; (3) conditions of production include the opening up of the text and authorial intention to an unknown, unlimited audience transcending time and place of authorship and production; (4) texts transcend being bound by local time and reference. To which I add the observation offered before: criticism may become part of the extended text beyond authorial intent.

22   *Hawthorne's Historical Allegory*, pp. 3–4. Religious typological allegory (as distinguished

from a literary symbolic mode) sees meaning as implicit in events and anticipatory or predictive of later events unfolding in a preordained chronological pattern; thus chronological position in history is indicative of nearness of completion of the grand pattern. This presumption is central to Hawthorne's deconstruction of historical allegory and informs his deconstruction of literary allegory. It may be mentioned here that biblical typology at the level of practice in Puritan New England was plural (that is, heterogeneous; cf., e.g., Wigglesworth with Cotton Mather). Becker adopts a familiar essentialist view of Puritan symbology; while that assumption may be historically challenged, Hawthorne seems himself to be challenging typological thinking on similar grounds (i.e., that it is monologically self-assured). As for more "traditional" allegory, Hawthorne seems perfectly aware of what twentieth-century critics have had to remind us: that "new critical" reductions of allegory to equivalences ($X = Y$) had never been strictly true of the mode; allegory has its own elaborate richness, which only the clumsy artist or critic ignored. Hawthorne's sense of allegory as a symbolic mode is closer to the complexity and ambiguity of Spenser's *Faerie Queene* than to the simplicity and directness of Bunyan's *Pilgrim's Progress*. We cannot tie Hawthorne to simplistic allegory or banal typology. Cf. E. Auerbach, Berek, Bronstein, Carton, Cowan, Doubleday (1972), Elder, Fletcher, Foster, Haviland, Honig, Keller, Lowance, Male (1981), Rees, and essays in *Typology*, ed. Bercovitch, and *Literary Uses of Typology*, ed. Miner.

23 I would say that Becker is at least partially right in the way he articulates Hawthorne's ambivalence toward Puritan historiography; see his comments on "The Gray Champion." But, again, Hawthorne's ambiguity would seem to account in some way for Becker's own ambivalence about "The Gray Champion," the discussion of which is representative of his own ambiguity. For a clearer exposition of the allegorical tradition, see Berek, Fletcher, Honig; cf. Cowan. For further consideration of Brumm's thesis, see Shurr.

24 On the problem of "American" allegory also see Dekker, Budick, and Dauber.

25 In his April 1842 review for *Graham's Magazine*, Poe playfully objected, when the "second edition" of *Twice-told Tales* came out, that they were really now "thrice-told"; see *E&R*, p. 568. Cf. the subtitle of the separate edition of "The Gentle Boy" as a "thrice-told tale" illustrated with a drawing by Sophia Peabody Hawthorne (discussed in chapter 3). See Chibka on "Wakefield" for an application of the designation the "tale told twice." Van Leer, in a provocative essay (which tends, however, to overstate most of its propositions), cogently observes that "Hawthorne's use of a 'twice-told' narration, his reformulation of other people's stories, demands that we attend to the teller as well as the tale. . . . Everywhere in the tales, the philosophical assumptions of Hawthorne's narrators are as important as the moral judgments they make" (p. 57).

26 See chapter 3 of *Romantic Arabesque* for a comparison of Bakhtin and Schlegel; Schlegel and Müller in fact articulated the binary of "monologisch" and "dialogisch," borrowed from them by Bakhtin.

27 Darrel Abel writes that readers of Hawthorne have long recognized in some way the centrality of an "author presence." In "all of Hawthorne's work we are sensible of an artist presence, sometimes incarnate in a character, sometimes not. The function of this presence is to observe events, to sympathize with the characters involved in them and thus to try to understand or identify with them, and to give expression and meaning to their actions and roles. Meaning is given by ideas in the artist mind, and amounts to creation of reality, since for Hawthorne all reality is subjectively defined" (*The Moral Picturesque*, p. 4). Abel sees more stability or "unity" in this author presence than I do. I prefer to "re-cognize" the author (to use Colacurcian language) in the terms suggested by Bakhtin

(or, for that matter, by Michel Foucault); see next chapter. For further discussion of the general problem, see Duban (1989) on Melville's narrators. The most fertile area of criticism for narrative voice(s) in Hawthorne has been *The Scarlet Letter* (and its preface); see (recently) Bayer, E. T. Hansen, Van Deusen, Van Leer. The most direct examination of the problem in the tales is Dunne's recent study of *Twice-told Tales*. Cf. (for a general study of narrative voice and distancing) West, "Hawthorne's Editorial Pose." For the debate on the usefulness of the concept/term "persona," see Elliott; Irvin Ehrenpreise; Buckley and Wilson; and Rubin-Dorsky, "A Persona Is Born," ch. 1 of *Adrift in the Old World*, esp. pp. 55–60, 259n., 270nn., along with his "Irving and the Genesis of the Fictional Sketch."

28   See chapters 1 and 6. The most extensive efforts in recent years are those of Weber, Luedtke, and, in his own individualistic way, Colacurcio, who is not much interested in self-reflexivity (see pp. 95, 279, 609n.). Weber is oriented in a scholarly direction rather than a critical one. His 1973 study was the first (and remains the only) full-length treatment of Hawthorne's abandoned "story cycle" projects: *Seven Tales of My Native Land, Provincial Tales*, and *The Story Teller*. Unfortunately, it is not translated into English and therefore is less well known by Americanists than it deserves. He has recently published a redaction, "The Outlines of 'The Story Teller.'" Luedtke devotes a chapter to the frame effects of *The Story Teller* and antecedents in Eastern story cycles (chapter 4, pp. 104–32). Although Baym is somewhat dismissive of the feasibility and the importance of the task of identifying or reconstructing the early collections, her succinct summary of the composition of *Provincial Tales* is highly useful. As should be apparent from the discussion to this point, I do not believe in the absolutist positions of some postmodernist, poststructuralist writers regarding the impossibility of recovery of the past. Cf. Neufeldt, pp. viiiff., Kloppenburg, and Warnke.

29   How these attitudes are known is a thorny problem glossed over by most commentators. Lanser adopts the basic premise of Genette that the unmarked narrator is equivalent to what he calls the "heterodiegetic author," a questionable assumption. Also see her discussion (cf. Stanzel) of the "degree zero" narratee, which is again fraught with problems. A simpler discussion is found in Rabinowitz; see especially the discussion of "Who Is Reading" (pp. 20ff.); his concept of audience includes *actual audience* and the author-oriented, "intended" hypothetical audience he calls the *authorial audience*. See chapter 1 of the present study for further discussion and bibliography; Wallace Martin offers a good analytic survey of recent theories of narrative; Lanser, Rabinowitz, and Martin have excellent bibliographies of narratology, as does Prince, who, all together, give a comprehensive overview through 1987. (Cf. note 27 above.)

30   Any rebirth of Hawthorne criticism must also acknowledge important interpretative questions raised by feminist critics, some of whom have been more successful in dealing with dream narrative and certain aspects of the psychological than most historicists. For a range of feminist approaches to aspects of Hawthorne and the "Woman Question," see especially Bauer, Baym, Berlant, Bronstein, DeSalvo, Fetterley, Fryer, C. D. Johnson, Tompkins, J. Warren. To these should now be added Ebert (see note 3 above); cf. Leverenz and Person.

31   For Colacurcio, Hawthorne is preeminently the historian, though he cites Levin and Hayden White on the "'literariness' of all historical writing" (p. 525) — a point not lost on Hawthorne either, as argued throughout this study. Colacurcio might well have cited L. H. Cohen's "The Romance of the Revolution," one of the best discussions we have of the relation of "romance" literary conventions and American historiography. Also see

Kloppenburg, Krieger, LaCapra, Levin (1959, 1967), *Literature of Fact*, Pease, Strout, Warnke, Weinstein, White (1973, 1976, 1987).

32   The most elaborate discussion of Hawthorne's framed narrative is that of Weber. See especially "Definition und theoretische Explikation der Rahmenerzählung," pp. 12–23. The second section of the book, on the "first seven years" (1825–1832), contains fairly detailed discussion of *Seven Tales of My Native Land* and *Provincial Tales*, including analyses of what he titles " 'Alice Doane,' " and of "The Hollow of the Three Hills," "My Kinsman, Major Molineux," four "biographical" sketches, "An Old Woman's Tale," a "second" discussion of "Alice Doane's Appeal" along with an "attempt to reconstruct a cyclical framed-narrative," that is, *The Story Teller.* I have, at a distance, been influenced by Weber's treatments of frames, framing techniques, and framed narratives in general, but I differ in the formulation of specific frame-effects and narrative-intrusion, and in interpretations of Hawthorne's works and their patterning.

33   Hawthorne's perception of the dynamics of the symbolizing process of human psychology is one that Jacques Lacan more than Freud helps us understand. I do not mean to dismiss entirely Freud's conceptions of conscious and subconscious activity nor to endorse wholly Lacan's more intricate conceptions of symbol, signifier, signified, and the quadralinear relations of *je, moi, autre,* and *Autre.* For the relevance of Lacan's ideas on symbolic activity and the model of the mind to Hawthorne's possible sense of it all — without getting unnecessarily involved in psychoanalytic theory per se — I would recommend to the general reader the discussions in *The Purloined Poe: Lacan, Derrida, and Psychoanalytic Reading*, especially the selections from Lacan's "Seminar on 'The Purloined Letter,' " from Derrida's "The Purveyor of Truth," and Barbara Johnson's article "The Frame of Reference: Poe, Lacan, Derrida," along with the editors' various introductions. This overview finds further clarification, historically and analytically, in Handwerk's fine study of irony and ethics in narrative, subtitled *From Schlegel to Lacan*; see especially the introduction and penultimate chapter on Lacan. The first two chapters on Schlegel set the historical groundwork leading to Lacan, the second one ("The Subject in Romantic Narrative") being of special interest.

34   On mediation (of various kinds) in Hawthorne's narratives, see Newberry and J. D. Crowley. The *Rahmenerzählung* as an "author-foregrounding genre" is presented in *Romantic Arabesque*. Prior to the 1980s, with the exception of Crowley and Weber, there was little serious interpretative criticism on Hawthorne's early framed narratives as a whole; but see Davidson's methodology in regard to Hawthorne's "last phase." For general discussion of framing, see next chapter.

35   The two main critics who have dealt with self-reflexivity as an important aspect of Hawthorne's artistry are Duban and Swann; but also see Janssen and West. Cf. John Carlos Rowe on *The Blithedale Romance.* Dauber comes at an aspect of self-reflexivity from a version of Geneva School phenomenological structuralism.

36   Author-foregrounding is a salient feature of the romantic sketch, American versions of which have received scant critical attention. But see Pauly, "The Literary Sketch in Nineteenth-Century America," and Rubin-Dorsky, "Washington Irving and the Genesis of the Fictional Sketch." Relevant also is Rubin-Dorsky's "A Crisis of Identity: *The Sketch-Book* and Nineteenth-Century American Culture," the thesis of which is given fuller general development in his *Adrift in the Old World.* Within a heavily moralistic-psychosexual framework, Rubin-Dorsky offers a provocative brief discussion of the development of a persona in the sketches of "Geoffrey Crayon" and the crisis of the concept of persona (including the term itself); he does not, however, centrally address the idea of

the genre of the sketch or the sketch-book (see p. 55 and p. 269nn.55, 60). See also Van Tassel; cf. (for contrast) the rather forced taxonomic efforts of Marler; then see Walter Evans on the dual tradition of the American short story.

37   Friedrich Schlegel's taxonomy for the arabesque *Roman* bifurcates at the first level into Poetic Romance and Prose Romance, the two basic types of the latter being philosophical and psychological romance. See *Romantic Arabesque*, pp. 220–23, 237–39.

1   *Paradigmatics of* Provincial Tales

1   See Lathrop's introductions to *Works;* the early chapters of Turner's biography; and J. D. Crowley's historical and textual notes to *Twice-told Tales (CE)*. Cf. notes 5 and 6 below.

2   See Lathrop, *Works*, 2:7–12, 12:7–10, 279–95. Two tales escaped the fire, as related by an author-narrator in an interpenetrating frame for "Alice Doane's Appeal," because they were in the possession of someone else. The combination frame-sketch-tale (published 1834 in the 1835 *Token*) is generally regarded as a "revision" of an earlier "Alice Doane" text.

3   The 1832 *Token* was published fall 1831; the 1835 *Token* fall 1834. Scholars have assumed in general that Hawthorne revised the Ur-Alice text (adding the frames and substituting narrative summaries) sometime between 1830 when Goodrich rejected the original version and the first half of 1834 (when the 1835 *Token* was being composed). Turner, S. L. Gross, Mathews, Markus, Baym, Brodwin, and others have offered various speculations on what specific revisions Hawthorne might have made and why he made them; see LBVN (pp. 2–3) for a summary review. But the position taken in the present study is that the 1835 "Alice Doane's Appeal" as we have it culminates a large pattern of narrative presence or intrusion in the *Provincial Tales*.

4   Northrop Frye observes that "national stories . . . as a rule shade insensibly from the legendary to the historical" (*Secular Scripture*, p. 8). Hawthorne in a sense reverses this pattern; or rather he emphasizes the double direction of the flow.

5   *Shape of Hawthorne's Career*, p. 30. In her précis of the scholarship on the *Provincial Tales*, Baym does not deal with suggestions that "The Hollow of the Three Hills" was part of the original manuscript, nor does she comment on the most highly speculative (I would say distortive) of all these canon considerations, that of Adams, who for "thematic unity" drops one of the five *known* works of *Provincial Tales* ("Alice Doane's Appeal"). See Chandler and Adkins (1945), the latter of whom believes that "Seven Vagabonds" was a first attempt to write an introduction to *The Story Teller* (p. 134). See also Janssen, "Hawthorne's Seventh Vagabond"; cf. Weber (1973), pp. 129–41, Duban ("Infidelity in Hawthorne's 'The Story Teller' "), Pauly ("Story Teller's Disaster"), and Duban, "Sceptical Context." Other pertinent studies (in addition to standard biographies) of the publication record and the stages of Hawthorne's early career include: Adams (1958), Adkins (1966), Doubleday (1966, 1972), Gilkes, S. L. Gross (1956, 1957, 1961), W. A. Jones, McDonald (1972, 1974), Pancost, Stewart (1945), Weldon. Associated with this general topic are studies of Hawthorne's early reading; see Kesselring, Mathews, Turner (1936), A. Warren.

6   I deal with some of the other candidates in the concluding chapter. CE, despite long tradition, lists "An Old Woman's Tale" as "attributed," with inadequate explanation. Pearce, one of the main *CE* editors, includes it in *T&S* while omitting "Sketches from Memory" II, which is even more clearly linked. Baym, in passing (p. 32), links "An Old Woman's Tale" to "The Hollow of the Three Hills" because of their mingling of the

visionary and the actual. Newman (LBVN), regarding "The Wives of the Dead," suggests that all three works make it impossible for the reader to differentiate between the actual and the imaginary and suggests further that the reader is forced in "An Old Woman's Tale" to supply an ending, "thereby giving his imagination the final role in the resolution of the plot's reality" (p. 329). Actually all four sketches emphasize the blending of readerly imagination with the writerly, with "Alice Doane's Appeal" explicitly foregrounding this "collaboration."

7   See pp. 1–45; quotation, p. 29. The introduction includes a useful discussion of the (inadequate) definition of *Novelle*, with which it is useful to frame (contextualize) Poe's famous definitions of the "tale" in his 1842 review of Hawthorne (see *E&R*). Ellis points up the faulty logic of misconceived binary exclusions and the "prescriptive power of the word" (e.g., weed vs. plant, tree vs. bush, *Märchen* vs. *Novelle*), so that obsessive concern with tale vs. sketch, novella vs. story, and the like are self-defeating. The historical documents in the development of the theory of the *Novelle* have been collected by Kunz and by Polheim.

8   Ellis, p. 38; my italics. M. M. Bakhtin, in "Discourse in the Novel," makes a number of pertinent observations regarding author and narrator(s). Among them are the following:

> (1) There are in fictional texts "words that are completely denied any authorial intentions" in the sense that "the author does not express *himself* in them . . . rather, he *exhibits* them as a unique speech-thing." A "prose writer can distance himself from the language of his own work, while at the same time distancing himself, in varying degrees, from the different layers and aspects of the work" (*Dialogic*, p. 299).
> (2) The "narrator's story or the story of the posited author is structured against the background of . . . the expected literary horizon." The "dialogic tension between two languages and two belief systems, permits authorial intentions to be realized in such a way that we can acutely sense their presence at every point in the work. The author is not to be found in the language of the narrator . . . but rather, the author utilizes now one language, now another, in order to avoid giving himself up wholly to either of them . . ." (*Dialogic*, p. 314).

9   See Clements and Gibaldi. Gustav Freytag's "triangular" diagrammatic representation of the "rising action" and "falling action" of a tragedy has had a pervasive schoolroom and critical influence. It is a useful but limited paradigm summarizing the dominant conceptualization of narrative unity since the Renaissance, one which is explicitly under assault in the works of Lawrence Sterne, Jean Paul Friedrich Richter, Ludwig Tieck, E. T. A. Hoffmann, and Poe, Melville, and Hawthorne. John Barth makes it a central object of playful analysis in *Lost in the Funhouse* (1968), *Chimera* (1972), and the *Friday-Book* (1984).

10 See Booth, Friedman, Prince, Genette, Iser, Chatman, and Lanser. Lanser attempts to accommodate her narratology to the hyperstructuated models of Genette (see chs. 3 and 4, and esp. the charts on pp. 144–45, 160, 163, 174, 177, 187, 200, 212–13; cf. 217, 224), which in my opinion are too complicated to be useful in practical critical discourse, and I do not employ his terminology; for a contrary view, see Rimmon-Kennan. Somewhat more useful for practical criticism is Stanzel. Also see Eco, Mailloux, Kent, Kermode. From among the growing number of collections of essays on narrative, see especially *On Narrative*, *The Reader in the Text*, *Reading Narrative*, and *Toward a Poetics of Fiction*. Also pertinent are Said on (a special sense of) beginnings, Kermode and Gerlach on endings, Brooks on plot and intention in narrative, and Phelan on "character, progression, and interpretation" of narrative.

11   In altered order, Expressive, Objective, Pragmatic, Mimetic. Lokke, in a spirited attack on the unexamined assumptions of taxonomies (pp. 1–25), formulates the schema as A-T-R + W and notes the rather questionable relation of some "real" WORLD to the rest of the paradigm. He writes: "The literary model — which seems to have governed our speculation in patent ways for about, to put it conservatively, fifty or sixty years, and in less obvious ways since pre-Socratic times — is the AUTHOR-TEXT-READER + WORLD model. Using artist, object (of art), audience, and the universe, this model, gracefully articulated in all its static grandeur, occupied 'central' prominence in the influential text of M. H. Abrams's *The Mirror and the Lamp*. . . . Outside the triangulation of the A-T-R lies the World, which, depending upon the momentary idiosyncracies of the discipline, the 'interpretative community,' or the user of the model, may or may not have relationships with the Author, the Text, or the Reader. . . . this supercontext, the World, or Universe, can enter the A-T-R formula only through the apex of the triangle: that is, the Author, Text, or Reader. The Author's, Text's, or Reader's relationship to the World exists only as a function of a prior suppressed or unexpressed taxonomy" (p. 2).

12   That is, the "reader" is to be conceived as a rhetorical-fictive norm. See Ong, "The Writer's Audience Is Always a Fiction."

13   For example, mid-twentieth-century Nazis and Stalinists, post-World War II neo-Nazis, certain Japanese cults, some tribes in Africa, several Islamic cultures — *or* most of the American westering pioneers and a number of America's present-day large-city street gangs.

14   Cf. Poe's "Tell-Tale Heart"; see paradigm 1. A complex variant is Poe's "The Fall of the House of Usher," which has an *initially* observing "I" narrator, who at first seems to corroborate the bizarre events of the narrative, but who is (or may be) drawn into the hallucinatory misperceptions of another.

15   That is, the outset of this segment of the discussion, prior to paradigm 1. An example of the implied version of this paradigm would be Poe's "The Cask of Amontillado." Montresor seems to be addressing the implied reader ("you" in paragraph one), but in the unfolding of the narrative is seen to be addressing an implied narratee listening to him give his deathbed confession, namely, a priest (a further comment in terms of "framing" follows below).

16   See Behler, p. 66, who cites Müller: "Demnach wollen wir versuchen, diese beiden Erscheinungen vermittelnd darzustellen" (*Schriften*, 2:32); cf. *Romantic Arabesque*, ch. 3, pp. 214–15ff.

17   The "new fiction" that Schlegel called the *Roman* is translated into English variously as "novel" and "romance." In contrast to the restrictive rules of the preceding era of "neoclassicism," the new age of the *Roman* was "*roman*tic," especially in the sense of framed indeterminacy or of a chaos that is yet framed or structured ("künstliches, gebildetes Chaos"). For a quick survey of ways in which romantic theory anticipates aspects of contemporary theory see Reising; cf. *Romantic Arabesque*.

18   Schrag, p. 13; italics mine. Schrag quotes Hayden White, "Foucault Decoded," p. 28: "The imagery used to characterize the epochs is not that of a 'river of time' or 'flow of consciousness,' but that of an 'archipelago,' a chain of epistemic islands, the deepest connections among which are unknown — and unknowable."

19   For an overview of the general issues, see Foucault's *The Order of Things*; Lyotard's *The Postmodern Condition* and *The Differend*. For an even more vigorous assault on representational language, see *Thousand Plateaus*, the "sequel" to *Anti-Oedipus*, by Deleuze and Guattari, and Deleuze's commentaries on Foucault.

20 As observed in *Romantic Arabesque*, the theoretical base of Bakhtin's major works varies to a degree from *Problems of Dostoevsky's Work* to *Rabelais and His World* to essays posthumously collected in English. Todorov's general introduction to Bakhtin's thought contextualizes these variations biographically and theoretically. For a succinct (if narrowly focused) overview of some of the major implications of the dialogic for applied criticism of American literature, see Bauer's *Feminist Dialogics*, especially the preface ("A Theory of Feminist Dialogics"), chapter 1 ("Gender in Bakhtin's Carnival"), and chapter 2 on Hawthorne's *Blithedale Romance*.

21 In a sense, the monological is really a special use of the dialogical, in which the particulars of context are denied or excluded, in order for the monological to constitute itself. A perusal of American histories from before Bancroft through World War II reveals an unself-conscious ignorance of bias, even pretension of scientific objectivity, paradoxically combined with nationalism and moral rectitude of a rather puritanistic sort. Except for Henry Adams's ironies, the big breakthroughs in American-authored historiography occurred late: Levin's *History as Romantic Art* (1959) and White's *Metahistory* (1973), to which should be added Cohen's *The Revolutionary Histories* (1980) and LaCapra's *Rethinking Intellectual History* (1983). See Kloppenburg, Warnke.

22 Bakhtin's theory of the *carnivalesque*, which is both historical and conceptual, strikingly illustrates this cross-grain emphasis. He associates the carnivalesque (as release, inversion, laughter, humor, irony) with rhetorical political strategy. The centripetal force of the uniform, the authoritarian, and the totalitarian is countered by the centrifugal force of carnival feast, parody, and the celebration of fools. "Carnival" stands at the "borderline" between art and life. In his study of Rabelais, Bakhtin suggests that literature embraces (or should embrace) the carnivalesque. Bakhtin sees Rabelais's carnivalesque portrayal of his society as centrifugal, subverting the idea of the divine right of kings, attacking the centralization of Aristotle's power in the academies, parodying the theology and ritual of the Catholic Church. Carnival represents momentary "freedom" opposed to the "official" feast of the Church. (Cf. remarks on the disaster cornice and the carnival cornice tradition of the Renaissance novella in the main text below.)

23 For a start, see glossary, *Dialogic Imagination*, p. 428; then see pp. 188ff. and 301–31, leading through author/narrator relations to "the speaking person in the novel" (pp. 331ff.). See also the opening pages of the first essay, "Epic and Novel"; and the first paragraphs of the "Chronotope" essay, pp. 84–85: "It can be said that it is precisely the chronotope that defines genre and generic distinctions." See Todorov, pp. 81–85 et passim. (But cf. Derrida, "Law of Genre.")

24 Todorov's words (p. 56) — to which we might add *hetero-intentionality*. Bakhtin writes of *heteroglossia* itself that it is, in the novel, "*another's speech in another's language*, serving to express authorial intentions but in a refracted way." We have thus "a special type of *double-voiced discourse*. It serves two speakers at the same time and expresses simultaneously two different intentions: direct intention of the character who is speaking, and the refracted intention of the author" (*Dialogic*, p. 324). Shortly after, he notes that "the internal dialogism of double-voiced prose discourse can never be exhausted thematically" (p. 326). Cf. pp. 332–33 (esp. on the speaking person in the novel as an *ideologue* and the speaker's words as *ideologemes*). See also pp. 375ff. on the "*Second Stylistic Line of development*" in the European novel characterized by *heteroglossia*.

25 All this seems to me to be a reasonably good definition, by contrast with the "tale proper," of the "sketch" as Hawthorne practiced it. These distinctions will be gradually developed throughout the remainder of the present study. See especially chapter 2.

The more important studies of Poe's critiques of Hawthorne are those of Belden and McKeithan.

26 For further analysis of the neglected *Tales of a Traveller,* see Hedges's consummate *Washington Irving: An American Study.* My essay on Irving and the American ghost story is focused on part 1 of the cycle, "Strange Stories by a Nervous Gentleman."

27 Weber in 1973 complains that in English there is very little criticism on the frame-tale tradition. Although it is still a relatively unexplored area, some studies have subsequently appeared. In addition to Weber, see Barth, and Clements and Gibaldi. For the framed-tale tradition and the literal "Arabesque," see Gittes and Gerhardt; the relation of this tradition to Poe and others is the subject of chapter 1 of *Romantic Arabesque.* A special issue on the short story cycle, ed. J. Gerald Kennedy, appeared in *Journal of the Short Story in English* No. 11 (1988); see Kennedy's introduction. From another point of view than the one taken here, but implicitly highlighting many similar points, Colacurcio groups such works as "The Haunted Mind," "Wakefield," "Alice Doane's Appeal" — with telling reference to Swann. For "frame-story," see Dittmar. Cf. Lemon; cf. Prince, *Dictionary of Narratology,* esp. on "embedded narrative" and its variants. For a more sociological definition of framing pertinent to literary analysis, see Goffman. See Raskin for an instrumental treatment of "script theory." Less linguistic and technical are Tannen's two essays on context framing.

28 One could call these "internal" frames as opposed to "external" frames, though normally the term applies to a frame within a frame. For example, in the *Decameron* a frame (Philomena prepares to tell her first story) within a larger frame (the retreat from the plague-stricken city of Florence) around another narrative (Philomena's story). For other considerations, see Alfred Weber's "Definition and Theoretical Explication of the Frame-Narrative" (pp. 12–23). Poe also attempted a *Rahmenerzählung,* the first version of which he titled *Eleven Tales of the Arabesque* (ante 1833), the second *Tales of the Folio Club* (c. 1834). A tale implicitly framed in the manner of "The Cask of Amontillado" (e.g., "Ligeia"), if also contained within the *Rahmenerzählung* of the Folio Club (as has been suggested on more than one occasion), would be multiply framed inside and out — in the manner of Hoffmann's *Serapionsbrüder.*

29 *Raven and the Whale,* pp. 41ff. The context of nineteenth-century American "chiaroscuro" was a bit different from what Clements and Gibaldi are trying to describe in Renaissance tale-cycles (though stemming from a similar impulse). The "chiaroscuro" of "John Waters" (Henry Clay) was, for example, more superficial and precious than what Poe and Hawthorne were doing. On a simple imagistic level, consider the light and dark symbolism of "Benito Cereno" or the central scenes of *The Marble Faun* (chs. 25–29), not to mention *The Scarlet Letter* (chs. 16–19).

30 Clements and Gibaldi observe that explicit external frames in the novella cornice tradition, besides the complex functions discussed in the main text above, have a variety of more basic (though not necessarily simple) functions. The frame may provide transition and entrée, a way of getting into and out of a story; it may add or suggest "truth" and verisimilitude; it may provide contrast or parallel of frame and story in setting, character, event, imagery — which may or may not create aesthetic distance. One of the functions of the frame in the late Middle Ages and Renaissance, they suggest, was to provide a shield from behind which authors could tell ribald stories (e.g., the following immoral tale has been transcribed, dear reader, just as I found it in an old chronicle).

31 2:195; *T&S,* 404; my italics. See Irwin's provocative discussion (*American Hieroglyphics,* pp. 258–65) of doubling in "Monsieur du Miroir."

2   *Following Darkness Like a Dream*

1   Baym makes a further division. Noting that among Hawthorne's early narratives were "a group of tales set in the American past and a number of biographical sketches of historical personages and events," she writes that "two distinct treatments of historical material . . . imply that at this stage of his career Hawthorne separated historical from imaginative writing quite sharply" (*Shape of Hawthorne's Career*, pp. 29–30). But I would argue that a writer who produced *historical* fiction and *biographies* of American *historical* figures might be said to exhibit a continuity and complementariness of interests rather than making a "sharp" separation of subject matter or mode. Baym (pp. 31–32) offers another sharp distinction, downplaying the historical entirely: ". . . Hawthorne was not interested in making history the subject of his fiction or in creating fictions for the purpose of commenting on the American past. (It is indeed arguable whether these were ever his purposes in fiction.)" This position is opposite to both Colacurcio's thesis that Hawthorne is preeminently an intellectual historian and my argument for the complementarity and interpenetration of categories like historical and imaginative in Hawthorne.

2   The ancient question regarding dreams is whether they are "true" (in the sense of prophetic) or "false" (in the sense of idiosyncratic fantasy). In the romantic period the "sleep-waking" state was considered by some to be a trance state between conscious and unconscious perception, making available to the cognitive faculties the design of the cosmic Unconscious; but it was countered in fiction by portrayal of the irrational "sleep-walking" state, in which the tormented personage was agitated into physical wandering under the influence of a disturbed subconscious. (Gollin, surprisingly, does not treat these matters.) The "truth" of dreams for Hawthorne is always psychological. For other perspectives on dreams or dreamland, see Herndon, B. Jones, Newlin.

3   The romantics were fascinated by these paradoxes and images of infinite regress. See comments on Ludwig Tieck in chapter 3 in the discussion of "Roger Malvin's Burial." Poe's famous lines, "Is *all* that we see or seem / But a dream within a dream?" (1849), are conventional for the period. The question of the dream within the dream may be said to be the collective theme of the provincial sketches discussed in this chapter.

4   As mentioned in the introduction, Friedrich Schlegel had given to such combined forms the name *Arabeske* (or more problematically, *Roman*); see *Romantic Arabesque*, ch. 3.

5   Elizabeth Hawthorne recalled that some of the narratives related to witchcraft, some to the sea. "Wives of the Dead" does not so strongly hint of actual supernatural occurrence as create an atmosphere of the preternatural. See Julian Hawthorne, 1:124ff.; Stewart, "Recollections of Hawthorne by His Sister"; and Lathrop, *Hawthorne*, p. 134.

6   "Epiphany" has a number of meanings in Greek: sudden appearance, vision, clarification, etc. It can be used in relation to God, angels, dream figures, dreamvisions, and so forth.

7   Schubert observes (pp. 23–24) that the narrative has a symbolic structural rhythm: three visions, three scenes, three hills, referred to six times. The trinitarian symbolism of Christianity would seem to be heavily implied, especially in the "demonic" inversions of the symbolism of love and hope by satanic witchcraft.

8   See Burhans and Skaggs for formal analyses. Downing emphasizes how the narrative struggles toward a significant meaning. See T. Martin, *Hawthorne*, pp. 49–51, for a comment on the suspension of historical time and the "Hawthornesque variation of the time-honored opening of the fairy tale"; cf. his "Method of Hawthorne's Tales." Bewley remarks in *Eccentric Design* the unity produced by the symbolic presence of the three hills corresponding to the three visions; and in "Hawthorne and the Deeper Psychology" he

makes a case for Hawthorne as symbolist rather than allegorist. (See further commentary on symbol versus allegory at the end of the chapter.) A good deal of what criticism there is on the narrative is preoccupied with seeing parallels with Hester Prynne ((Stewart, Bewley, S. L. Gross), though the similarities with any of Hawthorne's isolated and guilt-ridden figures are so patent and general as to require little comment. Fossum links the narrative with "Roger Malvin's Burial."

9   See pp. 45–46, a clear example of Colacurcio's nativist and historicist bias. Geist notes in passing that the lady is of "foreign birth." The implication is that the narrative, which is also not specifically located geographically, is not an "American" work, ignoring the fact that all of the white colonialists in North America are of foreign extraction: one of the key "American" experiences.

10   1:228–29; *T&S*, 7. Stein takes this passage as suggesting a literal compact with the devil (p. 56) but adds it is "the devil in her own soul." This point is more significant than may at first be apparent.

11   Dauber, pp. 48–51, 127ff. Von Abele sees the narrative's indefinitiveness as presaging the artistic "disintegration" of Hawthorne's later years — another (in my view presumptuous) psychobiographical reading of Hawthorne based on incomplete understanding of the narratology of Hawthorne's texts.

12   Gollin, p. 104; my italics. Gollin observes that "the narrative is consistent with Hawthorne's later comment about an alleged spiritual communication" (see *Works*, 10:395–96), partially quoted as an epigraph to this chapter.

13   Stock suggests a parallel with the Witch of Endor (1 Sam. 28); since Saul does not see the witch, only hears her, it may be a trick or a misperception. The primacy of sight in these matters is subverted in "Alice Doane's Appeal."

14   Pandeya, apparently unaware of the intricacies of Christian tradition, simply jumps to the demonic circle of black magic, omitting the key idea of satanic inversion of traditional positive symbols.

15   One critical suggestion is that the putrid and sunken hollow symbolizes the lady's heart (Bewley), as the general decay of the landscape symbolizes general spiritual decay (Pandeya). This kind of symbolic reading has also generated debate on whether Hawthorne's mode is primarily symbolic or allegorical.

16   Van Doren, p. 84; Doubleday, p. 216. This sentimental way of reading the text of "The Wives of the Dead" is a bit like Gollin's reading "An Old Woman's Tale" as the exemplification of the "charming idea" of a "gift" from the past out of a dream to a pair of poor lovers who have nothing in the present world except each other; see discussion in main text below.

17   Lang, "How Ambiguous Is Hawthorne?" (rpt. *Hawthorne*, ed. Kaul); for "Wives of the Dead," see pp. 87–89.

18   Lang continues: ". . . if we read the story on the realistic level, it is somewhat improbable (two simultaneous resurrections after two simultaneous deaths); read as a dream, it is perfectly natural: the widows would dream of their husbands' return" (p. 88). Thus the lamp becomes the poignant "symbol of hope" (p. 89) for the husbands' return — i.e., a forlorn one.

19   *Province*, p. 555n. Colacurcio's discussion covers pp. 100–107, 554–56 (notes 4–16). Carlson, in *Hawthorne's Functional Settings*, pp. 115–18, and "The Function of the Lamp," debates the symbolic function of light and the lamp with Stephenson; cf. Seltzer; see LBVN, pp. 327–32.

20   This may account for the underdeveloped and somewhat incoherent suggestion of a biblical allusion to Mary and Martha, wise and foolish "virgins," in the figures of Mary and Margaret. That the sketch evokes *some* sort of negative suggestion of religious

parallels involving death and resurrection can hardly be open to question. But these parallels cannot be pinned down, historically or allegorically, in the manner of Colacurcio's interpretations of "The Gray Champion," "Roger Malvin's Burial," "The Gentle Boy," or "My Kinsman, Major Molineux."

21 Colacurcio's resistance to such a double reading is curious in light of his comments on textuality and intertextuality in the framing argument of *Province of Piety*. For further commentary on his historical-literary method, see my modification of his reading of "My Kinsman, Major Molineux" in chapter 4.

22 Critics have speculated on the symbolic properties of the light in characterizing the two women: red light for the excitable Margaret, cool moonlight for Mary. See Stephenson and Carlson. The primary function, however, is to suggest a dream state.

23 The frosted window as illusive dreamvision portal occurs in "The Haunted Mind": ". . . the glass is ornamented with fanciful devices in frost work, and . . . each pane presents something like a frozen dream" (1:344; *T&S*, 201). Cf. the window and dreamvision by the moonlit church in "My Kinsman, Major Molineux."

24 LBVN (p. 329) suggests that the same "hypnagogic state" is dramatized in both "The Haunted Mind" and "Wives of the Dead."

25 See Lang, Carlson, and Stephenson on the possible significances of the two revelations from outside taking place in the lamplight and the twice repeated shining of the lamp upon the face of each sister.

26 One is reminded of Irving's "Rip Van Winkle" or "Dolph Heyliger." The traditional (historical) legendary aspect is obvious, as is the "historical" connection between legends and past events set in a New England locale. Unlike critics who make a sharp separation between the dreamvision works and the historical romances of *Provincial Tales*, M. D. Bell remarks "such quasi-historical sketches as 'An Old Woman's Tale' " (p. 203).

27 See discussion of the relation of "specter evidence," Satan, and the "imagination" in "Alice Doane's Appeal" in chapter 5.

28 Colarcurcio, looking for "historical" significance to the piece, notices that the dream figures wrangle over the "enormously disproportioned" old church steeple, source of some ancient controversy and "almost a schism in the church," now suggesting the "Tower of Babel" (12:116–17; *T&S*, 27). But Colacurcio admits that there is not enough in the text to do much with this detail (*Province*, p. 48). The Tower of Babel association, however, is suggestive regarding Hawthorne's subversion of traditional symbols; as in "Alice Doane's Appeal," the church steeple comes to have a negative suggestion.

29 Weber observes that we do not (as in "Alice Doane's Appeal") get the interior story in the old woman's words (Baym implies the opposite) but in the retrospective language of the narrator. Thus, says Weber, we get the perspective of two "narrator-figures," the old woman and the young storyteller. Weber leaves out the possible third perspective already mentioned—that of the older narrator on the boy remembering the old woman's tales. The device is not much developed. Interestingly, Weber creatively gives the old woman in the dream an *oven*-shovel, implying the connection with the frame-narrator in the chimney tale helping the old woman in the ashes. Neither Weber nor Gollin deals with "The Wives of the Dead," understandable in Weber's case since his subject is not dreams or "dream-sensation."

3   Framing the Negative Romance

1 Morse Peckham's once celebrated term to describe Byron and other skeptic-romantics is discussed in the introduction. Of particular interest is M. J. Hoffman's application and

revision of Peckham in "The Discovery of the Void: The House of Usher and Negative Romanticism," ch. 2 of *Subversive Vision*, pp. 19–29. By "balance" I do not necessarily mean absolute equipoise; the "balancing" may be unbalanced at any one point, tipping to one side, but never quite losing its overall state of dynamic equilibrium. That is, the overall system itself (text, authorial stance) is one of constantly shifting equilibrium; the effect is hardly monological.

2   The criticism on this tale recapitulates the large issues raised in the first two chapters, further contextualizing the Hawthorne Question. The majority of critics have tended to equate the young Hawthorne with the superpatriot narrator of "The Gray Champion" or, more often, ignore the tale and others like it. In addition, Wagenknecht questions the accuracy of Hawthorne's historiography and gently remonstrates that he sometimes puts historical and moral issues too simply as either/or questions. Wagenknecht writes that Hawthorne did not always bother to discriminate historically between, say, "the Pilgrims of Plymouth and the Puritans of the Massachusetts Bay Colony"; and "sometimes, as in 'The Gray Champion,' he presents the issue between his ancestors and their opponents in terms of black and white" (p. 175). Wagenknecht nicely, but apparently unconsciously, hits here on two key issues, to be disputed for the next thirty years: (1) the accuracy of Hawthorne's historicism and (2) the black-and-whiteness versus the grayness of such a story as "Gray Champion." As a historical note, however, it is only fair to Hawthorne to observe that the Plymouth Pilgrims came under Massachusetts Bay jurisdiction after two generations.

3   Prior to the mid-1960s, few critics had suggested that Hawthorne depicts the colonial antagonists with a more or less even hand, preferring neither one side nor the other. In 1965–66, three critics, reflecting the divergent interpretive opinion, take rather different, if not opposite, directions, running the gamut of interpretation. Terence Martin tempers his observation that Hawthorne frequently invokes the "power" of the past and sees colonial history as "prefiguring the spirit of the American Revolution" by also observing that Hawthorne's "sense of the past . . . is not at all simplistic"; for he portrays the Puritans in "The Gray Champion" and "Endicott and the Red Cross" as also cruel and intolerant, "blind to all liberties but their own" — even though Hawthorne's "portrayal of the defiant spirit of the colonists implies that they were preserving independence at this early date." (See *Hawthorne*, pp. 59–60.) At the same time, Fairbanks seems to accept Wagenknecht's black-and-white reading without qualification: "The triumphant Protestantism of 'The Gray Champion' and 'Endicott and the Red Cross' is almost exultant, still capable of thrilling the reader with its tableaux of liberty ranged against tyranny: 'Neither Pope nor Tyrant hath part in . . . [New England] now' " (p. 26). Just a year later, Crews, building on Pearce, says the opposite: "Without making grand claims for the importance or complexity of 'The Gray Champion,' we can say that it illustrates much of what we have been expounding as most Hawthornian. Its ostensible subject is a legend of democratic resistance to the power of James II. . . . Yet the tale really implies that authority can only be overmatched by greater authority." (See *Sins of the Fathers*, pp. 39–40.)

4   In the 1970s the critical perplexity continued; see, e.g., Becker (p. 32), M. D. Bell (*Historical Romance*, pp. 47–53; *CLHUS*, pp. 420–21); Doubleday (*Early Tales*, pp. 85–92). Baym writes that "The Gray Champion" begins *Twice-told Tales* in order to *assert* "an attitude toward history"; the narrative "establishes the volume as an American work." Such pronouncements are tied to her conclusions that Hawthorne's literary intention was to develop a mode of authorship that would pacify an audience (including its nationalistic demands), and that history actually acted as a constraint upon his imagination — a thesis

that informs the first half of *The Shape of Hawthorne's Career;* see esp. pp. 26–27ff., 31, 72–73, 80, 103, 105. LBVN (pp. 142ff.) confirms the point that the "pro-Puritan reading" represented the dominant interpretation.

5   Crews cites Pearce's earlier "Hawthorne and the Sense of the Past" as an "apt" characterization of Hawthorne's historical work. Pearce and Crews share the belief that the most compelling of Hawthorne's colonial tales are those that (in Crews's words) "make us feel a hidden oneness between the party of rebellion and the party of rule" (*Sins*, p. 38), though that is a distortion on one level of what Pearce actually says. For Pearce the two sides (Loyalist and Dissenter) are in some way "one." But the way in which the rival sides are one for Crews is quite different. See discussion of "My Kinsman, Major Molineux" in chapter 4.

6   Crews, p. 42. Cf. Colacurcio on this last point (history as inessential or irrelevant to any personal or cultural teleology), esp. his discussion of "My Kinsman." Also see Fossum and Stein.

7   *Divided Loyalties*, p. 52; see pp. 50–58; cf. his 1976 article. Newberry hints at the narrative complexity when he adds that the "theme of seminal American democracy or independence is not woven into the fabric of the tale but is instead urged by a narrative tone of voice moralizing in favor of the Puritans to the extent that it denounces the British. Yet this tone differs radically from the ironic one adopted by Hawthorne to observe the Puritans on their own merits."

8   The orthodox "definition" of "liberty" advocated by Winthrop in "A Model of Christian Charity." The Puritan definition of liberty Hawthorne places in deliberate contrast to the general normative meaning of the word. (Cf. other "provincial" tales like "The May-Pole of Merry Mount" or "Endicott and the Red Cross.") It may be noted, however, that Hawthorne's tale does reflect the gradual historical change in the latter part of seventeenth-century New England toward greater separation of religious and civil power.

9   William Goffe fled England to America (specifically to Massachusetts Bay), became involved in the Indian "King Phillip's War," and then returned home to England. See Orians, "The Angel of Hadley," and Brumm, "Regicide Judge"; cf. Doubleday, pp. 85–92; Newberry, *Divided Loyalties*, esp. pp. 54–55; see Colacurcio, pp. 212ff.; cf. Dekker (1984).

10 Crews strikingly observes, in connection with his remarks on the clash of patriarchal figures, that the "ancestry" of New England (that is, that of England) is precisely what the colonists are rejecting "not by meeting tyranny with freedom but by setting up a rival system of ancestor-worship" (*Sins*, p. 41).

11 Cf. the carefully contrasted machine image of political impetus (e.g., 1:25; *T&S*, 238–39). See Newberry's updated discussion in *Divided Loyalties*, pp. 50–58.

12 As suggested here *passim*. Cf. the incongruous "moral" of "Wakefield," which is nearly always taken straight by critics; see Chibka. Also see Janssen, "Impaled Butterflies."

13 Students, including undergraduates, unaware of the historical particulars of Lovewell's Fight, frequently puzzle over the negative innuendo of the narrator's opening remarks; the historical context confirms the *textual* innuendo. See Colacurcio's *rehistoricizing* of the tale (pp. 107–30) in tandem with his treatment of "My Kinsman, Major Molineux" (pp. 130–53). Beaver emphasizes the ambiguity of Hawthorne's "romance" in the first word of the title of his essay, "Towards Romance: The Case of 'Roger Malvin's Burial.'" See LBVN (pp. 277–82) for a summary of critical interpretations. Crews and Ehrlich (1974) represent a range of psychological readings. I would call special attention to Bewley, *Eccentric Design*, Slotkin, W. R. Thompson, "Biblical Sources," Stock, "History

and the Bible," Colacurcio, 107–30 and notes. LBVN summarizes and quotes from several accounts given of Lovewell's Fight (pp. 271–73).

14   Yet some critics have missed the point while others have made somewhat too much of it as a hidden feature of the narrative. See Crews's "Logic of Compulsion" essay (1964), revised for *Sins of the Fathers* (1966), pp. 80–95, for a systematic (or reductive, depending on one's point of view) Freudian overlay upon Waggoner's generalized discussion in *Hawthorne*. See Colacurcio's slightly waspish remarks (p. 557 n.20) upon the "discoveries" of Crews being "a bit too gleeful" given matters already "discovered" by Waggoner; Colacurcio also suggests that Crews's reading has over the years come to "appear a little tendentious and one-sided." Both these judgments seem a little harsh, though the general double narrative of fate and inner psychology *is* pretty obvious on the surface even to engineering undergraduates.

15   Cf. Poe's "The Black Cat" or "The Cask of Amontillado." Here, by burying guilt (denying the "unburied" Roger Malvin), Reuben suffers repressive trauma; by unburying the guilt (the ritual journey to the spot of "burial"), Reuben attempts to rebury it. In Poe's "Amontillado," "Usher," "Ligeia," and "Ulalume," similar enactments of burial, un-burial, return from the tomb, and sometimes reburial constitute the symbolic psychological matrix of the tales. Cf. the burial motif in "Wives of the Dead," discussed in chapter 2. For an interesting funereal rite contextualization of "Roger Malvin's Burial," see Mc-Cullen. A major difference between "Roger Malvin's Burial" and a typical Poe story is that Hawthorne's narrator, technically first-person but narrating as though from the third-person omniscient, makes it abundantly clear at several junctures that Reuben's problem is psychological. By contrast, in Poe everything is completely dramatized from an interior perspective, normally from the centrally involved first-person.

16   The German "Fate" story or drama, associated with the youthful Tieck (as in "The Fair Eckbert"), was highly controversial on the Continent before Hawthorne's time. Walzel notes Tieck's "speculations upon the involuntary restraint endured by human beings whose lives are directed by an inscrutable force of nature." The other main thrust of German romanticism was toward a combination of determinism and free will or toward an "innate belief in human mastery over fate" (pp. 263–71ff.), as in the Schlegels, Novalis, and Schleiermacher (p. 264). See Pochmann on Hawthorne and Tieck and Hawthorne's attempt to learn German and translate Tieck. See also Marks (1953).

17   Doubleday (1972) thinks Reuben's firing "expertly" at a vague motion in the thick veil of undergrowth, where he *knows* his wife and son are, is a "failure of technique" on Hawthorne's part. Doubleday thus implicitly rejects the earlier psychological readings by Waggoner (1955) and Crews (1964, 1966), which argue that Reuben's actions result from subconscious guilty "compulsion." Waggoner suggests the son is a "symbolic extension" (for Reuben) "of himself." See W. R. Thompson and Stock on biblical allusion and the significance of names in the tale; cf. Crews's "reply" ("Logic of Compulsion," 1964) to W. R. Thompson. Also see Donohue (1963) and McCullen. A rich (not necessarily convincing) biblical contextualization in terms of the Old Testament "akedah" (binding and intended sacrifice of Isaac) is found in Budick, pp. 39–54ff.

18   A circumstance that may account for some of the odder revisions, as in "Seven Vaga-bonds." Cf. Poe's bantering remarks on "twice-told" and "thrice-told" in his review of 1842.

19   *Man's Accidents*, pp. 123–25. Cf. Fossum's reading of the Gray Champion as a mediating figure between submission and rebellion with Newberry's thesis regarding the failed or displaced mediators of Hawthorne's fiction. Cf. Dauner.

20   See LBVN, pp. 131–35, for a summary of criticism. See especially W. R. Thompson's examination of "Patterns of Biblical Allusions" as ironically deployed to point up the defects of both Quaker and Puritan, and Crews's later more Freudian account (*Sins*, 1966), which, however, contains an odd interpretation of the "redemption" of the Quaker mother at the end. Crews notes the sadomasochistic relationship of the two religious groups that Hawthorne's narrator foregrounds, but he underplays their symbiosis. M. D. Bell (1971) argues that the Puritans' harshness was a necessity for survival in the New World, and that their intolerant children represent the New World metamorphosis, while Tobias, Ilbrahim, and Dorothy represent Old World values that will die out.

21   Male observes (*Tragic Vision*, pp. 45–48) that the main theme of the tale involves the difficulty of finding an "integrated" religious experience in America.

22   In an application of the "Bell thesis" of Puritan declination, P. M. Jones suggests that the theme of the "children's declension" is a shaping myth in Hawthorne's fiction; the "intolerant brood" of Puritan children in chapter 6 of *The Scarlet Letter* are like the "brood of baby-fiends" in the tale.

23   A criticism echoed by Matthiessen and even Adkins. The seminal essay on the revisions is that of S. L. Gross (1954), where he argues that in the trimmer version artistic unity is enhanced. Parker and Higgins (1981) criticize Gross's interpretation but offer only a disorderly reading deriving from Parker's concept of a pure first-printing text which is somehow truly genuine and therefore authoritative, with any and all subsequent revisions being "flaws" or deviations from the author's truest intention (unless restored by a scholarly composite text). In Parker's eyes, author's revisions seem to be erroneous tamperings with the first text; see *Flawed Texts and Verbal Icons*, esp. the introduction.

24   Others include such things as omitting the detail that one "apartment" of the Puritan meetinghouse also served "the purposes of a powder-magazine and armory" (*T&S*, 1484) and a comment that Tobias's strong features were "at variance" with his state of indecision (*T&S*, 1485).

25   But cf. Crews, who wants to read the final scene unironically and to see Catharine as redeemed, for which there is little evidence in the structure of the tale.

26   1:126; *T&S*, 138, has a comma after "kindnesses," which to a small degree alters the tonality.

27   W. R. Thompson's "Patterns of Biblical Allusions" underscores Hawthorne's subtlety in such matters. Hawthorne has the Puritans allude principally to the Old Testament and the Quakers to the New Testament, but each perversely with unconscious irony. Cf. the irony of the Puritans conferring "martyrdom" on non-Puritans mentioned before.

28   See the chapter "John Endicott as a Puritan Type" in *Divided Loyalties*, where Newberry conjoins the two Endicott tales (pp. 25–41) with "The Gentle Boy" (pp. 41–50) and "The Gray Champion" (pp. 50–58) as detailing "The Loss of England in the Seventeenth-Century Tales" (the chapter subtitle).

29   See LBVN, pp. 129–30; Newman also suggests that Hawthorne "relied on the Puritan annalists as well," such as Hutchinson, Hubbard, Neal, Boyles, and Cotton Mather.

30   The description of Pearson's character is paralleled at the end of Episode 1, when the narrator comments that the "insults" of Pearson's Puritan neighbors (after the Pearsons have taken in Ilbrahim) "irritated Pearson's temper for the moment; they entered also into his heart, and became imperceptible but powerful workers towards an end which his most secret thought had not yet whispered" (1:95, *T&S*, 115–16), namely, conversion. In the Riverside edition, a series of periods across the page immediately after this sentence indicates a break in the text; in *CE* as reprinted in *T&S* no indication of sectioning occurs;

the result is that the Library of America edition suggests that Hawthorne began the second section of the tale some thirty paragraphs later (after Ilbrahim's mother's central scene) and that there are only three formally marked major episodes in the tale.

4   Story of the Night Told Over

1   As mentioned, the rediscovery of "My Kinsman, Major Molineux" began in the 1950s with a series of landmark essays. Leavis (1951) argued that beneath its dreamlike, gothic surface lies a historical, pro-colonialist political allegory that is part of a larger such pattern in Hawthorne's early fiction. (The tale suggests America's passage from adolescence to political adulthood, with the dissenting colonialists standing for the emerging American nation, the colonial magistrates standing for the oppressive parental rule of Great Britain.) Lesser (1955) emphasized the psychoanalytic aspects, especially Oedipal conflict and dream structure, as did Franklin B. Newman (1955) and Male (1957), the latter of whom treated "The Gentle Boy" and "My Kinsman" together as versions of "The Search for a Home." Pearce in 1954 emphasized both the historical aspect and the moral dimension; in 1959 he offered a reconsideration in which he tried both to critique the limits of recent psychoanalytic criticism and to merge such criticism with the historical. (Also see Pearce's "The Twilight of Romance, 1948," and "Hawthorne and the Study of History," 1964.) D. G. Hoffman mapped out the tale in terms of folklore and archetypes — initiating a series of articles by others on the mythic aspects of the tale. These basic "allegorical" interpretations constitute the main orientations of the critical debate. The important critical contributions of the 1960s (for example, those of Broes, Rohrberger, Crews, Russell, Gross, Allison, and Yoder) play out along these lines in a pattern continuing to the present day. See LBVN, pp. 217–30. In the 1980s, the psychoanalytic and mythic have yielded somewhat to identifying historical references, especially to individuals, in an effort to recover the tale *for* history *from* dream, myth, romance. The most extreme of these efforts is that of Colacurcio, discussed in the main text below.

2   The mythic-oneiric level of "allegory" is here defined as incorporating together the following: some kind of deep dream experience as archetypal pattern, ancient motifs from Greek and Roman literature, Christian mythopoeic appropriations of ancient classics (as in Dante's *Divine Comedy*), and folk-myth archetypes.

3   Not to mention problems of humor, irony, and overall narrative tone. See Becker, pp. 166ff. for a discussion of allegory, symbolism, romance, and myth; unfortunately, Becker allows himself to be thrown off by Bewley's superficial treatment of these matters; see Bewley's essay on "Hawthorne and the Deeper Psychology" (Henry James's phrase); cf. *Eccentric Design*. See also Dauber, M. D. Bell, and Budick on symbol and allegory in Hawthorne (also see introduction).

4   For example, the veil suggests: (1) that we recognize the possibility — rather than the actuality — of universal sin; (2) that the recognition of human error is redemptive; (3) that such recognition may lead to prideful isolation; (4) that arrogant isolation is originary sin; (5) that we live in paradox; (6) that recognition of existential paradox is humanizing and redemptive; but (7) that, paradoxically it may cause despair and isolation. But cf. Abel (1951) on the theme of isolation. Newberry ("The Biblical Veil") suggests that the "veil as a type" should be "seen in an ironic, anachronistic relation to [Hooper's] prototype, Moses," as indicated by the career of Joseph Moody (to whom Hawthorne refers in a footnote to the story's title). According to Newberry, Colacurcio's claim that the context of the Great Awakening is necessary for understanding "The Minister's Black Veil" needs

to be reconsidered. While Colacurcio's thesis is "indispensable," the Great Awakening is yet an "ambiguous context for comprehending both Hooper's revival of Calvinistic primacy of sin and Hawthorne's own quarrel with it." By invoking the veil "type," Hawthorne seems to have "located a pivotal theological problem in the Bay Colony's orientation toward Old Testament typological models," reflecting "New England's tendency to dwell on the old dispensation generally" (pp. 170–71). Actually, the Great Awakening seems to be part of the parodic background context of "My Kinsman," as suggested toward the end of this chapter. In any case, all these hermeneutical complexities forcibly suggest that Hershel Parker's gloss in the *Norton Anthology of American Literature* is overly reductive.

5   See my discussion of "Romantic Irony in the United States"; representative Hawthorne tales and sketches are discussed pp. 278–83. Also see Lang and Male. Cf. Baym's reading of the Aubépine persona, which is the logical consequence of her immature/mature thesis, one diametrically opposite that offered here. See *Shape of Hawthorne's Career*, pp. 106–7.

6   Broes suggests that the kindly gentleman is not kindly at all but mendacious and malevolent. Critics have thus gone to opposite extremes, Male and Rohrberger characterizing the stranger as the embodiment of the "perfect" father figure and guide. I see him as ironically in-between somewhere; cf. Dauber on Aubépine.

7   The most extensive consideration of the parallels is D'Avanzo; but also see Herndon, Gross, and Turner ("Hawthorne's Literary Borrowings"). The parallels go further toward the elucidation of Hawthorne's tale than source critics have noted.

8   Quince introduces, in addition to the players of Pyramus and Thisbe, three other actors who "present" respectively a wall, moonshine, and a lion. The chief of these is Moonshine, who, accompanied by a dog (or an image of a dog), carries a (haw)thorn bush and a lantern with sides made of horn. He punningly announces: "This lanthorn doth the hornèd moon present, / Myself the man i' the moon do seem to be" (5.1.248–49). These images and references Hawthorne explicitly alludes to in order to underscore the night's "lunacy" in Boston (3:627, 640; *T&S*, 76, 86). Quince's prologue is so muddled that Theseus observes, "This fellow doth not stand upon points" (5.1.118); that is, Quince garbles his punctuation and syntactic units so much that his words come close to nonsense: "His speech was like a tangled chain — / nothing impaired, but all disordered" (5.1.125–26). This motif of disorder and confusion is especially important in Hawthorne's tale.

9   As noted, Oberon, Fairy King of the night world of imagination, was Hawthorne's name for the authorial self — or *an* authorial self. In act 2.1.32–34 a fairy says to Puck, conjoining the adjective "shrewd" with the name "Robin": "Either I mistake your shape and making quite, / Or else you are that shrewd and knavish sprite / Called Robin Goodfellow." To this identification, Puck replies: "Thou speak'st aright. / I am that merry wanderer of the night. / I jest to Oberon, and make him smile" (2.1.42–44). The nature of this "smile" as understood by Hawthorne is no simple matter, as the governing thesis of this study attempts to make clear in terms of the dialogic and romantic irony. Puck's concluding speeches emphasize the supernatural, mythic, and oneiric quality of the play and the play-within-the-play, which both take place under the moon. Now "are frolic," he says, the ". . . fairies, that do run / By the triple Hecate's team, / From the presence of the sun, / *Following darkness like a dream* . . ." (5.1.386–94; my italics), underscoring the confusion theme.

10 The fuller context of several of the lines used as epigraphs to this chapter are as follows.

Titania says to Oberon:

> Therefore the moon, the governess of floods,
> Pale in her anger, washes all the air,
> That rhéumatic diseases do abound.
> And thorough this distemperature we see
> The seasons alter. Hoary-headed frosts
> Fall in the fresh lap of the crimson rose,
> And on old Hiems' [winter's] thin and icy crown
> An odorous chapelet of sweet summer buds
> Is, as in mockery, set. The spring, the summer,
> The childing autumn, angry winter, change
> Their wonted liveries, and the mazed world,
> By their increase, now knows not which is which.
> (2.1.103–14)

In 3.2.370–71, we read: "When they next wake, all this derision / Shall seem a dream and fruitless vision. . . ." These lines, to which I made reference in the discussion of the dreamvision sketches in chapter 2, also describe "My Kinsman, Major Molineux," as do others also noted there.

The moon symbolism is more resonant than may at first be apparent. Just as Puck's concluding speech to the audience parallels Quince's opening speech to "Pyramus and Thisbe," *A Midsummer Night's Dream* opens with references to the moon, day turning into night, and dreaming away time. And Diana was sometimes referred to as three-formed, being worshipped as *Luna* (or *Cynthia*), the moon in heaven; *Diana* on earth; and *Proserpine* (or *Hecate*) in Hades—the three levels simultaneously suggested in Hawthorne's tale. (See Harrison's *Shakespeare*, p. 298.) Cf. the three realms evoked in the central scaffold scene of *The Scarlet Letter*. See Levy and Van Leer on Hawthorne's moonlight symbolism.

11   Broes and Allison suggest that Robin is ferried over a symbolic River Styx into Hades. They expand this rather evident suggestion in the tale to find echoes, if not direct allusions, to the underworld journeys of Odysseus, Aeneas, Heracles, and later Dante. Thus the appellation "shrewd" supposedly suggests Odysseus; the club Robin carries suggests Heracles; but the club is also somehow like the Cumaean bough Aeneas carries in Book 6 of the *Aeneid*; Robin's journey is like Aeneas's search for an older kinsman, and so forth. Broes goes on to add Spenser's Redcross Knight to the list of heroes, making the kindly stranger a villain with malicious intent, in short, Archimago. In addition (mainly because he carries a wallet), Robin is supposed to be like Christian in Bunyan's *Pilgrim's Progress*. Some of these analogues seem a bit fanciful, though I find the idea that Robin undergoes the trials of vanity and the story thus a kind of *Pilgrim's Progress* in reverse (like Hawthorne's "The Celestial Railroad") to have some merit. More to the point is that Hawthorne seems to be giving us a mock version of epic hero counterparts (including Theseus), an opinion shared by Kozikowski. Robin has also been seen as Dante (pilgrim) and Boston as Hades; Allison suggests that Robin is not Dante but a traitor in the final circle of hell; Broes suggests that the disagreement at the river is like that of Dante and the ferryman in the opening of the *Inferno*; Charon objects that Dante is alive, which suggests that Robin is morally alive in the city of the dead. Aristotle and Coleridge, Milton's *Comus* and *Paradise Lost* have all been suggested as literary and mythic parallels or allusions. Others, increasingly tenuous, include the young Ben Franklin of the *Autobiography* (Julian

Smith) and the literary character Arthur Mervyn in the novel of that name by Charles Brockden Brown (Van Der Beets and Withington).

The Golden Bough of Aeneas provides a link to some anthropological and folkloristic interpretations of the mythic undercurrents of the story. D. G. Hoffman, with specific reference to Sir James G. Frazer's anthropological study of myth, *The Golden Bough* (1922), argues that Hawthorne intuited archetypal patterns accessible to all of us. This is of course the old idea that we are all sensitive in some degree to all experience, but the artist is more sensitive than the average person and articulates both conscious and unconscious experiences symbolically as mythic narratives. The specifically American permutation of Robin's experience renders Americans as Yankee "bumpkins," that is, as provincials. Yankee "self-reliance," represented by Emerson and the New England provincials, says Hoffman, backfires.

12   Or perhaps the Minotaur, the half-human half-bull monster at the center of the labyrinth, who, like Satan, sports double horns. The Minotaur is an appropriate symbol for the inhumane colonists, half-human, half-bestial; and, of course, the sacrifice of the young to the Minotaur was a "political" tribute. It may be noted that Robin seems to "descend" through levels of the city to the harlot's house.

13   On the meaning of the laugh (and of laughter in general in Hawthorne) critics have differing views. Is it self-recognition, an ambiguous or ambivalent mixture of cruelty and pity and ridicule (for self and kinsman)? Robin hardly displays much concern for his kinsman's feelings (thereby his adolescent egocentricism is linked to egocentricism of political factions, religious factions, moral partisans). See a suggestive article by Fogle on "Weird Mockery"; also see Dusenbery. Cf. the narrative intrusion in *House of the Seven Gables*, ch. 18, where the dead body of Governor Pyncheon is mocked at length by a disembodied narrator.

A more deeply mythic reading of this scene and the folkloristic significance of the events that provoke Robin's laugh is the suggestion of P. Shaw that the tale reenacts the archetype of the scapegoat king, as in the Roman Saturnalia. The Saturnalia centered on the ritual overthrow of authority; salient features included disguise, mask, and mime, representing inversions of all kinds. Shaw's article ("Fathers, Sons, and the Ambiguities of Revolution") explicates an extended pattern of doubleness and inversion; cf. Bakhtin's discussion of *carnivalesque*. This interpretation is bolstered somewhat by Hawthorne's specific reference in the headnote to "The May-Pole of Merry Mount" (1836) to Joseph Strutt's *The Sports and Pastimes of the People of England* (1801): ". . . the facts, recorded on the grave pages of our New England annalists, have wrought themselves, almost spontaneously, into a sort of allegory. The masques, mummeries, and festive customs, described in the text, are in accordance with the manners of the age. Authority on these points may be found in Strutt's Book of English Sports and Pastimes" (1:70; *T&S*, 360). Cf. Vickery, J. N. Miller. The May celebration is associated by Strutt with "Robin" Hood, classic rebel to authority. That this rebelliousness does not describe Hawthorne's Robin does not seem to trouble source hunters; the possibility of *inverted* (mock) comparison, however, would seem to apply as much here as to other mythic comparisons. At the least, most of the myth and literary analogue critics see what is explicit in the text: from Robin's point of view (and the reader's) the town is nightmarish and the inhabitants fiendish — plainly negative aspects of the American provincial experience.

14   See Colacurcio on the significance of the money Robin gives the ferryman, discussed in a moment; that is, the specific event may be a 1730s riot, a point that has considerable significance for the interpretation of the story. See also Doubleday, who glosses the

allusions in the paragraph quoted above (p. 229). Cf. Nash on the insurrections and instability in the 1730s and early 1740s; also see Fliegelman. Another historical "mistake" is that Hawthorne slightly misstates the circumstances of the surrender of the old charter; technically, it was not "under James II" as stated in the frame introduction but under Charles II, in 1684. The narrator's point, however, is clear. Before 1684 the governors were elected. Afterwards they were appointed by the king—namely, by James II, for Charles II died in 1685. Cf. the opening frame of "The Gray Champion." The "space of about forty years" would set the story in the mid-1720s or early 1730s. Hawthorne is pretty insistent about the time; and Pearce mentions a reference in a magazine story in *1829* by W. L. Stone to "another Mollineaux" [*sic*] (*Historicism*, p. 138). See discussion of the historical interpretative excess that follows.

15   Although Newberry alludes to this effect, he resists the idea that the narrator *seduces* the reader into "forgetting" on a first reading the opening paragraph until the end. Pearce remarks what he considers the somewhat odd "moral abstraction" of the opening frame. John Russell, despite a somewhat too fixed interpretation of Robin as the allegorical *representation* of the six royal governors, offers an insightful observation on the dynamic of the story: the reader's experience via Robin allegorically parallels the political blindness and bewilderment of the magistrates.

16   For the problematic aspect of Hawthorne's theory of "progress," see, minimally, the *three* theories of history overtly articulated in *The House of the Seven Gables*. Cf. Levy (1971).

17   See *Historicism*, pp. 96–106. Blair calls Pearce's replies to Lesser an "attack," but Pearce's position is less an attack than a partial critique which tries to accommodate Lesser.

18   Pearce seems at this point to have accepted rather uncritically some basic Freudian premises for purposes of literary analysis. He credits Lesser for bringing to light matters that had been "inadequately attended to." Specifically, he observes that "perhaps he [Robin] does not want to find his kinsman, perhaps he is afraid to"; after all, Robin "does not pursue his [search] with any ardor." Especially striking for Pearce is "the fact that there is something more-or-less ambiguously sexual about the search—particularly in the episode of the whore who assures him that his kinsman is inside her dwelling, asleep." These observations are suddenly elevated into "facts," the import of which for Pearce is clear. "All these facts are made to point to the now obvious conclusion: that if Robin does find his kinsman, he will have to submit to a kind of authority from which he seems to have wanted to escape when he left home." It is therefore "no wonder that when he sits on the steps of the church, waiting to see his kinsman, 'he has a fantasy in which he imagines that his kinsman is already dead'" (*Historicism*, p. 99; quoting Lesser).

19   Crews's answer to these questions in the 1960s is yes, though in the case of "The Gentle Boy" and "The Gray Champion" he does not tell us precisely how all is Oedipal. At one point, he writes that "Oedipal strife is a common denominator among Hawthorne's most intense plots" (*Sins of the Fathers*, p. 79); and when he cannot identify Oedipal familial strife in Hawthorne's texts, he ranks them as lower in artistic merit and "intensity." Cf. my discussion, in the next chapter, of "Alice Doane's Appeal," the tale that is Crews's supreme example of Hawthorne's Oedipal theme. In fairness to Crews, it should be noted that in a series of essays since 1975 he has qualified his earlier Freudian methodology; and in a new issue of *Sins of the Fathers* (1989), he includes an "Afterword" in which he offers examples of his own misapplications of Freudian theory and "dogmatizing about the universal Oedipus complex," and instead emphasizes Hawthorne's "deliberate toying with his readers' expectations." Nevertheless, Crews's Freudian paradigm has had great influence, and critics less capable than he continue to apply the cookie-cutter.

20 Rohrberger, p. 34, who summarizes Franklin B. Newman; a good deal of Rohrberger's discussion is derivative; but her summary is concise and lucid. Part of her treatment (taken up in a moment) is important because she represents one of two opposing positions on what the psychoanalytic pattern suggests: that is, whether it is a positive or negative experience that Robin undergoes.

21 The "Absent One" may be dead, or simply missing, or away from home for perfectly ordinary reasons — literally "absent," like young Robin himself. Crews, with innuendo that goes far beyond the text, hints that some sexual conflict and guilt (incestuous and thus Oedipal) is suggested by this seemingly deliberately sentimental scene (pp. 75–76). Of course, the absent one may *be* Robin; if so, the father may here reveal his affection for the son gone out into the cold world beyond the hearth, though doubtless a psychoanalytic critic would see the quaver in the father's voice as a sign of guilt for rejecting the son. The point is that the scene is ambiguous at best and that no particular innuendo of Oedipal conflict is suggested; it has to be imported from the outside.

22 Male writes: "If Ilbrahim's search is for a mother, Robin's quest . . . is for a father" (*Hawthorne's Tragic Vision*, p. 48). Crews sees both as quests for the father, both as Oedipal; see esp. pp. 61–62, 78–79. Crews writes at the end of ch. 4 ("Submission and Revolt"): "In both stories literal fathers are supplanted by symbolic ones who are, on the whole, implicitly criticized. Ilbrahim suffers from paternal weakness and selfishness, and retreats to his mother's bosom to die; Robin acquires the confidence to challenge paternal strength, and so presumably falls heir to it" (p. 79). It is a little hard to see Ilbrahim's dead father (executed for conviction of conscience) as "weak"; and the psychological dynamics of Ilbrahim's "retreat" from Pearson as a weak paternal figure to, not Mrs. Pearson, but his maternally weak natural mother are a bit obscure. As for Robin, it may be observed that he never "challenges" either Molineux or his father.

23 Male, p. 50. His description and interpretation of the double-faced figure suggests the obsessive focus of the psychoanalytically oriented critics. The fiery red side of the bulky gentleman's face, writes Male, is "emblematic of the military" and "of the *petticoat*" (my italics), while the black side represents "sepulchral mourning." Actually, Hawthorne writes that "the red of one cheek was an emblem of fire and sword; the blackness of the other betokened the mourning that attends them" (3:637; *T&S*, 84). This description emphasizes the political situation (whispers of civil war) into which Robin has ignorantly and naively walked, more than some psychosexual one. A sounder approach might be found through adaptation of Fliegelman's historicism.

24 See 3:632; *T&S*, 80. Many critics play faster or looser with the text in certain predictable ways, depending on the hermeneutic paradigm the critic employs. C. D. Johnson, for example, writes that Robin's "journey is *identical* to that described by Puritan writers in that he learns that he can no longer depend on the props that had earlier sustained him" (p. 27; my italics). Her paradigm is Calvin's two-stage "justification/vivification" pattern; and she misreads Robin's dream reverie of home, asserting that Robin's father "excludes" him from the family, whereas, as we have seen, Hawthorne's text reads simply that the "latch tinkled into place."

25 Not the least of which are imputing to a Longfellow reference to Hawthorne's Molineux a meaning it demonstrably does *not* have — and presenting a quotation from a contemporary historical text about William Molineux as if it were from Hawthorne's text; see the opening paragraphs of Pearce's essay (pp. 137–40). Colacurcio, so astutely critical of most other critics, lets all this pass unremarked.

26 What evidence there is of a Molineux "legend" Pearce presents in a footnote and two

short paragraphs of speculation (pp. 138–39). Pearce also glosses over the fact that the historical Molineux was not a minor party official, as he is in Hawthorne's story, but a well-to-do Boston trader (p. 137).

27 6:519. To rise even higher than mere prelapsarian innocence in our moral development means for Hawthorne that we experience sin in order to become more understanding and forgiving: the principles of *caritas* and *sympathia*. The principle of *perspectiva* lies in the paradox of a "fortunate" fall itself. Pearce quotes (p. 184) the pronoun "we" as a reference to Adam (that is, he gives "we" as "he"), despite the syntactic logic against it, which suggests a somewhat different meaning; *CE* gives "we" (4:460) as well. Actually, "we" (those who come later and recognize the meaning of the past) gives more strength to Pearce's historical argument than "he." Of course, the typesetter may be at fault.

28 Cf. C. D. Johnson's application of a Calvinist variant of human transfiguration, the two-stage process mentioned in note 24 above, esp. the so-called half-journeys, which she calls "negative definitions of regeneration" (see pp. 15–20). See Stout's *New England Soul* for social contextualization.

29 Crews's analysis, though it goes beyond what Pearce suggests are the narrow limitations of psychoanalytic criticism, tends in my view to make critical pronouncements reflecting extremes of ideological criticism, as detailed in the present chapter. Pearce's full hypothesis, developed in the second half of the "Sense of the Past" essay, is that in the later major romances a "countertheme" becomes the major theme of Hawthorne's work but remains dependent on the early "Molineux theme." Hawthorne, he writes, is a writer whose fiction preeminently manifests the "meaning of history," which is evident as early as his writing the *Provincial Tales*. Yet, after "the years in which he was composing the *Provincial Tales*, Hawthorne moved *away* from the Molineux theme" into a countertheme that is "*not* the imputation of guilt and righteousness *through* history, but rather the discovery and acceptance of guilt (and righteousness too) *in* the *present*" (pp. 152–53; my italics). Put more simply, the two "themes" are one: the first shows assumption of "responsibility" through acknowledgment of the burden of the past in stories about the (American) past; the second shows the impingement of the past on the present, as in *The House of the Seven Gables*. The distinction is, perhaps, as Poe said of Coleridge on fancy and imagination, one without a difference, since for Pearce the stories of the past are didactic, intended to show us in the present how what we are is bound up in the past.

30 See Colacurcio, p. 565 and pp. 135ff., who builds on Doubleday, P. Shaw, and Grayson. Grayson sets the tale in 1730. (Of course, much of their speculation *assumes* that the *narrator* is speaking to us in 1832 — the date of the publication of the story — not from some indefinite authorial position.) Boston's economy was in terrible shape in the 1730s. About the same time, Ben Franklin was pushing for paper money in Philadelphia, with very different results.

31 "Proleptic" is a word sometimes misused to mean, not so much answering an objection before one's opponent has made it, as suggesting typological or teleological inevitability. Colacurcio seems to use it (often in quotation marks) sarcastically. Of course, if the 1730s Rum Riot presages the Revolution, then "proleptic" is quite ironically appropriate. Hawthorne dramatizes (the objections to) mob violence prior to the main event.

32 See pp. 136–37. The *other* view of the American Revolution — the British, the Tory — would see in revolution the reenactment of mankind's "Original Rebellion." Any act of violence against the duly ordained agents of preexistent order would in Tory eyes recommit the crucifixion of Christ (p. 138); the result is the same, typologically, religiously on both sides. Hawthorne, for Colacurcio, is as far from endorsing an essentially

Anglican (patriarchal and sacramental) view of history as any "idolatrous extension of Puritan typology" (p. 138). Thus those critical suggestions that the Major is a Christ figure cut both ways simultaneously (in another instance, I would say, of negative allegorical suggestion). How "minor" the incidents were is debatable; accounts suggest that the street riots of the 1730s and early 1740s were serious and dangerous. Hawthorne's technique, however, is clearly typological "reduction" of the American Revolution via the vehicle of a rum riot.

33 See pp. 135ff. esp. p. 140. Colacurcio argues unconvincingly from a texture of allusion in the tale to the idea of "Robinocracy" — thus Hawthorne's pun on a name. It may be observed that the term *democracy* was rarely used in American political discourse until the nineteenth century. (On Robinocracy, Colacurcio directs us to Bernard Bailyn.) At this point, we begin to leave Hawthorne's text for a series of creative one-for-one identifications, and Colacurcio's analysis, in my opinion, begins to lose its earlier cogency and pertinency.

34 The "joke is pretty broad," Colacurcio writes, "even though everybody seems to have missed it so far: the first man of whom Robin demands the whereabouts of his courtly kinsman turns out to be the leader of the Country Opposition, Molineux's deepest official enemy and (it seems likely) one of the principal organizers of the evening's political festivities" (p. 142).

35 Colacurcio, p. 568 n.93. See Julian Smith, "Historical Ambiguity," pp. 116–18; cf. Grayson, pp. 550–59. Colacurcio's main discussion is pp. 146–47; see p. 569 n.100 for sources; Colacurcio also cites Zobel, pp. 78–79, for the "political plausibility of such a route."

36 Colacurcio's method foregrounds the question of what constitutes "the tale" in the extended concept of "text." I have in this chapter on "My Kinsman, Major Molineux" conceived of the critical commentary as part of the extended text; and this now includes Colacurcio's (as it did not when I first began this study some years ago). But when has Hawthorne's originary text been so displaced from the center as to be supplanted? Despite this caveat, I find, in the main, the importation of certain historical figures and events to constitute less of a distortion of Hawthorne's text than the importation of distantly related mythic figures and patterns — or the imposition of either a programmatic psychology or a currently fashionable ideology.

37 See Colacurcio, pp. 568–69. We find in Colacurcio's notes gratuitous comments about the classic credulity of critics like Gross regarding the stranger (p. 568). Perhaps we have here a case of classic historicist credulity. That is, finding a historical roman à clef, the historicist is content that the critic's job is at last satisfactorily done.

38 Paralleling Hawthorne's familiar theme of the artist as voyeur. Also, if the "kindly stranger" is the "perfect father image," what better icon for the author of the characters' being and their textual world? Wordplay on *author*ity figures also suggests "author" as final authority in the romantic equation with God. Hawthorne's author figures range from eighteen-year-old youths (like the Story Teller) to men in their "prime" (as here).

5   *Power of Negative Suggestion*

1   In keeping with the analyses of the patterns of the other *Provincial Tales* examined in this study, I shall refer to the eleven parts of "Alice Doane's Appeal" as, first, a historical introduction, and the ensuing sections by the numbers 1 through 10. While actually reading the narrative of "Alice Doane's Appeal," one is likely to find the interpenetration

of the double structure fairly coherent. But it is hard to describe analytically. In describing the frame situation, I shall endeavor to use the historical present tense as is conventional for literary analysis. When describing the events and scenes of the interior gothic tale, I shall endeavor to use the past tense. This distinction will become problematic in the second half of the narrative, however, as frame and interior story interpenetrate; and I shall try to highlight this effect by alternating present and past tense as appropriate. In one sense the interior story frames the frame. When the text shifts to the narration of the interior tale by a second narrator and employs single quotation marks, I shall also employ single rather than double quotation marks to remind the reader of the narrative point of view. In order to keep clear the narrative function of the frame narrator as an "author" character, as distinguished from a "narrator" or from "Nathaniel Hawthorne," I shall use, where it seems appropriate, the phrases "author-narrator" or "author-figure." At other times, I refer to this personage and presence as the "storyteller," a phrase intended to suggest the "authorial" presence characterized in Hawthorne's self-reflexive narrative cycle *The Story Teller.*

2 See "Hawthorne's Gothic Discards," p. 115; *Shape*, pp. 25–27, 37–39. For an overview of shifting concepts of *apokalypsis*, see Robinson (1985).

3 Van Doren, p. 72. This criticism also reflects a very conventional notion of truthfulness and apocalypse. With the exception of Fossum ("Summons of the Past"), most critics before 1980 did not see the work as unified; until recently, critics have focused on the "gothic" provenance of the interior story, ignoring the framing effects either as awkward or as excessive employment of convention. Lundblad's relative lack of interest in the work even as "gothic" is representative (see subsection titled "Hawthorne and the Tradition of Gothic Romance," pp. 90–91ff.). Baym's discussion of the gothic element may be profitably juxtaposed with Markus's exploration of Hawthorne's "rejection" or ironic "counterexemplification" of gothic narrative style.

4 This judgment is principally based on remarks by Hawthorne's sister, Elizabeth Manning Hawthorne. She speculates that an "Alice Doane" was written in college, or perhaps just after college, in "the summer of 1825," although elsewhere she does not indicate that such a work was written so early. In any case, her slightly imprecise comments are chiefly responsible for the idea that an "Ur-text" of "Alice Doane's Appeal" existed and that the present text is a rewriting of that originary (and "simple") gothic tale. She is quoted by her nephew, Julian Hawthorne, 1:124ff., where he has her recalling "a tale of witchcraft," called ("I believe," says Elizabeth Hawthorne) "Alice Doane." In Randall Stewart's printing of her letters to John T. Field, however, the suggestion of an Ur-text of "Alice Doane's Appeal" does not appear; see "Recollections." On 16 December 1870, she writes: "Soon after Nathaniel left College he wrote some tales 'Seven Tales of My Native Land,' with the motto from Wordsworth 'We are Seven.' I think it was before Wordsworth's Poems were republished here. I read the Tales in Manuscript; some of them were very striking, particularly one or two Witch Stories" (p. 323). Lathrop has her recollecting that, of the *Seven Tales of My Native Land*, "some of them related to witchcraft, and some to the sea" (*A Study*, p. 134). Neither Julian Hawthorne nor Lathrop definitively indicates an original story called "Alice Doane" that was radically different from the text we have. Nor do Elizabeth Hawthorne's remarks about her brother's attitudes toward magazine publishers bear out Waggoner's contention (e.g., 1970) that Hawthorne was trying somewhat desperately to "salvage for publication" an earlier work. On the contrary, we know that Hawthorne was *not* desperate to publish. As his sister writes: ". . . I remember tales which I thought admirable; but it may be that they were never published; for he was

very impatient and *if there was any delay,* he would have them returned to him if he could, and I suppose put them in the fire" (Stewart, "Recollections," p. 331; my italics).

5   For example, Arvin, Becker, Dryden, Elder, Fogle, Hoeltje, C. D. Johnson, Male, Rohrberger, Schubert, Sutherland, Wagenknecht. And we find only a few sentences or brief paragraphs in Doubleday, Gollin, Lundblad, or Stein. Surprisingly, this neglect is also found in Millicent Bell's *Hawthorne's View of the Artist,* Normand's *Nathaniel Hawthorne: An Approach to an Analysis of Artistic Creation,* and Stubbs's *The Pursuit of Form: A Study of Hawthorne and the Romance.* More surprising perhaps, given its subject and the date of its publication, J. Auerbach's recent *Romance of Failure* contains only a couple of paragraphs on what one might suppose to be a key text in the argument. In the longer studies of Hawthorne, the most sensitive and sympathetic treatment is Colacurcio's, which acknowledges the central theme of the relation of romance and history as problems in narrative; but, as mentioned, Colacurcio minimizes self-reflexivity in Hawthorne. M. D. Bell, always sensitive to the innuendoes of Hawthorne's texts, struggles with the intricacies of "Alice Doane's Appeal" (pp. 68–76), which he characterizes as "consist[ing] of a number of loosely related fragments rather than [being] a coherent narrative" (*Hawthorne and Historical Romance,* p. 68). Dauber, while devoting only a couple of pages to "Alice Doane's Appeal," frames it within Hawthorne's self-reflexive concern for author-reader relationships (pp. 44–45).

Budick puts together a beautifully concise summation of many of the same issues I have addressed here under the subtitle "The Appeal to Indeterminacy," in her sixth chapter ("History's Veil and the Face of the Past"), pp. 99–102; she draws heavily upon Swann's pioneering essay but seems unaware of the critical dialogue on the tale during the 1980s. At the end of her brief discussion, she takes a sudden turn: ". . . Hawthorne is no Poe. Indeterminacy, this story tells us, is no simple philosophical or epistemological or literary critical matter. Hawthorne, therefore [*sic*], will not continue to entertain the frank, raw horror of gothic literature. . . ." He "will reject the gothicism of Poe and of his own early achievements, because he recognizes that the indeterminacy on which gothic literature depends, like the textual derestriction it affords, is double-edged. He does not doubt the power of the imagination so much as he fears it, his own every bit as much as the imaginations he investigates in his fictions" (p. 102). After the astute two and a half pages that precede, this paragraph comes as a startling conventional judgment and a less than coherent pronouncement on gothic. For contrast, cf. Carton on the "tension between overdetermination and indeterminacy" informing *The Scarlet Letter* (*Rhetoric,* pp. 193ff.).

6   Recent criticism has, in fact, advanced our understanding of the metafictional complexity and unity of the tale. Published in 1979, LBVN (for "Alice Doane's Appeal" see pp. 1–8) does not, of course, treat the reappraisals of the 1980s, such as those by Robinson and Colacurcio. But Newman downplays an important ongoing critical debate beginning with Elias and Coffey; and she misses Hennelly (1978), though his essay doubtless appeared too near the publication date of her own volume for inclusion. The same may be true for J. L. Williamson's essay; but she also misses what is perhaps the best of the contemporary treatments, that of Swann. Pertinent to the historical aspect elaborated in the present chapter are (in addition to Colacurcio): Brodwin, "Hawthorne and the Function of History"; Fossum, "Summons of the Past"; also see S. L. Gross, "Hawthorne's 'Alice Doane's Appeal' "; Schroeder, "Alice Doane's Story." Written in an allusive critical language that causes the critic to elide too many steps, Lauren Berlant's impressionistic examination of "Alice Doane's Appeal" as an "embodiment" of "national fantasy" ("America, Post-Utopia," 1989) is nevertheless a creative application of metaphoric

language and thinking, from a feminist psychoanalytic perspective, to landscape symbolism and historiographic sensibility. At least her attempt at "transcoding the national scene along gender lines" and "spatial considerations" in terms of the "utopian" and "political" dimensions of a "National Symbolic" represents a genuine attempt at *literary* and *cultural* criticism and avoids the grosser effronteries of most psychobiography. Particular additional studies are cited below where pertinent.

7   See Miyoshi for a succinct overview of the symbolic value of the theme of incest. The family represents the staid commercialism and religious pietism that are the backbone of European burgher states and anathema to the romantic hero. See Irwin (1975) for a more Lacanian interpretation of the incest motif in general and in Faulkner in particular. For an application to American fiction, with specific reference to "Alice Doane's Appeal," see J. D. Wilson.

8   *Sins*, pp. 59–60; my italics. In Hawthorne's text, the "vile and ineradicable weed," the wood-wax on the hill, is associated with Salem history and the "witch delusion"; but for Crews, obviously, the secret, hidden, "true" meaning is psychological. He also apparently attaches some special, secret meaning to the phrase "ceaseless flux of mind" (cf. his discussion of the missing family member in "My Kinsman, Major Molineux"). The meaning of this phrase is probably rather simply that one does not, at times, want to go back to earlier productions because one has changed, moved on (intellectually, artistically) from where one was: after all, Hawthorne's narrator is an "author." Baym incisively criticizes Crews's position: his description of the tale as one of turbulent agitation is apt, she says; but "every study of the Gothic that I have consulted mentions this motif [of incest] as a matter of course." It is "unfortunate, therefore," that Crews "extensively analyses 'Alice Doane's Appeal' as evidence that at the outset of his career, 'Hawthorne felt impelled to treat the most shameful of subjects, and to [do] so in a spirit of turbulent agitation.' . . . What Gothic story, one might rhetorically ask, is *not* done in a spirit of turbulent agitation" ("Hawthorne's Gothic Discards," p. 115). As mentioned, Crews has reexamined his position.

9   Amateur psychoanalysis of the author based on fictional texts and presumed "incestuous" attraction (based on a Manning family "incident") continues; see, for example, Ehrlich's *Family Themes* and Young's *Hawthorne's Secret*.

10 Swann, pp. 6, 8; among the "partial" readings he seeks to correct are those of Pearce in "Hawthorne and the Sense of the Past" and Henderson (see pp. 73, 74); others have suggested a "five-act structure."

11 The Riverside Edition omits a marker at the bottom of a page (12:284).

12 See Tieck's "The Fair-Haired Eckbert" (1796), trans. Thomas Carlyle (1827); fiction and reality blur as in a nightmare; nothing is as it seems; and Eckbert seems to discover, solipsistically, that he is all the other characters, including those he has murdered. The doppelgänger symbolism suggests that Leonard Doane is also the murderer of himself — or it might, had Hawthorne allowed the tale to work out according to certain gothic conventions instead of abruptly truncating it. The facial resemblance of the father to Brome who turns out to be the twin of Doane is but one exaggerated instance of the facial motif running throughout the narrative; certainly the dreamvision of the father's face falls into the conventional gothic pattern of disturbed filial relationships; cf. Poe on the inbred twins of "The Fall of the House of Usher."

13 Constituting further evidence, I would say, that an Ur-text of "Alice Doane's Appeal" which was radically different from the text we have is improbable. Cf. Robinson's analysis of the narrative balance of the work.

14   Cf. the male/female symbols of "The Village Uncle" and "Foot-prints on the Sea-shore." Typically in Hawthorne, the solitary, meditative male figure is somber, melancholy, while the female figures are less meditative, more immediately responsive to the gladsome aspects of environment. Hawthorne seems to have invested in this romantic convention beyond its purely literary aspects.

15   Previously mentioned; see the next chapter for further discussion. The etymological equivalence of the word *glory* to *halo* suggests the delusive sense of glory infecting the Puritans.

16   In this context, the statement that the former townspeople were the more horrible (to Leonard and Alice?) because of their ghastly "smile" of recognition parallels the same situation in "Young Goodman Brown" ("the smile of welcome gleamed darkly on every visage"). Hyatt Waggoner, puzzling over this scene, writes that there is "certainly a crucial confusion here," but "not in the mind of the reader" (*Critical Study*, p. 54). Once again, we have the psychobiographical explanation: Hawthorne's text is "confused" because it represents his "deepest experience" with Calvinism (in a tale also about "forbidden" psychosexual thoughts); the artist is not in full control.

17   Critics considering the possibility that the graveyard vision is spectral rather than genuinely apocalyptic include Elias, Coffey, Colacurcio; cf. Bell. The spectral idea was first applied to Hawthorne's fiction in a fine historical reading of "Young Goodman Brown" by Levin (1962), who rather condescendingly refers to critics extolling the ambiguity of the tale. Levin claims that a literalist historical reading clears up the ambiguities. It does not; in fact, Levin's reading further demonstrates how beautifully ambiguous the tale is. Levin comes to the rather curious conclusion that Brown lives in doubt, when his own argument demonstrates that the problem is that Brown has been absolutely convinced by the specter evidence of the forest. The Puritan texts he quotes are reprinted in his book, *What Happened in Salem?*

18   *New England Mind*, 1:257. The faculties are lucidly explained in detail in ch. 9, "The Nature of Man"; the imagination is particularly analyzed pp. 240–42, 246–48, 257–60.

19   This argument is of course contrary to Baym's that Hawthorne tried to "pacify" an audience adhering to the old Puritan distrust of imagination. Hawthorne's, in fact, is a very aggressive stance toward the audience, rather than a pacific one. In his gentlemanly way, he bullies the audience, pushing the reader about and leading us down false paths only to bring us up short again.

20   Thus the problem of specter evidence is useful to a dialogical reading. A further complexity of the problem of specter evidence is pertinent to the conclusion of Hawthorne's narrative. Cotton Mather, who is pictured as the Puritan archvillain in section 10 of "Alice Doane's Appeal," warned against putting too much confidence in specter evidence. David Levin ("Shadows of Doubt") speculates that Hawthorne must have known that "after the Mathers and Thomas Brattle had opposed even the admission of specter evidence (the Mathers on the ground that it was the Devil's testimony), the court had convicted almost no one and not a single convict had been executed. It seems certain, moreover, that Hawthorne had read Cotton Mather's biography of Sir William Phips, in which Mather the historian . . . clearly suggests that one of the Devil's purposes [in the witchcraft trials] had been the traducing of Faith." All this rather wonderfully complicates Hawthorne's *interpretation* of Cotton Mather — a matter significant to the overall interpretation of "Alice Doane's Appeal."

21   See A. H. Ehrenpreis, pp. 89–119, esp. 99–102. In suggesting George Bancroft or Joseph B. Felt as the "historian" alluded to, Brodwin ("Hawthorne and the Function of

History," pp. 118 and 126–27) apparently did not have access to Ehrenpreis's article; but his discussion of the focus and bias of these early nineteenth-century historians confirms the general historical trend (based on Robert Calef) initiated or popularized by Upham; see Hansen; also see Baym, *Shape of Hawthorne's Career*, pp. 38–39; Colacurcio, pp. 550 n.90, 552 n.102.

22   *Witchcraft at Salem*, pp. 171–72; my italics; Hansen cites Barrett Wendell, George Lyman Kittridge, Samuel Eliot Morison, Kenneth Murdock, and David Levin for support of his thesis of the injustice done to Cotton Mather (p. 228). His version of the exchanges between Calef and the Mathers suggests careful maneuvering on both sides; and the case against the psychological and political motives of Cotton Mather and others in power at the time cannot be simply dismissed. A modern reader probably cannot but side with the prevailing humane and rational orientation of Calef, whatever his personal animus toward the Mathers. Even Hansen adds that the distortion of the historical truth is "not all Upham's fault, nor that of later historians who have echoed him. It was, after all, Cotton Mather who chose to write *The Wonders of the Invisible World*, and chose to write it precisely as the witch hunt was ending. With this hasty, ill-considered, overwrought, partisan defense of his friends he was the first to fasten the false image of witch hunter on himself" (p. 172). Hansen omits the fact that Mather had been collecting instances of "witchcraft" prior to the Salem Witch Trials, had published a treatise on the matter, *Memorable Providences Relating to Witchcrafts and Possessions* (1689), saw in Salem corroboration of his suspicions, and seized the opportunity to be a key figure in the overall situation. For a modifying portrait, however, see the documents reprinted in *What Happened in Salem?* and Levin's discussion of the Mathers and Thomas Brattle in "Shadows of Doubt." Hawthorne's attitude is clearly complex. Whatever his possible contempt for Charles Upham, he was still uneasy about his own family's participation in the "witchcraft delusion," as is clear from several references in his writings, and as is exemplified by the well-known case of his changing the spelling of the Hathorne family name.

23   The Childe Harold and the Manfred aspects of the Byronic hero are everywhere evident in the *Story Teller* fragments, especially in the account of Oberon's return home in "Fragments from the Journal of a Solitary Man." Again, we have Elizabeth Hawthorne's testimony that Hawthorne burned many of his manuscripts, along with Hawthorne's own comments. At least, Hawthorne *said* he did; in the editorial prefaces and letters to publishers, it is sometimes hard to determine (a) the level of convention being followed in the playing out of the game or (b) the level of irony.

6   *The Oberonic Self*

1   See the different but complementary formulations by Evans and Marler; the insights of McElroy's promisingly titled "The Hawthorne Style of Fiction" are undeveloped.

2   Cf. Tharpe, "The Oral Storyteller in Hawthorne's Novels."

3   That the "relinquished work" referred to is *The Story Teller* is confirmed by the fact that some of the "Passages" were first published as "The Story Teller. No. I" in the *New-England Magazine* in November 1834. An early sketch titled "The Seven Vagabonds" (*Token*, 1833; collected in the expanded *Twice-told Tales*, 1842) clearly was once part of "Passages from a Relinquished Work," as we shall see in a moment. Two other sequences of sketches along with an uncollected "travel sketch" complete the schema insofar as we can retrieve it: the first sequence (in two parts) is "Sketches from Memory"

(Series 1, *New-England Magazine*, 1835, collected *Mosses*; Series 2, *New-England Magazine*, 1835, uncollected); the second is "Fragments from the Journal of a Solitary Man." The "Sketches from Memory" appeared sequentially in Park Benjamin's *New-England Magazine* in 1835. At the same time, other sketches of the New York-Erie-Detroit journey appeared. "My Visit to Niagara" (uncollected) and "Old News" (*Snow-Image*, 1851) appeared in *New-England Magazine* in 1835; then "Old Ticonderoga" appeared in the *American Monthly Magazine* in 1836 (collected in *The Snow-Image*, 1851); the *American Monthly* had just absorbed the *New England Magazine* and taken over its backlog; in 1837 "Fragments from the Journal of a Solitary Man" (uncollected) appeared in the *American Monthly*. All these travel sketches, widely dispersed, are related geographically and otherwise and were likely once part of one integrated sequence involving a single journey. See Weber (1973), pp. 142–49. Also see *Hawthorne's American Travel Sketches*, ed. Weber, Lueck, and Berthold (1989).

4 "Seven Vagabonds" was first published in *The Token*, collected in *Twice-told Tales*, part 2 (1842). Had the piece not been collected in the expanded *Twice-told Tales*, its most likely appearance would have been at the beginning of what became "Passages from a Relinquished Work" as collected in the expanded *Mosses from an Old Manse* (1854). See Dauber, Duban, Janssen, Luedtke, Pauly, Vance.

5 Such as Goldsmith's framed sequence *The Citizen of the World* (1760–61, 1762), which influenced Irving's *Salmagundi* and *Sketch-Book of Geoffrey Crayon*. Goldsmith was exploiting the rising interest of the West in Oriental literature and the Orient in general. It was at this time that the first Western translations of the *Arabian Nights* began to appear. See Luedtke; *Romantic Arabesque*, ch. 1.

6 Tennyson's celebrated image in "Ulysses" reflects a long tradition. Cf. the ambiguities of portals and arches (mentioned in previous chapters) elsewhere in Hawthorne's works (e.g., "Wives of the Dead," "Young Goodman Brown," "The Haunted Mind"). Or Clifford's arch-vision in the middle of *The House of the Seven Gables*, which causes him almost to fall from the apex of one of the gables—more than a little like Ishmael's "transcendent vision" in the crow's nest of the *Pequod* early in *Moby-Dick*, causing him almost to fall into the shark-infested sea below.

7 Hawthorne's often very subtle manipulation of the icon of the two gates of dreams may be illustrated by a brief consideration of two metafictional sketches, "A Virtuoso's Collection" and "The Hall of Fantasy," in both of which the narrator "literally" enters the imaginative realm of the fictive. (Cf. "The Clerk of the Weather," where ancient myth is literalized for the "presentday" narrator.) The Keeper of the Door to the Hall of Imagination is the icon of "The Hall of Fantasy," in which the realm of imagination suggests some kind of underworld descent. In this work, the arrangement of the figures is more clearly Dantesque than is at first evident in "A Virtuoso's Collection," heavily suggesting the Inferno. At the end, the mythic descent into the underworld and the association with Hermes is confirmed as the figures of Homer, Odysseus, Virgil, and Aeneas are mixed together in the Hall, blurring (as in Virgil) authors with fictional characters.

The narrator entering as a "real" person the domain of "fiction" is the actuating device of "A Virtuoso's Collection." The "I" narrator approaches a "new museum." To enter, he pays a doorkeeper of singular aspect. This transgression from the everyday world to the mythic or fantastic parallels the opening of "My Kinsman, Major Molineux" (Robin paying Charon to cross the river Styx). Here the narrator crosses the threshold and enters the imaginative world, which comes more and more to suggest Dante's Inferno. The first figure that the narrator meets in the Virtuoso's museum is said to be that of Opportunity, but the figure suggests the narrator of *Tanglewood Tales*, the covertly insinuated Hermes again, messenger of the gods, presented as the ordinary youth, Eustace Bright. Hermes brings the ancient myths and messages — but ambiguously. Inside the museum, we encounter topics of Hawthorne's own fictions, such as the great carbuncle and the elixir vitae. The Virtuoso turns out to be the Wandering Jew, a paradoxical figure of imagination, partially symbolizing commitment to the material world. His parting handshake with the narrator is telling: "The touch seemed like ice, yet I know not whether morally or physically. As I departed, he bade me observe that the inner door of the hall was constructed with the *ivory* leaves of the gateway through which Aeneas and the Sybil had been dismissed from Hades" (2:559; *T&S*, 713; my italics). It is not insignificant that "A Virtuoso's Collection" is the final text of *Mosses from an Old Manse*.

8   On this point, see Ortega y Gasset, Schlegel; cf. Thorslev.

9   The narrator's celebrity is framed, on the one hand, by an announcement of his preacher friend's intention to lead community prayer from the Book and "address sinners on the welfare of their immortal souls," and, on the other, by the peculiar circumstances of the stage appearance of the Story Teller. Abbott's "religious meeting" is announced in "tremulous characters" underneath the "flaming bills" that announce the Story Teller's performance, each notice appropriately suggesting the character of the performer and the taste of the public, with a slight hint of apocalypse in each case. The description of the play-bills ("Unprecedented Attraction! . . . in the hugest type that the printing-office could supply," etc.) may remind readers of the Duke and the Dauphin's theatrical-literary performances in *Huckleberry Finn*.

10   Schlegel writes that "philosophy is the proper home of irony"; but "poetry alone" rises "to the height of philosophy." There are "ancient and modern poems that breathe, throughout, in their entirety, and in everything, the divine breath of irony. In such, there lives a real *transcendental buffoonery*." Their "exterior form" is permeated by the "mimic" (or theatrical) "style of an ordinary good Italian *buffo*." *Lyceumsfragment* 42 (1797); my italics; my trans.; see *Werke*, 1:171.

11   As mentioned, another surviving fragment of *The Story Teller* is also found in *Mosses from an Old Manse*, immediately following "Relinquished Work." "Sketches from Memory," Series 1, was originally published in the *New-England Magazine* in 1835; it is composed of a series of three travel sketches: "The Notch of the White Mountains," "Our Evening Party Among the Mountains," and "The Canal Boat." Interspersed among these sketches would be "The Ambitious Guest" and "The Great Carbuncle." A second installment, "Sketches from Memory," Series 2, also published in the *New-England Magazine* in 1835, remained uncollected; it also has three sections: "The Inland Port," "Rochester," and "A Night Scene." The second series is not nearly so fully developed as the first, nor is it so manifest where the tales of *The Story Teller* were to be interspersed. See Weber (1973), "Zuordnung in der strukturanalytischen Untersuchung," pp. 362–64, for a chart of the probable sequence and possible specific contents of *The Story Teller*.

12   Millicent Bell, p. 137. See also Normand's more subjective treatment of the "Oberon" motif in *Nathaniel Hawthorne*, esp. "Part One: Oberon," pp. 3–84.

13   See Orgel (1965, 1969). Oberon appears in other works probably familiar to Hawthorne as well. He is featured in the prologue to Robert Green's *James IV*, which Shakespeare knew well; and he is a character in the romance *Huon of Bordeaux*, translated by Lord Berners, read by thousands in Shakespeare's time. Christoph Martin Wieland wrote an *Oberon* (1780) which Coleridge tried translating in 1797 and which John Quincy Adams

translated in full in 1799. Wieland's *Oberon* is structured around a quarrel between Oberon and Titania and their ultimate reconciliation; throughout, the province of dream and imagination is contested by the "real" world, and the two worlds are ultimately harmonized. Hawthorne's fascination with the masque and its allegorical potential is evident in many tales and sketches (including "Seven Vagabonds"). His use of the masque tradition is particularly evident in *The Blithedale Romance* (1852), where allusions to John Milton's dark poetic drama, *Comus — A Masque* (1634, 1637), qualify structure and theme. See Yates on masque and dance themes. It may also be mentioned here that the Oberon icon figures overtly and covertly in Jean Paul Friedrich Richter's influential *School for Aesthetics* (1804) as well as in his earlier romances.

14 For a brief overview of "objective subjectivity" see the discussion in chapter 2 of *Poe's Fiction* and in "The Development of Romantic Irony"; for a detailed discussion, see chapters 1 and 3 of *Romantic Arabesque* and the notes to these chapters.

15 Although Schlegel gives lip service to "poetry" as the genre or mode at the top of the literary hierarchy, he usually is referring to the concept of the "poetic," which can apply to prose fiction as well. In practical terms, he regards fiction (as *Roman*) as the highest pinnacle of actual literary achievement. Much the same attitude is found in Poe, notably in his reviews of Hawthorne.

16 As if a reminder of the critical issues at stake, just as this book was going to press a new psychobiographical study of Hawthorne, by Edwin Haviland Miller, was announced. The advertising matter carries the same passage from *The Snow-Image* I have just quoted and to which I referred in the introduction to this study. But Miller uses the passage for a diametrically opposite purpose: to uncover the biographical Hawthorne in his narratives — a feat achieved by largely ignoring narratology.

Works Cited

The following bibliography (through winter 1989–90) is focused on the subjects and issues of the present book. For more complete bibliographies of studies of Hawthorne per se, see Colacurcio and Newman (LBVN). Only a handful of items appearing in the interim between the submission of the manuscript and the publication of this book are cited as having special pertinence; no attempt has been made to incorporate the criticism of the last two and a half years in a comprehensive way.

The order of cited works by the same author is chronological. Full data for collections of essays recurrently cited are found under the volume titles; individual essays in these collections are listed under the author's name and bibliographical data is abbreviated. For certain journals that repaginate with each issue, like *ESQ* prior to 1972, the "no." of the issue is given before the date, followed by a comma, and then page numbers as "pp." For articles in *ESQ* after 1972, where pagination is consecutive for the volume, the volume number is given, followed by the date, followed by a colon and the page numbers.

Abel, Darrel. *The Moral Picturesque: Studies in Hawthorne's Fiction.* West Lafayette, Ind.: Purdue University Press, 1988.

Abernathy, P. L. "The Identity of Hawthorne's Major Molineux." *American Transcendental Quarterly*, No. 31 (1976), pp. 5–8.

Abrams, Meyer H. *The Mirror and the Lamp: Romantic Theory and the Critical Tradition.* 1953. Reprint. New York: Norton, 1958.

Adams, Richard P. "Hawthorne's *Provincial Tales.*" *New England Quarterly* 30 (1957): 39–57.

———. "Hawthorne: The Old Manse Period." *Tulane Studies in English* 8 (1958): 115–51.

Adkins, Nelson F. "The Early Projected Works of Nathaniel Hawthorne." *Papers of the Bibliographical Society of America* 39 (1945): 119–45.

———. "Notes on the Hawthorne Canon." *Papers of the Bibliographical Society of America* 60 (1966): 364–67.

Adorno, Theodor. *Negative Dialectics.* 1966. Reprint. Trans. E. B. Ashton. New York: Seabury Press, 1973.

———. *Aesthetische Theorie.* Frankfurt am Main: Suhrkamp, 1973. London: Routledge & Kegan Paul, 1984.

Allison, Alexander W. "The Literary Contexts of 'My Kinsman, Major Molineux.'" *Nineteenth-Century Fiction* 23 (1968): 304–11.

Arvin, Newton. *Hawthorne.* 1926. Reprint. New York: Russell & Russell, 1956.

Aspects of Narrative. [Selected papers from the English Institute.] Ed. J. Hillis Miller. New York: Columbia University Press, 1971.

Auerbach, Eric. "Figura." In *Scenes from the Drama of European Literature*, 19–43. 1959. Reprint. Minneapolis: University of Minnesota Press, 1984.

Auerbach, Jonathan. *The Romance of Failure: First-Person Fictions of Poe, Hawthorne, and James.* New York: Oxford University Press, 1989.

Bailyn, Bernard. *The Ideological Origins of the American Revolution.* Cambridge, Mass.: Harvard University Press, 1967.

Bakhtin, M. M. *Problems of Dostoevsky's Work.* 1922. Reprint. Ed. and trans. Caryl Emerson. Minneapolis: University of Minnesota, 1984.

———. *Rabelais and His World.* 1965. Reprint. Trans. Hélène Iswolsky. Bloomington: Indiana University Press, 1984.

———. *The Dialogic Imagination: Four Essays.* Ed. Michael Holquist. Trans. Caryl Emerson and Michael Holquist. Austin: University of Texas Press, 1981. See especially: "Discourse in the Novel" (1935); "Forms of Time and of the Chronotope in the Novel" (1938) plus "Concluding Remarks"; "From the Prehistory of Novelistic Discourse" (1940); "Epic and Novel" (1941).

Barth, John. "Tales Within Tales Within Tales." In *The Friday Book: Essays and Other Non-Fiction*, 218–38. New York: Putnam, 1984.

Bauer, Dale M. *Feminist Dialogics: A Theory of Failed Community.* Albany: State University of New York Press, 1988.

Bayer, John G. "Narrative Techniques and the Oral Tradition in *The Scarlet Letter.*" *American Literature* 52 (1980): 250–63.

Baym, Nina. "Hawthorne's Gothic Discards: *Fanshawe* and 'Alice Doane's Appeal.'" *Nathaniel Hawthorne Journal/1974:* 105–15.

———. *The Shape of Hawthorne's Career.* Ithaca, N.Y.: Cornell University Press, 1976.

———. "Concepts of the Romance in Hawthorne's America." *Nineteenth-Century Fiction* 38 (1984): 426–43.

Beattie, James. "On Fable and Romance." In *Dissertations Moral and Critical.* 2 vols. London, 1783. Reprint. New York: Garland, 1971.

Beaver, Harold. "Towards Romance: The Case of 'Roger Malvin's Burial.'" In *Nathaniel Hawthorne: New Critical Essays*, 31–47. Ed. A. Robert Lee. Totowa, N.J.: Barnes & Noble, 1982.

Becker, John E. *Hawthorne's Historical Allegory: An Examination of the American Conscience.* Port Washington, N.Y.: Kennikat Press, 1971.

Beer, Gillian. *The Romance.* London & New York: Methuen Critical Idiom, 1970.

Behler, Ernst. "The Theory of Irony in German Romanticism." In *Romantic Irony* (1988), 43–81.

Beldin, Henry Marvin. "Poe's Criticism of Hawthorne." *Anglia* 33 (1904): 376–404.

Bell, Michael Davitt. *Hawthorne and the Historical Romance of New England.* Princeton, N.J.: Princeton University Press, 1971.

———. *The Development of American Romance: The Sacrifice of Relation.* Chicago, Ill.: University of Chicago Press, 1980.

———. "Arts of Deception: Hawthorne, 'Romance,' and *The Scarlet Letter.*" In *New Essays on "The Scarlet Letter"* (1985), 29–56.

———. "Nathaniel Hawthorne." In *Columbia History of the United States*, 413–28. Ed. Emory Elliott et al. New York: Columbia University Press, 1988.

Bell, Millicent. *Hawthorne's View of the Artist.* New York: State University of New York Press, 1962.

Bercovitch, Sacvan. "The Problem of Ideology in American Literary History." *Critical Inquiry* 12 (1986): 631–53.

Berek, Peter. *The Transformation of Allegory from Spenser to Hawthorne.* Amherst, Mass.: Amherst College Press, 1962.

Berlant, Lauren. "Fantasies of Utopia in *The Blithedale Romance.*" *American Literary History* (1989): 30–62.

———. "America, Post-Utopia: Body, Landscape, and National Fantasy in Hawthorne's *Native Land.*" *Arizona Quarterly* 44 (1989): 14–54.

Bewley, Marius. *The Eccentric Design: Form in the Classic American Novel.* New York: Columbia University Press, 1959.

———. "Hawthorne and the Deeper Psychology." *Mandrake* 2 (1956): 366–73.

Bickman, Martin. *The Unsounded Centre: Jungian Studies in American Romanticism.* Chapel Hill: University of North Carolina Press, 1980.

Bier, Jesse. "Hawthorne on the Romance: His Prefaces Related and Examined." *Modern Philology* 53 (1955): 17–24.

Blackall, Eric. *The Novels of the German Romantics.* Ithaca, N.Y.: Cornell University Press, 1983.

Blair, Walter. "Nathaniel Hawthorne." In *Eight American Authors,* 85–128. Rev. ed. New York: Norton, 1971.

Booth, Wayne C. "Distance and Point-of-View: An Essay in Classification" (1961). In *Theory of the Novel* (1967), 87–107.

———. *The Rhetoric of Fiction.* Chicago: University of Chicago Press, 1961.

Bridge, Horatio. *Personal Recollections of Nathaniel Hawthorne.* 1893. Reprint. New York: Haskell House, 1968.

Britannica. "Novel" & "Romance." Edinburgh: Encyclopaedia Britannica, 1817.

Broadhead, Richard H. *Hawthorne, Melville, and the Novel.* Chicago: University of Chicago Press, 1976.

———. *The School of Hawthorne.* New York: Oxford University Press, 1986.

Brodwin, Stanley. "Hawthorne and the Function of History: A Reading of 'Alice Doane's Appeal.'" *Nathaniel Hawthorne Journal/1974:* 116–28.

Broes, Arthur T. "Journey into Moral Darkness: 'My Kinsman, Major Molineux' as Allegory." *Nineteenth-Century Fiction* 19 (1964): 171–84.

Bronstein, Zelda. "The Parabolic Ploys of *The Scarlet Letter.*" *American Quarterly* 39 (1987): 193–210.

Brooks, Peter. *Reading for Plot: Design and Intention in Narrative.* New York: Knopf, 1984.

Brown, Charles Brockden. "The Difference Between History and Romance." *Monthly Magazine and American Review* 2 (1800): 251.

Brubaker, B. R. "Hawthorne's Experiment in Popular Form: 'Mr. Higginbotham's Catastrophe.'" *Southern Humanities Review* 7 (1973): 155–66.

Brumm, Ursula. *American Thought and Religious Typology.* 1963. Reprint. Trans. John Hoagland. New Brunswick, N.J.: Rutgers University Press, 1970.

———. "A Regicide Judge as 'Champion' of American Independence." *Amerikastudien* 21 (1976): 177–86.

Buckley, Vincent, and Robert Wilson. "Persona: The Empty Mask." *Quadrant* (Australia) 19 (1975): 81–96.

Budick, Emily Miller. *Fiction and Historical Consciousness: The American Romance Tradition.* New Haven: Yale University Press, 1989.

Buell, Lawrence. *New England Literary Culture: From Revolution through Renaissance.* New York: Cambridge University Press, 1986.

Burhans, C. S. "Hawthorne's Mind and Art in 'The Hollow of the Three Hills.'" *Journal of English and Germanic Philology* 60 (1961): 286–95.

Carlson, Patricia Ann. "The Function of the Lamp in Hawthorne's 'The Wives of the Dead.'" *South Atlantic Bulletin* 40 (1975): 62–64.

——. *Hawthorne's Functional Settings*. Amsterdam: Rodopi, 1977.

Carton, Evan. "Hawthorne and the Province of Romance." *ELH* 47 (1980): 331–54. Revised in *Rhetoric of American Romance*.

——. *The Rhetoric of American Romance: Dialectic and Identity in Emerson, Dickinson, Poe, and Hawthorne*. Baltimore: Johns Hopkins University Press, 1985.

A Casebook on the Hawthorne Question. Ed. Agnes McNeill Donohue. New York: Crowell, 1963.

Cawelti, John G. *Adventure, Mystery, and Romance: Formula Stories as Art and Popular Culture*. Chicago: University of Chicago Press, 1976.

Chandler, Elizabeth. "A Study of the Sources of the Tales and Romances Written by Nathaniel Hawthorne Before 1853," *Smith College Studies in Modern Languages* 7 (1925–26): 1–63.

Charvat, William. "Romance" and "Criticism of Fiction." In *The Origins of American Critical Thought, 1810–1835*, 59–71, 134–63. 1936. Reprint. New York: A. S. Barnes, 1961.

Chase, Richard. *The American Novel and Its Tradition*. Garden City, N.Y.: Doubleday, 1957.

Chatman, Seymour. *Story and Discourse: Narrative Structure in Fiction and Film*. Ithaca, N.Y.: Cornell University Press, 1978.

Chibka, Robert L. "Hawthorne's Tale Told Twice: A Reading of 'Wakefield.'" *ESQ* 28 (1982): 220–32.

Clark, Harry Hayden. "Hawthorne's Literary and Aesthetic Doctrines as Embodied in His Tales." *Transactions of the Wisconsin Academy of Sciences, Arts, and Letters* 50 (1961): 251–75.

Clark, Robert. *History, Ideology, and Myth in American Fiction, 1823–1852*. London: Macmillan, 1984.

Clements, Robert J., and Joseph Gibaldi. *Anatomy of the Novella: The European Tale Collection from Boccaccio and Chaucer to Cervantes*. New York: New York University Press, 1977.

Coale, Samuel Chase. *In Hawthorne's Shadow: American Romance from Melville to Mailer*. Lexington: University Press of Kentucky, 1985.

Coffey, Dennis G. "Hawthorne's 'Alice Doane's Appeal': The Artist Absolved." *ESQ* 21 (1975): 230–40.

Cohen, Lester H. "The Romance of the Revolution." In *The Revolutionary Histories: Contemporary Narratives of the American Revolution*, 212–29. Ithaca, N.Y.: Cornell University Press, 1980.

Colacurcio, Michael J. *The Province of Piety: Moral History in Hawthorne's Early Tales*. Cambridge, Mass.: Harvard University Press, 1984.

Cowan, Bainard. "Text and Body: The Cultural Origin of Allegory" and "The Romantic Crisis of Allegory." In *Exiled Waters: "Moby-Dick" and the Crisis of Allegory*, 9–31, 32–59. Baton Rouge: Louisiana State University Press, 1982.

Cowie, Alexander. Introduction to *The Yemassee*, by William Gilmore Simms. ix–xxv. New York: American Book Co., 1937.

——. *The Rise of the American Novel*. New York: American Book Co., 1951.

Crews, Frederick C. *The Sins of the Fathers: Hawthorne's Psychological Themes*. 1966. Reprint. Berkeley: University of California, 1989. "Afterword," 273–86.

Crowley, J. Donald. "The Artist as Mediator: The Rationale of Hawthorne's Large-Scale Revisions in His Collected Tales and Sketches." In *Melville and Hawthorne in the Berkshires* (1966), 79–88, 156–57.

——. "The Unity of Hawthorne's *Twice-told Tales*." *Studies in American Fiction* 1 (1973): 35–61.

Dale, Peter Allan. *The Victorian Critic and the Idea of History*. Cambridge, Mass.: Harvard University Press, 1977.

Dauber, Kenneth. *Rediscovering Hawthorne*. Princeton, N.J.: Princeton University Press, 1977.

——. "Criticism of American Literature." *Diacritics* 7 (1977): 55–66. [Review-essay.]

Dauner, Louise. "The 'Case' of Tobias Pearson: Hawthorne and the Ambiguities." *American Literature* 21 (1950): 464–72.

D'Avanzo, Mario. "The Literary Sources of 'My Kinsman, Major Molineux': Shakespeare, Coleridge, Milton." *Studies in Short Fiction* 10 (1972): 121–36.

Davidson, Edward H. *Hawthorne's Last Phase*. 1949. Reprint. Hamden, Conn.: Archon, 1967.

Davis, David Brion. *Homicide in American Fiction, 1798–1860*. Ithaca, N.Y.: Cornell University Press, 1957.

Dekker, George. "Sir Walter Scott, the Angel of Hadley, and American Historical Fiction." *Journal of American Studies* 17 (1984): 211–27.

——. *The American Historical Romance*. New York: Cambridge University Press, 1987.

——. "Once More: Hawthorne and the Genealogy of American Romance." *ESQ* 35 (1989): 69–83. [Review-essay.]

Deleuze, Gilles, and Felix Guattari. *Anti-Oedipus: Capitalism and Schizophrenia*. 1972. Reprint. Trans. Robert Hurley, Mark Seem, and Helen R. Lane. Minneapolis: University of Minnesota Press, 1983.

——. *Thousand Plateaus*. 1980. English translation. Minneapolis: University of Minnesota Press, 1987.

de Man, Paul. "The Rhetoric of Temporality" (1969). Reprinted in *Blindness and Insight: Essays in the Rhetoric of Contemporary Criticism*, 187–228. 2d ed. Minneapolis: University of Minnesota Press, 1983.

Dennis, Carl. "How to Live in Hell: The Bleak Vision of Hawthorne's *My Kinsman, Major Molineux*." *University Review* 37 (1971): 250–58.

Derrida, Jacques. "The Purveyor of Truth" (1975). Abridged rpt. in *Purloined Poe* (1988), 173–212.

——. "The Law of Genre." 1969. Reprinted in *On Narrative*, 61ff.

DeSalvo, Louise. *Nathaniel Hawthorne*. Atlantic Highlands, N.J.: Humanities Press International, 1987.

Dickstein, Morris. "Popular Fiction and Critical Values: The Novel as a Challenge to Literary History." In *Reconstructing American Literary History* (1985), 29–66.

Dittmar, Linda. "Fashioning and Re-fashioning: Framing Narratives in the Novel and Film." *Mosaic* 16 (1983): 189–203.

Donohue, Agnes McNeill. " 'From Whose Bourn No Traveller Returns': A Reading of 'Roger Malvin's Burial.' " *Nineteenth-Century Fiction* 18 (1963): 1–19.

——. " 'The Fruit of That Forbidden Tree': A Reading of 'The Gentle Boy.' " In *Casebook on the Hawthorne Question* (1963), 158–70.

——. *Hawthorne: Calvin's Ironic Stepchild*. Kent, Ohio: Kent State University Press, 1985.

Doubleday, Neal Frank. "Hawthorne's Estimate of His Early Work." *American Literature* 37 (1966): 403–99.

——. *Hawthorne's Early Tales: A Critical Study*. Durham, N.C.: Duke University Press, 1972.

Downing, David W. "Beyond Convention: The Dynamics of Imagery and Response in Hawthorne's Early Sense of Evil." *American Literature* 51 (1980): 463–76.

Dryden, Edgar A. *Nathaniel Hawthorne: The Poetics of Enchantment*. Ithaca, N.Y.: Cornell University Press, 1977.

———. *The Form of American Romance*. Baltimore: Johns Hopkins University Press, 1988.

Duban, James. "The Sceptical Context of Hawthorne's 'Mr. Higginbotham's Catastrophe.'" *American Literature* 48 (1976): 292–301.

———. "The Triumph of Infidelity in Hawthorne's 'The Story Teller.'" *Studies in American Fiction* 7 (1979): 49–60.

———. "Chipping with a Chisel: The Ideology of Melville's Narrators." *Texas Studies in Literature and Language* 31 (1989): 341–85.

Dunne, Michael. "Varieties of Narrative Authority in Hawthorne's *Twice-told Tales* (1837)." *South Atlantic Review* 54 (1989): 33–49.

Dusenbery, Robert. "Hawthorne's Merry Company: The Anatomy of Laughter in the Tales and Stories." *PMLA* 82 (1967): 285–88.

Eco, Umberto. *A Theory of Semiotics*. Bloomington: Indiana University Press, 1976.

Ehrenpreis, Anne Henry. "Elizabeth Gaskell and Nathaniel Hawthorne." *Nathaniel Hawthorne Journal/1973*: 89–119.

Ehrenpreis, Irvin. "Personae." 1963. Reprinted in *Literary Meaning and Augustan Values*, 49–60. Charlottesville: University of Virginia Press, 1974.

Eigner, Edwin M. *The Metaphysical Novel in England and America: Dickens, Bulwer, Melville, and Hawthorne*. Berkeley: University of California Press, 1978.

Elder, Marjorie J. *Nathaniel Hawthorne: Transcendental Symbolist*. Athens: Ohio University Press, 1969.

Elias, Helen L. "Alice Doane's Innocence: The Wizard Absolved." *Emerson Society Quarterly* No. 62 (1971), pp. 28–32.

Ellenberger, Henri F. *The Discovery of the Unconscious: The History and Evolution of a Dynamic Psychiatry*. New York: Basic Books, 1970.

Elliot, Robert C. *The Literary Persona*. Chicago: University of Chicago Press, 1982.

Ellis, John M. *Narration in the German Novelle: Theory and Interpretation*. London and New York: Cambridge University Press, 1974.

Ellis, William. *The Theory of the American Romance: An Ideology in American Intellectual History*. Ann Arbor, Mich.: University Microfilms International, 1989.

Erlich, Gloria C. "Guilt and Expiation in 'Roger Malvin's Burial.'" *Nineteenth-Century Fiction* 26 (1971–72): 377–89.

———. *Family Themes in Hawthorne's Fiction: The Tenacious Web*. New Brunswick, N.J.: Rutgers University Press, 1984.

Evans, Walter. "Nineteenth-century American Theory of the Short Story: The Dual Tradition." *Orbis Literarium* 34 (1979): 314–27.

Fairbanks, Henry G. *The Lasting Loneliness of Nathaniel Hawthorne: A Study of the Sources of Alienation in Modern Man*. Albany, N.Y.: Magi Books, 1965.

Fetterley, Judith. *The Resisting Reader: A Feminist Approach to American Fiction*. Bloomington: Indiana University Press, 1978.

Fiedler, Leslie. *Love and Death in the American Novel*. 1960. Rev. ed. New York: Dell, 1966.

Fletcher, Angus. *Allegory: The Theory of a Symbolic Mode*. Ithaca, N.Y.: Cornell University Press, 1964.

———. *The Transcendental Masque: An Essay on Milton's Comus*. Ithaca, N.Y.: Cornell University Press, 1971.

Fliegelman, Jay. *Prodigals and Pilgrims: The American Revolution against Patriarchal Authority*. New York: Cambridge University Press, 1982.

Fogle, Richard Harter. *Hawthorne's Fiction: The Light and the Dark*. 1952. Rev. ed. Norman: University of Oklahoma Press, 1964.

——. "Weird Mockery: An Element of Hawthorne's Style." *Style* 2 (1968): 191–202. Rpt. in *The Permanent Pleasure: Essays in the Classics of Romanticism*, 124–36. Athens: University of Georgia Press, 1974.

——. "Hawthorne, Literary History, and Criticism." First published as "Literary History Romanticized" in *New Literary History* 1 (1970): 237–47. Reprinted in *Permanent Pleasure* (1974), 1–16.

——. "Art and Illusion: Coleridgean Assumptions in Hawthorne's Tales and Sketches." In *Ruined Eden of the Present* (1981), 109–27.

Folsom, James K. *Man's Accidents and God's Purposes: Multiplicity in Hawthorne's Fiction*. New Haven, Conn.: College and University Press, 1963.

Fossum, Robert H. *Hawthorne's Inviolable Circle: The Problem of Time*. Deland, Fla.: Everett/Edwards, 1972.

——. "The Summons of the Past: Hawthorne's 'Alice Doane's Appeal.'" *Nineteenth-Century Fiction* 23 (1968): 294–303.

Foster, Charles Howell. "Hawthorne's Literary Theory." *PMLA* 57 (1942): 241–54.

Foucault, Michel. *The Order of Things: An Archaeology of the Human Sciences*. 1966. Reprint. New York: Random House Vintage Books, 1973.

Franzosa, John. "Locke's Kinsman, William Molineux: The Philosophical Context of Hawthorne's Early Tales." *ESQ* 29 (1983): 1–15.

Friedman, Norman. "Point of View in Fiction: The Development of a Critical Concept." In *Theory of the Novel* (1967), 108–37.

Frye, Northrop. *Anatomy of Criticism*. 1957. Reprint. Princeton, N.J.: Princeton University Press, 1973.

——. *The Secular Scripture: A Study of the Structure of Romance*. Cambridge, Mass.: Harvard University Press, 1976.

Fryer, Judith. *The Faces of Eve: Women in the Nineteenth-Century American Novel*. New York: Oxford University Press, 1976.

Garber, Frederick. *Text, Self, and Romantic Irony: The Example of Byron*. Princeton, N.J.: Princeton University Press, 1988.

Geist, Stanley. "Fictitious Americans: A Preface to 'Ethan Brand.'" *Hudson Review* 5 (1952): 199–211.

Genette, Gerard. *Narrative Discourse: An Essay in Method*. 1972. Trans. Jane E. Lewin. Ithaca, N.Y.: Cornell University Press, 1980.

Gerhardt, Mia. *The Art of Story-Telling: A Literary Study of the Thousand and One Nights*. Leiden: E. J. Brill, 1963.

Gerlach, John. *Toward the End: Closure and Structure in the American Short Story*. Tuscaloosa: University of Alabama Press, 1985.

Gerould, Gordon Hall. *The Patterns of English and American Fiction: A History*. Boston: Little, Brown, 1942.

Gilkes, Lillian B. "Hawthorne, Park Benjamin, S. G. Goodrich: A Three-Cornered Imbroglio." *Nathaniel Hawthorne Journal/1971*: 83–112.

Gilmore, Michael. *The Middle Way: Puritanism and Theology in American Romantic Fiction*. New Brunswick, N.J.: Rutgers University Press, 1977.

Girgus, Sam B. *The Law of the Heart: Individualism and the Modern Self in American Literature*. Austin: University of Texas Press, 1979.

Gittes, K. S. "*The Canterbury Tales* and the Arabic Frame Tradition." *PMLA* 98 (1983): 237–51.

Goffman, Erving. *Frame Analysis*. New York: Harper & Row, 1974.

Gollin, Rita K. *Nathaniel Hawthorne and the Truth of Dreams.* Baton Rouge: Louisiana State University Press, 1979.

Grayson, Robert G. "The New England Sources of 'My Kinsman, Major Molineux.'" *American Literature* 54 (1982): 545–59.

Green, Martin. *Re-appraisals: Some Commonsense Readings in American Literature.* New York: Norton, 1965.

Greenwald, Elissa. *Realism and the Romance: Nathaniel Hawthorne, Henry James, and American Fiction.* Ann Arbor, Mich.: University Microfilms International, 1989.

Griffin, Nathaniel E. "The Definition of Romance." *PMLA* 38 (1923): 50–70.

Gross, Seymour L. "Hawthorne's Revisions of 'The Gentle Boy.'" *American Literature* 26 (1954): 196–208.

——. "Hawthorne's 'Alice Doane's Appeal.'" *Nineteenth-Century Fiction* 10 (1955): 232–36.

——. "Hawthorne's Income from *The Token.*" *Studies in Bibliography* 8 (1956): 236–38.

——. "Four Possible Additions to Hawthorne's 'Story Teller.'" *Publications of the Bibliographical Society of America* 51 (1957): 90–95.

——. "Hawthorne's 'My Kinsman, Major Molineux': History as Moral Adventure," *Nineteenth-Century Fiction* 24 (1969): 45–56.

——, and Alfred J. Levy. "Some Remarks on the Extant Manuscripts of Hawthorne's Short Stories." *Studies in Bibliography* 14 (1961): 254–57.

Gross, Theodore L. *The Heroic Ideal in American Literature.* New York: Free Press, 1971.

Gupta, R. K. "Hawthorne's Treatment of the Artist." *New England Quarterly* 45 (1972): 65–80.

Haggerty, George E. "Hawthorne's Gothic Garden." In *Gothic Fiction/Gothic Form,* 105–37. University Park: Pennsylvania State University Press, 1989.

Hamilton, A. C. "Elizabethan Romance: The Example of Prose Fiction." *ELH* 49 (1982): 287–99.

Handwerk, Gary J. *Irony and Ethics in Narrative: From Schlegel to Lacan.* New Haven, Conn.: Yale University Press, 1985.

Hansen, Chadwick. *Witchcraft at Salem.* New York: George Braziller, 1969.

Hansen, Elaine Tuttle. "Ambiguity and the Narrator in *The Scarlet Letter.*" *Journal of Narrative Technique* 5 (1975): 147–63.

Harris, Kenneth Marc. *Hypocrisy and Self-Deception in Hawthorne's Fiction.* Charlottesville: University Press of Virginia, 1988.

Haviland, Beverly. "The Sin of Synecdoche: Hawthorne's Allegory against Symbolism in 'Rappaccini's Daughter.'" *Texas Studies in Literature and Language* 29 (1987): 278–301.

Hawthorne, Julian. *Nathaniel Hawthorne and His Wife.* 2 vols. Boston: Houghton Mifflin, 1884.

Hawthorne, Nathaniel. *The Works of Nathaniel Hawthorne.* Ed. George Parsons Lathrop. 13 vols. Boston: Houghton Mifflin (Riverside Ed.), 1882–83.

——. *The American Notebooks.* Ed. Randall Stewart. New Haven, Conn.: Yale University Press, 1932.

——. *The Centenary Edition of the Works of Nathaniel Hawthorne.* Ed. William Charvat, Roy Harvey Pearce, Claude M. Simpson, Fredson Bowers, Matthew J. Bruccoli, L. Neal Smith, et al. Columbus: Ohio State University Press, 1962–.

——. *Tales and Sketches.* Ed. Roy Harvey Pearce. New York: Library of America, 1982.

——. *Nathaniel Hawthorne's Tales.* Ed. James McIntosh. New York: Norton, 1987.

Hawthorne Centenary Essays. Ed. Roy Harvey Pearce. Columbus: Ohio State University Press, 1964.

Hawthorne: A Collection of Critical Essays. Ed. A. N. Kaul. Englewood Cliffs, N.J.: Prentice-Hall, 1966.

Hawthorne: The Critical Heritage. Ed. J. Donald Crowley. New York: Barnes & Noble, 1970.

Hawthorne's American Travel Sketches. Ed. Alfred Weber, Beth L. Lueck, and Dennis Berthold. Hanover, N.H.: New England University Presses, 1989.

Hedges, William L. *Washington Irving: An American Study, 1802–1832.* Baltimore: Johns Hopkins University Press, 1965.

Henderson, Harry B., III. *Versions of the Past: The Historical Imagination in American Fiction.* New York: Oxford University Press, 1974.

Hennelly, Mark M., Jr. " 'Alice Doane's Appeal': Hawthorne's Case Against the Artist." *Studies in American Fiction* 6 (1978): 125–40.

Herndon, Jerry A. "Hawthorne's Dream Imagery." *American Literature* 46 (1975): 538–45.

Hoeltje, Hubert H. *Inward Sky: The Mind and Art of Nathaniel Hawthorne.* Durham, N.C.: Duke University Press, 1962.

Hoffman, Daniel G. *Form and Fable in American Fiction.* New York: Oxford University Press, 1961.

——. "Myth, Romance, and the Childhood of Man." In *Centenary Essays* (1964), 197–219.

Hoffman, Michael J. *The Subversive Vision: American Romanticism in Literature.* Port Washington, N.Y.: Kennikat Press, 1972.

Hollinger, David A. *In the American Province: Studies in the History and Historiography of Ideas.* Baltimore: Johns Hopkins University Press, 1985. Rev. ed., 1989.

Holmes, Edward M. "Hawthorne and Romanticism." *New England Quarterly* 33 (1960): 476–88.

Honig, Edwin. *Dark Conceit: The Making of Allegory.* Evanston, Ill.: Northwestern University Press, 1959.

Hurd, Richard. *Letters on Chivalry and Romance.* London, 1762. Reprint. New York: Garland, 1971.

Hutner, Gordon. *Secrets and Sympathy: Forms of Disclosure in Hawthorne's Novels.* Athens: University of Georgia Press, 1988.

Ideology and Classic American Literature. Ed. Sacvan Bercovitch and Myra Jehlen. New York: Cambridge University Press, 1986.

Irwin, John T. *Doubling and Incest/Repetition and Revenge: A Speculative Reading of Faulkner.* Baltimore: Johns Hopkins University Press, 1975.

——. *American Hieroglyphics: The Symbol of the Egyptian Hieroglyphics in the American Renaissance.* New Haven: Yale University Press, 1980.

Iser, Wolfgang. "Indeterminacy and the Reader's Response in Prose Fiction." In *Aspects of Narrative* (1971).

——. *The Implied Reader: Patterns of Communication in Prose Fiction from Bunyan to Beckett.* 1972. English ed. Baltimore: Johns Hopkins University Press, 1974.

——. *The Act of Reading: A Theory of Aesthetic Response.* Baltimore: Johns Hopkins University Press, 1978.

James, Henry. *Hawthorne.* 1879. Reprint. Garden City, N.Y.: Doubleday Dolphin Books, 1960.

——. Preface (1907) to *The American* (1877). Scribner's New York Edition, 1907. Rpt. in the Norton Critical Edition of *The American,* 1–15. Ed. James W. Tuttleton. New York, 1978.

Jameson, Fredric. "Magical Narratives: Romance as Genre." *New Literary History* 7 (1975): 135–63. Revised as "Magical Narratives: On the Dialectical Use of Genre Criticism." In *The Political Unconscious: Narrative as a Socially Symbolic Act.* Ithaca, N.Y.: Cornell University Press, 1981.

Janssen, James G. "Hawthorne's Seventh Vagabond: 'The Outsetting Bard.'" *ESQ* No. 62 (1971), pp. 22–28.

———. "Impaled Butterflies and the Misleading Moral in Hawthorne's Short Works." *Nathaniel Hawthorne Journal/1976: 269–75.*

Johnson, Barbara. "The Frame of Reference: Poe, Lacan, Derrida." First published in 1977 in "Literature and Psychoanalysis," *Yale French Studies* 55–56: 457–505. Reprinted in *Purloined Poe* (1988), 213–51.

Johnson, Claudia D. *The Productive Tension of Hawthorne's Art.* University: University of Alabama Press, 1981.

Johnson, Samuel. ["Modern Form of Romance."] *Rambler* No. 4 (1750). Reprinted in *Essays from the "Rambler," "Adventurer," and "Idler."* Ed. W. J. Bate. New Haven: Yale University Press, 1968.

Jones, Buford. "The *Faery Land* of Hawthorne's Romances." *ESQ* No. 48 (1967), pp. 106–24.

Jones, Phyllis M. "Hawthorne's Mythic Use of Puritan History." *Cithara* 12 (1972): 59–73.

Jones, Wayne Allen. "The Hawthorne Goodrich Relationship and a New Estimate of Hawthorne's Income from *The Token.*" *Nathaniel Hawthorne Journal/1975:* 31–36.

Keller, Karl. "Alephs, Zahirs, and the Triumph of Ambiguity." In *Literary Uses of Typology* (1977), 274–314.

Kennedy, J. Gerald, Jr. "Toward a Poetics of the Short Story Cycle." Intro. to special issue of *Journal of the Short Story in English,* No. 11 (1988).

Kent, Thomas. *Interpretation and Genre: The Role of Generic Perception in the Study of Narrative Texts.* Lewisburg, Penn.: Bucknell University Press, 1986.

Ker, William P. *Epic and Romance.* 1897. Reprint. New York: Dover, 1957.

Kermode, Frank. *The Sense of an Ending: Studies in the Theory of Fiction.* New York: Oxford University Press, 1967.

———. "An Approach through History." In *Toward a Poetics of Fiction* (1977).

———. *The Art of Telling: Essays on Fiction.* Cambridge, Mass.: Harvard University Press, 1983.

Kesselring, Marion. "Hawthorne's Reading, 1828–1850." *Bulletin of the New York Public Library* 53 (1949): 55–71, 121–38, 173–94. Reprint. Folcroft, Penn.: Folcroft Press, 1969.

Kiely, Robert. *The Romantic Novel in England.* Cambridge, Mass.: Harvard University Press, 1972.

Kimbrough, Robert. "'The Actual and the Imaginary': Hawthorne's Concept of Art in Theory and Practice." *Transactions of the Wisconsin Academy of Sciences, Arts, and Letters* 50 (1961): 277–93.

Kligerman, Jack. "A Stylistic Approach to Hawthorne's 'Roger Malvin's Burial.'" *Language and Style* 4 (1974): 188–94.

Kloppenburg, James. "Deconstruction and Hermeneutic Strategies for Intellectual History: The Recent Work of Dominick LaCapra and David Hollinger." *Intellectual History Newsletter* 9 (1987): 2–22.

Kozikowski, Stanley J. "'My Kinsman, Major Molineux' as Mock Heroic." *American Transcendental Quarterly* No. 31 (1976), pp. 20–21.

Krieger, Murray. "Fiction, History, and Empirical Reality." *Critical Inquiry* 1 (1974): 335–60.

Lacan, Jacques. "Seminar on 'The Purloined Letter.'" 1956. Abridged trans. in *Purloined Poe* (1988), 27–54.

LaCapra, Dominick. *Rethinking Intellectual History: Texts, Contexts, Language.* Ithaca, N.Y.: Cornell University Press, 1983.

Lang, Andrew. "Realism and Romance." *Contemporary Review* 53 (1887): 683–93.

Lang, Hans-Joachim. "How Ambiguous Is Hawthorne?" 1962. Reprinted in *Hawthorne*, ed. Kaul (1966), 86–96.

Lanser, Susan. *The Narrative Act: Point of View in Prose Fiction*. Princeton, N.J.: Princeton University Press, 1981.

Lathrop, George Parsons. *A Study of Hawthorne*. Boston: Osgood, 1876.

Leavis, Q. D. "Hawthorne as Poet." *Sewanee Review* 59 (1951): 179–205, 426–58. Reprinted in *Hawthorne*, ed. Kaul (1966), 25–63.

Lemon, Lee T. "Frame Story." In *A Glossary for the Study of English*. New York: Oxford University Press, 1971.

Lesser, Simon O. *Fiction and the Unconscious*. New York: Random House, 1957.

Leverenz, David. "Devious Men: Hawthorne." In *Manhood and the American Renaissance*, 227–58. Ithaca, N.Y.: Cornell University Press, 1989.

Levin, David. *History as Romantic Art: Bancroft, Prescott, Motley, and Parkman*. Stanford, Calif.: Stanford University Press, 1959.

——. *What Happened in Salem?* New York: Harcourt Brace, 1960.

——. "Shadows of Doubt: Specter Evidence in 'Young Goodman Brown.'" *American Literature* 34 (1962): 344–52.

——. *In Defense of Historical Literature: Essays on American History, Autobiography, Drama, and Fiction*. New York: Hill & Wang, 1967.

Levin, Harry. *The Power of Blackness: Hawthorne, Poe, and Melville*. New York: Knopf, 1958.

Levine, George. *The Realistic Imagination: English Fiction from Frankenstein to Lady Chatterley*. Chicago: University of Chicago Press, 1981.

Levine, Robert S. *Conspiracy and Romance: Studies in Brockden Brown, Cooper, Hawthorne, and Melville*. New York: Cambridge University Press, 1989.

Levy, Leo B. "'Time's Portraiture': Hawthorne's Theory of History." *Nathaniel Hawthorne Journal/1971*: 192–200.

——. "The Notebook Source and the 18th Century Concept of Hawthorne's Theory of Romance." *Nathaniel Hawthorne Journal/1973*: 120–29.

Lewis, C. S. *Allegory of Love*. 1936. Reprint. New York: Oxford University Press, 1958.

Literary Uses of Typology from the Middle Ages to the Present. Ed. Earl Miner. Princeton, N.J.: Princeton University Press, 1977.

The Literature of Fact. [Selected Papers from the English Institute.] Ed. Angus Fletcher. New York: Columbia University Press, 1976.

Lloyd-Smith, Allan Gardner. *The Analysis of Motives: Early American Psychology and Fiction*. Amsterdam: Rodopi, 1980.

——. *Uncanny American Fiction: Medusa's Face*. London: Macmillan, 1989.

Lokke, Virgil L. "Taxonomies Are Never Innocent." In *The Current in Criticism: Essays on the Present and Future of Literary Theory*, 1–25. Ed. Clayton Koelb and Virgil Lokke. West Lafayette, Ind.: Purdue University Press, 1987.

Lovejoy, D. S. "Lovewell's Fight and 'Roger Malvin's Burial.'" *New England Quarterly* 27 (1954): 527–31.

Lowance, Mason I., Jr. "Typology and Millennial Eschatology in Early New England." In *Literary Uses of Typology* (1977), 228–73.

——. *The Language of Canaan: Metaphor and Symbol in New England from the Puritans to the Transcendentalists*. Cambridge, Mass.: Harvard University Press, 1980.

Luedtke, Luther S. *Nathaniel Hawthorne and the Romance of the Orient*. Bloomington: Indiana University Press, 1989.

Lundblad, Jane. *Hawthorne and the European Literary Tradition.* 1947. Reprint. New York: Russell & Russell, 1965.

Lynch, James J. "The Devil in the Writings of Irving, Hawthorne, and Poe." *New York Folklore Quarterly* 8 (1952): 111–31.

Lyons, John O. *The Invention of the Self.* Carbondale: Southern Illinois University Press, 1978.

Lyotard, Jean-François. *The Postmodern Condition: A Report on Knowledge.* 1979. Trans. Geoff Bennington and Brian Massumi. Minneapolis: University of Minnesota Press, 1984.

———. *The Differend: Phrases in Dispute.* 1983. Trans. Georges Van Den Abbeele. Minneapolis: University of Minnesota Press, 1988.

McCall, Dan E. "Hawthorne's 'Familiar Kind of Preface.'" *ELH* 35 (1968): 422–39.

———. "'I Felt a Funeral in My Brain' and 'The Hollow of the Three Hills." *New England Quarterly* 42 (1969): 432–35.

McCullen, Joseph T., Jr. "Ancient Burial Rites for the Dead and 'Roger Malvin's Burial.'" *Southern Folklore Quarterly* 30 (1966): 313–22.

McDermott, Hugh. *Novel and Romance: The Odyssey to Tom Jones.* Totowa, N.J.: Barnes & Noble, 1989.

McDonald, John J. "The Old Manse Period Canon." *Nathaniel Hawthorne Journal/1972:* 13–39.

———. "'The Old Manse' and Its Mosses: The Inception and Development of *Mosses from an Old Manse.*" *Texas Studies in Literature and Language* 16 (1974): 77–108.

Macdonell, Diane. *Theories of Discourse: An Introduction.* Oxford: Basil Blackwell, 1986.

McElroy, John. "The Hawthorne Style of American Fiction." *ESQ* 19 (1972): 117–23.

McKeithan, D. M. "Poe and the Second Edition of Hawthorne's *Twice-told Tales.*" *Nathaniel Hawthorne Journal/1974:* 257–69.

McWilliams, John P., Jr. *Hawthorne, Melville, and the American Character: A Looking-Glass Business.* New York: Cambridge University Press, 1984.

Mailloux, Stephen. *Interpretative Conventions: The Reader in the Study of American Fiction.* Ithaca, N.Y.: Cornell University Press, 1982.

Male, Roy R. "'From the Innermost Germ': The Organic Principle in Hawthorne's Fiction." *ELH* 20 (1953): 218–36. Rev. rpt. in *Hawthorne's Tragic Vision.*

———. *Hawthorne's Tragic Vision.* Austin: University of Texas Press, 1957.

———. "Hawthorne's Literal Figures." In *Ruined Eden of the Present* (1981), 71–92.

Marks, Alfred H. "German Romantic Irony in Hawthorne's Tales." *Symposium* 7 (1953): 274–305.

———. "Hawthorne, Tieck, and Hoffmann: Adding to the Improbabilities of a Marvellous Tale." *ESQ* 35 (1989): 1–21.

Markus, Manfred. "Hawthornes 'Alice Doane's Appeal' — Eine Absage an den 'Gotischen' Erzählstil." *Germanisch-Romanisch Monatsschrift* 25 (1975): 338–49.

Marler, Robert F. "From Tale to Short Story: The Emergence of a New Genre in the 1850's." *American Literature* 46 (1974): 153–69.

Martin, Terence. "The Method of Hawthorne's Tales." In *Hawthorne Centenary Essays* (1964), 7–30.

———. *The Instructed Vision: Scottish Common-Sense Philosophy and the Origins of American Fiction.* Bloomington: Indiana University Press, 1962.

———. *Nathaniel Hawthorne.* 1965. Rev. ed. Boston: Twayne, 1983.

Martin, Wallace. *Recent Theories of Narrative.* Ithaca, N.Y.: Cornell University Press, 1986.

Matenko, Percy. "Tieck, Poe, and Hawthorne." In *Ludwig Tieck and America*, 71–88. Chapel Hill: University of North Carolina Press, 1954.

Mathews, James W. "Hawthorne and the Popular Tale: From Popular Lore to Art." *Publications of the Bibliographical Society of America* 68 (1974): 149–62.

Matthiessen, F. O. *American Renaissance: Art and Expression in the Age of Emerson and Whitman.* New York: Oxford University Press, 1941.

Mellow, James R. *Nathaniel Hawthorne in His Times.* Boston: Houghton Mifflin, 1980.

Melville and Hawthorne in the Berkshires. Ed. Luther Mansfield. Kent, Ohio: Kent State University Press, 1966.

Melville, Herman. "Hawthorne and His Mosses." 1850. Rpt. in *Recognition* (1969), 29–41, and *Hawthorne: Critical Heritage* (1970), 111–26.

Miller, E. H. *Salem Is My Dwelling Place: A Life of Nathaniel Hawthorne.* Iowa City: University of Iowa Press, 1991.

Miller, John N. "The Pageantry of Revolt in 'My Kinsman, Major Molineux.'" *Studies in American Fiction* 17 (1989): 51–64.

Miller, Perry. *The New England Mind.* 2 vols. Cambridge, Mass.: Harvard University Press. Vol. 1: *The Seventeenth Century,* 1939. Vol. 2: *From Colony to Province,* 1953.

——. *The Raven and the Whale: The War of Words and Wits in the Era of Poe and Melville.* New York: Harcourt, Brace & World, 1956.

——. "The Romance and the Novel." In *Nature's Nation,* 241–78. Cambridge, Mass.: Harvard University Press, 1967.

Mills, Nicolaus. *American and English Fiction in the Nineteenth Century: An Anti-Genre Critique.* Bloomington: Indiana University Press, 1973.

Miyoshi, Masao. *The Divided Self: A Perspective on the Literature of the Victorians.* New York: New York University Press, 1969.

Moore, Henrietta L. "Of Texts and Other Matters." Ch. 5 of *Space, Text and Gender,* 73–90. Cambridge: Cambridge University Press, 1986.

Moss, Sidney P. "The Problem of Theme in *The Marble Faun.*" *Nineteenth-Century Fiction* 18 (1964): 393–99.

Naples, Diane C. "'Roger Malvin's Burial' — a Parable for Historians?" *American Transcendental Quarterly* No. 13 (1972), pp. 45–48.

Nash, Gary. *The Urban Crucible: Social Change, Political Consciousness, and the Origin of the American Revolution.* Cambridge, Mass.: Harvard University Press, 1979.

The Native Muse: Theories of American Literature. Ed. Richard Ruland. 2 vols. New York: E. P. Dutton, 1972.

Neufeldt, Leonard N. *The Economist: Thoreau and Enterprise.* New York: Oxford University Press, 1988.

Newberry, Frederick. *Hawthorne's Divided Loyalties: England and America in His Works.* Rutherford, N.J.: Fairleigh Dickinson University Press, 1987.

——. "Hawthorne's 'Gentle Boy': Lost Mediators in Puritan History." *Studies in Short Fiction* 21 (1984): 363–83.

——. "The Biblical Veil: Sources and Typology in Hawthorne's 'The Minister's Black Veil.'" *Texas Studies in Literature and Language* 31 (1989): 169–95.

New Essays on "The Scarlet Letter." Ed. Michael J. Colacurcio. New York: Cambridge University Press, 1985.

Newlin, Paul A. "'Vague Shapes of the Borderland': The Place of the Uncanny in Hawthorne's Gothic Vision." *ESQ* 18 (1972): 83–96.

Newman, Franklin B. "'My Kinsman, Major Molineux,' An Interpretation." *University of Kansas City Review* 21 (1955): 203–12.

Newman, L. B. V. *A Reader's Guide to the Short Stories of Nathaniel Hawthorne*. Boston: G. K. Hall, 1979. [Cited as LBVN.]

Normand, Jean. *Nathaniel Hawthorne: An Approach to an Analysis of Artistic Creation*. 1964. Trans. Derek Coltman. Cleveland: Press of Case Western Reserve University, 1970.

Novel and Romance, 1700–1800: A Documentary-Record. Ed. Ioan Williams. New York: Barnes & Noble, 1970.

Novelle. Ed. Josef Kunz. Darmstadt: Wissenschaftliche Buchgesellschaft, 1968.

Ong, Walter J. "The Writer's Audience Is Always a Fiction." In *Interfaces of the Word: Studies in the Evolution of Consciousness and Culture*, 53–81. Ithaca, N.Y.: Cornell University Press, 1977.

On Narrative. Ed. W. J. T. Mitchell. Chicago: University of Chicago Press, 1981.

Orgel, Stephen. *The Jonsonian Masque*. Cambridge, Mass.: Harvard University Press, 1965.

———. Intro. to *Ben Jonson: The Complete Masques*, 1–39. New Haven, Conn.: Yale University Press, 1969.

Orians, G. Harrison. "The Romance Ferment after *Waverley*." *American Literature* 3 (1932): 408–31.

———. "The Angel of Hadley in Fiction: A Study of the Sources of Hawthorne's 'The Gray Champion.'" *American Literature* 4 (1932–33): 257–69.

———. "The Sources of 'Roger Malvin's Burial.'" *American Literature* 10 (1938): 313–18.

———. "The Sources and Themes of 'The Gentle Boy.'" *New England Quarterly* 14 (1941): 664–78.

Ortega y Gasset, José. *Meditations on Quixote*. Trans. Evelyn Rugg and Diego Marin. New York: Norton, 1961.

Pahl, Dennis. *Architects of the Abyss: The Indeterminate Fictions of Poe, Hawthorne, and Melville*. Columbia: University of Missouri Press, 1989.

Pancost, David W. "Evidence of Editorial Additions to Hawthorne's 'Fragments from the Journal of a Solitary Man.'" *Nathaniel Hawthorne Journal/1975*: 210–26.

Pandeya, Prabhat. "The Dream of Evil in 'The Hollow of the Three Hills.'" *Nathaniel Hawthorne Journal/1975*: 177–81.

Parker, Hershel. *Flawed Texts and Verbal Icons: Literary Authority in American Fiction*. Evanston, Ill.: Northwestern University Press, 1984.

Parker, Hershel, and Brian Higgins. "The Chaotic Legacy of the New Criticism and the Fair Augury of the New Scholarship." In *Ruined Eden of the Present* (1981), 27–45.

Pattison, Joseph C. "'The Celestial Railroad' as Dream-Tale." *American Quarterly* 20 (1968): 224–36.

Pauly, Thomas H. "'Mr. Higginbotham's Catastrophe' — The Story Teller's Disaster." *American Transcendental Quarterly* No. 14 (1972), pp. 171–74.

———. "The Literary Sketch in Nineteenth-Century America." *Texas Studies in Literature and Language* 17 (1975): 489–503.

———. "Hawthorne's Houses of Fiction." *American Literature* 48 (1976): 271–91.

Pearce, Roy Harvey. *Historicism Once More: Problems and Occasions for the American Scholar*. Princeton, N.J.: Princeton University Press, 1969. Includes: "Hawthorne and the Twilight of Romance" (1948); "Hawthorne and the Sense of the Past; or, The Immortality of Major Molineux" (1954), rpt. with a section of "Romance and the Study of History"; "Robin Molineux on the Analyst's Couch: A Note on the Limits of Psychoanalytic Criticism" (1959).

———. "Romance and the Study of History." In *Hawthorne Centenary Essays* (1964).

Pease, Donald E. *Visionary Compacts: American Renaissance Writings in Cultural Context*. Madison: University of Wisconsin Press, 1987. Ch. 2: "Hawthorne's Discovery of a Pre-Revolutionary Past."

Peckham, Morse. "Toward a Theory of Romanticism." *PMLA* 66 (1951): 5–23. Reprinted in *The Triumph of Romanticism: Collected Essays*, 3–26. Columbia: University of South Carolina Press, 1970.

Perosa, Sergio. *American Theories of the Novel, 1793–1903.* New York: New York University Press, 1983.

Person, Leland S., Jr. *Aesthetic Headaches: Women and a Masculine Poetics in Poe, Melville, and Hawthorne.* Athens: University of Georgia Press, 1988.

Pettet, E. C. *Shakespeare and the Romance Tradition.* 1949. Reprint. New York: Haskell House, 1982.

Phelan, James. *Reading People, Reading Plots: Characters, Progression, and the Interpretation of Narrative.* Chicago: University of Chicago Press, 1989.

Pochmann, Henry A. "Nathaniel Hawthorne." In *German Culture in America: Philosophical and Literary Influences, 1600–1900*, 381–88, 705–9. Madison: University of Wisconsin Press, 1957.

Poe, Edgar Allan. "Twice-Told Tales. By Nathaniel Hawthorne" (April 1842; May 1842); "Twice-Told Tales . . . Mosses from an Old Manse" (November 1847). Reprinted in *Essays and Reviews*, 568–88. Ed. G. R. Thompson. New York: Library of America, 1984.

Porte, Joel. *The Romance in America: Studies in Cooper, Poe, Hawthorne, Melville, and James.* Middletown, Conn.: Wesleyan University Press, 1969.

Post, Robert. "A Theory of Genre: Romance, Realism, and Moral Reality." *American Quarterly* 33 (1981): 367–90.

Prince, Gerald. "Notes Toward a Categorization of Fictional 'Narratees.'" *Genre* 4 (1971): 100–106.

——. *A Grammar of Stories.* The Hague: Mouton, 1973.

——. *Dictionary of Narratology.* Lincoln: University of Nebraska Press, 1987, 1989.

The Purloined Poe: Lacan, Derrida, and Psychoanalytic Reading. Ed. John P. Muller and William J. Richardson. Baltimore: Johns Hopkins University Press, 1988.

Rabinowitz, Peter J. *Before Reading: Narrative Conventions and the Politics of Interpretation.* Ithaca, N.Y.: Cornell University Press, 1987.

Raskin, Victor. *Semantic Mechanisms of Humor.* Dordrecht, Holland, and Boston: D. Reidel, 1984.

The Reader in the Text: Essays on Audience and Interpretation. Ed. Susan R. Suleiman and Inge Crosman. Princeton, N.J.: Princeton University Press, 1980.

Reading Narrative: Form, Ethics, Ideology. Ed. James Phelan. Chicago: University of Chicago Press, 1988.

The Recognition of Nathaniel Hawthorne: Selected Criticism Since 1828. Ed. B. Bernard Cohen. Ann Arbor: University of Michigan Press, 1969.

Reconstructing American Literary History. Ed. Sacvan Bercovitch. Cambridge, Mass.: Harvard University Press, 1986.

Rees, John O., Jr. "Hawthorne's Concept of Allegory: A Reconsideration." *Philological Quarterly* 54 (1975): 494–510.

Reeve, Clara. *The Progress of Romance.* 1785. Rpt. with *The History of Charoba, Queen of Aegypt*, ed. Esther M. McGill. New York: Facsimile Text Society, 1930.

Reising, Russell. *The Unusable Past: Theory and the Study of American Literature.* New York: Methuen, 1986.

Reynolds, David S. *Beneath the American Renaissance: The Subversive Imagination in the Ameri-*

can Renaissance. New York: Knopf, 1988; Cambridge, Mass.: Harvard University Press, 1989.

Rimmon-Kennan, Shlomith. *Narrative Fiction: Contemporary Poetics*. London: Methuen, 1983.

Ringe, Donald A. "Hawthorne's Psychology of the Head and Heart." *PMLA* 65 (1950): 120–32.

———. "Hawthorne's Night Journeys." *American Transcendental Quarterly* No. 10 (1977), pp. 27–32.

———. *American Gothic: Imagination and Reason in Nineteenth-Century Fiction*. Lexington: University Press of Kentucky, 1982.

Robillard, Douglas. "Hawthorne's 'Roger Malvin's Burial.'" *Explicator* 26 (1968), item 56.

Robinson, Douglas. "Metafiction and Heartfelt Memory: Narrative Balance in 'Alice Doane's Appeal.'" *ESQ* 28 (1982): 213–19.

———. *American Apocalypses: The Image of the End of the World in American Literature*. Baltimore: Johns Hopkins University Press, 1985.

Rohrberger, Mary. *Hawthorne and the Modern Short Story*. The Hague: Mouton, 1966.

Romantic Irony. Ed. Frederick Garber. Budapest: Akadémiai Kiadó for the International Comparative Literature Association, 1988.

Rowe, John Carlos. *Through the Custom-House: Nineteenth-Century American Fiction and Modern Theory*. Baltimore: Johns Hopkins University Press, 1982.

Rubin-Dorsky, Jeffrey. "Washington Irving and the Genesis of the Fictional Sketch." *Early American Literature* 21 (1986–87): 226–47.

———. "A Crisis of Identity: *The Sketch-Book* and Nineteenth-Century American Culture." *Prospects* 12 (1987): 255–91.

———. *Adrift in the Old World: Washington Irving's Psychological Pilgrimage*. Chicago: University of Chicago Press, 1988.

Ruined Eden of the Present: Hawthorne, Melville, Poe. Ed. G. R. Thompson and Virgil L. Lokke. West Lafayette, Ind.: Purdue University Press, 1981.

Ruland, Richard. "Beyond Harsh Inquiry: The Hawthorne of Henry James." *ESQ* 25 (1979): 95–117.

Russell, John. "Allegory and 'My Kinsman, Major Molineux.'" *New England Quarterly* 40 (1967): 432–40.

Said, Edward. *Beginnings: Intention and Method*. New York: Basic Books, 1975.

St. Armand, Barton Levi. "Hawthorne's 'Haunted Mind': A Subterranean Drama of the Self." *Criticism* 13 (1971): 1–25.

Saintsbury, George. *The Flourishing of Romance and the Rise of Allegory*. New York: Scribner's, 1897.

A Scarlet Letter Handbook. Ed. Seymour L. Gross. Belmont, Calif.: Wadsworth, 1960.

Schechter, Harold. "Death and Resurrection of the King: Elements of Primitive Mythology and Ritual in 'Roger Malvin's Burial.'" *English Language Notes* 8 (1973): 201–3.

Schlegel, Friedrich. *Werke*. 2 vols. Berlin and Weimar: Aufbau-Verlag Nationalen Forschungs- und-Gedenkstatten der klassichen deutscher Literatur, 1988.

Scholes, Robert, and Robert Kellogg. *The Nature of Narrative*. New York: Oxford University, 1968.

Schrag, Calvin O. *Radical Reflection and the Human Sciences*. West Lafayette, Ind.: Purdue University Press, 1980.

Schroeder, John. "Alice Doane's Story: An Essay on Hawthorne and Spenser." *Nathaniel Hawthorne Journal/1974*: 129–34.

Schubert, Leland. *Hawthorne, the Artist: Fine Art Devices in Fiction.* Chapel Hill: University of North Carolina Press, 1944.

Schulz, Dieter. "Imagination and Self-Improvement: The Ending of 'Roger Malvin's Burial.'" *Studies in Short Fiction* 10 (1973): 183–86.

——. "'Ethan Brand' and the Structure of American Quest Romance." *Genre* 7 (1975): 233–49.

Schwartz, Joseph. "Three Aspects of Hawthorne's Puritanism." *New England Quarterly* 36 (1963): 192–208.

Scott, Walter. "An Essay on Romance" (1824, 1827). Rev. ed. *Essays on Chivalry, Romance and the Drama* (1834). Reprint. Freeport: Books for Libraries Press, 1972. [Cf. *Britannica*, "Novel" and "Romance."]

——. *Sir Walter Scott on Novelists and Fiction.* Ed. Ioan Williams. London: Routledge & Kegan Paul, 1968.

Seltzer, John. "Psychological Romance in Hawthorne's 'Wives of the Dead.'" *Studies in Short Fiction* 16 (1979): 311–15.

Shakespeare: Major Plays and the Sonnets. Ed. G. B. Harrison. New York: Harcourt, Brace, 1948.

Shaw, Harry. *The Forms of Historical Fiction: Sir Walter Scott and His Successors.* Ithaca, N.Y.: Cornell University Press, 1983.

Shaw, Peter. "Fathers, Sons, and the Ambiguities of Revolution in 'My Kinsman, Major Molineux.'" *New England Quarterly* 49 (1976): 559–76.

——. "Their Kinsman, Thomas Hutchinson: Hawthorne, the Boston Patriots, and His Majesty's Royal Governor." *Early American Literature* 11 (1976): 183–90.

Shurr, William H. "Typology and Historical Criticism of the American Renaissance." *ESQ* 20 (1974): 57–63. [Review-essay.]

Simms, William Gilmore. *The Yemassee.* New York: American Book Co., 1937.

Simonson, Harold P. *Radical Discontinuities: American Romanticism and Christian Consciousness.* Rutherford, N.J.: Fairleigh Dickinson University Press, 1983. [East Brunswick, N.J.: Associated University Presses.]

Skaggs, Kenneth W. "The Structure of Hawthorne's 'The Hollow of the Three Hills.'" *Linguistics and Literature* 2 (1977): 1–18.

Slotkin, Richard. *Regeneration through Violence: The Mythology of the American Frontier.* Middletown, Conn.: Wesleyan University Press, 1973.

Smith, Allan Gardner. See Lloyd-Smith, A. G.

Smith, Julian. "Coming of Age in America: Young Ben Franklin and Robin Molineux." *American Quarterly* 17 (1965): 550–58.

——. "Hawthorne's *Legends of the Province House.*" *Nineteenth-Century Fiction* 24 (1969): 31–44.

——. "Historical Ambiguity in 'My Kinsman, Major Molineux.'" *English Language Notes* 8 (1970): 115–20.

Spengemann, William C. *The Adventurous Muse: The Poetics of American Fiction, 1789–1900.* New Haven, Conn.: Yale University Press, 1977.

Spengler, Oswald. *The Decline of the West: Form and Actuality.* 1918. Trans. Charles Francis Atkinson. 2 vols. New York: Knopf, 1926–28.

Stanzel, F. K. *A Theory of Narrative.* 1979. Trans. Charlotte Goedsche. Cambridge: Cambridge University Press, 1984.

Steele, Jeffrey. *The Representation of the Self in the American Renaissance.* Chapel Hill: University of North Carolina Press, 1987. "Hawthorne and the Psychology of Oppression," 151–59.

Stein, William Bysshe. *Hawthorne's Faust: A Study of the Devil Archetype.* Gainesville: University of Florida Press, 1953.

Stephenson, Edward R. "Hawthorne's 'The Wives of the Dead.' " *Explicator* 25 (1965), item 63.

Stewart, Randall. "Recollections of Hawthorne by His Sister Elizabeth." *American Literature* 16 (1945): 316–31.

——. *Nathaniel Hawthorne. A Biography.* New Haven, Conn.: Yale University Press, 1948.

Stock, Ely. "History and the Bible in Hawthorne's 'Roger Malvin's Burial.' " *Essex Institute Historical Collections* 100 (1964): 279–96.

——. "Witchcraft in 'The Hollow of the Three Hills.' " *American Transcendental Quarterly* No. 14 (1972), pp. 31–33.

Stout, Harry. *The New England Soul: Preaching and Religious Culture in Colonial New England.* New York: Oxford University Press, 1986.

Strout, Cushing. *The Veracious Imagination: Essays in American History, Literature, and Biography.* Middletown, Conn.: Wesleyan University Press, 1981.

Stubbs, John Caldwell. *The Pursuit of Form: A Study of Hawthorne and the Romance.* Urbana: University of Illinois Press, 1970.

Sundquist, Eric. *Home as Found: Authority and Genealogy in Nineteenth-Century American Fiction.* Baltimore: Johns Hopkins University Press, 1979.

Sutherland, Judith L. *The Problematic Fictions of Hawthorne, Poe, and James.* Columbia: University of Missouri Press, 1984.

Swann, C[harles]. S. B. "The Practice and Theory of Story Telling: Nathaniel Hawthorne and Walter Benjamin." *Journal of American Studies* 12 (1978): 185–202.

——. " 'Alice Doane's Appeal': or, How to Tell a Story." *Literature and History* 5 (1977): 4–25.

Tannen, Deborah. "What's in a Frame? Surface Evidence for Underlying Expectations." In *New Directions in Discourse Processing,* 137–81. Ed. Roy O. Freedle. Norwood, N.J.: Ablex, 1979.

——. "Framing and Reframing." In *That's Not What I Meant!* New York: Ballantine, 1986.

Tharpe, Coleman W. "The Oral Storyteller in Hawthorne's Novels." *Studies in Short Fiction* 16 (1979): 205–14.

Theorie und Kritik der deutschen Novelle von Wieland bis Musil. Ed. Karl Konrad Polheim. Tübingen: Reclam, 1970.

The Theory of the Novel. Ed. Philip Stevick. New York: Free Press, 1967.

Thompson, G. R. *Poe's Fiction: Romantic Irony in the Gothic Tales.* Madison: University of Wisconsin Press, 1973.

——. "Gothic Fiction of the Romantic Age: Context and Mode." In *Romantic Gothic Tales, 1790–1840,* 1–54. Ed. G. R. Thompson. New York: Harper & Row, 1979.

——. "The Apparition of This World: Transcendentalism and the American 'Ghost' Story." In *Bridges to Fantasy,* 90–107, 207–9. Ed. George Slusser, Robert Scholes, and Eric S. Rabkin. Carbondale: Southern Illinois University Press, 1982.

——. "Washington Irving and the American Ghost Story." In *The Haunted Dusk: American Supernatural Fiction, 1820–1920,* 13–36. Ed. Howard Kerr, John W. Crowley, and Charles Crow. Athens: University of Georgia Press, 1983.

——. *Circumscribed Eden of Dreams: Dreamvision and Nightmare in Poe's Early Poetry.* Baltimore, Md.: Enoch Pratt Free Library, Edgar Allan Poe Society, Library of the University of Baltimore, 1984.

——. "The Development of Romantic Irony in the United States." In *Romantic Irony* (1988), 267–89.

———. *Romantic Arabesque, Contemporary Theory, and Postmodernism* ("The Example of Poe's *Narrative*"). Nos. 3 & 4 of *ESQ* 35 (1989).

Thompson, W. R. "Biblical Sources of Hawthorne's 'Roger Malvin's Burial.'" *PMLA* 77 (1962): 92–96.

———. "Patterns of Biblical Allusions in Hawthorne's 'The Gentle Boy.'" *South Central Bulletin* 22 (1962): 3–10.

Thorslev, Peter. *The Byronic Hero: Type and Prototype*. Minneapolis: University of Minnesota Press, 1962.

Todorov, Tzvetan. *Mikhail Bakhtin: The Dialogical Principle*. 1981. Trans. Wlad Godzich. Minneapolis: University of Minnesota Press, 1984.

Tompkins, Jane. *Sensational Designs: The Cultural Work of American Fiction, 1790–1860*. New York: Oxford, 1985.

Toward a Poetics of Fiction. Ed. Mark Spilka. Bloomington: Indiana University Press, 1977.

Trilling, Lionel. "Manners, Morals, and the Novel." 1940. Rpt. in *The Liberal Imagination*, 205–22. New York: Viking, 1950.

Turner, Arlin. "Hawthorne's Literary Borrowings." *PMLA* 51 (1936): 543–62.

———. *Nathaniel Hawthorne: A Biography*. New York: Oxford University Press, 1980.

Tuve, Rosamund. "Romances." Ch. 5 of *Allegorical Imagery: Some Medieval Books and Their Posterity*, 335–36. Princeton, N.J.: Princeton University Press, 1966.

Typology and Early American Literature. Ed. Sacvan Bercovitch. Amherst: University of Massachusetts Press, 1972.

Vance, William L. "The Comic Element in Hawthorne's Sketches." *Studies in Romanticism* 3 (1964): 144–60.

Van Der Beets, Richard, and Paul Withington. "My Kinsman, Brockden Brown: Robin Molineux and Arthur Mervyn." *American Transcendental Quarterly* No. 1 (1969), pp. 13–15.

Van Doren, Mark. *Hawthorne: A Critical Biography*. 1949. Reprint. New York: Viking, 1957.

Van Deusen, Marshall. "Narrative Tone in 'The Custom House' and *The Scarlet Letter*." *Nineteenth-Century Fiction* 21 (1966): 61–71.

Van Leer, David. "Hester's Labyrinth: Transcendental Rhetoric in Puritan Boston." In *New Essays on "The Scarlet Letter"* (1985), 57–100.

Van Tassel, Mary M. "Hawthorne, His Narrator, and His Readers in 'Little Annie's Ramble.'" *ESQ* 33 (1987): 168–79.

Vickery, John B. "The Golden Bough at Merry Mount." *Nineteenth-Century Fiction* 12 (1957): 203–14.

Vinaver, Eugene. *Form and Meaning in Medieval Romance*. New York: Modern Humanities Research Association, 1966.

———. *The Rise of Romance*. Oxford: Clarendon Press, 1971.

Von Abele, Rudolph. *The Death of the Artist: A Study of Hawthorne's Disintegration*. The Hague: Nijhoff, 1955.

Von Frank, Albert J. *The Sacred Game: Provincialism and Frontier Consciousness in American Literature, 1630–1860*. New York: Cambridge University Press, 1985.

Wagenknecht, Edward. *Nathaniel Hawthorne: Man and Writer*. New York: Oxford University Press, 1961.

Waggoner, Hyatt. "Hawthorne's Beginning: 'Alice Doane's Appeal.'" *University of Kansas City Review* 16 (1950): 254–55.

———. *Hawthorne: A Critical Study*. 1955. Reprint. Cambridge, Mass.: Harvard University Press, 1963.

——. Intro. to *Hawthorne: Selected Tales and Sketches*, iii–xvi. 3rd ed. New York: Rinehart, 1970.

——. *The Presence of Hawthorne*. Baton Rouge: Louisiana State University Press, 1979.

Walzel, Oskar. *German Romanticism*. Trans. Alme Elise Lussky. 1932. Reprint. New York: Capricorn Books, 1966.

Warnke, Georgia. "History and Hermeneutics: Critique of Romantic Hermeneutics." In *Gadamer: Hermeneutics, Tradition, and Reason*, 5–34. Stanford, Calif.: Stanford University Press, 1987.

Warren, Austin. "Hawthorne's Reading." *New England Quarterly* 8 (1935): 480–97.

Warren, Joyce. "The Claims of the Other: Nathaniel Hawthorne." In *The American Narcissus: Individualism and Women in Nineteenth-Century Fiction*, 189–230. New Brunswick, N.J.: Rutgers University Press, 1984.

Weber, Alfred. *Die Entwicklung der Rahmenerzählungen Nathaniel Hawthornes "The Story Teller" und andere frühe Werke*. Berlin: Erich Schmidt, 1973.

——. "The Outlines of 'The Story Teller,' the Major Work of Hawthorne's Early Years." *Nathaniel Hawthorne Review* 15 (1989): 14–19.

Weinstein, Mark A. "The Creative Imagination in Fiction and History." *Genre* 9 (1976): 263–77.

Weldon, Roberta F. "From 'The Old Manse' to 'The Custom-House': The Growth of the Artist's Mind." *Texas Studies in Literature and Language* 20 (1978): 36–47.

West, Harry C. "Hawthorne's Editorial Pose." *American Literature* 44 (1972): 208–21.

Whelan, Robert Emmet, Jr. " 'Roger Malvin's Burial': The Burial of Reuben Bourne's Cowardice." *Research Studies* 37 (1969): 112–21.

White, Hayden. *Metahistory: The Historical Imagination in Nineteenth-Century Europe*. Baltimore: Johns Hopkins University Press, 1973.

——. "Foucault Decoded: Notes from Underground." *History and Thought* 12 (1973).

——. "The Fictions of Factual Representation." In *Literature of Fact* (1976), 21–44.

——. *The Content of the Form: Narrative Discourse and Historical Representation*. Baltimore: Johns Hopkins University Press, 1987.

Whyte, Lancelot Law. *The Unconscious Before Freud*. London: Social Science Paperbacks, 1967.

Williams, Ioan. *The Idea of the Novel in Europe 1600–1800*. London: Macmillan, 1978.

Williamson, James L. "Vision and Revision in 'Alice Doane's Appeal.' " *American Transcendental Quarterly* No. 40 (1978): 345–53.

Wilson, Anne. *Traditional Romance and the Tale*. New York: Rowan & Littlefield, 1976.

Wilson, James D. "Incest and American Romantic Fiction." *Studies in the Literary Imagination* 7 (1974): 31–50.

Wimsatt, W. K., Jr., and Monroe C. Beardsley. "The Intentional Fallacy." *Sewanee Review* 54 (1946): 468–88.

Wright, George F. *The Poet in the Poem: The Personae of Eliot, Yeats, and Pound*. Berkeley: University of California Press, 1960. See esp. pp. 1–59.

Yates, Norris. "Ritual and Reality: Mask and Dance Motifs in Hawthorne's Fiction." *Philological Quarterly* 34 (1955): 56–70.

Yoder, R. A. "Hawthorne and His Artist." *Studies in Romanticism* 7 (1968): 193–206.

Young, Philip. *Hawthorne's Secret: An Un-told Tale*. Boston: David Godine, 1984.

Zobel, Hiller B. *The Boston Massacre*. New York: Norton, 1971.

Index

Works by Nathaniel Hawthorne are listed under his name. The following abbreviations are used in parenthetical cross-references:

302 Index

Dialogical (*cont.*)
—as a theme in Hawthorne, 41, 42, 64
(YGB); 84; 29, 87, 92 (GC); 104–105, 112
(GB); 131–35, 145–46, 156 (MKMM);
161, 192, 201 (ADA); 210–31, 232, 233,
236, (Oberon)
See also Authoritarianism; *Either/or* readings;
Foucault; Frames; Monological; Müller;
Rahmenerzählung; Romantic irony;
Schlegel
Diana (as moon goddess), 126, 262 note 10.
See also Moon
Dickinson, Emily, 7
Diderot, Denis, 11
Digby, Richard, 92 (MAd). *See also* Legends/legendary
Disraeli, Benjamin, 3
Distanciation: and Hawthorne, 8, 19, 163
(ADA); and romanticism, 234; and self-
reflexive subversion, 169 (ADA); theoretical problems, 5–6, 244 note 21 (Ricoeur),
249 note 8 (Bakhtin). *See also* Aesthetic
criticism; Author/authorial; Mediation;
Narratology; Objective subjectivity; Romantic irony
Don Quixote. *See* Cervantes
Doppelgänger (double, mirror self, other
self), 48, 163; 166, 170–71, 182, 270 note
8 (ADA); author doubles, 210–12 (DMS);
47–48 (MdM); 222–28, 229–31 (STr);
Puritans and Quakers, 103–19 (GB). *See
also* Gothic; Psychological romance; Self
Dostoevsky, Fyodor, 41
Doubleday, Neal Frank, 67, 68 (WD); 80;
101, 104 (GB); 133; 150 (MKMM); 258
note 17 (RMB)
Double-faced figure. *See* Devil; "Joyce, Jr."
Double narrative. *See* Twice-told
Double-voiced discourse, 251 note 24
(Bakhtin)
"Douglas, Tragedy of." *See* "Passages from a
Relinquished Work" ("The Village Theatre": STr)
Dreams, 11, 50; Emerson's perplexity, 51–
52; theme in romantic literature, 163
—daydream, 99; and "dreaming awake," 48,
49, 160 (ADA)
—discourse on dream narrative, 51–56
—double dream, 57–58, 67–76 (WD); 71;
76–79 (OWT); 80, 82
—dream-experience, 53, 69 (Conrad); 53–
56 (Shakespeare); 120, 126, 127, 128–29,
136, 137–38, 153–54, 156, 158 (MKMM);

163, 182, 183, 195 (ADA); 229 (STr); and
the labyrinth, 127–28; sleepwaking/
sleepwalking, 52, 72; 253 note 2; and
"waking life," 50–51, 66, 70, 232
—dreamland, 165
—"Dream of Oberon," 231 (STr)
—dream-play tradition, 54, 122
—dream portals, 220, 253 note 2 (true and
false dreams); 255 note 23; 274 note 7
(gates of horn and ivory)
—dreamvision, 11, 25, 50; 56–58 (as genre);
71 (WD); 76 (OWT); 78, 120, 179; Story
Teller's dream of the artist self, 217–22,
229; as structure in "Alice Doane's Appeal," 160, 161, 166–67 (apocalyptic sequence), 182–89, 192–93, 195–98
—dream-within-a-dream, 55, 57, 58, 77, 80;
infinite regress theme, 82 (paralleled to
story structure), 82 (OWT); 126
(MKMM); 253 note 3
See also *Apokalypsis;* Conrad; Delphic oracle;
Delusion; Hermes; Imagination;
Other/ness; Poe; Shakespeare (*A Midsummer Night's Dream*)
Dyrden, Edgar A., 2
Dublin University Magazine: review of
Hawthorne, 8, 44, 159. *See also* Negated
terms: negative suggestion
Dudley, Thomas (colonial governor of Massachusetts), 89 (GC)

Edwards, Jonathan, 155. *See also* Great
Awakening
Egoism/egotism, 63–64 (YGB); 65 (HTH);
97–101 (RMB); and the dialogical, 234,
237. See also *Caritas;* individual titles
Either/or readings, 69, 80, 121–22, 145, 146,
147, 154, 241 note 13 (MKMM); 173
(ADA); 235. See also *Both/and* relationships; Inside/outside
Elizabeth I, Queen, 81
Ellipsis: as (non)closure. *See* Closure; "Alice
Doane's Appeal"
Ellis, John M.: on the German novelle, 26,
27, 28; on narrators' relation to narration,
26–28, 34
Eliot, George [Mary Ann Evans]: *Middlemarch,* 35
Emerson, Ralph Waldo: "The American
Scholar," 7; and dreams, 51–52; "Experience," 51; *Nature* (1836), 51; "New England Reformers," 7; *Society and Solitude,* 7

passim; of locale and time, 61, 129, 146–53 (MKMM); 165, 167, 169, 185, 189, 202, 269 note 5 (ADA); 229 (STr); and negative romance, 83. *See also* Dialogical; individual titles

Indian conflicts: King Philip's War, 118 (GC), 86, 91; Lovell's Fight, 94–96 (RMB); 183 (ADA)

Infinite regress. *See* Dreams: dream-within-a-dream

Inside/outside, 165, 212, 234, 241 note 13

Intention: Bakhtin on, 249 note 8, 251 note 24; and the dialogical, 41–43; and the "intentional fallacy," 35–36; presumption of Hawthorne's intentions, 6, 7–8, 17, 80 (Baym), 110, 111, 112, 256 note 4, 239 note 20 (Parker)

Intersubjectivity, 43, 47

Intertextuality, 16, 39; and genre, 43–44. See also *Rahmenerzählung*

In the American Province. See Hollinger

Irony, humor, parody. *See* Romantic irony

Irving, Washington, 11, 45, 235; "Buckthorne and His Friends," 45; Diedrich Knickerbocker and Geoffrey Crayon as frame narrators, 45; "Dolph Heyliger," 255 note 26; ghost story, popular genres, and framed narratives, 45; "Rip Van Winkle," 255 note 26; *Salmagundi*, 273 note 5; *The Sketch-Book of Geoffrey Crayon*, 273 note 5; *Tales of a Traveller*, 45, 89, 213

Isaac. *See* Abraham

Iser, Wolfgang, 30, 32

Isolation, 63–64, 98, 101, 104; 134 (MKMM)

Jacksonian Era, 143 (MKMM)

James, Henry: *The Ambassadors*, 35; on Hawthorne, 8; and the short story, 206; *The Turn of the Screw*, 18, 36, 123 ("trap for the unwary")

James II, King, 85, 88, 89, 132, 264 note 14

Janssen, James G.: on Hawthorne's concluding fictional "morals," 157

Jean Paul. *See* Richter

Jesus: and children, 107 (GB); and cosmic progress, 149. *See also* Manifest destiny; Rousseauism

Jonson, Ben: *Oberon, The Fairy Prince*, 232, 233

Journey motif: romantic circle out and back, 218, 219–28, 229. *See also* Arch-vision; Cervantes (road to Toboso); Christian

symbols: arch; Home and hearth; Pilgrim/wanderer; Rainbow

Joyce, James, 14–15, 57

"Joyce, Jr." (Boston revolutionary), 142, 143, 147, 155 (MKMM)

Jungian readings, 125, 147 (MKMM). *See also* Archetype; Myth

Kafka, Franz, 27

Keats, John: negative capability, 244 note 19

Keller, Gottfried, 27

"Kindly" stranger. *See* Hawthorne (MKMM)

King Philip's War. *See* Indian conflicts

King Street (Boston), 153 (MKMM)

Kleist, Heinrich von, 27

Lacan, Jacques: and Schlegel, 247 note 33

Labyrinth, 126–27, 152, 154 (MKMM); 205 (RMB). *See also* Shakespeare

Lamp. *See* Christian symbols

Lang, Hans Joachim, 67–68 (WD), 69, 75

Lanser, Susan, 30, 32

Laughter, 130, 134, 138, 154, 263 note 13 (MKMM); 172 (ADA); 183, 194, 211 (DMS)

Leavis, Q. D., 122, 144, 149 (MKMM)

Lectures upon Witchcraft. See Upham

Legends/legendary material, 24, 50, 58, 160; in relation to history, 84, 189, 236–37, 248 note 4, 255 note 26 (Irving); 172, 177, 189 (ADA). *See also* Historiography/history

Leninism (Bakhtin), 43

LeSage, Alain René: *The Limping Devil*, 207, 213, 221

Lesser, Simon O., 122, 141, 144, 145; *Fiction and the Unconscious*, 136

Liberalism/liberty, 109; as defined by American Calvinists, 39, 256 note 3, 257 note 8; as a problematic theme, 144–45, 149 (MKMM); 241 note 13 (MSt)

Light symbolism, 71, 75, 254 note 19, 255 notes 22 and 25 (WD); 170, 182, 185 (ADA); and "augury," 221; fading, 194; as a "ghostly glimmer round the reader," 186–87 (ADA); twilight, 195; as veiling, 186. *See also* Christian symbols; Rainbow

Literal and metaphoric, 53; and dream, 53. *See also* Allegory; Genre; Romance; Typology

Locke, John, 150, 155

11, 42, 158, 222; *School for Aesthetics*, 275
note 13
Rising glory of America. *See* Manifest destiny; Nationalism
Robinarchy, 151, 267 note 33 (MKMM). *See also* Bolingbroke
Robin Goodfellow: name symbolism, 129
(MKMM). *See also* Devil; Shakespeare:
Puck
Rohrberger, Mary, 122; on Oedipal conflict
and dream-experience (MKMM), 137–
41, 144, 145
Roman: as the "new fiction," 22, 37–38, 229,
234, 248 note 37, 250 note 17. *See also* Arabesque; Romantic irony
Romance: American romance tradition, 236,
242–43 note 17, 243 note 18; Hawthorne's historical romances, 24, 83, 94–
96; historiography and history, 19–20, 55,
56, 94–96 (RMB); 146–50 (RMB); 161,
166, 168, 173, 174 (ADA); and imagination, 166, 187, 209; novel/romance distinction, 209, 241–42 note 14; psychological romance (Hawthorne's term), 5,
18; and readership, 97 (RMB); romance
and realism, 123 (MKMM); Schlegel's
term, 22; traditional definitions, 11–12,
83. *See also* Borders/boundaries; Fact/fiction; Historiography/history; Negated
terms: negative romance; Neutral territory; Romanticism
Romantic irony, 9, 13, 20, 21, 55, 82, 231,
233, 237, 244 note 19; and allegory, 159;
and arabesque, 21–22, 45, 192; and Byronism, 181; and the centrifugal
(Bakhtin), 43; and the dialogical, 192; and
gender issues, 244 note 21; and humor
and parody, 43, 54 (*Midsummer Night's
Dream*); and negative romance, 83; and
Poe, 243 note 18; self-parody, 47–48
(MdM); 76, 210–12 (DMS), 212–31
(STr), 215 ("lighthearted desperation"),
224–28 (STr); and Schlegel, 274 note 10
("transcendental buffoonery"); and skepticism, 10; and subversion of genre conventions, 51, 56; and verisimilitude, 47
—in Hawthorne's works: 99 (RMB); 122,
123, 157 (MKMM); 177, 200–201 (ADA);
209–10 (MF); 210–12 (DMS); 221–22
(STr)
See also Dialogical; Genre; Metafiction;
Oberon; Objective subjectivity; Schlegel;
Sketch; Tale

Romanticism: aesthetic and narrative theory,
5, 12, 21, 234; anti-romanticism, 13; binarial problems, 4; conventions and clichés,
61, 65 (HTH); 79 (OWT); 107 (GB); 164
(opium); 174, 200–201 (ADA); 211–12
(DMS); 218–22, 233, 271 note 14; dialogical versus dialectical, 5, 15–17; and
Hawthorne, 21; and irony, 13; and narratology, 5; Puritan distrust of, 191–92;
romantic symbolism versus typology, 14;
themes subverted (childhood, courage,
fame, love, patriarchy, self-discovery), 94–
97, 98, 101, 103, 108, 205; visionary
theme, 218, 222–28. *See also* Arabesque;
Arch-vision; Byron and Byronism; Home
and hearth; Imagination; Journey motif;
Negated terms: negative romanticism;
Romantic irony; Schlegel
Rousseauism, 107
Rowson, Susanna H., 164
Rum riot. *See* Molasses Act; "My Kinsman,
Major Molineux"
Russian Orthodox Church (Bakhtin), 43

Sacrificial drama, 96, 101 (RMB); and
akedah, 258 note 18
Sadomasochism, 96–102, 102–19. *See also*
Psychological romance
Saint Peter's cathedral (Rome), 209 (MF)
Salem, 50, 61, 166, 167, 168, 173, 176, 177,
178, 183, 188, 190, 192, 193, 195, 196,
199–201 (Upham), 207, 208, 235, 272
note 22; salem/*shalom*, 174. *See also*
Witchcraft trials
Salem Witchcraft. See Upham
Sancho Panza. *See* Cervantes
Satan. *See* Devil
Saturnalia, 263 note 13 (MKMM)
Scapegoat king, 263 note 13 (MKMM)
Scarlet whore, 128; and Oedipal conflict,
139 (MKMM)
Scheherazade, 16, 45. *See also* Arabian
Nights
Schlegel, August Wilhelm, 127
Schlegel, Friedrich, 15, 21, 22, 37–38, 41,
42, 55, 229; and Adorno, 244 note 19 (and
Bakhtin); and *Don Quixote*, 235; and
Lacan, 247 note 33; and *A Midsummer
Night's Dream*, 54, 127; and Oberon, 233–
34, 235; *Roman* and the hierarchy of poetics, 275 note 15; "transcendental buffoonery," 274 note 8. See also *Roman*;
Romantic irony

G. R. Thompson is Professor of English at Purdue
University. Among his works are *Poe's Fiction: Romantic
Irony in the Gothic Tales, Circumscribed Eden of Dreams:
Dreamvision and Nightmare in Poe's Early Poetry*, and
Romantic Arabesque, Contemporary Theory, and Postmodernism.
He has also edited several volumes, including *Great Short
Works of Edgar Allan Poe, The Gothic Imagination: Essays in
Dark Romanticism, Romantic Gothic Tales, 1790–1840*, and
Essays and Reviews of Edgar Allan Poe. He has been editor of
the journal *Poe Studies* (1968–79) and *ESQ: A Journal of the
American Renaissance* (1972–78).

Library of Congress Cataloging-in-Publication Data
Thompson, G. R. (Gary Richard), b. 1937
The art of authorial presence : Hawthorne's provincial tales
/ G. R. Thompson.
Includes bibliographical references and index.
ISBN 0-8223-1306-5 (alk. paper). — ISBN 0-8223-1321-9
(pbk. : alk. paper)
1. Hawthorne, Nathaniel, 1804–1864—Knowledge—
History.   2. Hawthorne, Nathaniel, 1804–1864—
Technique.   3. Avant-garde (Aesthetics)—United States.
4. Romanticism—United States.   5. Regionalism in
literature.   6. New England in literature.   7. America
in literature.   8. Narration (Rhetoric)   I. Title.
PS1892.H5T47   1993
813'.3—dc20   92-33301 CIP